COMPUTERIZED ACCOUNTING WITH

QUICKBOOKS®

Online 2018

James B. Rosa, CPA
Queensborough Community College

Kathleen Villani, CPA
Queensborough Community College

PARADIGM
EDUCATION SOLUTIONS

St. Paul

Division President: Linda Hein
Vice President, Content Management: Christine Hurney
Director of Content Development, Computer Technology: Cheryl Drivdahl
Associate Developmental Editor: Katie Werdick
Tester: Janet S. Blum
Director of Production: Timothy W. Larson
Production Editor: Jen Weaverling
Cover and Design and Production Specialist: Jack Ross
Copy Editor: Lori Ryan
Indexer: Terry Casey
Vice President, Digital Solutions: Chuck Bratton
Digital Projects Manager: Tom Modl
Digital Solutions Manager: Gerry Yumul
Digital Production & Design Manager: Aaron Esnough
Vice President, Sales and Marketing: Scott Burns
Senior Director of Marketing: Lara Weber McLellan

Care has been taken to verify the accuracy of information presented in this book. However, the authors, editors, and publisher cannot accept responsibility for web, email, newsgroup, or chat room subject matter or content, or for consequences from the application of the information in this book, and make no warranty, expressed or implied, with respect to its content.

Trademarks: Intuit and QuickBooks are trademarks and service marks of Intuit Inc., registered in the United States and other countries. Microsoft is a trademark or registered trademark of Microsoft Corporation in the United States and/or other countries. Some of the product names and company names included in this book have been used for identification purposes only and may be trademarks or registered trade names of their respective manufacturers and sellers. The authors, editors, and publisher disclaim any affiliation, association, or connection with, or sponsorship or endorsement by, such owners.

Paradigm Publishing, Inc., is independent from Microsoft Corporation and not affiliated with Microsoft in any manner.

Cover Photo Credit: © Tarchyshnik Andrei/Shutterstock.com

We have made every effort to trace the ownership of all copyrighted material and to secure permission from copyright holders. In the event of any question arising as to the use of any material, we will be pleased to make the necessary corrections in future printings.

ISBN 978-0-76388-546-5 (print)
ISBN 978-0-76388-547-2 (digital)

© 2019 by Paradigm Publishing, Inc.
875 Montreal Way
St. Paul, MN 55102
Email: CustomerService@ParadigmEducation.com
Website: ParadigmEducation.com

Printed in the United States of America

28 27 26 25 24 23 22 21 20 19   1 2 3 4 5 6 7 8 9 10

Brief Contents

Contents

Preface

Computerized Accounting with QuickBooks® Online 2018, by James B. Rosa and Kathleen Villari, teaches you how to use QuickBooks Online, Intuit's cloud-based version of a popular general ledger software package for small- and medium-sized businesses. With this application, businesses can maintain a general ledger; track vendor, customer, and inventory activities; process payroll for company employees; prepare bank reconciliations; track time for employees; and complete other key accounting procedures. In addition to learning how to use QuickBooks Online with this textbook, you will review related accounting concepts as applied in the application.

Technology and the movement of software and data to the cloud provide excellent opportunities for interactive learning and assessing student performance. This textbook is accompanied by an ebook with live links to the QuickBooks Online application and student resources. Details about the ebook as well as instructor resources can be found on page xv.

Prerequisites

QuickBooks® Online 2018 provides detailed instruction and extensive practice for learning how to use the QuickBooks Online application. To get the most out of this textbook, you should be familiar with basic accounting principles and practices. You also should know how to use a personal computer with the Windows operating system. For effective use of this textbook, the Chapter Problem and Case Problem must be performed on a computer with internet access. It is recommended that you use Google Chrome as your browser.

Course Outcomes

A course that uses *QuickBooks® Online 2018* has two main objectives. The first objective is to teach you how to operate QuickBooks Online by entering common daily business transactions in the appropriate activity windows using sample company data. The second objective is to identify the behind-the-scenes accounting that QuickBooks Online records. This second objective is accomplished by reviewing the underlying accounting concepts through both narrative explanation and T-account illustrations. In the workplace, the better you understand the actual flow of the activity as it is recorded in the system, the more effective you will be in operating the software accurately and efficiently.

After completing a course that uses *QuickBooks® Online 2018*, you should be able to do the following:
- Understand differences and similarities between a manual accounting system and QuickBooks Online
- Set up and customize a new company file

- Identify and execute the four levels of operation within QuickBooks: New Company Setup, Lists, Activities, and Reports
- Set up and maintain Vendor, Customer, and Employee Lists; the Chart of Accounts List; and the Products and Services List
- Enter daily activities as appropriate at the Bill, Pay Bills, Check, Invoice, Receive Payment, Sales Receipts, Deposits, Sales Tax Center, Inventory Quantity Adjustment, Run Payroll, and Pay Taxes windows
- Transfer funds between accounts, record and pay credit card charges, and prepare a bank reconciliation
- View and print management reports, accounting reports, and financial statements
- Customize the appearance of windows, lists, and printed documents
- Set up and run payroll
- Use the time-tracking feature to create customer statements

Instructional Design

QuickBooks® Online 2018 teaches you how to use the QuickBooks Online application by integrating use of the textbook, the QuickBooks Online Test Drive, and your QuickBooks Online Plus account.

Textbook

Each chapter introduces common accounting concepts, walks through procedures with detailed step-by-step instructions, and then assesses your comprehension of chapter topics in the Chapter Review and Assessment. Procedures in this textbook are organized to follow the four levels of operation in QuickBooks: New Company Setup, Lists, Activities, and Reports. As each level of operation is presented in the chapters, it is denoted with a corresponding margin icon as a visual reminder of the level of operation. Screen captures from the application accompany instructional text to offer visual confirmation as you complete important steps. Reports and lists are included as model answers for you to compare against your completed work. More details about the textbook features can be found in the "Textbook and Chapter Features" section on page xii.

All screen captures in the textbook are as accurate as possible at the time of publication. However, Intuit may occasionally make changes to the design of the QuickBooks Online interface, and as a result, you may see minor changes in elements such as colors.

QuickBooks Online Test Drive

To allow you to practice accounting procedures, this textbook takes advantage of the QuickBooks Online Test Drive. The QuickBooks Online Test Drive is a free, interactive, preprogrammed QuickBooks Online account that is accessed on the internet. The Test Drive uses fictional data to populate a company file for Craig's Design and Landscaping Services, a fictional company that provides goods and services. The data for the vendors, customers, and goods and services is continually updated so that you can skip data entry and focus on learning and executing accounting tasks.

Each chapter of this textbook, with the exception of Chapter 2, teaches procedures using the Test Drive sample company. (Chapter 2 focuses on setting up a new account and guides you through using your own QuickBooks Online Plus account to learn the account setup procedures. You then practice the procedures of each chapter in the Case Problem at the end of each chapter using your own company file.) The textbook narrative and procedures are built on the assumption that the Test Drive data will not change significantly, though you may see minor changes that should not affect the work you do. For example, the sample company automatically sends, pays, and receives bills on schedules determined by Intuit. Depending on the day or month that you access the Test Drive, you may see different billing data in the system. The authors of the textbook have considered this and written exercises for you that do not rely on the timing of the data provided by Intuit whenever possible. Margin hints throughout the textbook remind you that the textbook instruction and screencaps may not exactly match what you see in the Test Drive and offer guidance about how to get the most from the Test Drive.

Once you log out of the Test Drive or close the internet browser, all changes to the Test Drive sample company file are lost. Any documents or reports generated in the Test Drive should be printed or saved as PDFs before exiting the Test Drive. Chapter work should be completed within one session so that all changes made to the Test Drive sample company are recorded in the final reports for that chapter.

Your QuickBooks Online Plus Account

QuickBooks® Online 2018 comes with free, one-year access to a fully functional QuickBooks Online Plus account. You will use this account to establish a company file in Chapter 1, set up the company file in Chapter 2, and then build on that company file in each Chapter Review and Assessment Case Problem. Once you master the procedures with the Test Drive sample company, you reinforce those skills by practicing in the Case Problem.

Because you set up the company file and control all the data entry, accuracy is essential. In the Test Drive, the data is reset each time you close the Test Drive, so if you make an error in one chapter, it will not affect the next chapter. In your company file, a mistake made in one chapter may cause problems in later chapters. Therefore, at the end of each Case Problem you will be instructed to print reports for your instructor to grade and review. The Case Problem does not need to be completed in one session as in the Test Drive—any changes made to your company file are saved and readily available the next time you log into your QuickBooks Online account.

Your company file is the best measurement for comprehension and execution of the procedures and concepts covered in this textbook. In addition to the practice you get in the Test Drive, building your own company file and completing the daily, monthly, and yearly accounting tasks will ensure that you have experience completing essential accounting tasks using QuickBooks Online.

Textbook and Chapter Features

The textbook contains a total of eleven chapters that should be completed sequentially. Each chapter is followed by a Chapter Review and Assessment.

Chapter Elements

Each chapter contains the following elements:

Chapter Openers present an overview of the skills that you will learn by completing the chapter.

Objectives outline learning goals for the chapter.

CHAPTER 4

Customers

Adding Customers, Creating Invoices, and Receiving and Depositing Payments

Objectives

- Identify the system default accounts for customers
- Update the Customer List
- Record sales on account in the Invoice window
- Record collections of accounts receivable in the Receive Payment window
- Record cash sales in the Sales Receipt window
- Deposit payments in the Deposit window
- Display and print customer-related reports

91

System Default Accounts

As we saw in Chapter 3, to process transactions expeditiously and organize data for reporting, QuickBooks Online establishes specific general ledger accounts as default accounts in each window. When you enter transactions, QuickBooks Online automatically increases or decreases certain account balances, depending on the nature of the transaction.

For example, for vendors, when you enter a transaction in the Bill window, QuickBooks Online automatically increases (credits) the Accounts Payable account; when you pay the bills in the Pay Bills window, QuickBooks Online automatically decreases (debits) the Accounts Payable account. Similarly, for customers, when you enter a transaction in the Invoice window, QuickBooks Online automatically increases (debits) the Accounts Receivable account because the Invoice window is used to record sales on account. When you record a collection of accounts receivable in the Receive Payment window, QuickBooks Online automatically decreases (credits) the Accounts Receivable account. You do not have to enter the account number or name for these default accounts because they have been preestablished by QuickBooks Online.

 Chapter Problem

In this chapter, you will enter and track customer transactions for Craig's Design and Landscaping Services. The company provides garden design and landscaping services both on account and for cash. Customers and clients remit payment for invoices; these funds are periodically deposited in the company checking account. Information for several customers has been entered in the Customer List. This information is contained in the QuickBooks Online Test Drive.

To access the QuickBooks Online Test Drive:
1. Open an internet browser, key https://QBO18.ParadigmEducation.com/TestDrive into the address bar, and then press the Enter key or click the Go arrow. This opens the Security Verification window.
2. Click the check box to the left of the text *I'm not a robot.* A window may appear with images. If so, follow the instructions to select images or part of an image and then click NEXT, SKIP, or VERIFY. (This may take several attempts.)
3. Click the Continue button. QuickBooks Online launches displaying the sample company Craig's Design and Landscaping Services.

To change the company name:
1. On the title bar, click the Gear icon. The Craig's Design and Landscaping Services window appears.
2. Click *Account and Settings* in the *Your Company* column. This opens the Account and Settings window.
3. Click the Edit icon in the *Company name* section or click anywhere in the section. The *Company name* section expands to display more information about the company, and you can now edit the company information.
4. In the *Company name* field, select the company name and key EX4 [*Your Name*] Craig's Design and Landscaping Services.

CUSTOMERS 93

Cloud icons indicate that a link to the QuickBooks Online application is available from the corresponding page in the ebook.

Magenta text identifies material to type.

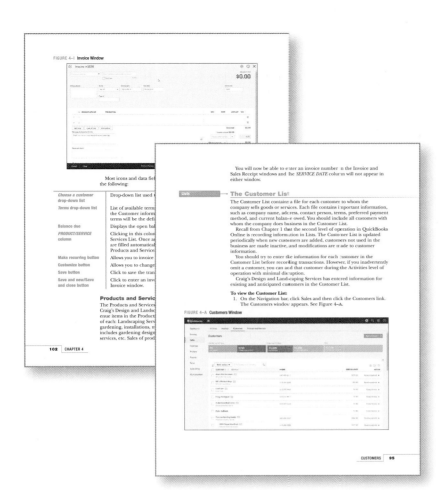

Step-by-Step Procedures with Screen Captures guide you to the desired outcome for each accounting procedure. Screen captures illustrate what the screen should look like at key points.

Explanatory Lists provide essential details about different links, buttons, and options at various windows.

QuickBooks Online Icon Images help you navigate the application's interface.

The Four Levels of QuickBooks margin icons identify which level—New Company Setup, Activities, Lists, or Reports—will be covered in the following section.

Accounting Concepts accompany and summarize each transaction in the traditional debit and credit format illustrated with T-accounts.

Practice Exercises provide an opportunity for you to repeat the preceding task or transaction without step-by-step guidance. Many Practice Exercises include a *QuickCheck* number, such as an invoice total, or a screen capture to check your work.

Hints in the margins provide alternative methods, reminders, and helpful tips for working in QuickBooks Online.

Key Terms and Definitions in the margins provide quick reference for chapter vocabulary.

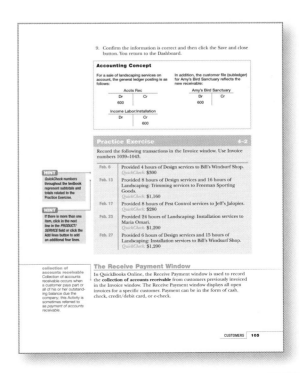

Chapter Review and Assessment Elements

The following elements are contained in the Chapter Review and Assessment pages of the textbook. You can find additional resources to reinforce your learning by using links in the ebook.

Study Tools include presentations with audio support and a glossary designed to help you review skills and concepts learned in the chapter. These tools are accessed through links in the ebook.

The **Procedure Review** provides a summary of the QuickBooks steps discussed in the chapter.

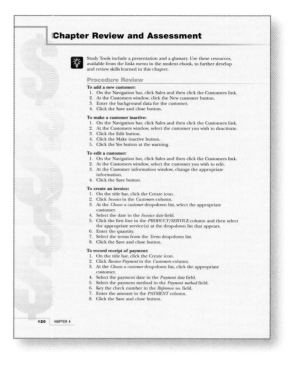

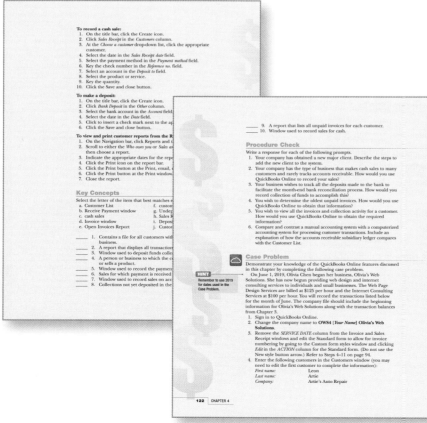

Key Concepts matching questions allow a quick assessment of comprehension.

Procedure Check short- and long-answer questions encourage active and critical thinking.

The **Case Problem** ensures that you master the topics of the chapter as you build the company file for Olivia's Web Solutions. Reports generated at the end of the Case Problem are the main assessment tools for each chapter.

Student eBook

The student ebook, available online at ParadigmEducation.com/ebooks, provides access to the *QuickBooks® Online 2018* content from any device (desktop, tablet, and smartphone), anywhere, through a live internet connection. The versatile ebook platform features dynamic navigation tools including a linked table of contents and the ability to jump to specific pages, search for terms, bookmark, highlight, and take notes. The ebook offers live links to the interactive content and resources that support the print textbook, including the QuickBooks Online Test Drive and student log-in web pages and Study Tools.

Instructor eResources eBook

All instructor resources are available digitally through a web-based ebook at ParadigmEducation.com/ebooks. The instructor materials include these items:

- Planning resources, such as lesson blueprints, and sample course syllabi
- Presentation resources, such as PowerPoint presentations with lecture notes
- Assessment resources, including PDF model answers for chapter work and end-of-chapter activities, answer keys for evaluating student work, and chapter-based quiz and exam banks

Technical Support for Students

Paradigm Education Solutions offers complimentary one-year access to QuickBooks Online Plus software to students who purchase *QuickBooks® Online 2018* courseware. The cloud-based application paired with the student ebook allows you to complete your work anywhere, inside and outside of the classroom. You can find the necessary license and product codes bundled with Paradigm Education Solutions' *QuickBooks® Online 2018* courseware. Please direct all technical support questions about QuickBooks Online Plus to Intuit at 1-800-488-7330 or Education@intuit.com.

Technical Support for Instructors

Intuit offers a free QuickBooks Online account to instructors when they register with Intuit's Education Program at www.intuiteducationprogram .com. The account is for the QuickBooks Online Accountant application, which is similar to QuickBooks Online Plus but with a few additional features. Instructors should direct all technical support questions about QuickBooks Online Accountant to Intuit at 1-888-333-3451 or Education@intuit.com. Any questions pertaining to Paradigm Education Solutions' *QuickBooks® Online 2018* courseware can be directed to ParadigmEducation.com.

About the Authors

James B. Rosa is a professor of accounting at Queensborough Community College of the City University of New York in Queens, New York. Jim received his bachelor's degree in accounting from Queens College of the City University of New York and his master's degree in business administration from the Peter J Tobin School of Business, St. John's University. Since 1987, Jim has taught principles and intermediate accounting, tax law, and accounting computer applications. Jim has been included in *Who's Who Among America's Teachers* three times. He is a certified public accountant in the state of New York. Jim is a coauthor of the textbooks *Computerized Accounting with QuickBooks® Online 2017* and *2018*; *Computerized Accounting with QuickBooks Pro 2000, 2003, 2005, 2007, 2008, 2009*, and *2010*, and *Computerized Accounting with QuickBooks 2011, 2012, 2013, 2014, 2015*, and *2018*, published by Paradigm Education Solutions.

Kathleen Villani is a professor of accounting and chairperson of the Business Department at Queensborough Community College of the City University of New York in Queens, New York. Kathleen received her bachelor's degree in accounting from Queens College of the City University of New York and her master's degree in business administration from Hofstra University. Since 1984, Kathleen has taught principles, intermediate, and cost accounting, along with accounting computer applications, microcomputer applications, and business organization and management. Kathleen has been included in *Who's Who Among America's Teachers* three times. She is a certified public accountant in the state of New York. Kathleen is a coauthor of the textbooks *Computerized Accounting with Quickbooks® Online 2017* and *2018*; *Computerized Accounting with QuickBooks Pro 2000, 2003, 2005, 2007, 2008, 2009*, and *2010* and *Computerized Accounting with QuickBooks 2011, 2012, 2013, 2014, 2015*, and *2018*, published by Paradigm Education Solutions. Kathleen previously worked as an auditor for New York State and for Ernst and Young and was a financial controller of a healthcare facility.

Acknowledgments

We would like to thank Janet Blum of Fanshawe College in London, Ontario for her important input as a tester of the exercises and case problems as well as Jeff Johnson and Desiree Carvel for their help preparing supplemental materials.

CHAPTER 1

QuickBooks Online

Creating Your Subscription Account and Accessing QuickBooks Online

Objectives

- Describe the differences and similarities between manual and computerized accounting

- Identify the four levels of operation within QuickBooks

- Compare the different versions and features of QuickBooks Online and the QuickBooks desktop software

- Create an account with QuickBooks Online

- Open QuickBooks Online

- Open and edit the Test Drive sample company file

- Exit QuickBooks Online

accounting The process of recording, summarizing, and presenting the financial information of a company in the form of financial statements.

Accounting for the financial activity of any company involves repetitive recording of day-to-day business activities. Recording common business activities such as paying bills, purchasing merchandise, selling merchandise, and processing payroll involves repeating the same steps again and again. Many of these activities can occur several times in the course of one day, requiring much repetitive recording.

When mainframe computers were introduced, certain processes such as payroll became simple to perform. Companies were created to process payrolls for local businesses using mainframe computers. Eventually, mainframe computers were used to process other accounting activities, such as maintaining the general ledger and journals. As personal computers became more common, computerized accounting software enabled routine business activities—including paying bills, buying and selling merchandise, and processing payroll—to be completed without the need for a mainframe computer.

financial statements Summaries of the financial information of a company. The most common are the income statement and the balance sheet.

As business activities are recorded using a computerized accounting software package, all necessary reports—from the journals to the general ledger to the payroll reports and the **financial statements**—are instantly prepared. This makes them available on a more timely basis. Also, if an error is noticed, it can be easily corrected and a revised report immediately printed.

Originally, only people trained in accounting commonly used accounting software. As more people began to use personal computers, business owners and non-accountants started to record business activities on their own using accounting software.

QuickBooks Online is an example of a cloud-based accounting application used to record all types of business and accounting activities and prepare a variety of reports, including financial statements. However, unlike many accounting software products, it is designed with the non-accountant in mind. Many of the data entry steps are described in everyday, non-accounting terms. Behind the scenes, QuickBooks Online uses traditional accounting procedures to record, summarize, and report financial information. Therefore, a basic understanding of accounting terms and procedures allows you to operate the software more efficiently. Throughout the textbook, to clarify the accounting principles behind the QuickBooks Online features, accounting terms are defined in the margins, and accounting concepts are presented after each QuickBooks Online activity.

transaction A monetary business event or activity.

general journal The document in which transactions are initially recorded chronologically. At the end of the month, transactions in the general journal are posted (rewritten) to the general ledger.

general ledger The document in which transactions are organized by account.

Accounting with QuickBooks Online versus Manual and Other Computerized Accounting Systems

In accounting, every **transaction** that involves money must be recorded. In a manual accounting system, all transactions are recorded chronologically in a **general journal**. At the end of the month, these transactions are posted (rewritten) in a book called the *general ledger*. The **general ledger** organizes the information by descriptive names, called *accounts*. Examples of accounts are Cash, Accounts Receivable, and Inventory (assets); Accounts Payable and Notes Payable (liabilities); Capital and Drawings, and Stock and Retained Earnings (equity); Fees Earned and Sales (revenue); and Rent, Insurance, Salaries, and Depreciation (expenses).

trial balance A report containing all the general ledger account names, their debit and credit balances, and the total debits and credits.

special journals Journals such as the purchases journal, sales journal, cash receipts journal, and cash payments journal. These journals can be used instead of the general journal to record similar transactions chronologically. At the end of the month, transactions in the special journals are posted (rewritten) to the general ledger.

After routine transactions and any necessary adjustments are recorded in the journal and posted to the general ledger, a **trial balance** is prepared to confirm that the general ledger is in balance, and then the financial statements are prepared.

To facilitate the recording of so many transactions in a manual accounting system, several journals are used. Similar transactions are recorded in each journal. Typically, a purchases journal is used to record purchases of merchandise on account; a sales journal is used to record sales of merchandise on account; a cash receipts journal is used to record collections of sales on account, cash sales, or any other cash receipt activity; and a cash payments journal is used to record payment of purchases on account, cash purchases, or any other cash payment activity. These journals are often referred to as **special journals**. Any transaction that is not appropriately recorded in a special journal is recorded in the general journal. Month-end adjusting journal entries and fiscal year-end closing entries are recorded in the general journal.

Many computerized accounting software packages follow the procedures used in a manual accounting system. Transactions are recorded in special journals and the general journal as appropriate, and transactions from the journals are then posted to the general ledger. Users of other accounting software packages need to analyze each transaction, determine the correct journal in which to record the transaction, enter the data, view the journal entry for correctness, and then post the journal entry to the general ledger.

QuickBooks Online is designed for the non-accountant as well as the accountant. QuickBooks Online does not record transactions in special journals; instead, it identifies transactions by business function: vendors, customers, employees, and banking. The language used in recording transactions is common business language: enter bills, pay bills, create invoices, receive payments, and so on. The user enters the transaction based on the nature of the activity. Then, behind the scenes, the application updates the appropriate accounting reports—the journal, general ledger, and trial balance—and financial statements, based on the activity entered into the system.

Four Levels of Operation

Although much of the accounting is conducted behind the scenes in QuickBooks Online, an understanding of the accounting concepts used by the application will help you determine how to record financial information correctly. The operations conducted by QuickBooks Online can be classified into four levels: New Company Setup, Lists, Activities, and Reports. See Figure 1–A.

FIGURE 1–A
Four Levels of Operation in QuickBooks

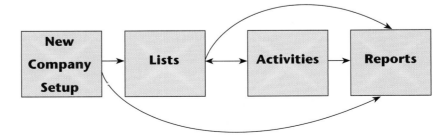

New Company Setup

The first level of operation is creating and setting up a new company file with the background information for the new company. This involves recording the company name, address, identification numbers, fiscal periods, type of business, accounts, and balances.

Lists

The second level of operation is recording information in Lists. These Lists include Chart of Accounts, Vendor, Customer, Products and Services, Terms, Employee, and so on. Information is initially recorded in Lists as part of the New Company Setup process but it can be revised by adding, deleting, or editing information.

The Lists in QuickBooks Online function similarly to a database. Certain information is stored in these Lists, and as business activities involving any item in the Lists are processed, the information can simply be recalled and plugged into the windows rather than requiring the data to be rekeyed.

Activities

The third level of operation is recording daily business activity in QuickBooks Online. This is where most of the routine accounting work is processed. Activities are identified using common language such as bill, check, invoice, receive payment, and so on. In addition, the information in Lists is frequently used to eliminate repetitive keying of data while recording daily activities.

Reports

At certain times, it is necessary to display and print a variety of reports and financial statements based on information entered into QuickBooks Online. The fourth level of operation is using QuickBooks Online to display and print an assortment of reports—for example, management reports related to each activity, such as vendor, customer, inventory, and payroll reports; accounting reports, such as the journal, general ledger, and trial balance; and financial statements, including the income statement and balance sheet.

Information that appears in the reports is gathered during other operations in QuickBooks Online. As data is entered in the New Company Setup, Lists, and Activities levels of operation, the information is simultaneously recorded in the Reports level. QuickBooks Online provides for both simple and more elaborate reporting. All the reports can be customized according to the user's needs.

Versions of QuickBooks and QuickBooks Online

Intuit, the maker of QuickBooks, offers two styles for QuickBooks. One style is to purchase the software and then install it on your computer. All levels of operation of QuickBooks are conducted and saved on your computer. This is referred to as the *desktop program*. The alternative style is to subscribe to the application on a monthly basis. This is the online application. You access QuickBooks Online via the internet. While you use your computer to access QuickBooks Online, all levels of operation of QuickBooks Online are conducted and stored on the QuickBooks (Intuit) servers. Each style offers several versions of the software.

QuickBooks Desktop Versions

The desktop program offers QuickBooks Pro, QuickBooks Premier, and QuickBooks Enterprise Solutions. The fundamentals of each version of the QuickBooks software are the same. QuickBooks Pro is the basic version of the software, while Premier and Enterprise Solutions offer additional features. Small business owners usually use QuickBooks Pro. Larger businesses that have large inventories, or businesses within some specific industries, may use QuickBooks Premier or Enterprise Solutions versions of the software.

QuickBooks Online Versions

HINT

Periodically, the QuickBooks Online graphic interface is updated. As a result, some of the figures in the textbook may be different than the graphic on your computer screen. Refer to your instructor for guidance if you encounter difficulty due to a graphic interface revision.

QuickBooks Online offers three versions: QuickBooks Online Simple Start, QuickBooks Online Essentials, and QuickBooks Online Plus. As with the desktop program, the different versions of QuickBooks Online offer additional features.

Although the functionality of the online program is similar to the desktop program, the graphic interface of the menus, data entry windows, and reports differs significantly. In this textbook, you will learn how to use QuickBooks Online using the QuickBooks Online Plus version accessed via the internet.

Because the software is accessed online, it is common for the software graphics to be updated periodically. Therefore, the graphics displayed on the computer may be different than the figures in the textbook sometimes. Usually, the concepts remain the same. In the event that you have difficulty following the steps in the textbook due to a graphic revision, refer to your instructor for guidance.

Create Your Account with QuickBooks Online

Included with this textbook is a year-long subscription to QuickBooks Online. This version of QuickBooks Online has no limitations in comparison with the paid subscription versions of QuickBooks Online. The student subscription allows you to access the software for one year while you learn computerized accounting as presented in this textbook.

HINT

The preferred internet browsers for QuickBooks Online are Google Chrome and Mozilla Firefox. Google Chrome was used for the illustrations in this textbook.

You will access QuickBooks Online via the internet and then set up your own account to access the application. To set up your account and access the student trial, you will need the license number and product number provided with this textbook. When you create your account, you also begin to set up a company file. This company file will be used throughout Chapter 2 and in the end-of-chapter Case Problems to practice using the features of QuickBooks Online.

To create your account with QuickBooks Online and begin to set up a new company file:
1. Open an internet browser, key https://QBO18.ParadigmEducation.com/AccountSetUp into the address bar, and then press the Enter key or click the Go arrow. You move to the Set Up Your Account window. See Figure 1–B.

FIGURE 1–B Set Up Your Account Window

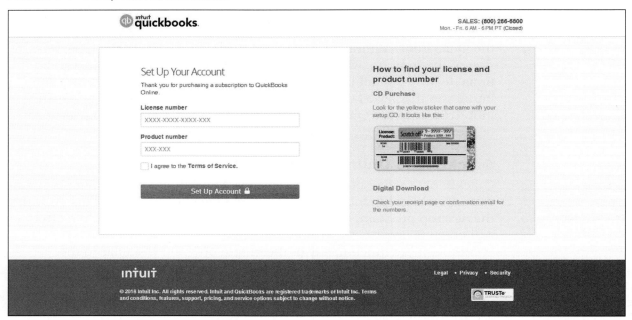

2. Refer to the QuickBooks Online Subscription Card included with the textbook and key the license number and product number in the appropriate fields.
3. Click to insert a check mark to the left of *I agree to the Terms of Service.*
4. Click the Set Up Account button. You move to the Sign Up for QuickBooks window. See Figure 1–C.

FIGURE 1–C Sign Up for QuickBooks Window

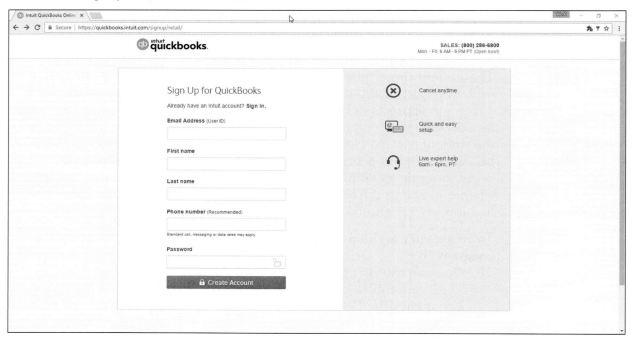

5. Complete the Sign Up for QuickBooks window and then click the Create Account button. You are moved to the No two businesses are alike window.

   Be sure to remember the email address and password that you entered at the Sign Up for QuickBooks window, and keep the QuickBooks Online Subscription Card in a safe place.
6. In the *What's your business called?* field, key Olivia's Web Solutions.
7. In the *How long have you been in business?* field, click the drop-down arrow to see the different options.
8. Click *Less than 1 year* from the drop-down list. See Figure 1–D.

FIGURE 1–D No Two Businesses Are Alike Window—Completed

9. Click the Next button. You move to the What would you like to do in QuickBooks? window.
10. Do not select anything at the What would you like to do in QuickBooks? window.
11. Click the All set button. If a pop-up window appears, click the X in the pop-up window to close it. QuickBooks Online opens to the Dashboard for your company file. See Figure 1–E.

FIGURE 1–E QuickBooks Online Dashboard

Along the top of the Dashboard is the title bar, which includes the company name on the left and the icons on the right. The icons include the Create icon ⊕, the Search Transactions icon 🔍, the Gear icon ⚙, and the Help icon ⓘ.

The Dashboard includes several panels that provide information on the profit and loss, expenses, bank accounts, and so on. Along the left of the Dashboard is the Navigation bar.

Notice the internet browser tab labeled *QuickBooks.* This tab will display different names as you move around QuickBooks Online, but this tab must stay open at all times while completing chapter work. If you close this tab while working in the Test Drive sample company file—which you will soon open—you will exit out of QuickBooks Online, and your work will be lost. Be very careful to never click the X on this tab regardless of the name on the tab.

You can, however, use the back and forward arrows in your browser to move around QuickBooks Online, but it is usually better to use the Navigation bar or the links within the windows.

12. On the title bar, click the Create icon. The Create window appears. See Figure 1–F.

FIGURE 1–F
Create Window

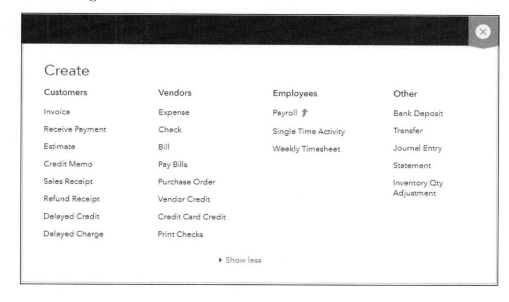

The Create window displays four columns of information: *Customers, Vendors, Employees,* and *Other*. Each column contains links for easy access to information and activities for each category.

Notice on the title bar that the Create icon ⊕ changed to the Close icon ⊗. To close the Create window, click the Close icon or on any blank space outside the Create window but within QuickBooks Online.

13. On the title bar, click the Gear icon. The Olivia's Web Solutions (Company) window appears. If a pop-up message appears, click the X to close the message. Then click the Gear icon, if necessary, to open the Olivia's Web Solutions (Company) window. The Olivia's Web Solutions window displays four columns of information: *Your Company, Lists, Tools,* and *[Your Name]*. See Figure 1–G.

FIGURE 1–G
Olivia's Web Solutions
(Company) Window

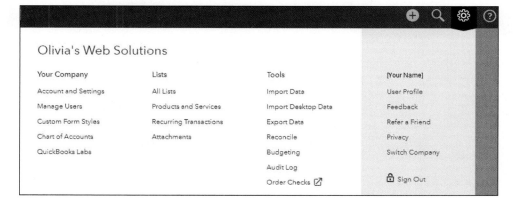

14. Click *Sign Out* in the *[Your Name]* column. You have exited out of QuickBooks Online.
15. Close the internet browser.

Opening QuickBooks Online

After you have created your QuickBooks Online account and set up your company file, the process for opening QuickBooks Online is much shorter.

To open and close QuickBooks Online:
1. Open an internet browser, key https://intuit.com into the address bar, and then press the Enter key or click the Go arrow. This opens the Intuit home page.
2. Along the top of the Intuit home page, click the Sign In button. A window appears displaying several buttons in three sections: *Individuals, Small Business,* and *Accountants.* See Figure 1–H.

FIGURE 1–H
Intuit Sign In Button Choices

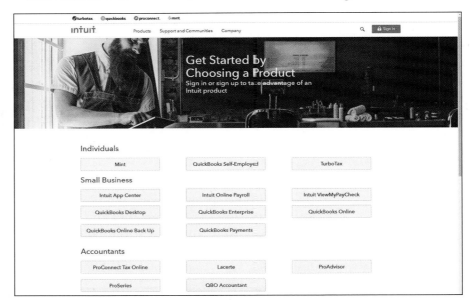

3. In the *Small Business* section, click the QuickBooks Online button. The Sign in window appears.
4. Key in your user ID and password.
5. Click the Sign in button. If a window appears requesting additional verification information, click Skip or enter the information and click Continue. QuickBooks Online launches, and the QuickBooks Dashboard for Olivia's Web Solutions company file appears.

   When you purchase the desktop program of QuickBooks, you are able to store several company files on your computer. When you subscribe to QuickBooks Online, you can have only one company file (unless you pay a separate fee for each new company file). This company file will open each time you sign in to QuickBooks Online.
6. On the title bar, click the Gear icon. The Company window appears.
7. Click *Sign Out* in the *[Your Name]* column. You have exited out of QuickBooks Online.
8. Close the internet browser.

Opening the Test Drive

As previously noted, in QuickBooks Online you can have access to only one company file. To help you learn how to use QuickBooks Online, Intuit provides a Test Drive sample company file. You do not need to subscribe to QuickBooks Online to access the Test Drive sample company file—anyone can access it free of charge. You can experiment with the Test Drive sample company file and perform a variety of activities and enter transactions, but when you close the Test Drive file, the transactions are not saved. To set up your own company file and record and save activities, you must subscribe to QuickBooks Online by paying a monthly fee. If you want to use QuickBooks Online for more than one company file, you must pay a separate monthly fee for each company file.

The Test Drive sample company file will be used throughout this textbook (except in Chapter 2) to illustrate the different aspects of the QuickBooks Online software. The sample company file in the Test Drive is for Craig's Design and Landscaping Services.

In Chapter 2, you will learn how to set up a new company file using Olivia's Web Solutions, the company you began to set up to create your QuickBooks Online account. In all other chapters, you will use the Test Drive sample company file to learn the content of the chapter, and at the end of each chapter, you will have the opportunity to practice using QuickBooks Online with the Olivia's Web Solutions company file you created.

> **HINT**
>
> This textbook provides access to QuickBooks Online for one year for no extra charge and allows you to create one company file.

Open the Test Drive

To open the QuickBooks Online Test Drive:

1. Open an internet browser, key https://QBO18.ParadigmEducation.com/TestDrive into the address bar, and then press the Enter key or click the Go arrow. This opens the Security Verification page.
2. Click the check box to the left of the text *I'm not a robot*. A window may appear with images. If so, follow the instructions to select images and then click NEXT, SKIP, or VERIFY. (This may take several attempts.)
3. Click the Continue button. The QuickBooks Online Test Drive opens with the sample company Craig's Design and Landscaping Services displayed. See Figure 1–I.

FIGURE 1–I

QuickBooks Online—Craig's Design and Landscaping Services Dashboard

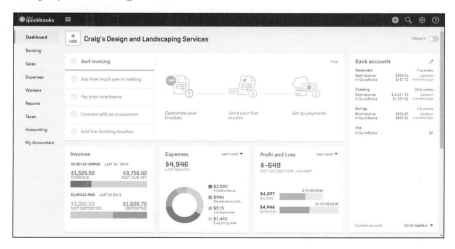

To change the company name:

1. On the title bar, click the Gear icon. This opens the Craig's Design and Landscaping Services (Company) window.

2. At the Craig's Design and Landscaping Services window, click *Account and Settings* in the *Your Company* column. This opens the Account and Settings window.

    At the Account and Settings window, there are four tabs on the left: Company, Sales, Expenses, and Advanced. When you subscribe to QuickBooks Online, you will also see the Billing & Subscriptions tab. Sometimes there will also be a Payments tab. By default, the Company tab is selected. There are five sections on the Company tab: *Company name, Company type, Contact info, Address*, and *Communications with Intuit*. See Figure 1–J.

FIGURE 1–J Account and Settings Window—Company Tab Selected

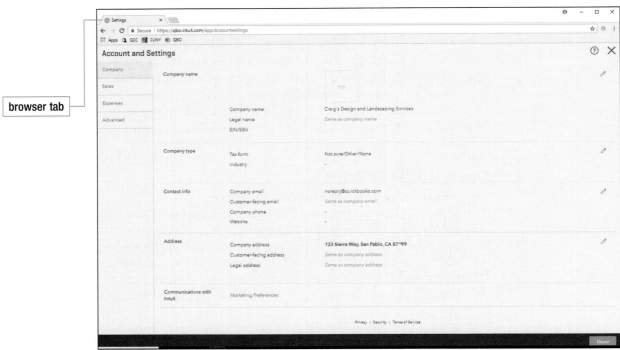

Notice the browser's QuickBooks tab displays Settings. Never click the X on the browser tab, or it will exit out of QuickBooks Online and all work will be lost.

3. On the Company tab, click the Edit icon [✏] in the *Company name* section or click anywhere in the section. The *Company name* section expands to display more information about the company, and you can now edit the company information.

4. In the *Company name* field, key EX1 [*Your Name*] Craig's Design and Landscaping Services, where *Your Name* is your first and last name. See Figure 1–K.

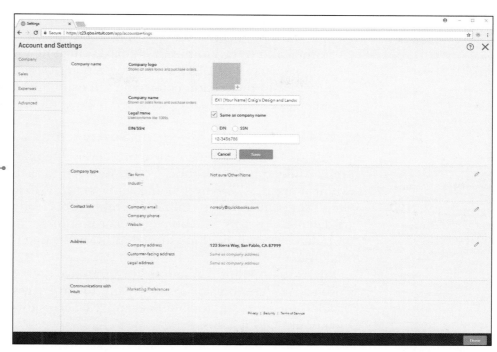

The company name will display in the heading of reports you will create and print in later chapters. Including the exercise's chapter number and your name as well as the company name (e.g., EX1 [*Your Name*] Craig's Design and Landscaping Services, or OWS1 [*Your Name*] Olivia's Web Solutions) will help you keep track of your reports.

5. Confirm the information is correct and then click the Save button.

The changes are saved, and you return to the Account and Settings window with the *Company name* section updated and condensed. If the *Company name* section does not display, click the Company tab on the left. See Figure 1–L.

FIGURE 1–L

Account and Settings
Window—Company Tab
Selected—Company
Name Section—Edit
Completed

HINT
Do not click the X on the browser tab or you will exit out of QuickBooks Online.

6. Confirm the information is correct and then click the Done button in the lower right corner of the window, or click the X in the upper right corner. You return to the Dashboard, which now displays the updated company name of EX1 [*Your Name*] Craig's Design and Landscaping Services. In the section below, you will exit QuickBooks Online, and all changes to the Test Drive sample company file will be lost.

Multi-User and Single-User Software

multi-user software
QuickBooks Online feature that allows up to five users and two accountants to have access to the company file.

QuickBooks Online is designed so that several people can use one company file at the same time. This is referred to as **multi-user software**. Assume a business has three bookkeepers, each with a separate computer. When using QuickBooks Online, the multi-users feature allows each bookkeeper to access the company records at the same time on separate computers. All information entered individually updates the company file for all users.

QuickBooks Online Plus allows for up to five users in a company, as well as two accountants outside the company, to have access to a company file. For additional fees, up to 25 users can have access to a company file in QuickBooks Online Plus.

single-user software
A type of software that allows only one person to access the company file.

Software that allows only one person to access the account is referred to as **single-user software**.

Exiting QuickBooks Online

HINT
Any work you do in the Test Drive sample company is not saved when you exit out of the company file.

At the end of each session, you should exit QuickBooks Online and close the browser.

To exit QuickBooks Online and close the browser:
1. On the title bar, click the Gear icon.
2. At the Company window, click *Sign Out* in the *Profile* column. This closes the company file and exits QuickBooks Online.
3. Close your browser.

Chapter Review and Assessment

 Study Tools include a presentation and a glossary. Use these resources, available from the links menu in the student ebook, to further develop and review skills learned in this chapter.

Procedure Review

To create your account with QuickBooks Online and begin to set up a new company file:

1. Open an internet browser, key https://QBO18.ParadigmEducation .com/AccountSetUp into the address bar, and then press the Enter key or click the Go arrow. You move to the Set Up Your Account window.
2. Refer to the QuickBooks Online Subscription Card included with the textbook and key the license number and product number in the appropriate fields.
3. Click to insert a check mark to the left of *I agree to the Terms of Service*.
4. Click the Set Up Account button. You move to the Sign Up for QuickBooks window.
5. Complete the Sign Up for QuickBooks window and then click the Create Account button. You are moved to the No two businesses are alike window.

    Be sure to remember the email address and password that you entered at the Sign Up for QuickBooks window, and keep the QuickBooks Online Subscription Card in a safe place.
6. In the *What's your business called?* field, key the company name.
7. In the *How long have you been in business?* field, select an appropriate option from the drop-down list.
8. Click the Next button. You move to the What would you like to do in QuickBooks? window.
9. Do not select anything at the What would you like to do in QuickBooks? window.
10. Click the All set button. If a pop-up window appears, click the X in the pop-up window to close it. QuickBooks Online opens to the Dashboard for your company file.

To open and close QuickBooks Online:

1. Open an internet browser, key https://intuit.com into the address bar, and then press the Enter key or click the Go arrow. This opens the Intuit home page.
2. Along the top of the window, click the Sign In button. A window appears displaying several buttons in three sections: *Individuals*, *Small Business*, and *Accountants*.
3. In the *Small Business* section, click the QuickBooks Online button. The Sign in window appears.
4. Key your user ID and password.

5. Click the Sign in button. The Let's make sure it's you window may appear. If it does, select your preferred method of verification and then click the Continue button. QuickBooks Online launches, and the company file's Dashboard appears.
6. On the title bar, click the Gear icon. The Company window appears.
7. Click *Sign Out* in the *[Your Name]* column. You have exited out of QuickBooks Online.
8. Close the internet browser.

To open and close the QuickBooks Online Test Drive:
1. Open an internet browser, key https://QBO18.ParadigmEducation.com/TestDrive into the address bar, and then press the Enter key or click the Go arrow. This opens the Security Verification window.
2. Click the check box to the left of the text *I'm not a robot*. A window may appear with images. If so, follow the instructions to select images and then click NEXT, SKIP, or VERIFY. (This may take several attempts.)
3. Click the Continue button. The QuickBooks Test Drive sample company file opens. Any work you record in the QuickBooks Test Drive sample company file is not saved when you close the Test Drive.
4. On the title bar, click the Gear icon.
5. At the Company window, click *Sign Out* in the *Profile* column.
6. Close your browser.

To change the company name:
1. On the title bar, click the Gear icon. This opens the Company window.
2. Click *Account and Settings* in the *Your Company* column. This opens the Account and Settings window with the Company tab selected.
3. Click the Edit icon in the *Company name* section. The section expands to display more information about the company, and you can now edit the company information.
4. In the *Company name* field, change the company name to the desired name.
5. Click the Save button. The changes are saved, and you return to the Account and Settings window with the *Company name* section updated and condensed. If the *Company name* section does not update, click the Company tab on the left.
6. Click the Done button in the lower right corner of the window. You return to the Dashboard, which now displays the updated company name.

Key Concepts

Select the letter of the item that best matches each definition.

a. company name	f. Reports
b. Test Drive	g. New Company Setup
c. Activities	h. online
d. QuickBooks Online	i. Gear
e. desktop	j. Lists

_____ 1. A software application used to record business and accounting activities, designed with the non-accountant in mind.

_____ 2. The level of operation that creates and sets up a new company file.

_____ 3. The level of operation that stores information that can later be recalled rather than requiring the data to be rekeyed.

_____ 4. The level of operation at which most routine work is processed.

_____ 5. The level of operation at which information can be displayed and printed.

_____ 6. A sample company file provided by Intuit to help you learn QuickBooks Online.

_____ 7. The name that appears on the Dashboard of QuickBooks Online and in the heading of reports.

_____ 8. The version of QuickBooks that you access via the internet.

_____ 9. The version of the QuickBooks software that you install on your computer.

_____ 10. An icon on the title bar used to change the company name and sign out of QuickBooks Online.

Procedure Check

Write a response for each of the following prompts.

1. What is QuickBooks Online?
2. Identify the four levels of operation for QuickBooks Online and provide a brief description of each.
3. Identify the two styles of QuickBooks and provide a brief description of each. What is the major difference between the two styles?
4. List the steps for opening and closing the Test Drive.
5. List the steps for opening and closing QuickBooks Online. After opening QuickBooks Online, in the classroom environment, why would you change the company name?
6. Discuss the advantages of using a computerized accounting software package instead of using non-computerized accounting methods. Discuss the specific advantages of using QuickBooks Online.

Case Problem

Demonstrate your knowledge of the QuickBooks Online features discussed in this chapter by completing the following case problem.

On June 1, 2019, Olivia Chen started her business, Olivia's Web Solutions, as an internet consultant and web page designer.

1. Sign in to QuickBooks Online.
2. Change the company name to **OWS1 [*Your Name*] Olivia's Web Solutions**.
3. Close QuickBooks Online.
4. Close the internet browser.

CHAPTER 2

New Company Setup

Setting Up the Company File; Updating the Chart of Accounts List and Products and Services List; and Printing Accounting Reports

Objectives

- Set up a new company file and update company information
- Customize and update the Chart of Accounts List
- Record the opening journal entry
- Update the Products and Services List
- Display and print accounting reports

In Chapter 1, you learned that there are four levels of operation for QuickBooks Online: New Company Setup, Lists, Activities, and Reports. In this chapter you will continue the first level of operation—New Company Setup.

When you created your account with QuickBooks Online, you also began to set up the company file for Olivia's Web Solutions.

In this chapter you will learn how to continue the setup of this company file so that it can be used to record the activities for the company.

QuickBooks Online versus Manual Accounting: New Company Setup

In a manual accounting system, a company's records are set up by creating the Chart of Accounts and the general ledger. The **Chart of Accounts** is the list of accounts (assets, liabilities, equity, revenues, and expenses) the company intends to use as it conducts its business. The **general ledger** is the book of all accounts with their respective opening balances. If desired, subsidiary ledgers can also be created and beginning balances recorded. The subsidiary ledgers typically include accounts receivable and accounts payable. If the perpetual inventory system is used, an inventory subsidiary ledger is also created.

In QuickBooks Online, a company's records are set up by creating a new company file and establishing the Chart of Accounts List. As the opening balances are entered, QuickBooks simultaneously sets up the general ledger. QuickBooks sets up the Customer List and Vendor List; these lists are equivalent to the accounts receivable and accounts payable subsidiary ledgers. QuickBooks also sets up the Products and Services List, a list that is equivalent to an inventory subsidiary ledger. However, in QuickBooks, the Products and Services List includes service revenue items in addition to inventory items.

In this chapter, you will set up the company file by customizing the company information, establishing preferences, customizing and updating the Chart of Accounts List, and updating the Product and Services List. You will then enter a journal entry to record the opening balances for a few accounts.

 ## Chapter Problem

On June 1, 2019, Olivia Chen started her business, Olivia's Web Solutions, as an internet consultant and web page designer. She began by depositing $25,000 cash in a bank account in the business's name. She also contributed a computer system. The computer has an outstanding note balance of $2,500 that will be assumed by the business. You will set up the company file using New Company Setup and record the opening balances for the cash, computer, note payable, and capital accounts. Olivia anticipates spending the beginning of the month setting up her office and expects to provide web design and internet consulting services later in the month, which you will learn to record in Chapter 3.

Before setting up a new company file, gather all the information you need, including company information (name, address, tax identification numbers) and general ledger account names, account numbers, and opening balances. Enter this information into QuickBooks Online as you set up the new company file.

New Company Setup

In New Company Setup, the first level of operation in QuickBooks, you will enter the information needed to set up a company file for Olivia's Web Solutions. In Chapter 1, you began New Company Setup when you created your account. You will now continue with New Company Setup.

To continue New Company Setup:

1. Sign in to QuickBooks Online. QuickBooks Online opens to the Dashboard for OWS1 [*Your Name*] Olivia's Web Solutions. See Figure 2–A.

FIGURE 2–A QuickBooks Online—Dashboard

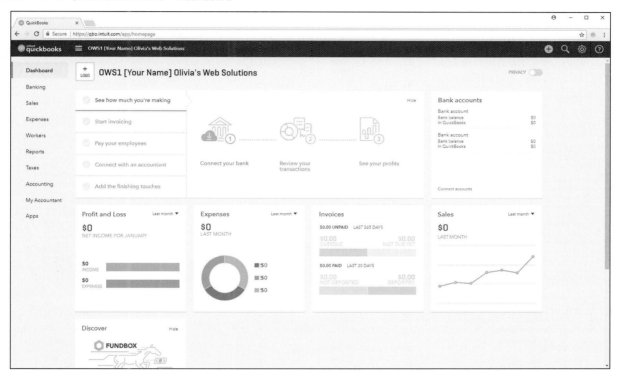

HINT

If your company name does not display OWS1 [*Your Name*] Olivia's Web Solutions, then you did not do the Case Problem at the end of Chapter 1. You can go back to Chapter 1 and complete the Case Problem at the end of the chapter or continue with these steps.

2. On the title bar, click the Gear icon ⚙. If a pop-up message appears, close it and click the Gear icon again, if necessary. The OWS1 [*Your Name*] Olivia's Web Solutions (Company) window displays.

3. Click *Account and Settings* in the *Your Company* column. The Account and Settings window appears with the Company tab selected.

4. Click the Edit icon in the *Company name* section or click anywhere in the section. The *Company name* section expands, and you can now edit the information.

5. In the *Company name* field, key EX2 [*Your Name*] Olivia's Web Solutions.

6. In the *Legal name* field, confirm there is a check mark in the check box to the left of *Same as company name*. If necessary, click the check box to insert a check mark. The legal name is the name that will be used on tax forms. If the company name and legal name are not the same, you can make any necessary changes. For our sample company, the company name and legal name are the same.

7. In the *EIN/SSN* field, click the *EIN* radio button and then key 55-5656566 in the text box.

8. Confirm the information is correct and click the Save button. The *Company name* section of the Account and Settings window updates with the information. If the information does not display, click the Company tab.

9. Click the Edit icon in the *Company type* section or click anywhere in the section. The *Company type* section expands, and you can now edit the information.

10. In the *Tax form* field, click *Sole proprietor (Form 1040).*

11. Confirm the information is correct and then click the Save button. The *Company type* section updates with the information.

12. Scroll down and click the Edit icon in the *Contact info* section or click anywhere in the section. The *Contact info* section expands, and you can now edit the information.

13. In the *Company phone* field, key 516-555-5000.

14. Confirm the information is correct and click the Save button. The *Contact info* section of the Account and Settings window updates with the information.

15. Scroll down and click the Edit icon in the *Address* section or click anywhere in the section. The *Address* section expands, and you can now edit the information.

16. Key or select the following information in the indicated fields:
    Street: 547 Miller Place
    City: Westport
    State: NY
    Zip: 12993

17. Confirm the information is correct and then click the Save button. The *Address* section of the Account and Settings window updates with the information. See Figure 2–B.

FIGURE 2–B Account and Settings Window—Company Tab Updated

18. Confirm the information is correct and then click the Done button. You return to the Dashboard.

Establishing Preferences

When you set up your account, QuickBooks Online enables or disables features. These features are referred to as *preferences*. The preferences can be enabled or disabled at the Account and Settings window as well. Sometimes if you are unable to perform a task in QuickBooks Online, it may be because a preference has not yet been enabled. In this chapter, you will use the Account and Settings window to enable the inventory preference, increase the time-out period, and enable the account number preference. In later chapters, you will enable additional preferences.

HINT

An alternative way to access the Account and Settings window is to click the company name—EX2 [*Your Name*] Olivia's Web Solutions—on the Dashboard.

To enable the inventory preference:

1. On the title bar, click the Gear icon. The EX2 [*Your Name*] Olivia's Web Solutions window appears.
2. At the EX2 [*Your Name*] Olivia's Web Solutions window, in the *Your Company* column, click *Account and Settings*. The Account and Settings window appears.
3. Click the Sales tab on the left.

    There are seven sections on the Sales tab: *Customize, Sales form content, Products and services, Messages, Reminders, Online delivery,* and *Statements.* The *Products and services* section is where you enable the inventory preference. See Figure 2–C.

FIGURE 2–C Account and Settings Window—Sales Tab

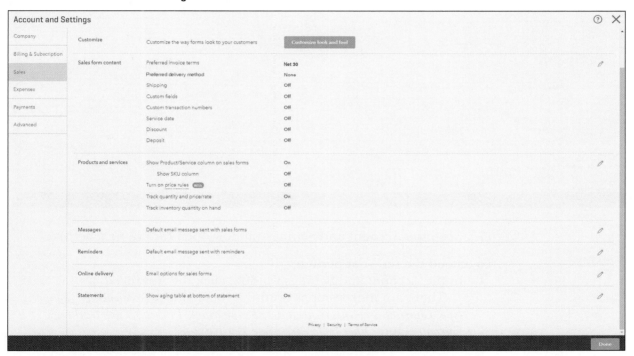

4. Click the Edit icon in the *Product and services* section or click anywhere in the section. The *Product and services* section expands, and you can now edit the information.
5. Insert check marks in the check boxes to the left of *Show Product/Service column on sales forms, Track quantity and price/rate,* and *Track inventory quantity on hand* if they are not already there. See Figure 2–D.

FIGURE 2–D
**Products and Services
Section Completed**

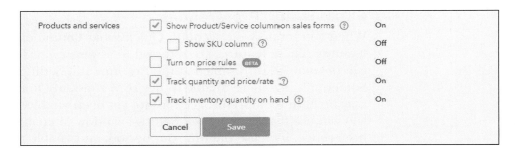

6. Confirm the information is correct and then click the Save button. If a pop-up message appears, click the OK button. The changes are saved and the inventory preference is now enabled. See Figure 2–E.

FIGURE 2–E Account and Settings Window—Sales Tab—Updated

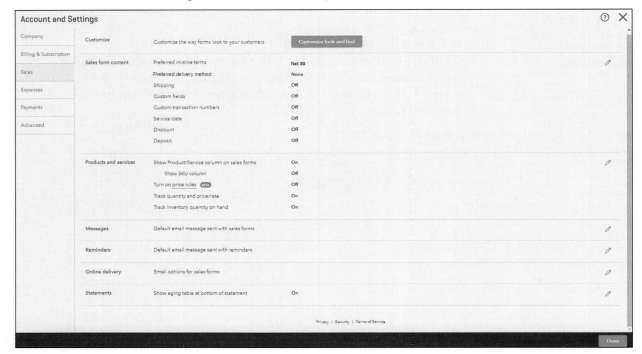

7. Keep the Account and Settings window open for the next activity.

To extend the time-out period:
1. In the Account and Settings window, click the Advanced tab.
   There are nine sections on the Advanced tab: *Accounting, Company type, Chart of accounts, Categories, Automation, Projects, Time tracking, Currency,* and *Other preferences.* See Figure 2–F.

FIGURE 2–F   Account and Settings Window—Advanced Tab

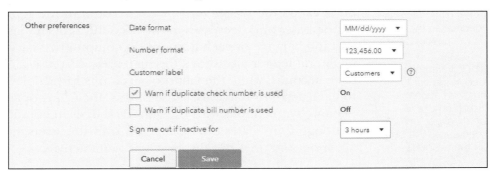

Notice in the *Chart of accounts* section, the *Enable account numbers* option is set to *Off.* You will enable this preference in the "Customizing and Updating the Chart of Accounts List" section of this chapter.

Notice also in the *Other preferences* section there is a *Sign me out if inactive for* option that is set to *1 hour.* By default, if QuickBooks Online is inactive for one hour, you will automatically be signed out. You can extend this time to a maximum of three hours.

2. Click the Edit icon in the *Other preferences* section or click anywhere in the section. The *Other preferences* section expands, and you can now edit the information.

3. At the *Sign me out if inactive for* field, click the drop-down arrow and then click *3 hours.* See Figure 2–G.

FIGURE 2–G
Other Preferences
Section—Completed

4. Confirm the information is correct and then click the Save button. The change is saved, and you will now be automatically signed out if you are inactive for three hours instead of one hour. See Figure 2–H.

FIGURE 2–H Account and Settings Window—Advanced Tab—Updated

5. Click the Done button or click the X to close the Account and Settings window.

Lists

Chart of Accounts List

debit Dollar amount recorded in the *left* column of an account. Depending on the account, it either increases or decreases the balance in the account.

credit Dollar amount recorded in the *right* column of an account. Depending on the account, it either increases or decreases the balance in the account.

Recall from Chapter 1 that the second level of operation in QuickBooks Online is recording information in Lists. The Chart of Accounts List is the list of accounts a company uses as it conducts its business. In a manual accounting system, all the individual accounts are placed together in a book called the *general ledger*. Each account in the general ledger shows all increases and decreases in the account, reflected as **debits** and **credits**, and the balance of each account. In computerized accounting systems, a general ledger also shows the increases, decreases, and balance for each account, while the Chart of Accounts List displays the balance next to each account name. Because of this, the Chart of Accounts List has become synonymous with the general ledger in computerized systems, although it indicates the balance for only the assets, liabilities, and equity accounts and does not display all account activity.

In QuickBooks Online, the Chart of Accounts List consists of the account number, name, account type, detail type, and balance. The account numbers are optional but are used in this textbook for the Case Problem at the end of the chapter. The account name is whatever name you assign to an account, and it appears in various windows and on reports. The balance is determined by the original amount entered (if any) when the account is first created and then subsequently updated by Activities entered in the windows.

The account type identifies the account as an asset, liability, equity, or income and expense account. The account types are used to determine where to place the account name and balance on the financial statements.

The account types include:

Assets: 　Accounts Receivable (A/R) 　Other Current Assets 　Bank 　Fixed Assets 　Other Assets **Liabilities:** 　Accounts Payable (A/P) 　Credit Card 　Other Current Liabilities 　Long Term Liabilities	**Equity:** 　Equity **Income and Expenses:** 　Income 　Cost of Goods Sold 　Expenses 　Other Income 　Other Expense

The detail type is a specific subcategory of the account type. It is determined by QuickBooks Online and cannot be changed. The detail type subcategorizes the account on the financial statements. For example, a Prepaid Insurance account would first be identified as an Other Current Asset account type, and then QuickBooks Online would subcategorize the Prepaid Insurance account as a Prepaid Expense in the detail type.

As you set up the Chart of Accounts List, QuickBooks Online uses the account types to identify certain accounts as system default accounts. These default accounts, which will be explained in more detail in the following section, "System Default Accounts," determine which account should be used when a transaction is recorded. For example, the Accounts Payable account type is used to identify the Accounts Payable liability account when purchase on account transactions are recorded. The Accounts Receivable account type is used to identify the Accounts Receivable asset account when sales on account transactions are recorded. QuickBooks Online does not use the account name to identify a system default account because the account name is customized by the user. Instead, when the software looks for an account, it looks for the account type and detail type.

To review the Chart of Accounts List:

1. On the Navigation bar, click Reports. The Reports window appears. See Figure 2–I.

FIGURE 2–I

Reports Window—All Reports

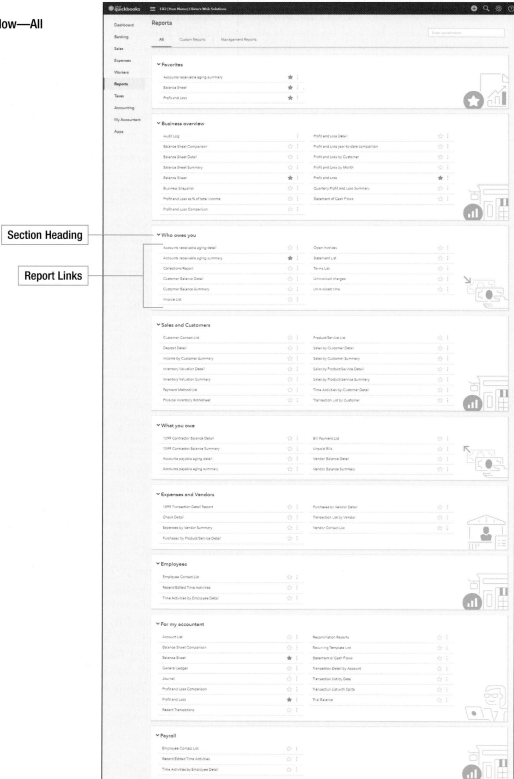

Section Heading

Report Links

Along the top of the Reports window are three links: All, Custom Reports, and Management Reports. The default is the All link as noted by the green underline. In the Reports window, reports are listed in nine sections. The section headings are: *Favorites, Business overview, Who owes you, Sales and Customers, What you owe, Expenses and Vendors, Employees, For my accountant,* and *Payroll.* Listed below each of these section headings are the reports associated with the section heading.

Look at the reports listed under the *For my accountant* section. These are the reports an accountant would typically need.

2. In the *For my accountant* section, click *Account List.* If the *Customize reports instantly* message appears, click the X to close it. The Account List Report displays. See Figure 2–J.

FIGURE 2–J Account List Report

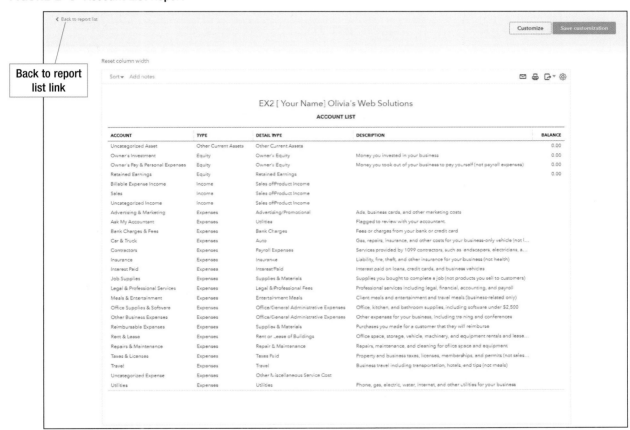

Back to report list link

Notice the Back to report list link. Each time you open a report, you will see this link in the upper left corner of the report.

3. Keep the Account List Report open for the next activity.

These are the accounts that were automatically created by QuickBooks Online when you created the company file in Chapter 1. If your accounts do not match, you will have an opportunity to correct the Account List after you learn the procedures in this chapter.

Notice the Account List Report displays five columns: *ACCOUNT, TYPE, DETAIL TYPE, DESCRIPTION,* and *BALANCE.* Between each of these column headings is a dotted line. To widen or narrow the columns, hover the mouse pointer over the dotted line. The pointer becomes parallel lines with arrows pointing left and right. Click and drag to the left or to the right to make the column wider or narrower.

At the top of every report is a report bar that contains some or all of the following links, icons, and buttons: Sort, Add notes, Email icon, Print icon, Export icon, and Settings icon. Each report window also contains a Customize button and a Save customization button. See Figure 2–K.

FIGURE 2–K
Report Bar

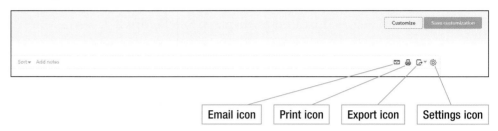

To view a specific account:

1. With the Account List Report open, place the mouse pointer over the Sales account. The Sales account name displays in blue font and is underlined.
2. Click *Sales* to select it. The Account window for Sales displays.

The Account window contains the following account fields:

Account Type	Use the drop-down list to display and choose the account type. QuickBooks Online uses the account type to identify the account as an asset, liability, equity, income, or expense account; to identify it as a system default account; and for placement in financial statements.
Detail Type	The detail type subcategorizes the type of the account and is also used to identify system default accounts and for placement in financial statements. Detail types are predefined by QuickBooks and cannot be changed by the user.
Name	The user determines the account name. The software uses the account type, not the account name, for necessary identification (default accounts and placement in financial statements). The name keyed in this field appears in various windows and on reports.
Number	An account number is optional. This preference must be enabled for this field to display.
Description	This field is optional. A description entered here appears on certain reports.
Is sub-account	Accounts can be identified as subaccounts of other accounts. To activate this field, click to insert a check mark in the check box. Once this field is activated, use the drop-down list to determine in which account this will become a subaccount.
Balance and *as of*	Enter a balance and the appropriate date in these fields for assets, liabilities, and equity accounts only. In this textbook, the beginning balances will be entered in the journal.

3. Click the *Detail Type* drop-down arrow, and notice the *Sales of Product Income* detail type for this account. See Figure 2–L.

FIGURE 2–L

Account Window—Sales of Product Income

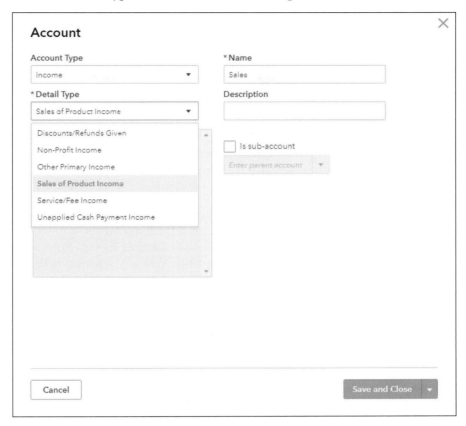

4. Close the Account window by clicking the X or the Cancel button.
5. Close the Account List Report by clicking Dashboard on the Navigation bar.

System Default Accounts

As previously noted, QuickBooks Online establishes system default accounts and uses those accounts when recording transactions in the Activities windows. QuickBooks Online looks for these system default accounts in the Chart of Accounts List; if it cannot find an account, it will create one. Some system default accounts are Accounts Receivable, Undeposited Funds, Accounts Payable, Sales Tax Payable, Inventory, and Cost of Goods Sold. Other system default accounts include equity accounts (Capital and Accumulated Earnings) and payroll accounts (Payroll Liabilities and Payroll Expenses). When you created the company file and established some of the company preferences, QuickBooks Online created some of the system default accounts.

Some of the system default accounts can be customized to an account name of your choosing, or even deleted, and some cannot. If you enable a preference or enter a transaction for a system default account you have renamed or deleted, QuickBooks Online will automatically re-create the system default account.

System default accounts that cannot be deleted, used for anything else, or renamed are:

> Credit Card Receivables
> Undeposited Funds
> Inventory/Stock Assets
> Cost of Goods Sold/Cost of Sales
> Reconcile/Reconciliation Discrepancies
> Unapplied Cash Payment Income

System default accounts that cannot be deleted or used for anything else but that can be renamed are:

> Opening Balance Equity
> Retained Earnings

In this textbook, you will leave as is the accounts that you cannot rename, with two exceptions. Although QuickBooks Online already created them as system default accounts, you will create several Inventory accounts and several other Cost of Goods Sold accounts that the software will not be able to identify. You will leave as is the Inventory and Cost of Goods Sold accounts that QuickBooks Online created. In a later chapter, you will see that you can use the accounts you created, and not the system default accounts created by QuickBooks Online, in the transactions.

Customizing and Updating the Chart of Accounts List

When you set up your company in QuickBooks Online, a Chart of Accounts List was automatically created with accounts common to all types of businesses. Refer to Figure 2–J on page 29 for the accounts QuickBooks Online created for Olivia's Web Solutions.

You will customize the Chart of Accounts List for Olivia's Web Solutions by first enabling the account numbers preference and then adding and editing new accounts with account numbers and names.

Enabling the Account Numbers Preference

By default, QuickBooks Online does not use account numbers. Notice in the Chart of Accounts List and in the Account window (see Figure 2–J on page 29 and Figure 2–L on page 31) that there aren't any account numbers, nor is there a field to record an account number.

When you don't use account numbers, QuickBooks Online lists the accounts in alphabetical order within each account type. When you do use account numbers, QuickBooks Online lists the accounts in numerical order.

To add account numbers to the Chart of Accounts List, you must enable the account numbers preference in the Account and Settings window.

To enable the account numbers preference:
1. On the title bar, click the Gear icon. The EX2 [*Your Name*] Olivia's Web Solutions window appears.
2. At the EX2 [*Your Name*] Olivia's Web Solutions window, in the *Your Company* column, click *Account and Settings*. The Account and Settings window appears.
3. Click the Advanced tab.

4. Click the Edit icon in the *Chart of accounts* section or click anywhere in the section. The *Chart of accounts* section expands, and you can now edit the information.
5. Click the check box to the left of *Enable account numbers* to insert a check mark.
6. Click the check box to the left of *Show account numbers* to insert a check mark. The account numbers will now display in reports and transactions. See Figure 2–M.

FIGURE 2–M

Chart of Accounts Section Expanded— Account Numbers Enabled

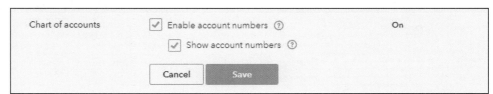

7. Confirm the information is correct and then click the Save button. The account *NUMBER* column will now appear in the Chart of Accounts window, the Account window, and the Account List Report.
8. Click the Done button or click the X to close the Account and Settings window.

Adding an Account

Now you will add new accounts to the Chart of Accounts List that QuickBooks Online created. You will then update the Chart of Accounts List by editing the accounts created by QuickBooks Online.

There are several ways that you can access reports and information in QuickBooks Online. You first viewed the Accounts List as a report. To add new accounts, you will now access the Chart of Accounts List using the Gear icon.

HINT

An alternative to using the Gear icon to access the Chart of Accounts window is to click the Accounting tab on the Navigation bar.

To add a new account:
1. On the title bar, click the Gear icon. The EX2 [*Your Name*] Olivia's Web Solutions window appears.
2. At the EX2 [*Your Name*] Olivia's Web Solutions window, in the *Lists* column, click *All Lists*. The Lists window appears. See Figure 2–N.

FIGURE 2–N Lists Window

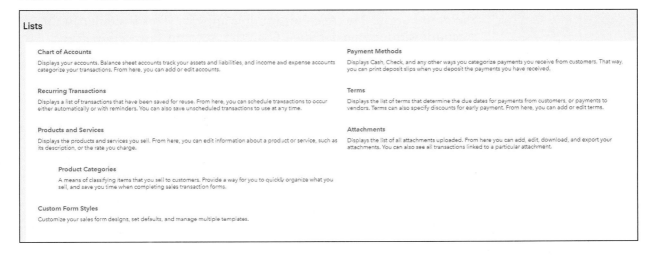

3. At the Lists window, click *Chart of Accounts.* The first time you access the Chart of Accounts List, a window will appear with a See your Chart of Accounts button. You will only see this button the first time you access the Chart of Accounts List.
4. Click the See your Chart of Accounts button. The Chart of Accounts window appears. See Figure 2–O.

FIGURE 2–O Chart of Accounts Window

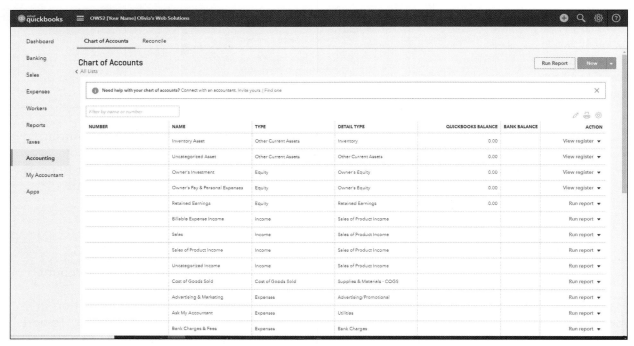

Notice that the Chart of Accounts window has the same column headings as the Account List Report: *NUMBER* (after the account numbers preference was enabled), *NAME,* (account) *TYPE, DETAIL TYPE,* and *QUICKBOOKS BALANCE.* The Chart of Accounts window also has a *BANK BALANCE* column and an *ACTION* column. In the *ACTION* column, when you click the drop-down arrow, *Edit* and *Delete* options appear. You will use these options later.

5. In the upper right corner of the Chart of Accounts window, click the New button. The Account window appears. This is similar to the Account window you accessed from the Account List Report (see Figure 2–L on page 31), but in this Account window, you can also add new accounts. Notice now there is a *Number* field.

6. At the Account window, click the drop-down arrow in the *Account Type* field. The drop-down list of account types appears. See Figure 2–P.

FIGURE 2–P
Account Window—
Account Type Selected

7. Select *Bank* from the *Account Type* drop-down list.
8. In the *Detail Type* drop-down list, click *Checking*.
9. Key in the following information in the indicated fields so that your screen matches Figure 2–Q.
   Name: Cash - Checking
   Number: 1010

FIGURE 2–Q
Account Window—
Checking Completed

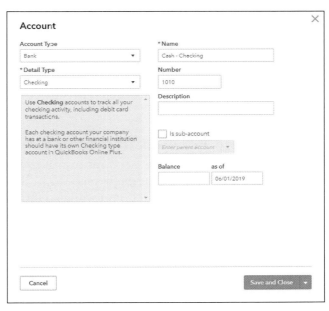

10. Confirm the information is correct, click the Save and Close button arrow, and then click *Save and New* from the drop-down list. The information is saved, and the button will change to Save and New. The Account window resets for the next account.

11. Use the information in Table 2–1 to add new accounts to the Chart of Accounts List.

TABLE 2–1

Chart of Accounts List—New Accounts

HINT

In the *Account Type* field, instead of looking for the type in the drop-down list, key the first letter of the account type to find it quickly.

Account Type	Detail Type	Account Name	Number
Accounts receivable (A/R)	Accounts Receivable (A/R)	Accounts Receivable	1200
Other Current Assets	Undeposited Funds	Undeposited Funds	1250
Other Current Assets	Inventory	Inventory of Scanners	1265
Other Current Assets	Prepaid Expenses	Computer Supplies	1300
Other Current Assets	Prepaid Expenses	Prepaid Advertising	1410
Other Current Assets	Prepaid Expenses	Prepaid Insurance	1420
Fixed Assets	Fixed Asset Computers	Computers - Cost	1725
Fixed Assets	Fixed Asset Furniture	Furniture - Cost	1825
Fixed Assets	Fixed Asset Software	Software - Cost	1925
Accounts payable (A/P)	Accounts Payable (A/P)	Accounts Payable	2010
Other Current Liabilities	Loan Payable	Notes Payable	2020
Equity	Owner's Equity	Olivia Chen, Drawings	3020
Income	Service/Fee Income	Web Page Design Fees	4010
Income	Service/Fee Income	Internet Consulting Fees	4020
Income	Sales of Product Income	Sale of Scanners	4065
Cost of Goods Sold	Supplies & Materials - COGS	Cost of Scanners Sold	5065
Expenses	Supplies & Materials	Office Supplies Expense	6325
Expenses	Utilities	Telephone Expense	6450

12. Close the Account window.
13. Close the Chart of Accounts by clicking Dashboard on the Navigation bar.

Editing Account Names and Adding Account Numbers

After you enable the account numbers preference, you can then enter account numbers for each account in the Chart of Accounts List. In the following activities, you will also change some of the account names assigned by QuickBooks Online to an account name of your choice.

To edit account names and add account numbers to the Chart of Accounts List:
1. On the Navigation bar, click Accounting. The Chart of Accounts window appears.
2. In the row that displays the account name *Inventory Asset*, click the drop-down arrow to the right of *View register* in the *ACTION* column. The drop-down menu appears. See Figure 2–R.

FIGURE 2–R
View Register
Drop-Down Menu

Notice that for asset, liability, and equity accounts, the *ACTION* column displays *View register* with options to *Edit* or *Delete* the account or to *Run report* to generate an Account QuickReport (discussed in Chapter 5). For the retained earnings, revenue, and expense accounts, the *ACTION* column displays *Run report* in addition to options to *Edit* or *Delete* the account.

3. At the drop-down menu on the Inventory Asset row, click *Edit.* The Account window appears, and you are able to edit the account name and add the account number.

4. In the *Name* field, delete *Inventory Asset* and key Inventory of Computers.

5. In the *Number* field, key 1260. See Figure 2–S.

FIGURE 2–S
Account Window—
Inventory of
Computers—Completed

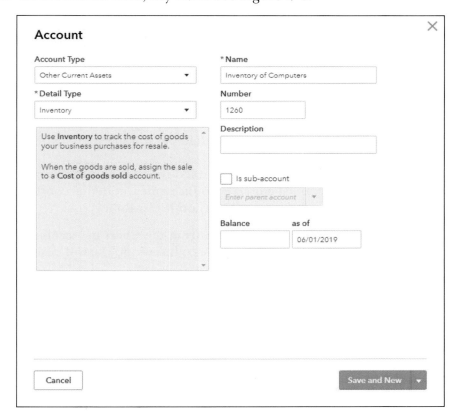

HINT
If the button displays Save and New, click the button arrow and click *Save and Close.* The button changes to Save and Close.

6. Confirm the information is correct and then click the Save and Close button. You return to the updated Chart of Accounts window.

7. Use the information in Table 2–2 to edit each of the accounts created by QuickBooks Online, changing the account names and adding the account numbers as listed below.

TABLE 2–2

Chart of Accounts List— Edit Account Names and Add Account Numbers

Original	Edited	
Account Name	Account Name	Number
Opening Balance Equity	Olivia Chen, Capital	3010
Retained Earnings	Accumulated Earnings	3030
Sales	Sale of Computers	4060
Cost of Goods Sold	Cost of Computers Sold	5060
Advertising & Marketing	Advertising Expense	6050
Insurance	Insurance Expense	6100
Interest Paid	Interest Expense	7000
Legal & Professional Fees	Accounting Expense	6020
Office Supplies & Software	Online Service Expense	6350
Rent and Lease	Rent Expense	6400
Repairs & Maintenance	Repair Expense	6425
Job Supplies	Computer Supplies Expense	6300
Utilities	Utilities Expense	6500

HINT

If an account is not available, refer to Figure 2–T on page 39 for information to create the account.

8. Keep the Chart of Accounts open for the next activity.

Deleting an Account

There are several accounts that were created by QuickBooks Online that Olivia's Web Solutions does not need. In this section, you will delete these accounts. In general, when you take the steps to delete an account, you are not actually deleting it; rather, QuickBooks Online makes the account inactive.

After you have enabled the account numbers preference, added new accounts, edited account names, added account numbers, and deleted accounts, view the Account List Report.

To delete an account from the Chart of Accounts List:

1. At the Chart of Accounts window, scroll down to the Billable Expense Income account.
2. In the *ACTION* column of the Billable Expense Income row, click the drop-down arrow to the right of *Run report*.
3. At the drop-down menu, click *Delete*.
4. At the *Delete Account* warning, click the Yes button. QuickBooks Online does not delete the account but makes it inactive.
5. Delete the following accounts:
    Owners Investment
    Owners Pay & Personal Expenses
    Sales of Product Income
    Ask My Accountant
    Meals and Entertainment
    Other Business Expenses
    Purchases
    Reimbursable Expense
    Taxes & Licenses

To view the Account List Report:

1. On the Navigation bar, click Reports. The Reports window appears.
2. Scroll down to the *For my accountant* section and then click *Account List*. The Account List Report displays. See Figure 2–T.

    If your accounts do not match this Account List, go back and add, edit, or delete accounts as needed.

FIGURE 2–T Account List Report—Updated

Sort▾ Add notes

EX2 [Your Name] Olivia's Web Solutions ✎
ACCOUNT LIST

ACCOUNT #	ACCOUNT	TYPE	DETAIL TYPE	DESCRIPTION	BALANCE
1010	Cash - Checking	Bank	Checking		0.00
1200	Accounts Receivable	Accounts receivable (A/R)	Accounts Receivable (A/R)		0.00
1250	Undeposited Funds	Other Current Assets	Undeposited Funds		0.00
1260	Inventory of Computers	Other Current Assets	Inventory		0.00
1265	Inventory of Scanners	Other Current Assets	Inventory		0.00
1300	Computer Supplies	Other Current Assets	Prepaid Expenses		0.00
1410	Prepaid Advertising	Other Current Assets	Prepaid Expenses		0.00
1420	Prepaid Insurance	Other Current Assets	Prepaid Expenses		0.00
	Uncategorized Asset	Other Current Assets	Other Current Assets		0.00
1725	Computers - Cost	Fixed Assets	Fixed Asset Computers		0.00
1825	Furniture - Cost	Fixed Assets	Fixed Asset Furniture		0.00
1925	Software -Cost	Fixed Assets	Fixed Asset Software		0.00
2010	Accounts Payable	Accounts payable (A/P)	Accounts Payable (A/P)		0.00
2020	Notes Payable	Other Current Liabilities	Loan Payable		0.00
3010	Olivia Chen, Capital	Equity	Opening Balance Equity		0.00
3020	Olivia Chen, Drawings	Equity	Owner's Equity		0.00
3030	Accumulated Earnings	Equity	Retained Earnings		0.00
4010	Web Page Design Fees	Income	Service/Fee Income		
4020	Internet Consulting Fees	Income	Service/Fee Income		
4060	Sale of Computers	Income	Sales of Product Income		
4065	Sale of Scanners	Income	Sales of Product Income		
	Uncategorized Income	Income	Sales of Product Income		
5060	Cost of Computers Sold	Cost of Goods Sold	Supplies & Materials - COGS		
5065	Cost of Scanners Sold	Cost of Goods Sold	Supplies & Materials - COGS		
6020	Accounting Expense	Expenses	Legal & Professional Fees	Professional services including legal, fina...	
6050	Advertising Expense	Expenses	Advertising/Promotional	Ads, business cards, and other marketing...	
6100	Insurance Expense	Expenses	Insurance	Liability, fire, theft, and other insurance fo...	
6300	Computer Supplies Expense	Expenses	Supplies & Materials	Supplies you bought to complete a job (n...	
6325	Office Supplies Expense	Expenses	Supplies & Materials		
6350	Online Service Expense	Expenses	Office/General Administrative E...	Office, kitchen, and bathroom supplies, in...	
6400	Rent Expense	Expenses	Rent or Lease of Buildings	Office space, storage, vehicle, machinery,...	
6425	Repair Expense	Expenses	Repair & Maintenance	Repairs, maintenance, and cleaning for o...	
6450	Telephone Expense	Expenses	Utilities		
6500	Utilities Expense	Expenses	Utilities	Phone, gas, electric, water, internet, and ...	
7000	Interest Expense	Expenses	Interest Paid	Interest paid on loans, credit cards, and b...	
	Bank Charges & Fees	Expenses	Bank Charges	Fees or charges from your bank or credit ...	
	Car & Truck	Expenses	Auto	Gas, repairs, insurance, and other costs fo...	
	Contractors	Expenses	Payroll Expenses	Services provided by 1099 contractors, s...	
	Travel	Expenses	Travel	Business travel including transportation, h...	
	Uncategorized Expense	Expenses	Other Miscellaneous Service Cost		

3. Close the Account List Report by clicking Dashboard on the Navigation bar.

Displaying and Hiding Inactive Accounts

When QuickBooks Online makes an account inactive, the account is no longer displayed in the Chart of Accounts window. You can choose to display inactive accounts in the Chart of Accounts window.

To display inactive accounts:
1. On the Navigation bar, click Accounting. The Chart of Accounts window displays.
2. Click the Settings gear ⚙ above the *ACTION* column.
3. At the *Settings* drop-down menu, in the *Other* section, click the check box to the left of *Include inactive* to insert a check mark.
4. Click the Settings gear to close the drop-down menu.
5. Scroll down the Chart of Accounts window and notice in the *ACTION* column, some rows display *Make active*. These are the inactive accounts.
6. Hide the inactive accounts again by repeating Steps 2–4 to remove the check mark to the left of *Include inactive*.
7. Close the Chart of Accounts window by clicking Dashboard on the Navigation bar.

Updating the Products and Services List

In addition to the Chart of Accounts List, QuickBooks Online uses the Products and Services List, which contains a file for each type of service or inventory item sold by the company. You will now update the Products and Services List by adding two service items that Olivia's Web Solutions will provide: Internet Consulting Services, which will be billed at a rate of $100 per hour, and Web Page Design Services, which will be billed at a rate of $125 per hour.

To add service items to the Products and Services List:
1. On the title bar, click the Gear icon and then click *Products and Services* in the *Lists* column. The Products and Services window appears.
2. At the Products and Services window, click the New button. The Product/Service information window appears.
3. Click *Service*. This opens the Product/Service information—Service window.
4. In the *Name* field, key Internet Consulting Services.
5. Under the *Sales information* section, click to insert a check mark in the check box to the left of *I sell this product/service to my customers*, if necessary.
6. In the *Description on sales forms* field, key Internet Consulting Services.
7. In the *Sales price/rate* field, key 100.
8. In the *Income account* field, select *4020 Internet Consulting Fees*. See Figure 2–U.

FIGURE 2–U
Product/Service
Information—Service
Window—Completed

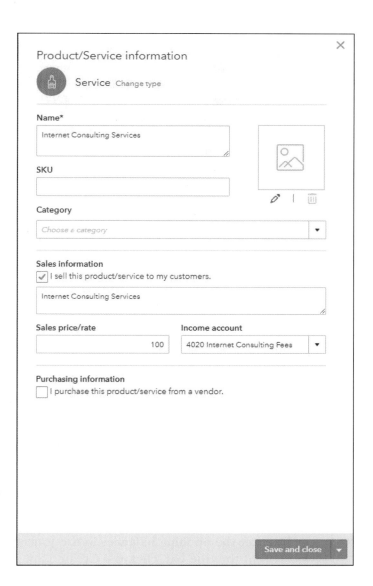

9. Confirm the information is correct, click the Save and close button arrow, and then click *Save and new* from the drop-down list. The service item is saved, and the fields are cleared to enter a new service.

10. Complete the window using the following information:

Name:	Web Page Design Services
Sales information:	(Insert a check mark.)
Description:	Web Page Design Services
Sales price/rate:	125
Income account:	4010 Web Page Design Fees

11. Confirm the information is correct and then click the Save and close button. The two new service items appear in the Products and Services List. See Figure 2–V.

FIGURE 2–V Products and Services Window—Updated

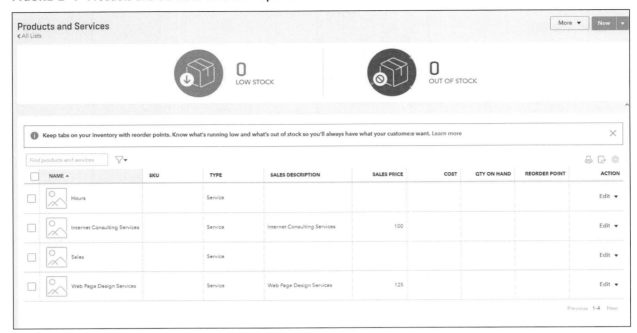

12. To close the Products and Services window, click Dashboard on the Navigation bar.

Entering Opening Balances

You have customized and updated the Chart of Accounts List and the Products and Services List for Olivia's Web Solutions. You will now enter the two opening balances in one journal entry.

To enter the opening balances in the Journal Entry window:

1. On the title bar, click the Create icon ⊕. The Create icon turns into an X, and the Create window appears. See Figure 2–W.

FIGURE 2–W
Create Window

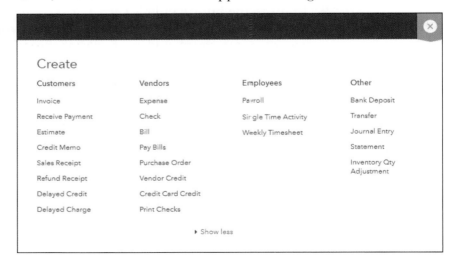

2. At the Create window, in the *Other* column, click *Journal Entry*. The Journal Entry window appears. See Figure 2–X.

FIGURE 2–X Journal Entry Window

The Journal Entry window includes the following elements:

Journal date field	Enter the date for which you want the journal entry recorded.
Journal no. field	Enter a number of your choice or leave the field blank.
ACCOUNT column	Choose the general ledger account.
DEBITS column	Enter the amount to debit to the account.
CREDITS column	Enter the amount to credit to the account.
DESCRIPTION column	Add a description that will appear on reports or leave the field blank.
Move Rows icon	Click and drag this icon to rearrange the order of the rows.
Delete Row icon	Click this icon to delete all information in this row.
Add lines/Clear all lines	Click either of these buttons to add or delete rows.

3. In the *Journal date* field, choose *06/01/2019*.
4. In the *Journal no.* field, key *Opening bal. 1*.
5. In the first line of the *ACCOUNT* column, click the drop-down arrow and then click *1010 Cash - Checking*.
6. In the *DEBITS* column, key 25000.
7. Move to the second line in the *ACCOUNT* column, click the drop-down arrow, and click *3010 Olivia Chen, Capital*.

> **HINT**
>
> You can key in the account number for each account or use the drop-down list.

8. In the *CREDITS* column, *25,000.00* should appear; if it does not, key 25000.

9. In the *DESCRIPTION* column of the second row, key To record owner's investment in company. The *DESCRIPTION* column is optional; you do not have to enter an explanation. See Figure 2–Y.

FIGURE 2–Y Journal Entry Window—Completed

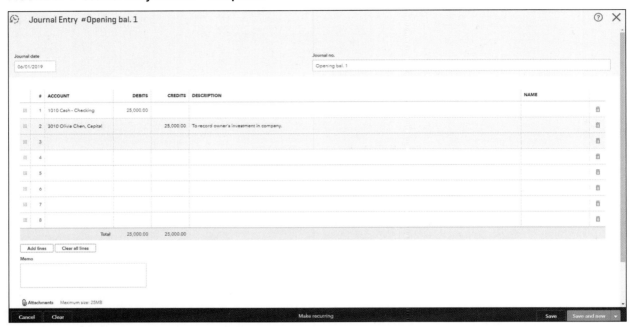

10. Confirm the information is correct, click the Save and new button arrow, and then click *Save and close* from the drop-down list.

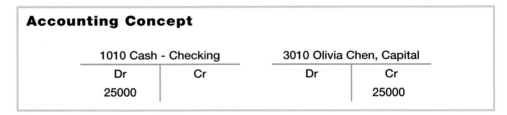

Accounting Concept

1010 Cash - Checking		3010 Olivia Chen, Capital	
Dr	Cr	Dr	Cr
25000			25000

Reports

Displaying and Printing Accounting Reports

Upon completing the New Company Setup and entering the beginning balances at the Journal Entry window, you should display and print the accounting reports.

There are several accounting reports, which you will learn about in the coming chapters. For this chapter, you will display and print the Account List Report and the Journal Report.

Account List Report

You viewed the Account List Report earlier in this chapter. Remember the Account List Report is the Chart of Accounts List in report format. You will now display and print the report.

To display and print the Account List Report:

1. On the Navigation bar, click Reports.
2. Scroll to the *For my accountant* section and then click *Account List.* The Account List Report displays.
3. On the report bar, click the Print icon. The Print, email, or save as PDF window appears. See Figure 2–Z

FIGURE 2–Z Print, Email, or Save as PDF Window

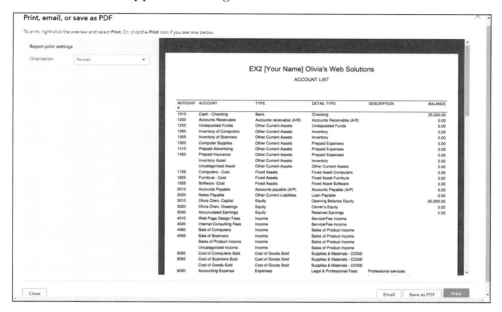

4. Click the Print button at the bottom of the window. The Print window appears. The *Destination* field is where you can select your printer. See Figure 2–AA.

FIGURE 2–AA Print Window

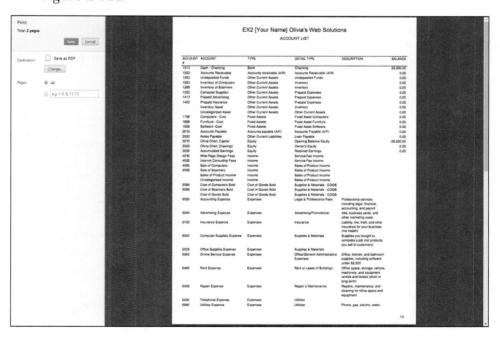

5. In the *Destination* field, click the Change button. The Select a destination window appears.

6. Select to save the report as a PDF or select your printer from the list of local destinations. If you select a printer, there will be a Print button; if you select to save as a PDF, there will be a Save button. If you click the Save button, you will be moved to the Save As dialog box where you can save the PDF file.
7. Click the Print button to print the report. You return to the Print, email, or save as PDF window. In the printout, notice the Account List Report now has balances for some of the accounts. See Figure 2–BB.

FIGURE 2–BB
Account List Report

EX2 [Your Name] Olivia's Web Solutions
ACCOUNT LIST

ACCOUNT #	ACCOUNT	TYPE	DETAIL TYPE	DESCRIPTION	BALANCE
1010	Cash - Checking	Bank	Checking		25,000.00
1200	Accounts Receivable	Accounts receivable (A/R)	Accounts Receivable (A/R)		0.00
1250	Undeposited Funds	Other Current Assets	Undeposited Funds		0.00
1260	Inventory of Computers	Other Current Assets	Inventory		0.00
1265	Inventory of Scanners	Other Current Assets	Inventory		0.00
1300	Computer Supplies	Other Current Assets	Prepaid Expenses		0.00
1410	Prepaid Advertising	Other Current Assets	Prepaid Expenses		0.00
1420	Prepaid Insurance	Other Current Assets	Prepaid Expenses		0.00
	Inventory Asset	Other Current Assets	Inventory		0.00
	Uncategorized Asset	Other Current Assets	Other Current Assets		0.00
1725	Computers - Cost	Fixed Assets	Fixed Asset Computers		0.00
1825	Furniture - Cost	Fixed Assets	Fixed Asset Furniture		0.00
1925	Software -Cost	Fixed Assets	Fixed Asset Software		0.00
2010	Accounts Payable	Accounts payable (A/P)	Accounts Payable (A/P)		0.00
2020	Notes Payable	Other Current Liabilities	Loan Payable		0.00
3010	Olivia Chen, Capital	Equity	Opening Balance Equity		-25,000.00
3020	Olivia Chen, Drawings	Equity	Owners Equity		0.00
3030	Accumulated Earnings	Equity	Retained Earnings		0.00
4010	Web Page Design Fees	Income	Service/Fee Income		
4020	Internet Consulting Fees	Income	Service/Fee Income		
4060	Sale of Computers	Income	Sales of Product Income		
4065	Sale of Scanners	Income	Sales of Product Income		
	Sales of Product Income	Income	Sales of Product Income		
	Uncategorized Income	Income	Sales of Product Income		
5060	Cost of Computers Sold	Cost of Goods Sold	Supplies & Materials - COGS		
5065	Cost of Scanners Sold	Cost of Goods Sold	Supplies & Materials - COGS		
	Cost of Goods Sold	Cost of Goods Sold	Supplies & Materials - COGS		
6020	Accounting Expense	Expenses	Legal & Professional Fees	Professional services including legal, financial, accounting, and payroll	
6050	Advertising Expense	Expenses	Advertising/Promotional	Ads, business cards, and other marketing costs	
6100	Insurance Expense	Expenses	Insurance	Liability, fire, theft, and other insurance for your business (not health)	
6300	Computer Supplies Expense	Expenses	Supplies & Materials	Supplies you bought to complete a job (not products you sell to customers)	
6325	Office Supplies Expense	Expenses	Supplies & Materials		
6350	Online Service Expense	Expenses	Office/General Administrative Expenses	Office, kitchen, and bathroom supplies, including software under $2,500	
6400	Rent Expense	Expenses	Rent or Lease of Buildings	Office space, storage, vehicle, machinery, and equipment rentals and leases (short or long-term)	
6425	Repair Expense	Expenses	Repair & Maintenance	Repairs, maintenance, and cleaning for office space and equipment	
6450	Telephone Expense	Expenses	Utilities		
6500	Utilities Expense	Expenses	Utilities	Phone, gas, electric, water, internet, and other utilities for your business	
7000	Interest Expense	Expenses	Interest Paid	Interest paid on loans, credit cards, and business vehicles	
	Bank Charges & Fees	Expenses	Bank Charges	Fees or charges from your bank or credit card	
	Car & Truck	Expenses	Auto	Gas, repairs, insurance, and other costs for your business-only vehicle (not loan payments)	
	Contractors	Expenses	Payroll Expenses	Services provided by 1099 contractors, such as landscapers, electricians, and web designers	
	Purchases	Expenses	Supplies & Materials		
	Travel	Expenses	Travel	Business travel including transportation, hotels, and tips (not meals)	
	Uncategorized Expense	Expenses	Other Miscellaneous Service Cost		

Notice that the Inventory Asset account was edited to 1260 Inventory of Computers, the Cost of Goods Sold account was edited to 5060 Cost of Computers Sold, the Sales of Product Income account was created for 4065 Sale of Scanners, and the Purchases account was deleted (made inactive), but when the Products and Services List was opened, QuickBooks looked for these accounts, could not find them, and re-created them. The Billable Expense Income Account may also appear. If any of these accounts is renamed or deleted (made inactive), QuickBooks will continue to re-create the accounts. It is best to leave them in the Chart of Accounts as QuickBooks creates them. In addition, you cannot delete the Uncategorized Asset account. In this textbook, the accounts that QuickBooks creates that cannot be renamed or deleted will remain in the Chart of Accounts, but they will not have account numbers and will not be used in any activities (transactions).

8. Click the Close button at the Print, email, or save as PDF window. You return to the Account List Report.

9. Close the Account List Report by clicking Dashboard on the Navigation bar.

Journal Report

The Journal Report reflects all transactions recorded in QuickBooks Online. In this chapter, one journal entry was recorded in the Journal Entry window. The Journal Report will display this journal entry.

To display and print the Journal Report:

1. On the Navigation bar, click Reports.

2. Scroll to the *For my accountant* section and then click *Journal*. The Journal Report window appears.

3. At the Journal Report window, key 06/01/2019 in each of the two date fields at the top of the window and press the Tab key. The Journal Report updates. This report reflects the one journal entry recorded in the Journal Entry window. See Figure 2–CC.

FIGURE 2–CC Journal Report

4. Click the Print icon.

5. At the Print, email, or save as PDF window, click the Print button.

6. At the Print window, select the correct option in the *Destination* field and then click the Print button.

7. Click the Close button to close the Print, email, or save as PDF window.
8. Close the Journal Report by clicking Dashboard on the Navigation bar.

Exiting QuickBooks Online

HINT

Be sure to complete the Case Problem at the end of Chapter 2 before moving on to Chapter 3.

At the end of each session, you should exit QuickBooks Online and close the browser.

To exit QuickBooks Online and close the browser:
1. On the title bar, click the Gear icon.
2. At the Company window, click *Sign Out*. This closes the company file and exits QuickBooks Online.
3. Close your browser.

Chapter Review and Assessment

 Study Tools include a presentation and a glossary. Use these resources, available from the links menu in the student ebook, to further develop and review skills learned in this chapter.

Procedure Review

To begin New Company Setup:

1. Sign in to QuickBooks Online. QuickBooks Online opens to the Dashboard for your company file.
2. On the title bar, click the Gear icon. If a pop-up messages appears, click the X to close it, and click the Gear icon again, if necessary. The Company window displays.
3. At the Company window, in the *Your Company* column, click *Account and Settings*. The Account and Settings window appears with the Company tab selected.
4. Click the Edit icon in the *Company name* section or click anywhere in the section. The section expands, and you can now edit the information.
5. In the *Company name* field, key the company name.
6. In the *Legal name* field, there should be a check mark in the check box to the left of *Same as company name*. If not, click the check box to insert a check mark.
7. In the *EIN/SSN* field, click the *EIN* radio button and then key in the company's employer identification number.
8. Click the Save button. If the new information does not display, click the Company tab to refresh the information.
9. Click the Edit icon in the *Company type* section or click anywhere in the section. The section expands, and you can now edit the information.
10. In the *Tax form* field, choose the company type.
11. Click the Save button.
12. Click the Edit icon in the *Contact info* section or click anywhere in the section. The *Contact info* section expands, and you can now edit the information.
13. In the *Company phone* field, key the phone number.
14. Click the Save button. The *Contact info* section of the Account and Settings window updates.
15. Click the Edit icon in the *Address* section or click anywhere in the section. The *Address* section expands, and you can now edit the information.
16. Key the address information in the appropriate fields.
17. Click the Save button. The *Address* section of the Account and Settings window updates.
18. Click the Done button. You return to the Dashboard.

To enable the inventory preference:
1. On the title bar, click the Gear icon. The Company window appears.
2. At the Company window, in the *Your Company* column, click *Account and Settings*. The Account and Settings window appears.
3. Click the Sales tab.
4. Click the Edit icon in the *Products and services* section or click anywhere in the section. The *Products and services* section expands, and you can now edit the information.
5. Insert check marks in the check boxes to the left of *Show Product/ Service column on sales forms, Track quantity and price/rate,* and *Track inventory quantity on hand,* if they are not already there.
6. Click the Save button. The changes are saved, and the inventory preference is now enabled.
7. Click the Done button. You return to the Dashboard.

To extend the time-out period:
1. On the title bar, click the Gear icon. The Company window appears.
2. At the Company window, in the *Your Company* column, click *Account and Settings*. The Account and Settings window appears.
3. Click the Advanced tab.
4. Click the Edit icon in the *Other* section or click anywhere in the section. The *Other* section expands, and you can now edit the information.
5. At the *Sign me out if inactive for* field, click the drop-down arrow and then choose a period of time.
6. Click the Save button. The change is saved, and you will now be automatically signed out if you are inactive for the specified period of time.
7. Click the Done button. You return to the Dashboard.

To enable the account numbers preference:
1. On the title bar, click the Gear icon. The Company window appears.
2. At the Company window, in the *Your Company* column, click *Account and Settings*. The Account and Settings window appears.
3. Click the Advanced tab.
4. Click the Edit icon in the *Chart of accounts* section or click anywhere in the section. The *Chart of accounts* section expands, and you can now edit the information.
5. Click the check box to the left of *Enable account numbers* to insert a check mark and turn on the account numbers preference.
6. Click the check box to the left of *Show account numbers* to insert a check mark. The account numbers will display in reports and transactions.
7. Click the Save button. The account number will now display in the Chart of Accounts window, the Account window, and the Account List Report.
8. Click the Done button. You return to the Dashboard.

To add a new account to the Chart of Accounts List:
1. On the title bar, click the Gear icon. The Company window appears.
2. At the Company window, in the *Lists* column, click *All Lists*. The Lists window appears.

3. At the Lists window, click *Chart of Accounts.*
4. In the upper right corner of the Chart of Accounts window, click the New button. The Account window appears.
5. At the Account window, select the account type from the *Account Type* drop-down list.
6. Select the detail type in the *Detail Type* drop-down list.
7. Key in the account name and number.
8. Click the Save and Close button.

To edit the account names and add account numbers to the Chart of Accounts List:
1. On the Navigation bar, click Accounting. The Chart of Accounts window appears.
2. Scroll to the account you want to edit. In the *ACTION* column, click the drop-down arrow to the right of *View register* or *Run report.* A drop-down menu appears.
3. At the drop-down menu, click *Edit.* The Account window appears.
4. Edit the account name and add the account number.
5. Click the Save and Close button.

To delete an account from the Chart of Accounts List:
1. On the Navigation bar, click Accounting. The Chart of Accounts window appears.
2. Scroll to the account you want to delete. In the *ACTION* column, click the drop-down arrow to the right of *View register* or *Run report.*
3. At the drop-down menu, click *Delete.*
4. At the *Delete Account* warning, click the Yes button. QuickBooks Online does not always delete the account but may make it inactive.

To display inactive accounts:
1. On the Navigation bar, click Accounting. The Chart of Accounts window appears.
2. Click the Settings gear above the *ACTION* column.
3. At the drop-down menu, in the *Other* section, click the check box to the left of *Include inactive* to insert a check mark.
4. Click the Settings gear to close the drop-down menu.
5. Scroll down the Chart of Accounts window and notice in the *ACTION* column that some rows display *Make active.* These are the inactive accounts.
6. Hide the inactive accounts by repeating Steps 2–4 to remove the check mark to the left of *Include inactive.*

To add a service item to the Products and Services List:
1. On the title bar, click the Gear icon. The Company window appears.
2. At the Company window, click *Products and Services* in the *Lists* column.
3. At the Products and Services window, click the New button. The Product/Service information window appears.
4. Click *Service* to open the Product/Service information—Service window.
5. Complete the window.
6. Click the Save and Close button.

To enter the opening balances in the Journal Entry window:
1. On the title bar, click the Create icon. The Create icon turns into an X, and the Create window appears.
2. At the Create window, in the *Other* column, click *Journal Entry*. The Journal Entry window appears.
3. In the *Journal date* field, choose the date.
4. In the *Journal no.* field, key a number or accept the number in the field.
5. In the first line of the *ACCOUNT* column, click the drop-down arrow and choose the account to debit.
6. In the *DEBITS* column, key the amount.
7. Move to the second line in the *ACCOUNT* column, click the drop-down arrow, and then choose the account to credit.
8. In the *CREDITS* column, the amount may appear; if it does not, key the amount.
9. In the *DESCRIPTION* column, key a description.
10. Click the Save and Close button.

To display and print an accounting report:
1. On the Navigation bar on the left, click Reports.
2. Scroll to the *For my accountant* section and then click a report name (e.g., the Account List Report, the Journal Report) to display the report.
3. Enter dates, if necessary.
4. On the report bar, click the Print icon. The Print, email, or save as PDF window appears.
5. Click the Print button. The Print window appears.
6. In the *Destination* field, click the Change button.
7. Select your printer or select to save the report as a PDF file. If you select a printer, there will be a Print button; if you select to save as a PDF, there will be a Save button. If you click the Save button, you will be moved to the Save As dialog box, where you can save the PDF file.
8. Click the Print button to print the report. You are returned to the Print, email, or save as PDF window.
9. Click the Close button. You are returned to the Report window.
10. To close the report, click Dashboard on the Navigation bar.

Key Concepts

Select the letter of the item that best matches each definition.

a. system default accounts
b. account type
c. account numbers
d. inactive accounts
e. Account List
f. preferences
g. Journal Entry window
h. time-out period
i. detail type
j. Journal Report

_____ 1. Accounts created by QuickBooks Online that are used to record transactions in the Activities windows.

_____ 2. A preference in a company file that identifies accounts; must be activated on the Advanced tab of the Account and Settings window.

_____ 3. Features in QuickBooks Online that must be enabled to be used.

_____ 4. Used in QuickBooks Online to identify an account as an asset, liability, equity, or income and expense account.

_____ 5. A report in QuickBooks Online that lists all the accounts on the Chart of Accounts List.

_____ 6. Accounts that are no longer listed on the Chart of Accounts List.

_____ 7. The window where you record opening balances in the accounts.

_____ 8. A specific subcategory of the account type that is predetermined by QuickBooks Online and cannot be changed by a user.

_____ 9. The amount of time you have been inactive after which QuickBooks Online will automatically log you out; set to one hour by default but can be extended to three hours.

_____ 10. The report in QuickBooks Online that lists all transactions, including transactions recorded in the Journal Entry window.

Procedure Check

Write a response for each of the following prompts.

1. What are the first steps you would take in New Company Setup?
2. What is the difference between the Chart of Accounts List and the Account List?
3. What are the steps to enable the inventory preference?
4. What are the steps to enable the account numbers preference?
5. What are system default accounts? Can you edit system default account names and numbers? Can you delete system default accounts?
6. Your manager is just learning QuickBooks Online. She has asked you to explain what QuickBooks Online New Company Setup means. Provide the manager with a written explanation of the QuickBooks Online New Company Setup process. Also, describe any additional steps you may take after New Company Setup before you begin recording routine activities.

Case Problem

Demonstrate your knowledge of the QuickBooks Online features discussed in this chapter by completing the following case problem.

On June 1, 2019, Olivia Chen began her business, Olivia's Web Solutions. In the first month of business, Olivia set up the office and began the New Company Setup procedure in QuickBooks Online. She would like to update the Chart of Accounts List. In addition, Olivia would like to record the computer system that she contributed to the company along with the outstanding note balance of $2,500 that will be assumed by the business.

1. Sign in to QuickBooks Online.
2. Change the company name to **OWS2 [*Your Name*] Olivia's Web Solutions**.

3. Use the information in Table 2–3 below to add accounts to the Chart of Accounts List.

Account Type	Detail Type	Account Name	Number
Other Current Assets	Inventory	Inventory of HTML Software	1270
Other Current Assets	Inventory	Inventory of Desktop Pub. Software	1275
Other Current Assets	Prepaid Expenses	Office Supplies	1305
Income	Sales of Product Income	Sale of HTML Software	4070
Income	Sales of Product Income	Sale of Desktop Pub. Software	4075
Income	Discounts/Refunds Given	Sales Discounts	4100
Cost of Goods Sold	Supplies & Materials - COGS	Cost of HTML Software Sold	5070
Cost of Goods Sold	Supplies & Materials - COGS	Cost of Desktop Pub. Software Sold	5075
Cost of Goods Sold	Supplies & Materials - COGS	Inventory Adjustment	5900
Other Income	Interest Earned	Interest Income	6900

4. Use the information in Table 2–4 below to edit account names and add account numbers to the Chart of Accounts List.

Original	Edited	
Account Name	Account Name	Number
Bank Charges	Bank Service Charges Expense	6060
Travel	Travel and Entertainment Expense	6475

5. Delete the following accounts:
   Car & Truck
   Contractors

6. Make a journal entry to record the computer system that Olivia Chen is contributing to the company, along with the notes payable, as follows:

Date: June 1, 2019
No.: Opening bal. 2
Debit: 1725 Computers - Cost $5,000
Credit: 2020 Notes Payable 2,500
Credit: 3010 Olivia Chen, Capital 2,500

7. Display and print the following reports for June 1, 2019:
   a. Account List
   b. Journal

CHAPTER 3

Vendors

Adding Vendors and Creating and Paying Bills

Objectives

- Identify the system default accounts for vendors
- Update the Vendor List
- Record purchases on account in the Bill window
- Record vendor credits in the Vendor Credit window
- Record payment of accounts payable in the Pay Bills window
- Record cash purchases in the Check window
- Display and print vendor-related reports

QuickBooks Online allows you to track all vendor transactions. A **vendor** is someone from whom a company buys goods or services, either on account or for cash. You should establish a file for each vendor before entering transactions for that vendor. The collection of all vendor files comprises the Vendor List.

vendor Someone from whom a company buys goods or services, either on account or for cash.

Once a vendor file is established, transactions such as receiving a bill from a vendor, paying that bill, or paying for a cash purchase can be entered in the Bill, Pay Bills, and Check windows. As transactions are recorded in the activities windows, QuickBooks Online simultaneously updates the vendor's file in the Vendor List and any related reports with information about the transaction for a particular vendor.

In this chapter, you will record and pay bills received by our sample company, Craig's Design and Landscaping Services, for non-inventory purchases of goods and services, such as operating expenses and assets acquisitions. In addition, you will record cash purchases when bills have not been previously received or entered.

QuickBooks Online versus Manual Accounting: Vendor Transactions

In a manual accounting system, all purchases of goods on account are recorded in a multi-column **purchases journal**. At the conclusion of the month, the totals are posted to the asset, expense, and liability Accounts Payable accounts affected by the transactions. As each purchase transaction is recorded, the appropriate vendor's account in the accounts payable subsidiary ledger is updated for the new liability on a daily basis. Payments for open accounts payable balances and payments for cash purchases of goods or services are recorded in a multi-column **cash payments journal**. As in the purchases journal, monthly totals are posted to the general ledger accounts, while payment information is recorded daily in the vendor's subsidiary ledger record.

purchases journal A journal used to record all purchases of goods on account; can be in a single-column or multi-column format.

cash payments journal A journal used to record all cash payment activities, including payment of accounts payable.

In QuickBooks Online, the Vendor List serves as the accounts payable subsidiary ledger for the company. The Vendor List contains a file for all companies and individuals from whom the company buys goods and services. Relevant information, such as name, address, contact, phone numbers, and so on, should be entered at the time the vendor's file is created in the Vendor List.

When the company receives a bill for goods or services, the bill is recorded in the Bill window. The Bill window is equivalent to the multi-column purchases journal. QuickBooks Online automatically updates the Chart of Accounts List and general ledger; at the same time, it updates the vendor's file in the Vendor List for the new liability. When the bill is to be paid, you enter the transaction in the Pay Bills window. The Pay Bills window is equivalent to the part of the cash payments journal that records payment of open accounts payable. This transaction also updates the Chart of Accounts List and general ledger and at the same time updates the vendor's file in the Vendor List for the payment of the liability.

For a cash payment for a bill not previously entered, you use the Check window. This is equivalent to the part of the cash payments journal that records payment for cash purchases of goods or services. Again, the Chart of Accounts List, the general ledger, and the vendor's file in the Vendor List are simultaneously updated.

System Default Accounts

To process transactions expeditiously and organize data for reporting, QuickBooks Online establishes specific general ledger accounts as default accounts in each activity window. When you enter transactions, QuickBooks Online automatically increases or decreases certain account balances depending on the nature of the transaction. For example, when you enter a vendor invoice in the Bill window, QuickBooks Online automatically increases (credits) the Accounts Payable account because the Bill window is used to record purchases on account. When you write a check in the Pay Bills window, QuickBooks Online automatically decreases (debits) the Accounts Payable account. Therefore, you do not have to enter the account number or name for these default accounts because they have already been established by QuickBooks Online.

Throughout the textbook, the default accounts for each type of transaction, such as vendor, customer, inventory, and payroll, will be identified.

Chapter Problem

In this chapter, you will enter and track vendor transactions for Craig's Design and Landscaping Services, a sole proprietorship providing garden design and landscaping services to both residential and commercial clients. The file for Craig's Design and Landscaping Services is contained in the QuickBooks Online Test Drive. Beginning February 1, 2019, Craig's Design wishes to begin tracking vendor transactions. Information for several vendors is contained in the Vendor List of the Test Drive sample company file. Please keep in mind that once you exit the Test Drive, all changes to the sample file are lost.

To access the QuickBooks Online Test Drive:
1. Open an internet browser, key https://QBO18.ParadigmEducation .com/TestDrive into the address bar, and then press the Enter key or click the Go arrow. This opens the Security Verification window.
2. Click the check box to the left of the text *I'm not a robot*. A window may appear with images.
3. If the images appear, follow the instructions to select images or part of an image and then click the Verify button. (This may take several attempts.)
4. Click the Continue button. QuickBooks Online launches, displaying the sample company, Craig's Design and Landscaping Services.

To change the company name:
1. On the title bar, click the Gear icon . The Craig's Design and Landscaping Services window appears.
2. At the Craig's Design and Landscaping Services window, in the *Your Company* column, click *Account and Settings*. This opens the Account and Settings window.
3. Click the Edit icon in the *Company name* section or click anywhere in the section. The *Company name* section expands to display more information about the company, and you can now edit the company information.

4. In the *Company name* field, select the company name and key EX3 [*Your Name*] Craig's Design and Landscaping Services.
5. Click the *EIN* radio button and then key 12-3456788 in the *EIN* field.
6. Confirm the information is correct and then click the Save button. The changes are saved, and the Account and Settings window displays with the *Company name* section updated and condensed. If the *Company name* section does not display, click the Company tab.
7. Confirm the information is correct and then click the Done button in the lower right corner of the window or click the X at the right of the Account and Settings window. The Dashboard now displays the updated company name of EX3 [*Your Name*] Craig's Design and Landscaping Services. This company name will now appear in the headings of reports.

To extend the time-out period of time:
1. On the title bar, click the Gear icon. The Company window appears.
2. At the Company window, in the *Your Company* column, click *Account and Settings*. This opens the Account and Settings window.
3. At the Account and Settings window, click the Advanced tab.
4. Click the Edit icon in the *Other preferences* section or click anywhere in the section.
5. In the *Sign me out if inactive for* field, click the drop-down arrow and then click *3 hours*.
6. Click the Save button. The change is saved, and you will now be automatically signed out if you are inactive for three hours instead of one hour.
7. Click the Done button or click the X to close the Account and Settings window.

Each time you open the Test Drive, the default date for transactions is the current date. The dates of previous transactions entered in the Test Drive sample company file will range from up to five months prior to the current date.

In each chapter you will be instructed as to what date(s) to use. You should use the day and month provided but adjust the year to reflect the year in which you are working. The textbook will use the year 2019 in examples and figures, but you should use the year you access the Test Drive sample company.

Lists

The Vendor List

The Vendor List contains a file for each vendor with which the company does business. For example, the utility company that supplies electricity, the company that provides advertising, and the company from which equipment for the business is purchased are all vendors. The Vendor List contains important information on each vendor, such as company name, address, contact person, terms, tax ID, and current balance owed. All vendors the company does business with should be included in the Vendor List.

You should enter the information for each vendor in the Vendor List before recording transactions. However, if you inadvertently omit a vendor, you can add that vendor during the Activities level of operation with minimal disruption.

You will periodically revise the Vendor List to add new vendors, make vendors inactive, or make modifications as background information on vendors changes. These adjustments to the vendor files in the Vendor List are referred to as *updating* the Vendor List, and they are part of the second level of operation in QuickBooks Online.

Craig's Design and Landscaping Services has entered information for existing and anticipated vendors in the Vendor List of the company file.

To review the Vendor List:

1. On the Navigation bar, click Expenses and then click the Vendors link, which is located towards the top of the window. The Vendors window appears with the Vendor List displayed. See Figure 3–A.

FIGURE 3–A Vendors Window

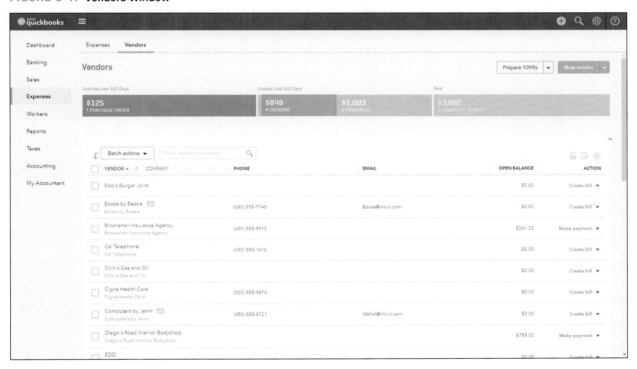

The Vendors window includes the following elements:

Unbilled Last 365 Days filter	Lists all open purchase orders for period.
Unpaid Last 365 Days filter	Lists all open bills for the period, including overdue bills.
Paid filter	Lists all bills paid in past 30 days.
New vendor button	Used to add or import a new vendor.
Batch actions button	Used to send an email to all selected vendors.
***ACTION* column**	Used to initiate various actions for a selected vendor, such as creating a bill, writing a check, making a payment, etc.
Print icon	Used to print a list of the vendors.

To view a specific vendor file:

1. At the Vendors window, click *Brosnahan Insurance Agency*. This opens the vendor file with the Transaction List tab displayed. See Figure 3–B.

FIGURE 3–B Vendor File—Brosnahan Insurance Agency

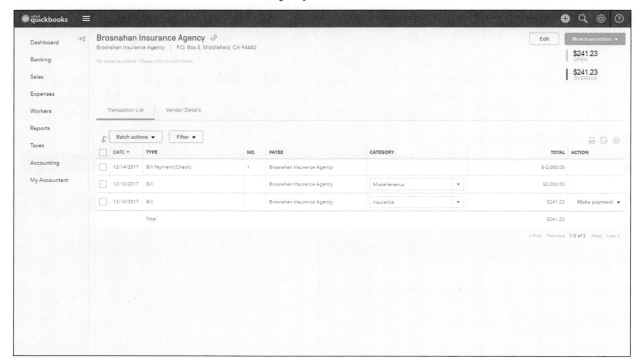

Note the following elements of the vendor file window:

Edit button	Allows you to edit vendor information, such as company name, address, phone numbers, etc.
Open/Overdue amounts	Lists the dollar total of all open and overdue bills.
Transaction List tab	Displays all recent transactions for this vendor.
Vendor Details tab	Displays vendor profile information contained in the file.
Filter button	Allows you to display transactions by type or date.

2. Click Expenses on the Navigation bar to return to the Vendors window.
3. Close the Vendors window by clicking Dashboard on the Navigation bar.

Adding a Vendor

Craig's Design has just hired a new accountant who will provide accounting services each month for the business. The company wishes to add this vendor to the Vendor List by creating a vendor file.

To add a vendor:

1. On the Navigation bar, click Expenses and then click the Vendors link, if necessary. The Vendors window opens, displaying a list of vendors, along with information for each vendor on the list.
2. At the Vendors window, click the New vendor button. The Vendor Information window appears. See Figure 3–C.

FIGURE 3–C

Vendor Information Window

HINT

QuickBooks Online defaults to the current date. Be sure to change the date in the *as of* field to match the exercise. Remember to use the day and month provided, but always use the current year in which you are using the Test Drive sample company.

HINT

Use the Tab key to move to each field and Shift + Tab to move back a field.

3. Enter the data below at the Vendor Information window in the indicated fields. The Vendor Information window should look similar to Figure 3–D.

First name:	[Your First Name]
Last name:	[Your Last Name]
Company:	[Your Name] Accounting Service
Display name as:	[Your Name] Accounting Service
Address:	45888 Main Street
	Middlefield CA 94303
Phone:	650-555-2222
Mobile:	650-555-2223
Terms:	Net 30
Opening balance:	0
as of:	February 1, 2019
Account no.:	99-2019-XX

4. Confirm the information is correct and then click the Save button.
5. Close the Vendors window by clicking Dashboard on the Navigation bar.

FIGURE 3–D
Vendor Information
Window—Completed

Making a Vendor Inactive

Craig's Design wishes to deactivate Books by Bessie in the Vendor List because the company has ceased to operate. In QuickBooks Online, you cannot delete a vendor; you can only make it inactive.

To make a vendor inactive:

HINT

You can also make
a vendor inactive by
opening the vendor file,
clicking the Edit button,
and then clicking the
Make inactive button.

1. On the Navigation bar, click Expenses and then click the Vendors link, if necessary.
2. At the Vendors window, click in the *ACTION* column drop-down list for *Books by Bessie* and then click *Make inactive*.
3. At the warning message, *Are you sure you want to make Books by Bessie inactive?*, click the Yes button. The vendor file is removed from the Vendor List. See Figure 3–E.
4. Close the Vendors window by clicking Dashboard on the Navigation bar.

FIGURE 3–E Vendor List—Books by Bessie Removed

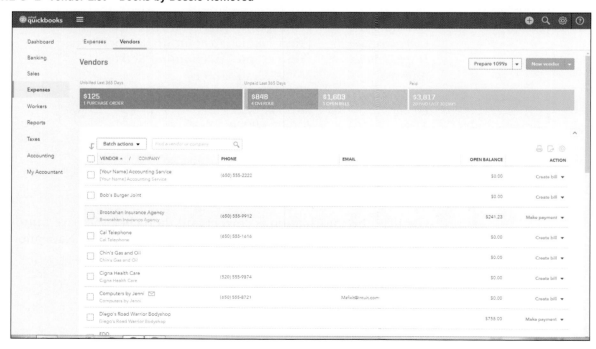

If you wish to reactivate the vendor, click Vendors on the Navigation bar. At the Vendors window, click the Settings gear above the *ACTION* column, then insert a check mark in the *Include inactive* check box. Any vendor previously made inactive will be restored to the Vendor List. However, the vendor will be marked *(deleted)*. To make the vendor active again, click *Make active* in the *ACTION* column for that vendor.

Editing a Vendor

Craig's Design needs to enter terms in the PG&E vendor file.

To edit a vendor file:
1. On the Navigation bar, click Expenses and then click the Vendors link, if necessary.
2. At the Vendors window, click *PG&E*.
3. Click the Edit button. This opens the Vendor Information window.
4. In the *Terms* field, select *Net 30* from the drop-down list. See Figure 3–F.

FIGURE 3–F
Vendor Information Window—Updated

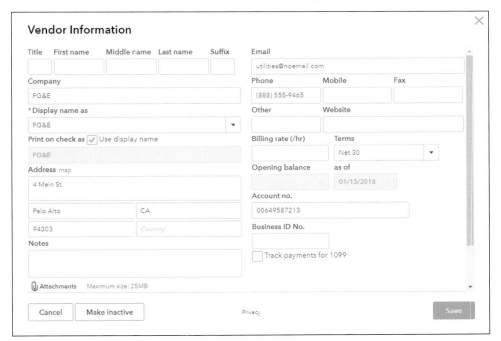

5. Confirm the information is correct and then click the Save button. You return to the vendor's file.
6. On the Navigation bar, click Expenses to return to the Vendors window.

Add the following new vendor:

First name:	Bernard
Last name:	Williams
Company:	Williams Auto & Truck
Display name as:	Williams Auto & Truck
Address:	19 Main Street
	Middlefield CA 94303
Phone:	650-555-2240
Mobile:	650-555-2241
Terms:	Net 30
Opening balance:	0
as of:	February 1, 2019
Account no.:	55-8988

Make the following vendor inactive:
    Mahoney Mugs

Edit the following vendor:
    New phone numbers for Lee Advertising

Phone:	650-555-0002
Mobile:	650-555-0003

QuickCheck: The updated Vendor List appears in Figure 3–G.

FIGURE 3–G Updated Vendor List—Partial

Activities

The Bill Window

purchase on account
When a company receives a bill for goods or services from a vendor but plans to pay it at a later date.

In QuickBooks Online, the Bill window is used to record a **purchase on account**. This window allows you to identify the vendor sending the bill, the invoice date, due date, terms of payment, and nature of purchase (expense, asset, or item). QuickBooks Online uses the default Accounts Payable account from the Chart of Accounts List to post all open bill liabilities. Certain recurring bills can be set up to be recorded automatically as they become due. QuickBooks Online records a transaction that is a purchase on account as follows:

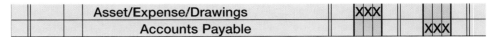

		Asset/Expense/Drawings		XXX				
		Accounts Payable				XXX		

At the same time as the bill information is updated, QuickBooks Online updates the vendor's file in the Vendor List to reflect the new liability.

Recall from Chapter 1 that the third level of operation in QuickBooks Online is Activities. In this case, the Activity is the recording of purchases on account in the Bill window. Accounts Payable is the default general ledger posting account. All transactions entered in this window will result in a credit to the Accounts Payable account. The *ACCOUNT* column in the Bill window is used to indicate the asset, expense, or drawings account to be debited.

The QuickBooks Online Bill window appears in Figure 3–H.

FIGURE 3–H Bill Window

The Bill window has two details sections: Account and Item. When the Bill window opens, the *Account details* section displays. This allows you to record purchases for expenses, assets, and drawings. The *Item details* section is used when inventory items are purchased on account. Inventory purchases will be covered in Chapter 6.

Make special note of the following elements in the Bill window:

Choose a vendor **drop-down list**	Drop-down list used to choose a vendor from the Vendor List.
Terms **drop-down list**	List of available terms for payment. If you have entered terms in the Vendor Information window for the selected vendor, it will be the default selection.
Balance Due	Displays the open balance for the selected vendor.
Account details **section**	Fields in this section are used to enter the general ledger account, description, amount, etc., for the purchase of non-inventory items.
Item details **section**	Fields in this section are used to enter the purchase of inventory items.
Save button	Click to save the transaction and remain in the Bill window to enter a bill for the same vendor.
Save and new/ Save and close button	Click to save the transaction and enter a bill for a different vendor or to exit the Bill window.

Entering a Bill

On February 2, 2019, Craig's Design received a bill for utilities services from PG&E in the amount of $200, Bill no. 125-55. The bill is due March 4, 2019.

HINT

You can also access the Bill window from the *ACTION* column for a vendor while at the Vendors window.

HINT

You may get a warning asking, *Do you want to prefill this bill and overwrite your entries using values from this contact's last bill?* If you click the Yes button, QuickBooks Online will prefill the account chosen for the vendor from a previously entered transaction.

To enter a bill:

1. On the title bar, click the Create icon ⊕. The Create window appears.
2. In the *Vendors* column, click *Bill*. This displays the Bill window.
3. At the *Choose a vendor* drop-down list, click *PG&E*. This displays the Bill window with the background information for PG&E completed.
4. Confirm the *Terms* field reads *Net 30*.
5. In the *Bill date* field, choose *02/02/2019*. (Click the calendar icon and then click through the months to find February 2, 2019.) The *Due date* field should fill in automatically based upon information in the vendor's file.
6. In the *Bill no.* field, key 125-55.
7. Confirm that the *ACCOUNT* column reads *Utilities:Gas and Electric*.
8. In the *AMOUNT* column, key 200. See Figure 3–I.

FIGURE 3-I Bill Window—Completed

HINT

If a message appears offering more information about paying bills online, click the No thanks button.

9. Confirm the information is correct and then click *Save and close* from the Save and new button list. Recall that Save and close saves the information, closes the window, and returns you to the last window you accessed. Save and new saves the transaction and clears the fields for a new transaction.

10. Close the Bill window by clicking Dashboard on the Navigation bar.

Accounting Concept

For a purchase of an expense on account, the general ledger posting is as follows:

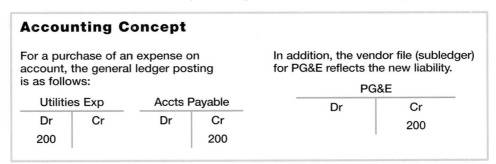

In addition, the vendor file (subledger) for PG&E reflects the new liability.

Updating the Vendor List While in an Activity Window

On February 2, 2019, Craig's Design received a bill for prepaid advertising services from Cuza and Carl Associates in the amount of $500, Bill no. X-145. The bill is due March 4, 2019, with terms Net 30. Cuza and Carl Associates is a new vendor.

To update the Vendor List from the Bill window:
1. On the title bar, click the Create icon.
2. In the *Vendors* column, choose *Bill*. The Bill window appears, but no vendor information has been prefilled.

3. At the *Choose a vendor* drop-down list, click *Add new.* The New Vendor window appears. See Figure 3–J.

4. In the *Name* field, key Carrie Cuza.
5. Click *Details.* The Vendor Information window opens with the correct text in the first and last name fields.
6. Enter the following information in the indicated fields:

Company:	Cuza and Carl Associates
Display name as:	Cuza and Carl Associates
Address:	23 Main Street
	Middlefield CA 94303
Phone:	650-555-8855
Mobile:	650-555-8856
Terms:	Net 30
Opening balance:	0
as of:	February 1, 2019
Account no.:	CD569

7. Confirm the information is correct and then click the Save button. The Bill window displays with vendor information for Cuza and Carl Associates.
8. In the *Bill date* field, choose *02/02/2019.*
9. In the *Bill no.* field, key X-145.
10. Click *Account details,* if the section is not already expanded, and then click *Prepaid Expenses* in the *ACCOUNT* column.
11. In the *AMOUNT* column, key 500. See Figure 3–K.
12. Confirm the information is correct and then click *Save and close* from the Save and new button list.

HINT

You may need to scroll down the *ACCOUNT* column to reach the Prepaid Expenses account.

FIGURE 3–K Bill Window—Completed

Correcting Errors

Recall that on February 2, 2019, Craig's Design purchased prepaid advertising from Cuza and Carl Associates, Bill no. X-145, in the amount of $500. As it turns out, the correct amount was $600. Craig's Design wishes to correct the transaction.

HINT

If Cuza and Carl Associates does not appear in the Vendor List, click Dashboard and then return to the Vendors window.

To correct a previously entered transaction:
1. On the Navigation bar, click Expenses and then click the Vendors link, if necessary.
2. At the Vendors window, click *Cuza and Carl Associates*. The vendor's file will open with the prior bill listed.
3. Click any field of the listed bill. This will open the original transaction.
4. In the *AMOUNT* column, change the amount to *600*.
5. Confirm the information is correct and then click *Save and close* from the Save and new button list.
6. Click Expenses on the Navigation bar to return to the Vendors window.

There are several ways to correct an error in a recorded transaction. One way is to open the window that contains the transaction. To access previous transactions recorded in that window, click the Recent Transactions icon at the upper left corner, and a list of the previous transactions displays. When you select the transaction from the list, it will open in the window. You can then make the necessary correction and save the transaction by choosing *Save and close*. An alternative to correcting an error in a transaction is to delete the transaction by selecting *Delete* from the *More* drop-down list at the bottom of the window and re-entering the correct transaction.

Record the following transactions in the Bill window:

Feb. 3	Received bill from Hall Properties for the month's rent, Bill no. F-19, $900. Due upon receipt. (Charge to Rent or Lease account.)
Feb. 9	Received bill from Brosnahan Insurance Agency for one-year insurance policy, Bill no. 01-21, $2,400. Net 10, due February 19, 2019. (Charge to Prepaid Expenses account.)
Feb. 13	Received bill from Williams Auto & Truck for the purchase of a used truck, Bill no. 555588, $3,700. Net 30, due March 15, 2019. (Charge to Truck: Original Cost account.)
Feb. 23	Received bill from [*Your Name*] Accounting Service for accounting service, Bill no. Feb19, $300. Net 30, due March 25, 2019. (Charge to Legal & Professional: Accounting account.)

HINT

Click *Save and new* to save the transaction and clear the fields for a new transaction.

Processing a Vendor Credit

vendor credit
A reduction of accounts payable as a result of a return or an allowance by a vendor.

QuickBooks Online allows you to process a **vendor credit** from a vendor using the Vendor Credit window. The resulting credit reduces the balance owed to that vendor.

On February 24, 2019, Craig's Design received a $100 credit from Williams Auto & Truck for a damaged part to the truck purchased on February 13, using Reference no. VC 245.

To record a vendor credit:
1. On the title bar, click the Create icon.
2. Click *Vendor Credit* in the *Vendors* column.
3. From the *Choose a vendor* drop-down list, click *Williams Auto & Truck*. The *Mailing address* field will automatically populate with the vendor's information.
4. In the *Payment date* field, choose February 24, 2019.
5. In the *Ref no.* field, key VC 245.
6. In the *ACCOUNT* column, click *Truck: Original Cost.*
7. In the *AMOUNT* column, key 100. See Figure 3–L.

HINT

Do not place a negative number in the *AMOUNT* column.

8. Confirm the information is correct and then click *Save and close* from the Save and new button list.
9. Close the Vendors window by clicking Dashboard on the Navigation bar.

FIGURE 3–L Vendor Credit Window—Completed

Accounting Concept

For credit for the damaged part, the general ledger posting is as follows:

Accts Payable		Truck:Cost	
Dr	Cr	Dr	Cr
100			100

In addition, the vendor file for Williams Auto & Truck reflects the reduced liability amount:

Williams Auto & Truck			
Dr		Cr	
VC	100	Bill	3,700
		Bal	3,600

The Pay Bills Window

In QuickBooks Online, the Pay Bills window is used to record the **payment on account**. These are the bills previously recorded in the Bill window. This window displays all open bills as of a selected date. Bills can be paid in full, or a partial payment can be made. Payment can be in the form of a check, a credit card, or an online payment. In addition, several bills can be paid at one time.

The Pay Bills window is designed only for payments of existing bills. The default accounts are Accounts Payable and Cash/Credit Card. The transaction is recorded as follows:

payment on account
Payment of an outstanding account payable.

		Accounts Payable			XXX			
		Cash/Credit Card					XXX	

At the same time, the vendor's file in the Vendor List is updated to reflect the payment. The QuickBooks Online Pay Bills window appears in Figure 3–M.

FIGURE 3–M Pay Bills Window

This window allows you to select a bill or bills to be paid, pay all or part of each bill, and designate checks to be printed by the computer. Note the following elements in the Pay Bills window:

Payment account **drop-down list**	Allows you to select the method of payment. Default choices are: Checking and Savings bank accounts or Mastercard and Visa credit cards. Once chosen, the account balance will be displayed.
Starting check no. **field**	Appears if a bank account is selected as the payment account displaying the next check number.
Payment date **field**	Indicates the date of payment that will appear on the payment check and all reports.
Filter button	Allows you to customize the display as to date ranges and payees
Save button	Click to save the transaction and remain in the Pay Bills window.

Activities identified as purchases on account were recorded in the Bill window. Subsequently, activities identified as payment of the outstanding accounts payable (previously recorded in the Bill window) are then recorded in the Pay Bills window. Accounts Payable and Cash/Credit Card are the default general ledger posting accounts. All transactions entered in this window result in a debit to the Accounts Payable account and a credit to a Cash account or a Credit Card.

Paying a Bill in Full

HINT

You can also access open bills by clicking *Make payment* in the *ACTION* column for a vendor while in the Vendors window.

On February 10, 2019, Craig's Design wishes to pay Hall Properties for the rent bill received on February 3, 2019 (Check no. 71). Do not print the check.

To pay a bill in full:

1. On the title bar, click the Create icon.
2. Click *Pay Bills* in the *Vendors* column. The Pay Bills window appears.
3. In the *Payment account* field, click *Checking*. The *Starting check no.* should be *71*. Make sure the *Print later* check box is unchecked.
4. Click the Filter button. A pop-up window appears with filter options.
5. In the *Payee* field, click *Hall Properties* and then click the Apply button.
6. In the *Payment date* field, choose *02/10/2019*.
7. Click the check box to the left of the payee name to insert a check mark. You will notice the *PAYMENT* column fills for the full amount of the bill. See Figure 3–N.

FIGURE 3–N Pay Bills Window—Vendor Bill Selected

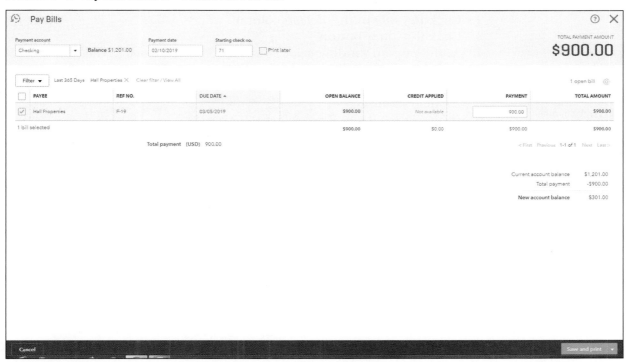

8. Confirm the information is correct and then click *Save and close* from the Save and print button list.
9. Close the Vendors window by clicking Dashboard on the Navigation bar.

Accounting Concept

For a payment of an existing Accounts Payable, the general ledger posting is as follows:

Accts Payable		Cash-Checking Acct	
Dr	Cr	Dr	Cr
900			900

In addition, the vendor file (subledger) for Hall Properties reflects the payment:

Hall Properties			
Dr		Cr	
Payment	900	Bill	900
		0	

Even though a check is not printed, the bill is now considered paid for accounts payable and general ledger purposes. The vendor balance owed has been reduced along with the cash balance in the checking account.

Making a Partial Payment of a Bill

QuickBooks Online allows a partial payment to be made toward an outstanding bill. On February 23, 2019, Craig's Design wishes to make a partial payment of $100 toward the Cuza and Carl Associates outstanding bill of $600 (Check no. 72).

To make a partial payment:

1. On the title bar, click the Create icon.
2. Click *Pay Bills* in the *Vendors* column.
3. Click the Filter button.
4. At the pop-up window, select *Cuza and Carl Associates* in the *Payee* field and then click the Apply button. Bill no. X-145 for $600 displays.
5. Confirm the *Payment account* field reads *Checking* and the *Starting check no.* field reads *72*.
6. In the *Payment date* field, select *02/23/2019*.
7. In the *PAYMENT* column, key 100. When you move to another field, the bill is automatically checked off for payment. See Figure 3–O.
8. Confirm the information is correct and then click *Save and close* from the Save and print button list.
9. Close the Vendors window by clicking Dashboard on the Navigation bar.

HINT

Depending on when you access the Test Drive, other bills may appear for this vendor. If other bills appear, ignore them.

FIGURE 3–O Pay Bills Window—Partial Payment

Practice Exercise 3-3

Record the following transaction in the Pay Bills window:

Feb. 27	Made a partial payment of $100 toward [*Your Name*] Accounting Service bill of $300 (Check no. 73).

The Check Window

cash purchase
Payment of any bill or item other than accounts payable.

In QuickBooks Online, the Check window is used to record a **cash purchase** that has not been previously entered into the system. The Check window is useful for companies that usually pay on account but occasionally receive bills and remit payments immediately, or for companies that do not purchase goods or services on account and therefore do not need to track vendor data. Accounts Payable is not used, which allows for a cash purchase to be recorded in one step. The data fields in this window are similar to those in the Bill window—payee (vendor name), date, expense, asset, or item purchased.

The default account is Cash. The transaction is recorded as follows:

		Asset/Expense/Drawing		XXX	
		Cash			XXX

A transaction entered in this window is not tracked through the Accounts Payable or Vendor reports.

Activities identified as cash purchases are recorded in the Check window. In this window, the Cash accounts are the default credit posting accounts because all transactions result in a cash payment. All transactions entered in this window result in a credit to a Cash account. The account field in this window is used to indicate the asset, expense, or drawings account to be debited.

Writing a Check

On February 28, 2019, Craig's Design receives a bill for $50 for truck fuel from Chin's Gas and Oil. The company pays the bill with Check no. 74.

To write a check:

1. On the title bar, click the Create icon.
2. Click *Check* in the *Vendors* column.
3. At the *Choose a payee* drop-down list, click *Chin's Gas and Oil.*
4. Confirm the *Choose an account* drop-down list reads *Checking* and the *Check no.* field reads *74.*
5. In the *Payment date* field, choose *02/28/2019.*
6. In the *ACCOUNT* column, click *Automobile:Fuel,* if it is not already displayed.
7. In the *AMOUNT* column, key *50.*
8. Confirm the *Print later* check box is unchecked. See Figure 3–P.

HINT

If another transaction appears or automatically fills, click the Clear all lines button in the *Account details* section.

FIGURE 3–P Check Window—Completed

HINT

Errors can be corrected in the Check window, or you can click the *Void* or *Delete* option from the *More* menu at the bottom of the window.

9. Confirm the information is correct and then click the Save and new button. Even though a check is not printed, the bill is now considered paid.
10. Keep the Check window open for the next activity.

Accounting Concept

For a cash payment of an expense, the general ledger posting is as follows:

Automobile:Fuel		Cash - Checking	
Dr	Cr	Dr	Cr
50			50

The vendor file is unaffected because payment was made immediately.

If you click the Recent Transaction icon, you will see the payments recorded in the Check window as well as the payments recorded in the Pay Bills window. The payments are recorded in check number sequence. Since checks are not being printed, the program automatically assigns the next check number.

Practice Exercise 3-4

Record the following transaction in the Check window:

Feb. 28	Received bill from Cal Telephone for telephone service, $50. Pay immediately with Check no. 77 as checks 75 and 76 have been used by the Test Drive (charge to Utilities:Telephone account).

HINT
Make sure the *Print later* check box is not checked.

Reports

Vendor Reports and Accounting Reports

Reports, the fourth level of operation in QuickBooks Online, reflect the information and activities recorded in the various Lists and Activities windows. QuickBooks Online can display and print a variety of internal management reports as well as typical accounting and financial reports, many of which should be printed monthly.

Vendor Reports

The Accounts Payable and vendor-related reports help a company manage its liability payments, ensure timely and correct remittances, control cash flow, and retain an accurate record of all vendor-related transactions. Among these reports are the Unpaid Bills Report, the Vendor Balance Detail Report, and the Vendor Contact List Report.

Unpaid Bills Report

The Unpaid Bills Report lists all unpaid bills for each vendor as of a specific date. The report lists each open bill (with date and invoice number) for a vendor, along with any vendor credits applied. The report may be customized to show all vendors or only those with outstanding bills.

To view and print the Unpaid Bills Report:
1. On the Navigation bar, click Reports and then click the All link, if necessary.
2. Scroll to the *What you owe* section and then click *Unpaid Bills*.

HINT
The All link will remain as the default choice after you exit the Reports menu.

HINT

Amounts in the *PAST DUE* column may vary depending on when you access the Test Drive.

3. Accept *All Dates* in the *Report period* field and *Current* in the *Aging method* field. Leave the *Min. Days Past Due* field blank.
4. Click the Run report button. The report displays. See Figure 3–Q.

FIGURE 3–Q Unpaid Bills Report

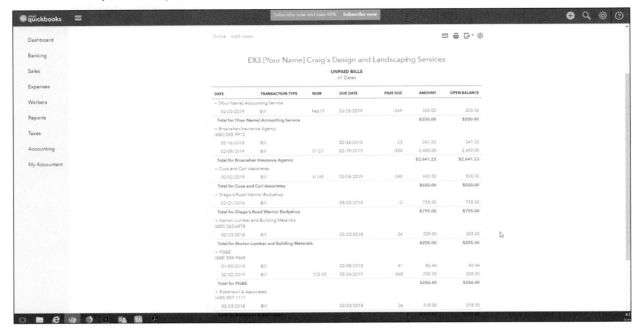

HINT

If you wish to save the report as a PDF, click the Save as PDF button.

5. To print the report, click the Print icon on the report bar. The Print, email, or save as PDF window appears.
6. Choose *Landscape* orientation from the *Orientation* drop-down list and then click the Print button.
7. At the Print window, click the Print button. You return to the Print, email, or save as PDF window.
8. Click the Close button. You return to the report.
9. Close the Unpaid Bills Report by clicking Dashboard on the Navigation bar.

Vendor Balance Detail Report

The Vendor Balance Detail Report displays all transactions for each vendor and shows the remaining balance owed. This report is similar to an accounts payable subsidiary ledger in a manual system. The report shows all vendor-related transactions—that is, all bills, payments, and credit memos for each vendor—in chronological order.

To view and print the Vendor Balance Detail Report:
1. On the Navigation bar, click Reports.
2. Scroll to the *What you owe* section and then click *Vendor Balance Detail*. The Vendor Balance Detail Report appears.
3. Click the Print icon.

4. Choose *Portrait* from the *Orientation* drop-down list and then click the Print button.
5. At the Print window, click the Print button. See Figure 3–R.

FIGURE 3–R Vendor Balance Detail Report

EX3 [Your Name] Craig's Design and Landscaping Services
VENDOR BALANCE DETAIL
All Dates

DATE	TRANSACTION TYPE	NUM	DUE DATE	AMOUNT	OPEN BALANCE	BALANCE
[Your Name] Accounting Service						
02/23/2019	Bill	Feb19	03/25/2019	300.00	200.00	200.00
Total for [Your Name] Accounting Service				**$300.00**	**$200.00**	
Brosnahan Insurance Agency						
02/16/2018	Bill		02/26/2018	241.23	241.23	241.23
02/09/2019	Bill	01-21	02/19/2019	2,400.00	2,400.00	2,641.23
Total for Brosnahan Insurance Agency				**$2,641.23**	**$2,641.23**	
Cuza and Carl Associates						
02/02/2019	Bill	X-145	03/04/2019	600.00	500.00	500.00
Total for Cuza and Carl Associates				**$600.00**	**$500.00**	
Diego's Road Warrior Bodyshop						
02/21/2018	Bill		03/23/2018	755.00	755.00	755.00
Total for Diego's Road Warrior Bodyshop				**$755.00**	**$755.00**	
Norton Lumber and Building Materials						
02/23/2018	Bill		02/23/2018	205.00	205.00	205.00
Total for Norton Lumber and Building Materials				**$205.00**	**$205.00**	
PG&E						
01/09/2018	Bill		02/08/2018	86.44	86.44	86.44
02/02/2019	Bill	125-55	03/04/2019	200.00	200.00	286.44
Total for PG&E				**$286.44**	**$286.44**	
Robertson & Associates						
02/23/2018	Bill		02/23/2018	315.00	315.00	315.00
Total for Robertson & Associates				**$315.00**	**$315.00**	
Williams Auto & Truck						
02/13/2019	Bill	556588	03/15/2019	3,700.00	3,700.00	3,700.00
02/24/2019	Vendor Credit	VC 245		-100.00	-100.00	3,600.00
Total for Williams Auto & Truck				**$3,600.00**	**$3,600.00**	
TOTAL				**$8,702.67**	**$8,502.67**	

6. At the Print, email, or save as PDF window, click the Close button.
7. Close the Vendor Balance Detail Report by clicking Dashboard on the Navigation bar.

Vendor Contact List Report

The Vendor Contact List Report displays information for all vendors that has been entered in each vendor's file. This report displays the name of each vendor, along with the vendor's phone number(s), email address, mailing address, and account number.

To view the Vendor Contact List Report:
1. On the Navigation bar, click Reports and then scroll to the *Expenses and Vendors* section.
2. Click *Vendor Contact List*.
3. Compare the report with Figure 3–S.

FIGURE 3-S Vendor Contact List Report

4. Close the Vendor Contact List Report by clicking Dashboard on the Navigation bar.

Drilling Down to a Transaction Window

HINT

You can view a vendor file by choosing the vendor name from the Vendor List or by "drilling down" to the vendor file from within a vendor report.

While viewing reports, it is frequently helpful to see the originating transaction or document that gave rise to the report figures. Most of the reports provide a drill-down feature. When reviewing a report, QuickBooks Online, like many computerized accounting programs, allows you to "drill down" from a report to the original window where data has been entered. If the transaction is incorrect, you can edit or remove the transaction at that time. Any changes to the transactions are automatically reflected in subsequent reports.

When Craig's Design reviewed the Unpaid Bills Report, it discovered that the bill from PG&E was entered incorrectly as $200; the correct amount was $250.

To drill down from a report and correct an error:
1. On the Navigation bar, click Reports and then click the All link, if necessary.
2. Scroll to the *What you owe* section and then click *Unpaid Bills.*
3. Confirm that *All Dates* displays in the *Report period* field.
4. Find the PG&E bill of 02/02/2019 and click *Bill.* The word becomes a link to the original bill entry. See Figure 3-T.

FIGURE 3–T PG&E Bill

5. Change the amount in the *AMOUNT* column to *250*.
6. Click the Save and close button to return to the report with the correction in place. See Figure 3–U.

FIGURE 3–U Corrected Unpaid Bills Report

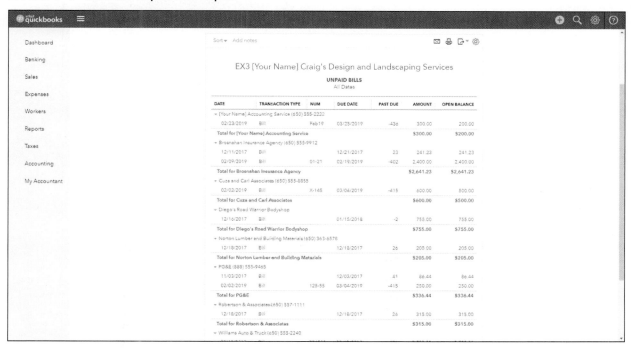

7. To print the corrected report, click the Print icon on the report bar. The Print, email, or save as PDF window appears.
8. Choose *Landscape* from the *Orientation* drop-down list and then click the Print button.
9. At the Print window, click the Print button.
10. At the Print, email, or save as PDF window, click the Close button.
11. Close the Unpaid Bills Report by clicking Dashboard on the Navigation bar.

Accounting Reports

As activities are entered in the windows, behind-the-scenes accounting activity is recorded in general journal format, posted to the general ledger, and incorporated into the financial statements. QuickBooks Online can display and print these standard accounting reports, such as the Journal Report. The Journal Report displays, in general journal format, all transactions recorded during a specified period of time.

To view and print the Journal Report:
1. On the Navigation bar, click Reports.
2. Scroll to the *For my accountant* section and then click *Journal*.
3. In the *Report period* fields, choose *02/01/2019* and *02/28/2019*. The Journal Report displays.
4. Click the Print icon.
5. At the Print, email, or save as PDF window, click the Print button.
6. At the Print window, click the Print button. See Figure 3–V.

FIGURE 3–V
Journal Report

EX3 [Your Name] Craig's Design and Landscaping Services

JOURNAL

February 2019

DATE	TRANSACTION TYPE	NUM	NAME	MEMO/DESCRIPTION	ACCOUNT	DEBIT	CREDIT
02/02/2019	Bill	125-55	PG&E		Accounts Payable (A/P)		$250.00
					Utilities:Gas and Electric	$250.00	
						$250.00	$250.00
02/02/2019	Bill	X-145	Cuza and Carl Associates		Accounts Payable (A/P)		$600.00
					Prepaid Expenses	$600.00	
						$600.00	$600.00
02/03/2019	Bill	F-19	Hall Properties		Accounts Payable (A/P)		$900.00
				Building Lease	Rent or Lease	$900.00	
						$900.00	$900.00
02/09/2019	Bill	01-21	Brosnahan Insurance Agency		Accounts Payable (A/P)		$2,400.00
					Prepaid Expenses	$2,400.00	
						$2,400.00	$2,400.00
02/10/2019	Bill Payment (Check)	71	Hall Properties	55642	Checking		$900.00
					Accounts Payable (A/P)	$900.00	
						$900.00	$900.00
02/13/2019	Bill	556588	Williams Auto & Truck		Accounts Payable (A/P)		$3,700.00
					Truck:Original Cost	$3,700.00	
						$3,700.00	$3,700.00
02/23/2019	Bill	Feb19	[Your Name] Accounting Service		Accounts Payable (A/P)		$300.00
					Legal & Professional Fees:Accounting	$300.00	
						$300.00	$300.00
02/23/2019	Bill Payment (Check)	72	Cuza and Carl Associates	CD569	Checking		$100.00
					Accounts Payable (A/P)	$100.00	
						$100.00	$100.00
02/24/2019	Vendor Credit	VC 245	Williams Auto & Truck		Accounts Payable (A/P)	$100.00	
					Truck:Original Cost		$100.00
						$100.00	$100.00
02/28/2019	Check	74	Chin's Gas and Oil		Checking		$50.00
					Automobile:Fuel	$50.00	
						$50.00	$50.00
02/28/2019	Check	77	Cal Telephone		Checking		$50.00
					Utilities:Gas and Electric	$50.00	
						$50.00	$50.00
TOTAL						$9,350.00	$9,350.00

7. Click the Close button at the Print, email, or save as PDF window.
8. Close the Journal Report by clicking Dashboard on the Navigation bar.

The *TRANSACTION TYPE* column in Figure 3–V indicates the window where the activity was recorded. In this column, the *Bill* entries represent transactions entered in the Bill window. Notice that each of these *Bill* transactions has a credit to Accounts Payable because this is the default for that account. The *Vendor Credit* entry represents the vendor credit entered in the Vendor Credit window. The *Bill Payment (Check)* entries represent transactions entered in the Pay Bills window. Each of these transactions is a debit to Accounts Payable and a credit to Cash (Checking); these two accounts are the default for this window. The *Check* entries are from the Check window and are all credits to Cash (Checking) because that is the default account for this window.

Exiting QuickBooks Online

HINT

Any work you do in the Test Drive sample company file is not saved when you exit out of the company file.

At the end of each session, you should exit QuickBooks Online and close the browser.

To exit QuickBooks Online and close the browser:
1. On the title bar, click the Gear icon.
2. At the Company window, click *Sign Out* in the *Profile* column. This closes the company file and exits QuickBooks Online.
3. Close your browser.

Chapter Review and Assessment

 Study Tools include a presentation and a glossary. Use these resources, available from the links menu in the student ebook, to further develop and review skills learned in this chapter.

Procedure Review

To add a vendor:
1. On the Navigation bar, click Expenses and then click the Vendors link. The Vendors window opens.
2. At the Vendors window, click the New vendor button. The Vendor Information window opens.
3. Enter the background data for the vendor.
4. Click the Save button.

To make a vendor inactive:
1. On the Navigation bar, click Expenses and then click the Vendors link.
2. At the Vendors window, click in the *ACTION* column drop-down list for the selected vendor and then click *Make inactive*.
3. At the warning message, click the Yes button.

To edit a vendor:
1. On the Navigation bar, click Expenses and then click the Vendors link.
2. At the Vendors window, click the name of the vendor you wish to edit.
3. Click the Edit button.
4. Change the appropriate information in the Vendor Information window.
5. Click the Save button.

To enter a bill:
1. On the title bar, click the Create icon. The Create window appears.
2. In the *Vendors* column, click *Bill*. This displays the Bill window.
3. At the *Choose a vendor* drop-down list, click the name of the vendor sending the bill.
4. Confirm or change the *Terms*, if necessary.
5. In the *Bill date* field, choose the appropriate date.
6. Enter the bill number in the *Bill no.* field.
7. Select the account to be debited in the *ACCOUNT* column.
8. Enter the bill amount in the *AMOUNT* column.
9. Click the Save and close button.

To update the Vendor List while in an Activity window:
1. On the title bar, click the Create icon.
2. In the *Vendors* column, choose *Bill*.
3. At the *Choose a vendor* drop-down list, click *Add new*. The New Vendor window appears.
4. In the *Name* field, key the vendor name and then click *Details*.
5. Complete the Vendor Information window.
6. Click the Save button.

To process a vendor credit:
1. On the title bar, click the Create icon.
2. In the *Vendors* column, click *Vendor Credit.*
3. At the *Choose a vendor* drop-down list, click the name of the vendor. The Vendor Credit window opens.
4. Enter the date in the *Payment date* field.
5. In the *ACCOUNT* column, choose the posting account.
6. In the *AMOUNT* column, enter the amount of the credit.
7. Click the Save and close button.

To pay a bill:
1. On the title bar, click the Create icon.
2. In the *Vendors* column, click *Pay Bills.*
3. In the *Payment account* field, click *Checking.* The starting check number should automatically fill. Confirm the *Print later* check box is unchecked if you do not want to print the check.
4. Click the Filter button.
5. At the pop-up window, select the payee name and then click the Apply button.
6. In the *Payment date* field, enter the date.
7. Click the check box to the left of the payee name to insert a check mark. The *PAYMENT* column fills for the full amount of the bill. To make a partial payment, enter the amount in the *PAYMENT* column.
8. Click the Save and close button.

To write a check:
1. On the title bar, click the Create icon.
2. Click *Check* in the *Vendors* column.
3. At the *Choose a payee* drop-down list, choose the appropriate payee.
4. Choose the appropriate bank account.
5. In the *Payment date* field, enter the date.
6. In the *Check no.* field, enter the check number.
7. In the *ACCOUNT* column, choose the account to be debited.
8. In the *AMOUNT* column, enter the amount of the payment.
9. Click the Save and close button.

To view and print vendor reports:
1. On the Navigation bar, click Reports.
2. Scroll to either the *What you owe* or *Expenses and Vendors* section and then choose a report.
3. Indicate the appropriate dates and settings for the report, if necessary, and then click the Run report button.
4. Click the Print icon on the report bar.
5. Click the Print button at the Print, email, or save as PDF window.
6. Click the Print button at the Print window.

Key Concepts

Select the letter of the item that best matches each definition.

a. Journal Report
b. Check window
c. system default account
d. Vendor List
e. Unpaid Bills Report

f. vendor credit
g. Pay Bills window
h. vendor
i. Bill window
j. Vendor Contact List

_____ 1. Someone from whom the business buys goods or services.

_____ 2. Contains a file for all vendors with whom the company does business.

_____ 3. A report that lists all unpaid vendor bills at a specific date.

_____ 4. A reduction of the vendor's liability due to a credit for return or allowance.

_____ 5. An activity window used to record vendor bills to be paid at a later date.

_____ 6. A report that displays transactions in general journal format for a specified period of time.

_____ 7. A report that lists all vendors from which the company buys goods and services.

_____ 8. A pre-identified general ledger account that increases or decreases automatically depending on the type of transaction entered.

_____ 9. An activity window used to record the cash purchase of goods or services from a vendor.

_____ 10. An activity window used to pay bills previously entered in the Bill window.

Procedure Check

Write a response for each of the following prompts.

1. Your company has changed its telephone carrier. Describe the steps to add the new vendor to the system.

2. Upper management requests a list of all businesses from which the company buys goods or services. How would you use QuickBooks Online to quickly produce this information?

3. You receive a batch of bills that must be paid immediately. You do not need to maintain an Accounts Payable record of these payments. How would you use QuickBooks Online to expeditiously enter these payments into the system and write the appropriate payment checks?

4. A vendor calls your company to complain that a bill sent 45 days ago remains unpaid. How would you use QuickBooks Online to verify this complaint?

5. You wish to view all the bills received from a vendor and all payments to that vendor. How would you use QuickBooks Online to obtain the required information?

6. Compare and contrast a manual accounting system with a computerized accounting system for processing vendor transactions. How does the accounts payable subsidiary ledger compare with the Vendor List?

Case Problem

Demonstrate your knowledge of the QuickBooks Online features discussed in this chapter by completing the following case problem.

On June 1, 2019, Olivia Chen started her business, Olivia's Web Solutions, as an internet consultant and web page designer. She began by depositing $25,000 cash in a bank account in the business name. She also contributed a computer system. The computer has an outstanding note balance of $2,500 that will be assumed by the business. In the previous chapter, the cash, computer, note payable, and capital have all been recorded in the opening balances of the books. Olivia anticipates spending the beginning of the month setting up her office and expects to provide web design and internet consulting services later in the month. You will record the vendor transactions listed below for the month of June.

1. Sign in to QuickBooks Online.
2. Change the company name to **OWS3 [*Your Name*] Olivia's Web Solutions**.
3. Add the following vendors to the Vendor List:

First name:	Alvin
Last name:	Clinton
Company:	ARC Management
Display name as:	ARC Management
Address:	668 Lakeville Ave.
	Garden City NY 11678
Phone:	516-555-6363
Mobile:	516-555-6364
Terms:	Net 30
Opening balance:	0
as of:	June 1, 2019

First name:	Customer
Last name:	Service
Company:	Comet Computer Supplies
Display name as:	Comet Computer Supplies
Address:	657 Motor Parkway
	Center Island City NY 11488
Phone:	631-555-4444
Mobile:	631-555-4445
Terms:	Net 15
Opening balance:	0
as of:	June 1, 2019

First name:	Chris
Last name:	Chrbet
Company:	Chrbet Advertising
Display name as:	Chrbet Advertising
Address:	201 East 10th Street
	New York NY 10012
Phone:	212-555-8777
Mobile:	212-555-8778

HINT

Remember, the textbook is using 2019 as the current year. Unlike the Test Drive, you can use the 2019 year for the Case Problems for all chapters except Chapters 10 and 11.

Terms:	Net 30
Opening balance:	0
as of:	June 1, 2019

First name:	Customer
Last name:	Service
Company:	Eastel
Display name as:	Eastel
Address:	655 Fifth Ave.
	New York NY 10012
Phone:	212-555-6565
Mobile:	212-555-6566
Terms:	Net 30
Opening balance:	0
as of:	June 1, 2019

First name:	Customer
Last name:	Service
Company:	Eastern Mutual Insurance
Display name as:	Eastern Mutual Insurance
Address:	55 Broadway Rm55
	New York NY 10001
Phone:	212-555-6563
Mobile:	212-555-6564
Terms:	Net 30
Opening balance:	0
as of:	June 1, 2019

First name:	Manny
Last name:	Lewis
Company:	Lewis Furniture Company
Display name as:	Lewis Furniture Company
Address:	1225 Route 110
	Farmingdale NY 11898
Phone:	631-555-6161
Mobile:	631-555-6162
Terms:	Net 30
Opening balance:	0
as of:	June 1, 2019

First name:	Customer
Last name:	Service
Company:	LI Power Company
Display name as:	LI Power Company
Address:	5444 Northern Avenue
	Plainview NY 11544
Phone:	516-555-8888
Mobile:	516-555-8889
Terms:	Net 15
Opening balance:	0
as of:	June 1, 2019

First name:	Customer
Last name:	Service
Company:	Netsoft Development
Display name as:	Netsoft Development
Address:	684 Mountain View Road
	Portland OR 68774
Phone:	974-555-7873
Mobile:	974-555-7874
Terms:	Net 30
Opening balance:	0
as of:	June 1, 2019

First name:	Customer
Last name:	Service
Company:	Office Plus
Display name as:	Office Plus
Address:	45 Jericho Turnpike
	Jericho NY 11654
Phone:	516-555-3214
Mobile:	516-555-3213
Terms:	Net 30
Opening balance:	0
as of:	June 1, 2019

First name:	Olivia
Last name:	Chen
Company:	(blank)
Display name as:	Olivia Chen
Address:	(blank)
Phone:	(blank)
Mobile:	(blank)
Terms:	(blank)
Opening balance:	(blank)
as of:	(blank)

4. Using the appropriate window, record the following transactions for June 2019:

Jun. 1	Received bill for rent for the month of June from ARC Management, $800, paid immediately. Check no. 1. Do not print check.
Jun. 4	Received a one-year insurance policy on account from Eastern Mutual Insurance, Bill no. 87775, $1,800, Net 30 Days.
Jun. 4	Purchased software on account from Netsoft Development, Bill no. 38745, $3,600, Net 30 Days. (Debit account 1925 Software - Cost.)
Jun. 7	Purchased office furniture on account from Lewis Furniture Company, Bill no. O-9887, $3,200, Net 30 Days. (Debit account 1825 Furniture - Cost.)

Jun. 8	Purchased six months of advertising services on account from Chrbet Advertising, Bill no. O-989, $1,200, Net 30 Days.
Jun. 11	Purchased computer supplies on account from Comet Computer Supplies, Bill no. 56355, $600, Net 15 Days.
Jun. 14	Received bill for online internet services from Systems Service, $150, paid immediately (Check no. 2). Systems Service is a new vendor.

Add the new vendor:

First name:	Jeremy
Last name:	Jones
Company:	Systems Service
Display name as:	Systems Service
Address:	36 Sunrise Lane
	Hempstead NY 11004
Phone:	516-555-2525
Mobile:	516-555-2526
Terms:	Net 30
Opening balance:	0
as of:	June 1, 2019

Jun. 15	Purchased office supplies on account from Office Plus, Bill no. 3665, $450, Net 30 Days.
Jun. 18	Received telephone bill from Eastel, Bill no. 6-2568, $350, Net 30 Days.
Jun. 21	Received utilities bill from LI Power Company, Bill no. OWS-23556, $125, Net 15 Days.
Jun. 21	Returned office supplies to Office Plus for a $75 credit, Ref. no. VC789.
Jun. 21	Paid in full Eastern Mutual Insurance, Bill no. 87775 (Check no. 3). Do not print check.
Jun. 25	Paid in full Comet Computer Supplies, Bill no. 56355 (Check no. 4).
Jun. 28	Paid in full LI Power Company, Bill no. OWS-23556 (Check no. 5).
Jun. 30	Made a partial payment of $2,000 to Netsoft Development, Bill no. 38745 (Check no. 6).
Jun. 30	Made a partial payment of $1,500 to Lewis Furniture Company, Bill no. O-9887 (Check no. 7).
Jun. 30	The owner, Olivia Chen, withdrew $500 for personal use (Check no. 8).

5. Display and print the following reports for June 1, 2019, to June 30, 2019:
   a. Unpaid Bills
   b. Vendor Balance Detail
   c. Vendor Contact List
   d. Journal

CHAPTER 4

Customers

Adding Customers, Creating Invoices, and Receiving and Depositing Payments

Objectives

- Identify the system default accounts for customers
- Update the Customer List
- Record sales on account in the Invoice window
- Record collections of accounts receivable in the Receive Payment window
- Record cash sales in the Sales Receipt window
- Deposit payments in the Deposit window
- Display and print customer-related reports

QuickBooks Online allows you to track all customer transactions. A **customer** is a person or business to which a company sells goods or services, either on account or for cash. A file for each customer should be established before entering transactions for a particular customer. The collection of all customer files comprises the Customer List.

Once a customer file is established, transactions such as creating an invoice for a customer, receiving payment from that customer, or making a cash sale can be entered in the Invoice, Receive Payment, Sales Receipt, and Deposit windows. As transactions are recorded in these activities windows, QuickBooks Online simultaneously updates the customer's file in the Customer List to include information about the transactions for that customer. At the same time, QuickBooks Online updates any related reports.

In this chapter, our sample company, Craig's Design and Landscaping Services, will create invoices for design and landscaping services, receive payments for invoices, make cash sales, and deposit funds.

QuickBooks Online versus Manual Accounting: Customer Transactions

In a manual accounting system, all sales of goods or services on account are recorded in a multi-column **sales journal**. At the conclusion of the month, the totals are posted to the accounts receivable and revenue accounts affected by the transactions. As each sales transaction is recorded, the appropriate customer's account in the accounts receivable subsidiary ledger is updated for the new receivable. Collections of open accounts receivable balances and cash sales of goods or services are recorded in a multi-column **cash receipts journal**. As was done with the sales journal, monthly totals are posted to the general ledger accounts while payment information is recorded daily in the customer's subsidiary ledger record.

In QuickBooks Online, the Customer List serves as the accounts receivable subsidiary ledger for the company. The Customer List contains a file for all companies and individuals to whom the company sells goods and services. Relevant information, such as company name, address, contact, and so on, is entered when the customer's file is created in the Customer List.

When the company creates an invoice for goods or services, the invoice is created in the Invoice window. The Invoice window is equivalent to the multi-column sales journal. This transaction updates the Chart of Accounts List and general ledger while simultaneously updating the customer's file in the Customer List for the new receivable. When the customer pays the invoice, the company enters this transaction in the Receive Payment window. The Receive Payment window is equivalent to the part of the cash receipts journal that records collection of open accounts receivable. QuickBooks Online automatically updates the Chart of Accounts List, general ledger, and the customer's file in the Customer List for the payment of the receivable.

To record a check received for an invoice not previously entered, the Sales Receipt window is used. This window is equivalent to the remainder of the cash receipts journal, which records all cash receipts other than collection of accounts receivable. Again, the Chart of Accounts List, general ledger, and the customer's file in the Customer List are simultaneously updated.

customer A person or business to which a company sells goods or services, either on account or for cash.

sales journal A journal used to record all sales of goods or services on account; can be in single-column or multi-column format.

cash receipts journal A journal used to record collections of open accounts receivable balances and cash sales of goods or services.

System Default Accounts

As we saw in Chapter 3, to process transactions expeditiously and organize data for reporting, QuickBooks Online establishes specific general ledger accounts as default accounts in each window. When you enter transactions, QuickBooks Online automatically increases or decreases certain account balances, depending on the nature of the transaction.

For example, for vendors, when you enter a transaction in the Bill window, QuickBooks Online automatically increases (credits) the Accounts Payable account; when you pay the bills in the Pay Bills window, QuickBooks Online automatically decreases (debits) the Accounts Payable account. Similarly, for customers, when you enter a transaction in the Invoice window, QuickBooks Online automatically increases (debits) the Accounts Receivable account because the Invoice window is used to record sales on account. When you record a collection of accounts receivable in the Receive Payment window, QuickBooks Online automatically decreases (credits) the Accounts Receivable account. You do not have to enter the account number or name for these default accounts because they have been preestablished by QuickBooks Online.

 Chapter Problem

In this chapter, you will enter and track customer transactions for Craig's Design and Landscaping Services. The company provides garden design and landscaping services both on account and for cash. Customers and clients remit payment for invoices; these funds are periodically deposited in the company checking account. Information for several customers has been entered in the Customer List. This information is contained in the QuickBooks Online Test Drive.

To access the QuickBooks Online Test Drive:
1. Open an internet browser, key https://QBO18.ParadigmEducation .com/TestDrive into the address bar, and then press the Enter key or click the Go arrow. This opens the Security Verification window.
2. Click the check box to the left of the text *I'm not a robot.* A window may appear with images. If so, follow the instructions to select images or part of an image and then click NEXT, SKIP, or VERIFY. (This may take several attempts.)
3. Click the Continue button. QuickBooks Online launches displaying the sample company Craig's Design and Landscaping Services.

To change the company name:
1. On the title bar, click the Gear icon. The Craig's Design and Landscaping Services window appears.
2. Click *Account and Settings* in the *Your Company* column. This opens the Account and Settings window.
3. Click the Edit icon in the *Company name* section or click anywhere in the section. The *Company name* section expands to display more information about the company, and you can now edit the company information.
4. In the *Company name* field, select the company name and key EX4 [*Your Name*] Craig's Design and Landscaping Services.

5. Click the *EIN* radio button and then key 12-3456788 in the *EIN* field.
6. Confirm the information is correct and then click the Save button. The changes are saved and you return to the Account and Settings window with the *Company name* section updated and condensed. If the section does not update, click the Company tab on the left.
7. Confirm the information is correct and then click the Done button in the lower right corner of the window.

To extend the time-out period of time:
1. On the title bar, click the Gear icon. The Company window appears.
2. At the Company window, in the *Your Company* column, click *Account and Settings*. This opens the Account and Settings window.
3. At the Account and Settings window, click the Advanced tab.
4. Click the Edit icon in the *Other preferences* section or click anywhere in the section.
5. In the *Sign me out if inactive for* field, click the drop-down arrow and then click *3 hours*.
6. Click the Save button. The change is saved, and you will now be automatically signed out if you are inactive for three hours instead of one hour.
7. Click the Done button or click the X to close the Account and Settings window.

Craig's Design and Landscaping Services wishes to have the invoice number displayed in and the *SERVICE DATE* column removed from the Invoice and Sales Receipt windows.

To display the invoice number and remove the *SERVICE DATE* column:
1. On the title bar, click the Gear icon.
2. In the *Your Company* column, click *Custom Form Styles*.
3. At the Custom form styles window, click the New style button arrow and select *Invoice*.
4. At the Create invoices that turn heads and open wallets window, click the Content tab. The sample invoice on the right dims and divides into three sections for easy editing.
5. Click the Edit icon in the top (header) section. The header section becomes active for edits.
6. At the left side of the window in the *Form* section, click to insert a check mark next to *Use custom transaction numbers* and remove the check mark next to *Form numbers*.
7. Click the Done button to return to the Custom form styles window.
8. Click the Gear icon and then click *Account and Settings* in the *Your Company* column.
9. In the Account and Settings window, click the Sales tab and then click the Edit icon in the *Sales form content* section or click anywhere in the section.
10. Remove the check mark next to *Service date* to turn off that option and then click the Save button.
11. Close the Custom form styles window by clicking Dashboard on the Navigation bar.

You will now be able to enter an invoice number in the Invoice and Sales Receipt windows and the *SERVICE DATE* column will not appear in either window.

Lists

The Customer List

The Customer List contains a file for each customer to whom the company sells goods or services. Each file contains important information, such as company name, address, contact person, terms, preferred payment method, and current balance owed. You should include all customers with whom the company does business in the Customer List.

Recall from Chapter 1 that the second level of operation in QuickBooks Online is recording information in Lists. The Customer List is updated periodically when new customers are added, customers not used in the business are made inactive, and modifications are made to customer information.

You should try to enter the information for each customer in the Customer List before recording transactions. However, if you inadvertently omit a customer, you can add that customer during the Activities level of operation with minimal disruption.

Craig's Design and Landscaping Services has entered information for existing and anticipated customers in the Customer List.

To view the Customer List:
1. On the Navigation bar, click Sales and then click the Customers link. The Customers window appears. See Figure 4–A.

FIGURE 4–A Customers Window

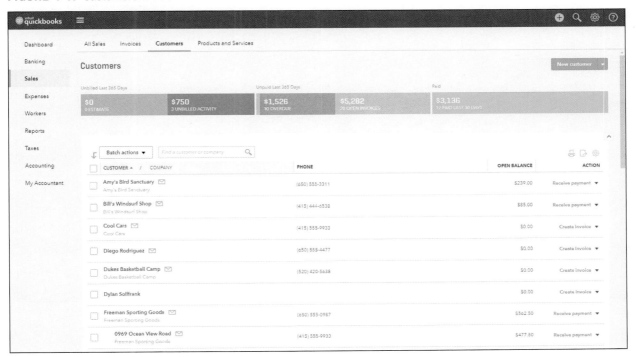

The Customers window contains the following elements:

Unbilled Last 365 Days filter	Lists all open estimates and employee time that has not yet been invoiced to customers (see Chapter 11) for period.
Unpaid Last 365 Days filter	Lists all open invoices for the period, including overdue invoices.
Paid filter	Lists all invoices collected in the past 30 days.
New customer button	Used to add or import a new customer.
Batch actions button	Used to send an email or statement to all selected customers.
***ACTION* column**	Used to initiate various actions for a selected customer, such as creating an invoice, creating a sales receipt, receiving a payment, etc.
Print icon	Used to print a list of the customers.

To view a specific customer file:

1. At the Customers window, click *Amy's Bird Sanctuary* to open the file. See Figure 4–B.

FIGURE 4–B Customer File—Amy's Bird Sanctuary

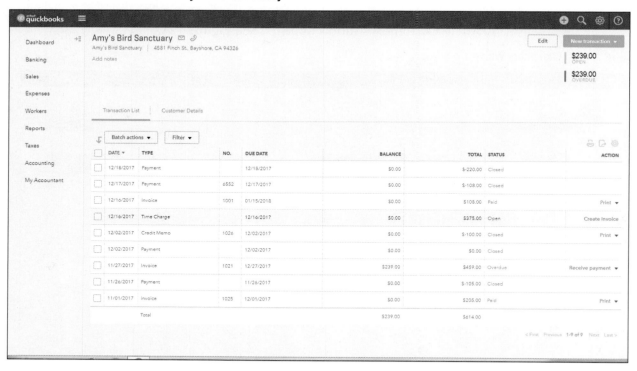

The customer file window contains the following elements:

Edit button	Allows you to edit customer information, such as customer name, address, phone numbers, etc.
New Transaction button	Allows you to enter a transaction, such as invoice, payment, etc., for this customer.
Open/Overdue boxes	Lists the dollar amount of open and overdue invoices.
Transaction List tab	Lists all recent transactions for this customer.
Customer Details tab	Displays customer profile information contained in the file.
Filter button	Allows you to modify the display of transactions, either by type or date range.

2. Click Sales on the Navigation bar to return to the Customers window.
3. Close the Customers window by clicking Dashboard on the Navigation bar.

Adding a Customer

Craig's Design has just been hired by a new client, Maria Omari, to provide design and landscaping services for Omari's new residence.

To add a new customer:
1. On the Navigation bar, click Sales and then click the Customers link, if necessary. The Customers window opens with a list of customers and information displayed for each customer.
2. At the Customers window, click the New customer button. The Customer information window appears. See Figure 4–C.

FIGURE 4–C
Customer Information Window

3. Key the data below in the Customer information window. See Figure 4–D.

First name:	Maria
Last name:	Omari
Display name as:	Maria Omari
Phone:	650-555-9999
Mobile:	650-555-9998
Billing address:	210 NE Lowry Ave.
	Middlefield CA 94303

FIGURE 4–D
Customer Information Window—Partially Complete

HINT

To move from field to field, press the Tab key or Shift + Tab.

4. Click the Payment and billing tab and enter the information below. See Figure 4–E.

Preferred payment method:	Check
Terms:	Net 30
Preferred delivery method:	None
Opening balance:	0
as of:	02/01/2019

FIGURE 4–E
Customer Information Window—Payment and Billing Tab Completed

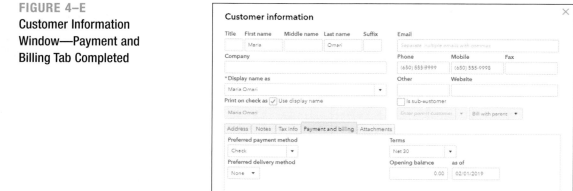

5. Confirm the information is correct and then click the Save button.
6. Click Sales on the Navigation bar to return to the Customers window.

Making a Customer Inactive

Craig's Design wishes to make Cool Cars inactive on the Customer List because the company has gone out of business. In QuickBooks Online, you cannot delete a customer, but you can make the customer inactive.

To make a customer inactive:
1. Open the Customers window, if necessary.
2. In the *ACTION* column for Cool Cars, click *Make inactive.*
3. At the warning message, *Are you sure you want to make Cools Cars inactive?*, click the Yes button. The customer file is removed from the Customer List. See Figure 4–F.

FIGURE 4–F
Customers Window—
Cool Cars Inactive

4. Close the Customers window by clicking Dashboard on the Navigation bar.

If you wish to reactivate the customer, return to the Customers window, click the Settings gear above the *ACTION* column, and then click the *Include inactive* check box. Any customer previously made inactive will be restored to the Customer List but marked *(deleted).* You can make the customer active again by clicking *Make active* in the *ACTION* column.

HINT

If you make a customer with an open balance inactive, QuickBooks Online will automatically credit that customer's account for the unpaid balance.

Editing a Customer

Craig's Design needs to edit the file for Gevelber Photography because the contact person has changed.

To edit a customer file:
1. On the Navigation bar, click Sales and then click the Customers link, if necessary.
2. At the Customers window, click *Gevelber Photography.*
3. Click the Edit button. This opens the Customer information window.
4. In the *First name* field, delete the current name and then key Laura. See Figure 4–G.
5. Confirm the information is correct and then click the Save button.
6. Click Sales on the Navigation bar to return to the Customers window.

FIGURE 4–G
Customer Information
Window—Updated
First Name

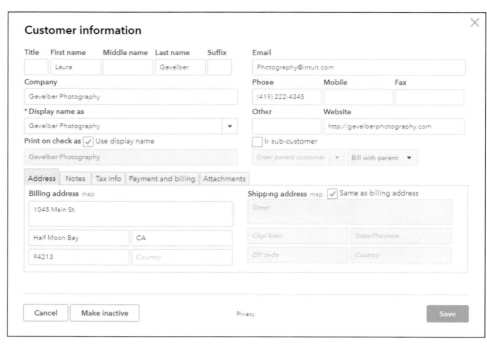

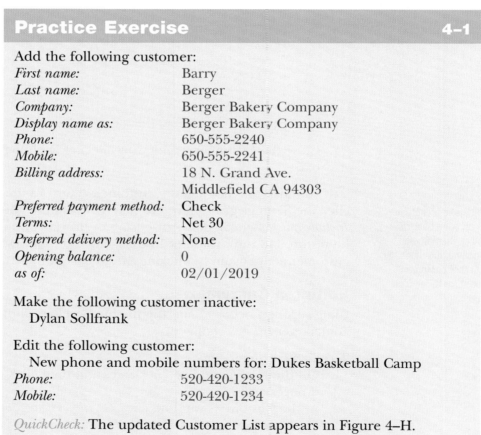

Practice Exercise 4–1

Add the following customer:

First name:	Barry
Last name:	Berger
Company:	Berger Bakery Company
Display name as:	Berger Bakery Company
Phone:	650-555-2240
Mobile:	650-555-2241
Billing address:	18 N. Grand Ave.
	Middlefield CA 94303
Preferred payment method:	Check
Terms:	Net 30
Preferred delivery method:	None
Opening balance:	0
as of:	02/01/2019

Make the following customer inactive:
Dylan Sollfrank

Edit the following customer:
New phone and mobile numbers for: Dukes Basketball Camp

Phone:	520-420-1233
Mobile:	520-420-1234

QuickCheck: The updated Customer List appears in Figure 4–H.

FIGURE 4-H Updated Customer List

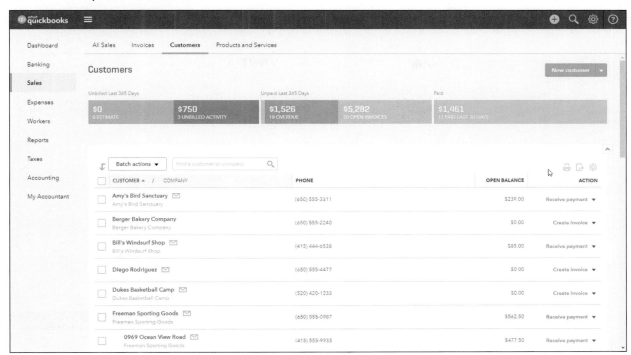

Activities

The Invoice Window

sale on account
A sale on account occurs when a company sells goods or services to a customer but does not receive payment until a future date.

Recall from Chapter 1 that the third level of operation in QuickBooks Online is Activities. In QuickBooks Online, any Activity identified as a **sale on account** is recorded in the Invoice window. Accounts Receivable is the default general ledger posting account. All transactions entered in this window result in a debit to the Accounts Receivable account. The account to be credited, usually a revenue account, is determined based on the item chosen.

QuickBooks records a sale on account as follows:

| Accounts Receivable | XXX | |
| Revenue | | XXX |

At the same time that a sale on account is recorded, QuickBooks Online updates the customer's file in the Customer List to reflect the new receivable. The QuickBooks Online Invoice window appears in Figure 4–I.

FIGURE 4–1 Invoice Window

Most icons and data fields are self-explanatory, but take special note of the following:

Choose a customer drop-down list	Drop-down list used to choose a customer from the Customer List.
Terms drop-down list	List of available terms for payment. If you have entered terms in the Customer information window for the selected customer, those terms will be the default selection.
Balance due	Displays the open balance for the selected customer.
PRODUCT/SERVICE column	Clicking in this column allows you to access the Products and Services List. Once an item is selected, the description and rate are filled automatically based on the information entered in the Products and Services List.
Make recurring button	Allows you to invoice this customer automatically at selected intervals.
Customize button	Allows you to change the format of the invoice.
Save button	Click to save the transaction and remain in the Invoice window.
Save and new/Save and close button	Click to enter an invoice for a different customer or to exit the Invoice window.

Products and Services

The Products and Services List contains a list of services and products sold. Craig's Design and Landscaping Services has established two primary revenue items in the Products and Services List, with various subcategories of each: Landscaping Services includes exterior services, such as weekly gardening, installations, maintenance and repair, etc.; Design Services includes gardening design, such as lighting, concrete work, general design services, etc. Sales of products will be covered in Chapter 6.

HINT

You can also access the Products and Services List by clicking Sales on the Navigation bar.

To view the Products and Services List:
1. On the title bar, click the Gear icon.
2. In the *Lists* column, click *Products and Services.* See Figure 4–J.

FIGURE 4–J Products and Services List

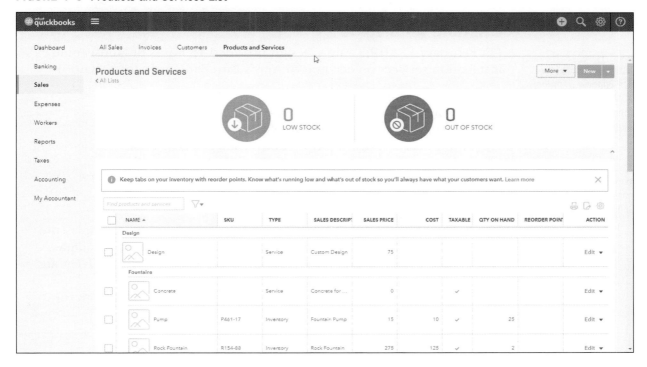

3. To view the data for the Custom Design service, double-click the item. The Product/Service information window appears. See Figure 4–K.

FIGURE 4–K
Product/Service Information Window

Design is indicated as a service, rather than inventory. The window also contains sales information, the sales price/rate, and a default general ledger income account. QuickBooks Online uses this data when you create an invoice for a customer for this service.

4. Close the Product/Service information window.
5. Close the Products and Services List by clicking Dashboard on the Navigation bar.

Creating an Invoice

HINT

You can also access the Invoice window from the *ACTION* column at the Customers window for this customer.

On February 1, 2019, Craig's Design provided 12 hours of landscaping installation services on account to Amy's Bird Sanctuary, Invoice no. 1038.

To create an invoice:
1. On the title bar, click the Create icon.
2. In the *Customers* column, click *Invoice*.
3. At the *Choose a customer* drop-down list, click *Amy's Bird Sanctuary*. The information for that customer will fill in automatically.

HINT

If a pop-up message appears, click the X to close it.

4. At the *Terms* drop-down list, accept the default choice, *Net 30*.
5. In the *Invoice date* field, choose *02/01/2019*.
6. Confirm the Invoice no. is *1038*.
7. In the *PRODUCT/SERVICE* column, click the first line to display the drop-down list, then click *Installation of landscape design*. The data from the Products/Services List will complete the *DESCRIPTION* and *RATE* columns.
8. In the *QTY* column, key 12. When you move to the next field, the *AMOUNT* column will automatically fill. See Figure 4–L.

FIGURE 4–L Invoice Window—Completed

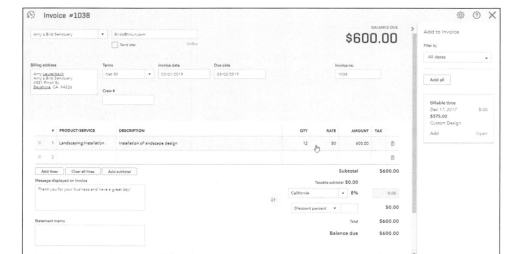

HINT

If you wish to view recent invoices, click the Recent Transactions icon in the upper left corner of the Invoice window.

As stated earlier, the default account to debit in the Invoice window is Accounts Receivable. An account to be credited is not indicated in the Invoice window. The information for Landscaping in the Products/Services List indicated the revenue account that should be credited when entering this service in an activity window. Once you choose the service in the Invoice window, QuickBooks Online knows from the Products/Services List to credit the appropriate revenue account for this transaction.

9. Confirm the information is correct and then click the Save and close button. You return to the Dashboard.

Accounting Concept

For a sale of landscaping services on account, the general ledger posting is as follows:

In addition, the customer file (subledger) for Amy's Bird Sanctuary reflects the new receivable:

Accts Rec			Amy's Bird Sanctuary	
Dr	Cr		Dr	Cr
600			600	

Income Labor:Installation	
Dr	Cr
	600

Practice Exercise 4–2

Record the following transactions in the Invoice window. Use Invoice numbers 1039–1043.

Feb. 6	Provided 4 hours of Design services to Bill's Windsurf Shop. *QuickCheck: $300*
Feb. 13	Provided 8 hours of Design services and 16 hours of Landscaping: Trimming services to Freeman Sporting Goods. *QuickCheck: $1,160*
Feb. 17	Provided 8 hours of Pest Control services to Jeff's Jalopies. *QuickCheck: $280*
Feb. 23	Provided 24 hours of Landscaping: Installation services to Maria Omari. *QuickCheck: $1,200*
Feb. 27	Provided 6 hours of Design services and 15 hours of Landscaping: Installation services to Bill's Windsurf Shop. *QuickCheck: $1,200*

HINT

QuickCheck numbers throughout the textbook represent subtotals and totals related to the Practice Exercise.

HINT

If there is more than one item, click in the next line in the *PRODUCT/ SERVICE* field or click the Add lines button to add an additional four lines.

collection of accounts receivable Collection of accounts receivable occurs when a customer pays part or all of his or her outstanding balance due the company; this Activity is sometimes referred to as *payment of accounts receivable*.

The Receive Payment Window

In QuickBooks Online, the Receive Payment window is used to record the **collection of accounts receivable** from customers previously invoiced in the Invoice window. The Receive Payment window displays all open invoices for a specific customer. Payment can be in the form of cash, check, credit/debit card, or e-check.

The Receive Payment window is designed only for collection of existing invoices. The default accounts are Accounts Receivable and Cash or Undeposited Funds (discussed later in this chapter). The transaction is recorded as follows:

		Cash (or Undeposited Funds)		XXX		
		Accounts Receivable			XXX	

At the same time, the customer's file in the Customer List is updated to reflect the payment. The QuickBooks Online Receive Payment window appears in Figure 4–M.

FIGURE 4–M Receive Payment Window

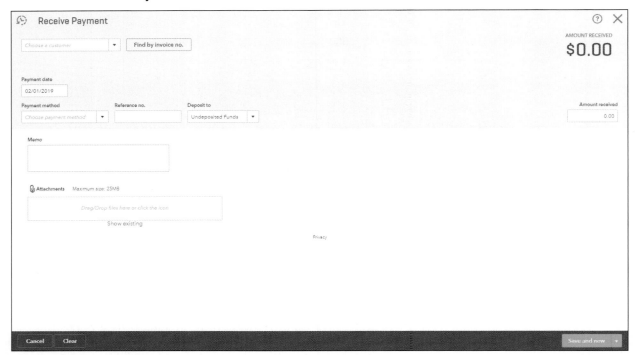

Once a customer is selected, a list of open invoices displays. Note the following elements at the Receive Payment window:

Find by invoice no. button	Used to enter the invoice number. Once entered, the customer and the invoice information display.
Payment method drop-down list	Allows you to indicate the customer's method of payment. Choices include check, cash, and various credit cards.
Reference no. field	Used to enter a check number or credit card transaction number.
Deposit to drop-down list	Indicates the general ledger posting account for the payment. In this text, the default account will be Undeposited Funds.
Outstanding Transactions list	Lists the open invoices for the selected customer. (See Figure 4–N.)
Filter button	Allows you to customize the display as to date range. (See Figure 4–N.)

Activities identified as sales on account were recorded in the Invoice window. Subsequently, activities identified as collection of an outstanding account receivable (previously recorded in the Invoice window) are now recorded in the Receive Payment window. Cash or Undeposited Funds and Accounts Receivable are the default general ledger posting accounts. All transactions entered in this window result in a debit to the Cash or Undeposited Funds account and a credit to the Accounts Receivable account.

Receiving a Payment in Full

HINT

You can also access the Transactions List by clicking *Receive payment* in the *ACTION* column for this customer in the Customers window.

On February 13, 2019, Craig's Design receives a $600 payment from Amy's Bird Sanctuary for Invoice no. 1038, their Check no. 6544.

To record a receipt of payment:
1. On the title bar, click the Create icon.
2. In the *Customers* column, click *Receive Payment*.
3. At the *Choose a customer* drop-down list, click *Amy's Bird Sanctuary*. The file will open with the Outstanding Transactions list displaying all open invoices. See Figure 4–N.

FIGURE 4–N Amy's Bird Sanctuary—Outstanding Transactions

HINT

QuickBooks Online had automatically assigned the next invoice number 1038 when you recorded the sale on account in the Invoice window.

4. In the *Payment date* field, choose *02/13/2019*.
5. At the *Payment method* drop-down list, click *Check*.
6. In the *Reference no.* field, key 6544.
7. Confirm the *Deposit to* field displays *Undeposited Funds* as the posting account.
8. Click to insert a check mark next to *Invoice #1038*. The *PAYMENT* column will automatically fill in for the full amount. See Figure 4–O.

FIGURE 4-O   Receive Payment Window—Completed

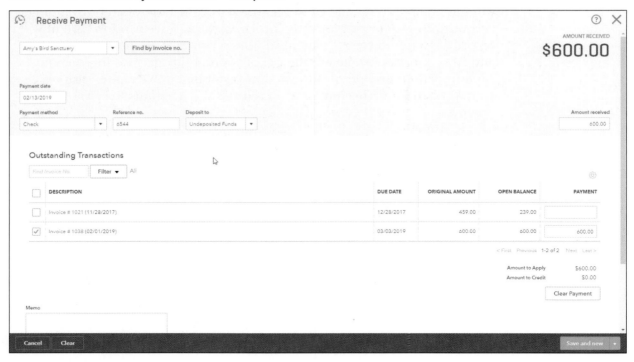

9. Confirm the information is correct and then click *Save and close* from the Save and new button list. You will return to the Dashboard.

    Remember, clicking *Save and close* posts the transaction and returns you to the last window you accessed. If you wish to remain at the Receive Payment window and record a payment from a different customer, click the Save and new button.

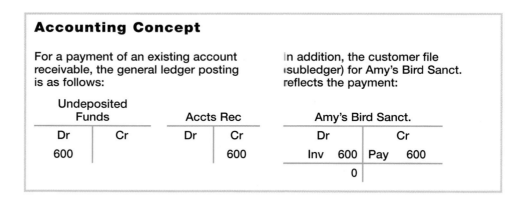

Accounting Concept

For a payment of an existing account receivable, the general ledger posting is as follows:

In addition, the customer file (subledger) for Amy's Bird Sanct. reflects the payment:

	Undeposited Funds			Accts Rec			Amy's Bird Sanct.	
Dr		Cr	Dr		Cr	Dr		Cr
600					600	Inv	600	Pay	600
							0	

Entering a Partial Payment of an Invoice

The Receive Payment window allows you to record partial payments of open invoices. On February 23, 2019, Freeman's Sporting Goods remits $500 toward its open Invoice no. 1040 in the amount of $1,160, its Check no. 1255. No discount is allowed.

HINT

The collection procedure described here allows you to access the Receive Payment window from the Customer List.

To record a partial payment of an invoice:

1. On the Navigation bar, click Sales and then click the Customers link, if necessary. The Customers window appears with the Customer List displayed.
2. Click *Freeman Sporting Goods.* The customer file appears.
3. In the *ACTION* column for Invoice 1040, click *Receive payment.* Notice that Invoice #1040 has been checked for payment and the *PAYMENT* column displays $1,160.
4. In the *Payment date* field, choose *02/23/2019.*
5. At the *Payment method* drop-down list, click *Check.*
6. In the *Reference no.* field, key 1255.
7. Confirm the *Deposit to* field displays *Undeposited Funds* as the posting account.
8. In the *PAYMENT* column, delete the existing amount and then key 500. See Figure 4–P.

FIGURE 4–P Receive Payment Window—Partial Payment

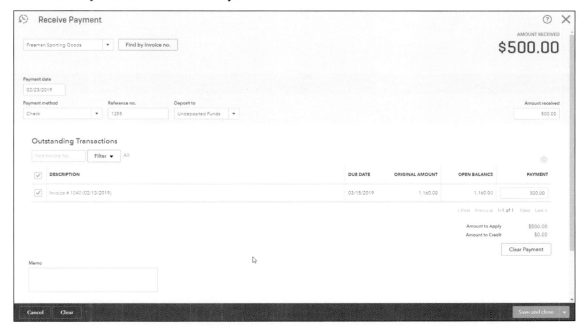

9. Confirm the information is correct and then click the Save and close button. You return to the Freeman Sporting Goods customer file.
10. Close the customer file by clicking Dashboard on the Navigation bar.

Recording Payment for More Than One Invoice

QuickBooks Online allows you to record a payment of several invoices at the same time. On February 27, 2019, Bill's Windsurf Shop remits $1,585 in full payment of Invoice nos. 1027, 1039, and 1043, its Check no. 655.

To record payment of more than one invoice:

1. On the title bar, click the Create icon.
2. Click *Receive Payment* in the *Customers* column.
3. At the *Choose a customer* drop-down list, click *Bill's Windsurf Shop.* The Outstanding Transactions list displays all open invoices.
4. In the *Payment date* field, select *02/27/2019.* See Figure 4–Q.

FIGURE 4–Q Bill's Windsurf Shop—Outstanding Transactions

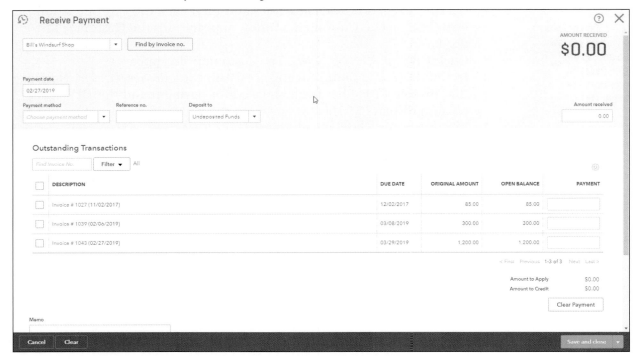

5. Click *Check* at the *Payment method* drop-down list.
6. Key 655 in the *Reference no.* field.
7. In the *Amount received* field, key 1585. When you move to the next field, the amount is applied to all invoices. See Figure 4–R.
8. Confirm the information is correct and then click the Save and new button.

FIGURE 4–R Receive Payment Window—Completed

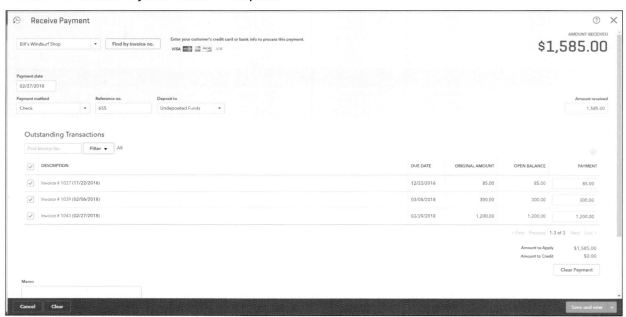

Record the following transactions in the Receive Payment window:

| Feb. 28 | Received $954.75 from Paulsen Medical Supplies in full payment of Invoice no. 1015, their Check no. 674. |
| Feb. 28 | Received $600 from Maria Omari in partial payment of Invoice no. 1042, her Check no. 124. |

The Sales Receipt Window

In QuickBooks Online, you use the Sales Receipt window to record a **cash sale**, or a sale for which payment is received immediately. Since you do not use Accounts Receivable, this window allows you to record a cash sale in one step. The data fields in this window are similar to those of the Invoice window: customer, date, item sold, service provided, and so on.

The Sales Receipt window is used for all cash sales of goods and services. As with the Receive Payment window, the default account is Cash or Undeposited Funds because all transactions result in a cash receipt. The transaction is recorded as follows:

| | | Cash (or Undeposited Funds) | | XXX | | |
| | | Revenue | | | XXX | |

A transaction entered in this window is not tracked through the Accounts Receivable or Customer Reports.

The account to be credited is based on the item selected. As in the Invoice window, when an item is selected, QuickBooks Online uses the information from the Products and Services List to determine which account should be credited.

Recording a Cash Sale

On February 24, 2019, Craig's Design provided eight hours of custom design services to Berger Bakery Company, Invoice no. 1044. It paid in full with Check no. 25545.

To record a cash sale:
1. On the title bar, click the Create icon.
2. In the *Customers* column, click *Sales Receipt*.
3. At the *Choose a customer* drop-down list, click *Berger Bakery Company*.
4. In the *Sales Receipt date* field, select *02/24/2019*.
5. Confirm that the *Sales Receipt no.* is *1044*.
6. At the *Payment method* drop-down list, select *Check*.
7. In the *Reference no.* field, key 25545.
8. Confirm the *Deposit to* field reads *Undeposited Funds*.
9. In the *PRODUCT/SERVICE* column, choose *Custom Design*. QuickBooks Online will automatically complete the *DESCRIPTION* column.

10. In the *QTY* column, key 8. See Figure 4–S.

FIGURE 4–S Sales Receipt Window—Completed

11. Confirm the information is correct and then click the *Save and close* option from the Save and send button list.

The Transaction List tab in the customer file will reflect the cash sale. However, the transaction will not be reflected in the Accounts Receivable reports.

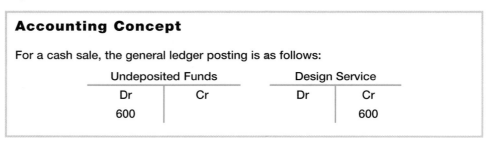

Accounting Concept

For a cash sale, the general ledger posting is as follows:

Undeposited Funds			Design Service	
Dr	Cr		Dr	Cr
600				600

Activities

The Deposit Window

Most accounting textbooks assume that when cash is received, it is immediately posted to a Cash account. However, many businesses post to the Cash account only when funds are actually deposited in the checking account. This may occur several days after the funds are received. For these businesses, the receipt of funds is posted to a current asset account, titled Undeposited Funds, until a deposit is made. At that point, a second transaction is recorded to show the undeposited funds transferred to the Cash - Checking account. Debits to the Cash - Checking account should coincide with deposits recorded on the bank statement. This allows the company to more easily track deposits during the month-end bank reconciliation process.

When the Undeposited Funds account is used, cash receipts are recorded as follows:

		Undeposited Funds	XXX	
		Accounts Receivable/Revenue		XXX

This entry results from activities entered in the Receive Payment and Sales Receipt windows.

When funds previously received and recorded in the Receive Payment or Sales Receipt window are subsequently deposited in the bank, the Deposit window is used. The default accounts are Cash and Undeposited Funds. The transaction is recorded as follows:

		Cash	XXX	
		Undeposited Funds		XXX

Activities identified as deposits of funds are recorded in the Deposits window. In this window, Cash and Undeposited Funds are the default general ledger posting accounts. All transactions entered in this window result in a debit to the Cash account and a credit to the Undeposited Funds account.

Depositing All Receipts

In the Receive Payment and Sales Receipt windows, the default posting account for the receipt of cash is the Undeposited Funds account rather than the Cash - Checking account. In this chapter, Craig's Design and Landscaping Services will deposit all receipts at one time at month-end. In a real-world setting, deposits are made more frequently, depending on collection volume. The Deposit window allows you to deposit each receipt individually, deposit several receipts, or deposit all receipts at one time. On February 28, 2019, the company deposits all collections for the month.

HINT

In this textbook, the Undeposited Funds account will remain as the default debit posting account.

To deposit all receipts collected and previously recorded as Undeposited Funds:
1. On the title bar, click the Create icon.
2. Click *Bank Deposit* in the *Other* column. The Deposit window displays, showing all undeposited receipts.
3. Confirm *Checking* appears in the *Account* field.
4. In the *Date* field, choose *02/28/2019*.
5. Because all payments will be deposited, click the Select all button. See Figure 4–T.

FIGURE 4–T Deposit Window—All Payments Selected

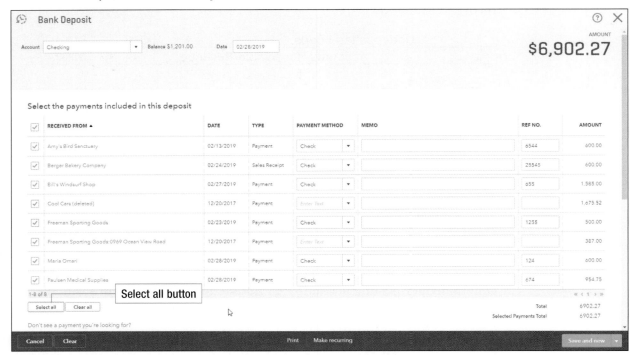

6. Confirm the information is correct and then click *Save and close* from the Save and new button list.

HINT

If you make an error in the deposit, click the Recent Transactions icon at the top left corner of the window to view the deposit.

Accounting Concept

The deposit of receipts as a separate transaction is recorded as follows:

Checking		Undeposited Funds	
Dr	Cr	Dr	Cr
6,902.27		6,902.27	6,902.27
			0

Reports

Customer Reports and Accounting Reports

Recall from Chapter 1 that Reports, the fourth level of operation, display the information and activities recorded in the various Lists and Activities windows. QuickBooks Online can display and print a variety of internal management reports as well as typical accounting and financial reports, many of which should be printed monthly.

Customer Reports

The Accounts Receivable and Customer Reports help the company to manage its collections, control cash flow, and retain an accurate record of all customer-related transactions. Among these reports are the Open Invoices Report, the Customer Balance Detail Report, and the Customer List Report.

Open Invoices Report

The Open Invoices Report lists all unpaid invoices for each customer at a specific date. The report lists each open invoice, with date and invoice number, for a customer; it also lists the terms and due date. The report may be customized to show all customers or only those with outstanding bills.

To view and print the Open Invoices Report:
1. On the Navigation bar, click Reports and then click the All link, if necessary.
2. Scroll to the *Who owes you* section and click *Open Invoices.* If a *Customize reports instantly* pop-up window appears, click the X to close it.
3. In the *Report period* field, choose *02/28/2019.*
4. Click the Run report button. The report displays. See Figure 4–U.

FIGURE 4–U Open Invoices Report

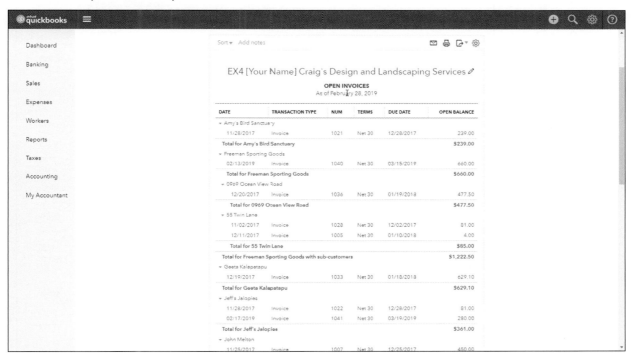

5. To print the report, click the Print icon on the report bar. The Print, email, or save as PDF window appears.
6. Choose *Landscape* from the *Orientation* drop-down list and then click the Print button.
7. At the Print window, click the Print button.
8. Close the Print, email, or save as PDF window.
9. Close the Open Invoices Report by clicking Dashboard on the Navigation bar.

Customer Balance Detail Report

The Customer Balance Detail Report displays all transactions for each customer with the remaining balance owed. This report is similar to an accounts receivable subsidiary ledger in a manual accounting system.

To view and print the Customer Balance Detail Report:

1. On the Navigation bar, click Reports.
2. Scroll to the *Who owes you* section and then click *Customer Balance Detail.* The report shows all invoices, payments, and credit memos for each customer in chronological order.
3. Click the Print icon on the report bar.
4. At the Print, email, or save as PDF window, click the Print button.
5. At the Print window, click the Print button. See Figure 4–V.
6. Close the Print, email, or save as PDF window.
7. Close the Customer Balance Detail Report by clicking Dashboard on the Navigation bar.

FIGURE 4–V

Customer Balance Detail Report

EX4 [Your Name] Craig's Design and Landscaping Services

CUSTOMER BALANCE DETAIL

All Dates

DATE	TRANSACTION TYPE	NUM	DUE DATE	AMOUNT	OPEN BALANCE	BALANCE
Amy's Bird Sanctuary						
11/28/2017	Invoice	1021	12/28/2017	459.00	239.00	239.00
Total for Amy's Bird Sanctuary				$459.00	$239.00	
Freeman Sporting Goods						
02/13/2019	Invoice	1040	03/15/2019	1,160.00	660.00	660.00
Total for Freeman Sporting Goods				$1,160.00	$660.00	
0969 Ocean View Road						
12/20/2017	Invoice	1036	01/19/2018	477.50	477.50	477.50
Total for 0969 Ocean View Road				$477.50	$477.50	
55 Twin Lane						
11/02/2017	Invoice	1028	12/02/2017	81.00	81.00	81.00
12/11/2017	Invoice	1005	01/10/2018	54.00	4.00	85.00
Total for 55 Twin Lane				$135.00	$85.00	
Total for Freeman Sporting Goods with sub-customers				$1,772.50	$1,222.50	
Geeta Kalapatapu						
12/19/2017	Invoice	1033	01/18/2018	629.10	629.10	629.10
Total for Geeta Kalapatapu				$629.10	$629.10	
Jeff's Jalopies						
11/28/2017	Invoice	1022	12/28/2017	81.00	81.00	81.00
02/17/2019	Invoice	1041	03/19/2019	280.00	280.00	361.00
Total for Jeff's Jalopies				$361.00	$361.00	
John Melton						
11/25/2017	Invoice	1007	12/25/2017	750.00	450.00	450.00
Total for John Melton				$750.00	$450.00	
Kookies by Kathy						
11/01/2017	Invoice	1016	12/01/2017	75.00	75.00	75.00
Total for Kookies by Kathy				$75.00	$75.00	
Maria Omari						
02/23/2019	Invoice	1042	03/25/2019	1,200.00	600.00	600.00
Total for Maria Omari				$1,200.00	$600.00	
Mark Cho						
12/20/2017	Invoice	1035	01/19/2018	314.28	314.28	314.28
Total for Mark Cho				$314.28	$314.28	
Red Rock Diner						
10/12/2017	Invoice	1024	11/11/2017	156.00	156.00	156.00
12/18/2017	Invoice	1023	01/17/2018	70.00	70.00	226.00
Total for Red Rock Diner				$226.00	$226.00	
Rondonuwu Fruit and Vegi						
12/19/2017	Invoice	1034	01/18/2018	78.60	78.60	78.60
Total for Rondonuwu Fruit and Vegi				$78.60	$78.60	
Shara Barnett						
Barnett Design						

Customer Contact List Report

The Customer Contact List Report displays information for all customers that has been entered in each customer's file in the Customers window. This report displays the customer name, billing address, contact person, phone number, and email address.

To view the Customer Contact List Report:
1. On the Navigation bar, click Reports.
2. Scroll to the *Sales and Customers* section and click *Customer Contact List.* This displays the report. See Figure 4–W.

3. Close the Customer Contact List Report by clicking Dashboard on the Navigation bar.

Accounting Reports

As activities are entered in the windows, behind-the-scenes accounting activity is recorded in general journal format, posted to the general ledger, and flowed into the financial statements. You can display and print standard accounting reports showing this activity, such as the Journal Report. The Journal Report displays, in general journal format, all transactions recorded during a specified period of time.

To view and print the Journal Report:
1. On the Navigation bar, click Reports.
2. Scroll to the *For my accountant* section and then click *Journal.*
3. In the date fields, choose *02/01/2019* to *02/28/2019.*
4. To print the report, click the Print icon on the report bar.
5. Choose *Landscape* from the *Orientation* drop-down list and then click the Print button.
6. At the Print window, click the Print button. Your printout should look like Figure 4–X.
7. Close the Print, email, or save as PDF window.
8. Close the Journal Report by clicking Dashboard on the Navigation bar.

FIGURE 4–X Journal Report

EX4 [Your Name] Craig's Design and Landscaping Services

JOURNAL

February 2019

DATE	TRANSACTION TYPE	NUM	NAME	MEMO/DESCRIPTION	ACCOUNT	DEBIT	CREDIT
02/01/2019	Invoice	1038	Amy's Bird Sanctuary		Accounts Receivable (A/R)	$600.00	
				Installation of landscape design	Landscaping Services:Labor:Installation		$600.00
						$600.00	**$600.00**
02/06/2019	Invoice	1039	Bill's Windsurf Shop		Accounts Receivable (A/R)	$300.00	
				Custom Design	Design income		$300.00
						$300.00	**$300.00**
02/13/2019	Invoice	1040	Freeman Sporting Goods		Accounts Receivable (A/R)	$1,160.00	
				Custom Design	Design income		$600.00
				Tree and Shrub Trimming	Landscaping Services		$560.00
						$1,160.00	**$1,160.00**
02/13/2019	Payment	6544	Amy's Bird Sanctuary		Undeposited Funds	$600.00	
					Accounts Receivable (A/R)		$600.00
						$600.00	**$600.00**
02/17/2019	Invoice	1041	Jeff's Jalopies		Accounts Receivable (A/R)	$280.00	
				Pest Control Services	Pest Control Services		$280.00
						$280.00	**$280.00**
02/23/2019	Invoice	1042	Maria Omari		Accounts Receivable (A/R)	$1,200.00	
				Installation of landscape design	Landscaping Services:Labor:Installation		$1,200.00
						$1,200.00	**$1,200.00**
02/23/2019	Payment	1255	Freeman Sporting Goods		Undeposited Funds	$500.00	
					Accounts Receivable (A/R)		$500.00
						$500.00	**$500.00**
02/24/2019	Sales Receipt	1044	Berger Bakery Company		Undeposited Funds	$600.00	
				Custom Design	Design income		$600.00
						$600.00	**$600.00**
02/27/2019	Invoice	1043	Bill's Windsurf Shop		Accounts Receivable (A/R)	$1,200.00	
				Custom Design	Design income		$450.00
				Installation of landscape design	Landscaping Services:Labor:Installation		$750.00
						$1,200.00	**$1,200.00**
02/27/2019	Payment	655	Bill's Windsurf Shop		Undeposited Funds	$1,585.00	
					Accounts Receivable (A/R)		$1,585.00
						$1,585.00	**$1,585.00**
02/28/2019	Payment	674	Paulsen Medical Supplies		Undeposited Funds	$954.75	
					Accounts Receivable (A/R)		$954.75
						$954.75	**$954.75**
02/28/2019	Payment	124	Maria Omari		Undeposited Funds	$600.00	
					Accounts Receivable (A/R)		$600.00
						$600.00	**$600.00**
02/28/2019	Deposit				Checking	$6,902.27	
					Undeposited Funds		$1,675.52
					Undeposited Funds		$387.00
					Undeposited Funds		$600.00
					Undeposited Funds		$500.00
					Undeposited Funds		$600.00
					Undeposited Funds		$1,585.00
					Undeposited Funds		$954.75
					Undeposited Funds		$600.00
						$6,902.27	**$6,902.27**
TOTAL						**$16,482.02**	**$16,482.02**

The *TRANSACTION TYPE* column indicates the window where the activity was recorded. The *Invoice* transaction type is from the Invoice window. Each of these transactions has a debit to Accounts Receivable because this is the default for that window. The *Payment* transaction type is from the Receive Payment window. All these transactions are a debit to Undeposited Funds and a credit to Accounts Receivable, which are the default accounts for this window. The *Sales Receipt* transaction type is from the Sales Receipt window. All these transactions have a debit to Undeposited Funds because that is the default account for this window. The *Deposit* transaction type is from the Deposit window. These transactions are a debit to Cash and a credit to Undeposited Funds by default.

Exiting QuickBooks Online

Any work you do in the Test Drive sample company file is not saved when you exit out of the company file.

At the end of each session, you should exit QuickBooks Online and close the browser.

To exit QuickBooks Online and close the browser:
1. On the title bar, click the Gear icon.
2. At the Company window, click *Sign Out* in the *Profile* column. This closes the company file and exits QuickBooks Online.
3. Close your browser.

Chapter Review and Assessment

 Study Tools include a presentation and a glossary. Use these resources, available from the links menu in the student ebook, to further develop and review skills learned in this chapter.

Procedure Review

To add a new customer:
1. On the Navigation bar, click Sales and then click the Customers link.
2. At the Customers window, click the New customer button.
3. Enter the background data for the customer.
4. Click the Save and close button.

To make a customer inactive:
1. On the Navigation bar, click Sales and then click the Customers link.
2. At the Customers window, select the customer you wish to deactivate.
3. Click the Edit button.
4. Click the Make inactive button.
5. Click the Yes button at the warning.

To edit a customer:
1. On the Navigation bar, click Sales and then click the Customers link.
2. At the Customers window, select the customer you wish to edit.
3. At the Customer information window, change the appropriate information.
4. Click the Save button.

To create an invoice:
1. On the title bar, click the Create icon.
2. Click *Invoice* in the *Customers* column.
3. At the *Choose a customer* drop-down list, select the appropriate customer.
4. Select the date in the *Invoice date* field.
5. Click the first line in the *PRODUCT/SERVICE* column and then select the appropriate service(s) at the drop-down list that appears.
6. Enter the quantity.
7. Select the terms from the *Terms* drop-down list.
8. Click the Save and close button.

To record receipt of payment:
1. On the title bar, click the Create icon.
2. Click *Receive Payment* in the *Customers* column.
3. At the *Choose a customer* drop-down list, click the appropriate customer.
4. Select the payment date in the *Payment date* field.
5. Select the payment method in the *Payment method* field.
6. Key the check number in the *Reference no.* field.
7. Enter the amount in the *PAYMENT* column.
8. Click the Save and close button.

To record a cash sale:
1. On the title bar, click the Create icon.
2. Click *Sales Receipt* in the *Customers* column.
3. At the *Choose a customer* drop-down list, click the appropriate customer.
4. Select the date in the *Sales Receipt date* field.
5. Select the payment method in the *Payment method* field.
6. Key the check number in the *Reference no.* field.
7. Select an account in the *Deposit to* field.
8. Select the product or service.
9. Key the quantity.
10. Click the Save and close button.

To make a deposit:
1. On the title bar, click the Create icon.
2. Click *Bank Deposit* in the *Other* column.
3. Select the bank account in the *Account* field.
4. Select the date in the *Date* field.
5. Click to insert a check mark next to the appropriate payment.
6. Click the Save and close button.

To view and print customer reports from the Reports menu:
1. On the Navigation bar, click Reports and then click the All link.
2. Scroll to either the *Who owes you* or *Sales and Customers* section and then choose a report.
3. Indicate the appropriate dates for the report.
4. Click the Print icon on the report bar.
5. Click the Print button at the Print, email, or save as PDF window.
6. Click the Print button at the Print window.
7. Close the report.

Key Concepts

Select the letter of the item that best matches each definition.

a. Customer List	f. customer
b. Receive Payment window	g. Undeposited Funds
c. cash sales	h. Sales Receipt window
d. Invoice window	i. Deposit window
e. Open Invoices Report	j. Customer Balance Detail Report

_____ 1. Contains a file for all customers with whom the company does business.

_____ 2. A report that displays all transactions for a customer.

_____ 3. Window used to deposit funds collected.

_____ 4. A person or business to which the company provides services or sells a product.

_____ 5. Window used to record the payment of invoices.

_____ 6. Sales for which payment is received immediately.

_____ 7. Window used to record sales on account.

_____ 8. Collections not yet deposited in the bank.

_____ 9. A report that lists all unpaid invoices for each customer.
_____ 10. Window used to record sales for cash.

Procedure Check

Write a response for each of the following prompts.

1. Your company has obtained a new major client. Describe the steps to add the new client to the system.
2. Your company has the type of business that makes cash sales to many customers and rarely tracks accounts receivable. How would you use QuickBooks Online to record your sales?
3. Your business wishes to track all the deposits made to the bank to facilitate the month-end bank reconciliation process. How would you record collection of funds to accomplish this?
4. You wish to determine the oldest unpaid invoices. How would you use QuickBooks Online to obtain that information?
5. You wish to view all the invoices and collection activity for a customer. How would you use QuickBooks Online to obtain the required information?
6. Compare and contrast a manual accounting system with a computerized accounting system for processing customer transactions. Include an explanation of how the accounts receivable subsidiary ledger compares with the Customer List.

Case Problem

Demonstrate your knowledge of the QuickBooks Online features discussed in this chapter by completing the following case problem.

On June 1, 2019, Olivia Chen began her business, Olivia's Web Solutions. She has now begun providing web design and internet consulting services to individuals and small businesses. The Web Page Design Services are billed at $125 per hour and the Internet Consulting Services at $100 per hour. You will record the transactions listed below for the month of June. The company file should include the beginning information for Olivia's Web Solutions along with the transaction balances from Chapter 3.

HINT

Remember to use 2019 for dates used in the Case Problem.

1. Sign in to QuickBooks Online.
2. Change the company name to **OWS4 [*Your Name*] Olivia's Web Solutions**.
3. Remove the *SERVICE DATE* column from the Invoice and Sales Receipt windows and edit the Standard form to allow for invoice numbering by going to the Custom form styles window and clicking *Edit* in the *ACTION* column for the Standard form. (Do not use the New style button arrow.) Refer to Steps 4–11 on page 94.
4. Enter the following customers in the Customers window (you may need to edit the first customer to complete the information):

First name:	Leon
Last name:	Artie
Company:	Artie's Auto Repair

Display name as:	Artie's Auto Repair
Phone:	516-555-1221
Mobile:	516-555-1231
Billing address:	32 West 11th Street
	New Hyde Park NY 11523

Preferred payment method:	Check
Terms:	Net 30
Preferred delivery method:	None
Opening balance:	0
as of:	06/01/2019

First name:	Customer
Last name:	Service
Company:	Long Island Water Works
Display name as:	Long Island Water Works
Phone:	516-555-4747
Mobile:	516-555-4748
Billing address:	87-54 Bayview Ave.
	Glen Cove NY 11563

Preferred payment method:	Check
Terms:	Net 30
Preferred delivery method:	None
Opening balance:	0
as of:	06/01/2019

First name:	Johnny
Last name:	Schneider
Company:	Schneider Family
Display name as:	Schneider Family
Phone:	516-555-8989
Mobile:	516-555-8990
Billing address:	363 Farmers Rd.
	Syosset NY 11547

Preferred payment method:	Check
Terms:	Net 30
Preferred delivery method:	None
Opening balance:	0
as of:	06/01/2019

First name:	Miguel
Last name:	Perez
Company:	Miguel's Restaurant
Display name as:	Miguel's Restaurant
Phone:	516-555-3236
Mobile:	516-555-3237
Billing address:	30 Willis Avenue
	Roslyn NY 11541

Preferred payment method:	Check
Terms:	Net 30
Preferred delivery method:	None
Opening balance:	0
as of:	06/01/2019

First name:	David
Last name:	Singh
Company:	Singh Family
Display name as:	Singh Family
Phone:	516-555-3233
Mobile:	516-555-3239
Billing address:	363 Marathon Parkway
	Little Neck NY 11566

Preferred payment method:	Check
Terms:	Net 30
Preferred delivery method:	None
Opening balance:	0
as of:	06/01/2019

First name:	Allen
Last name:	Scott
Company:	Breathe Easy A/C Contractors
Display name as:	Breathe Easy A/C Contractors
Phone:	516-555-6868
Mobile:	516-555-6869
Billing address:	556 Atlantic Ave.
	Freeport NY 11634

Preferred payment method:	Check
Terms:	Net 30
Preferred delivery method:	None
Opening balance:	0
as of:	06/01/2019

First name:	William
Last name:	Way
Company:	Thrifty Stores
Display name as:	Thrifty Stores
Phone:	718-555-2445
Mobile:	718-555-2446
Billing address:	23 Boston Ave.
	Bronx NY 11693

Preferred payment method:	Check
Terms:	Net 30
Preferred delivery method:	None
Opening balance:	0
as of:	06/01/2019

First name:	Jerry
Last name:	Sehorn
Company:	Sehorn & Smith
Display name as:	Sehorn & Smith
Phone:	212-555-3339
Mobile:	212-555-3338
Billing address:	510 Fifth Ave.
	New York NY 10022
Preferred payment method:	Check
Terms:	Net 30
Preferred delivery method:	None
Opening balance:	0
as of:	06/01/2019
First name:	Joseph
Last name:	Porter
Company:	South Shore School District
Display name as:	South Shore School District
Phone:	516-555-4545
Mobile:	516-555-4546
Billing address:	3666 Ocean Ave.
	South Beach NY 11365
Preferred payment method:	Check
Terms:	Net 30
Preferred delivery method:	None
Opening balance:	0
as of:	06/01/2019

HINT

All cash receipts should be deposited to Undeposited Funds.

5. Using the appropriate window, record the following transactions for June 2019:

Jun. 11   Provided 8 hours of Internet Consulting Services and 10 hours of Web Page Design Services on account to Long Island Water Works, Invoice no. 1001, Net 30 Days.

Jun. 14   Provided 8 hours of Web Page Design Services on account to Sehorn & Smith, Invoice no. 1002, Net 30 Days.

Jun. 15   Provided 8 hours of Web Page Design Services on account to the Schneider Family, Invoice no. 1003.

Jun. 17   Provided 4 hours of Internet Consulting Services and 8 hours of Web Page Design Services on account to Miguel's Restaurant, Invoice no. 1004, Net 30 Days.

Jun. 18   Provided 4 hours of Internet Consulting Services to the Singh Family, Sales Receipt no. 1005. Received payment immediately, Check no. 687. Deposit to Undeposited Funds.

Jun. 21   Provided 8 hours of Web Page Design Services on account to Breathe Easy, Invoice no. 1006, Net 30 Days.

Jun. 25   Received payment in full from Long Island Water Works for Invoice no. 1001, Check no. 124554.

Jun. 25	Provided 12 hours of Web Page Design Services on account to Thrifty Stores, Invoice no. 1007, Net 30 Days.
Jun. 28	Provided 8 hours of Internet Consulting Services on account to Artie's Auto Repair, Invoice 1008, Net 30 Days.
Jun. 28	Received payment in full from Sehorn & Smith for Invoice no. 1002, Check no. 3656.
Jun. 29	Provided 12 hours of Internet Consulting Services on account to South Shore School District, Invoice no. 1009, Net 30 Days.
Jun. 29	Received payment in full from Miguel's Restaurant for Invoice no. 1004, Check no. 3269.
Jun. 30	Provided 8 hours of Internet Consulting Services on account to Sehorn & Smith, Invoice no. 1010, Net 30 Days.
Jun. 30	Received partial payment of $250 from Breathe Easy for Invoice no. 1006, Check no. 1455.
Jun. 30	Deposited all receipts for the month.

6. Display and print the following reports for June 1, 2019, to June 30, 2019:
   a. Open Invoices
   b. Customer Balance Detail
   c. Customer Contact List
   d. Journal

CHAPTER 5

Period-End Procedures

Adding Accounts, Recording Adjusting Journal Entries, and Customizing Reports

Objectives

- Update the Chart of Accounts List
- Record adjustments in the Journal Entry window
- View the effect of period-end adjustments on the trial balance
- Display and print period-end accounting reports
- Change the reports display using the Customize report button
- Display and print accounting reports and financial statements
- Explore the Register feature and generate an Account QuickReport

QuickBooks Online allows you to record journal entries in general journal format as seen in Chapter 2. In Chapters 3 and 4 you saw that QuickBooks Online records daily activities in windows such as Bill, Pay Bills, Check, Invoice, Receive Payment, and so on. However, behind the scenes, QuickBooks Online also records the activities in general journal format using debits and credits. The accounts used to record the activities come from the Chart of Accounts List.

At certain periods, such as the end of the month or the end of the fiscal year, some account balances will need to be adjusted based on information that does not appear in the daily activities so that the financial statements can be properly prepared in accordance with **generally accepted accounting principles (GAAP)**. These adjustments to the accounts are called **adjusting journal entries** and are recorded in the Journal Entry window. As you record the daily activities and adjusting journal entries, QuickBooks Online simultaneously updates the accounting records and financial statements.

In this chapter, you will make adjusting journal entries for the Test Drive sample company, Craig's Design and Landscaping Services.

QuickBooks Online versus Manual Accounting: General Journal Entries

In a manual accounting system, the general journal is the document in which transactions are initially recorded chronologically. For each transaction, the dollar value of at least one account must be recorded as a debit amount, and the dollar value of at least one account must be recorded as a credit amount. The total dollar value of debits must equal the total dollar value of credits. Companies have the option of recording all transactions exclusively in the general journal or, alternatively, they can record frequent similar transactions in special journals. In either case, at month-end, the transactions from all journals are posted to the general ledger.

Periodically, certain adjustments that are not daily business activities must be made to the accounts to update the balances. These adjustments, called *adjusting journal entries*, are always recorded in the general journal. They are then posted to the general ledger to update the balances in the accounts. The adjusted balances are used to prepare the financial statements. These adjusting journal entries must always be made on the date the financial statements are prepared, but they can be recorded more often. Most large companies typically prepare the adjusting journal entries monthly.

QuickBooks Online does not follow the format of the special journals for daily transactions. Instead, all activities are recorded in different windows depending on the nature of the activity. Behind the scenes, QuickBooks Online records the activity in general journal format, as seen in the Journal Report in Chapters 3 and 4. However, for adjusting journal entries, QuickBooks Online uses the Journal Entry window in a manner similar to that of a manual accounting system. As you save information entered in each of the windows (including the Journal Entry window), the general ledger balances, the Chart of Accounts List balances, the trial balance, and the financial statements are simultaneously updated. Because balances are easily updated in a computerized accounting system, even small companies can now record adjusting journal entries monthly.

generally accepted accounting principles (GAAP) Principles used to prepare the financial statements of a company. They consist of both formal accounting regulations and procedures mandated by regulatory agencies and traditionally used accounting procedures.

adjusting journal entries Adjustments made to accounts at certain periods, such as the end of the month or the end of the fiscal year, to bring the balances up to date.

Chapter Problem

In this chapter, you will record the adjusting journal entries for the end of the month, on February 28, 2019, for Craig's Design and Landscaping Services. The file for Craig's Design and Landscaping Services is contained in the QuickBooks Online Test Drive.

To begin, open the Test Drive sample company file for Craig's Design and Landscaping Services. Change the company name in the file to **EX5 [*Your Name*] Craig's Design and Landscaping Services** and key 12-3456788 in the *EIN* field. You may also want to extend the time-out period to three hours.

Lists

The Chart of Accounts List

Recall from Chapter 1 that the second level of operation in QuickBooks is recording background information in Lists. As you know, the Chart of Accounts List is the list of accounts a company uses as it conducts its business. All the individual accounts are placed together in a book called the *general ledger*. The Chart of Accounts List needs to be revised periodically when new accounts need to be added, accounts not used in the business need to be deleted, or modifications need to be made to an account. When you make these revisions to the accounts, you are updating the Chart of Accounts List. This was illustrated in Chapter 2.

As you have seen, in QuickBooks Online, each account on the Chart of Accounts List consists of the account number, name, account type, detail type, and balance. The account numbers are optional but are used in this textbook for the Case Problem at the end of each chapter. The name you assign an account is the name that appears in the windows and reports. The balance is determined in the general ledger and includes the original amount entered (if any) when the account is first created and then subsequently updated by Activities entered in the windows.

For each account, there is an account type and a detail type. First you select the account type, and then you select the detail type. The detail type is a subcategory of the account type. The account types and the detail types are determined by QuickBooks Online and cannot be changed. The software uses the account type and detail type to determine where to place the account name and balance on the financial statements and to establish the system default accounts. It is important to select the correct types; otherwise, the accounts may be placed incorrectly on the financial statements.

As shown in Chapters 3 and 4, QuickBooks Online also identifies certain accounts as system default accounts and then uses them to identify the transactions recorded in the windows.

Review the Chart of Accounts List for Craig's Design and Landscaping Services to see the accounts that have been set up.

To review the Chart of Accounts List as a report:
1. On the Navigation bar, click Reports.
2. In the *For my accountant* section, click *Account List*.

   Recall the Chart of Accounts List is called the *Account List Report* when viewed in report format. If the *Customize reports instantly* message appears, close it. The Account List Report displays. See Figure 5–A.

FIGURE 5–A

Account List Report

EX5 [Your Name] Craig's Design and Landscaping Services

ACCOUNT LIST

ACCOUNT	TYPE	DETAIL TYPE	DESCRIPTION	BALANCE
Checking	Bank	Checking		1,201.00
Savings	Bank	Savings		800.00
Accounts Receivable (A/R)	Accounts receivable (A/R)	Accounts Receivable (A/R)		5,281.52
Inventory Asset	Other Current Assets	Inventory		596.25
Prepaid Expenses	Other Current Assets	Prepaid Expenses		0.00
Uncategorized Asset	Other Current Assets	Other Current assets		0.00
Undeposited Funds	Other Current Assets	Undeposited Funds		2,062.52
Truck	Fixed Assets	Vehicles		13,495.00
Truck:Depreciation	Fixed Assets	Accumulated Depreciation		0.00
Truck:Original Cost	Fixed Assets	Vehicles		13,495.00
Accounts Payable (A/P)	Accounts payable (A/P)	Accounts Payable (A/P)		-1,602.67
Mastercard	Credit Card	Credit Card		-157.72
Visa	Credit Card	Credit Card		0.00
Arizona Dept. of Revenue Payable	Other Current Liabilities	Sales Tax Payable		0.00
Board of Equalization Payable	Other Current Liabilities	Sales Tax Payable		-370.94
Loan Payable	Other Current Liabilities	Other Current Liabilities		-4,000.00
Notes Payable	Long Term Liabilities	Other Long Term Liabilities		-25,000.00
Opening Balance Equity	Equity	Opening Balance Equity		9,337.50
Retained Earnings	Equity	Retained Earnings		0.00
Billable Expense Income	Income	Service/Fee Income		
Design income	Income	Other Primary Income		
Discounts given	Income	Discounts/Refunds Given		
Fees Billed	Income	Service/Fee Income		
Landscaping Services	Income	Other Primary Income		
Landscaping Services:Job Materials	Income	Other Primary Income		
Landscaping Services:Job Materials...	Income	Other Primary Income		
Landscaping Services:Job Materials...	Income	Other Primary Income		
Landscaping Services:Job Materials...	Income	Other Primary Income		
Landscaping Services:Job Materials...	Income	Other Primary Income		
Landscaping Services:Labor	Income	Other Primary Income		
Landscaping Services:Labor:Installa...	Income	Other Primary Income		
Landscaping Services:Labor:Mainte...	Income	Other Primary Income		
Other Income	Income	Other Primary Income		
Pest Control Services	Income	Other Primary Income		
Refunds-Allowances	Income	Discounts/Refunds Given		
Sales of Product Income	Income	Sales of Product Income		
Services	Income	Service/Fee Income		
Unapplied Cash Payment Income	Income	Unapplied Cash Payment Income		
Uncategorized Income	Income	Service/Fee Income		
Cost of Goods Sold	Cost of Goods Sold	Supplies & Materials - COGS		
Advertising	Expenses	Advertising/Promotional		
Automobile	Expenses	Auto		
Automobile:Fuel	Expenses	Auto		
Bank Charges	Expenses	Bank Charges		
Commissions & fees	Expenses	Other Miscellaneous Service Cost		
Disposal Fees	Expenses	Other Miscellaneous Service Cost		
Dues & Subscriptions	Expenses	Dues & subscriptions		
Equipment Rental	Expenses	Equipment Rental		
Insurance	Expenses	Insurance		
Insurance:Workers Compensation	Expenses	Insurance		
Job Expenses	Expenses	Other Miscellaneous Service Cost		
Job Expenses:Cost of Labor	Expenses	Other Miscellaneous Service Cost		
Job Expenses:Cost of Labor:Installa...	Expenses	Other Miscellaneous Service Cost		
Job Expenses:Cost of Labor:Mainte...	Expenses	Other Miscellaneous Service Cost		
Job Expenses:Equipment Rental	Expenses	Equipment Rental		
Job Expenses:Job Materials	Expenses	Supplies & Materials		
Job Expenses:Job Materials:Decks ...	Expenses	Supplies & Materials		
Job Expenses:Job Materials:Founta...	Expenses	Supplies & Materials		
Job Expenses:Job Materials:Plants ...	Expenses	Supplies & Materials		
Job Expenses:Job Materials:Sprinkl...	Expenses	Supplies & Materials		
Job Expenses:Permits	Expenses	Other Miscellaneous Service Cost		
Legal & Professional Fees	Expenses	Legal & Professional Fees		
Legal & Professional Fees:Accounting	Expenses	Legal & Professional Fees		
Legal & Professional Fees:Bookkeeper	Expenses	Legal & Professional Fees		
Legal & Professional Fees:Lawyer	Expenses	Legal & Professional Fees		
Maintenance and Repair	Expenses	Repair & Maintenance		
Maintenance and Repair:Building R...	Expenses	Repair & Maintenance		
Maintenance and Repair:Computer ...	Expenses	Repair & Maintenance		
Maintenance and Repair:Equipmen...	Expenses	Repair & Maintenance		
Meals and Entertainment	Expenses	Entertainment Meals		
Office Expenses	Expenses	Office/General Administrative Expenses		
Promotional	Expenses	Advertising/Promotional		
Purchases	Expenses	Supplies & Materials		
Rent or Lease	Expenses	Rent or Lease of Buildings		
Stationery & Printing	Expenses	Office/General Administrative Expenses		
Supplies	Expenses	Supplies & Materials		
Taxes & Licenses	Expenses	Taxes Paid		
Travel	Expenses	Travel		
Travel Meals	Expenses	Travel Meals		
Unapplied Cash Bill Payment Expense	Expenses	Unapplied Cash Bill Payment Expense		
Uncategorized Expense	Expenses	Other Miscellaneous Service Cost		
Utilities	Expenses	Utilities		
Utilities:Gas and Electric	Expenses	Utilities		
Utilities:Telephone	Expenses	Utilities		
Interest Earned	Other Income	Interest Earned		
Other Portfolio Income	Other Income	Other Miscellaneous Income		
Depreciation	Other Expense	Depreciation		
Miscellaneous	Other Expense	Other Miscellaneous Expense		
Penalties & Settlements	Other Expense	Penalties & Settlements		

HINT

Recall that in a report, you can click and drag the vertical dotted bar before the column heading to change the width of the column.

HINT

When account numbers aren't used, QuickBooks Online puts the accounts in alphabetical order within each account type.

The Account List Report column headings include: *ACCOUNT, TYPE, DETAIL TYPE, DESCRIPTION,* and *BALANCE.* When account numbers are used, the numbers appear in the first column. Recall that account numbers are not used in the Test Drive sample company file, but they are used in the Case Problem at the end of each chapter.

3. Scroll through the accounts listed in the Account List Report and note the following:
   - Balances are listed only for the assets, liabilities, and equity accounts.
   - The balances are not listed for the income and expenses accounts.
   - The Prepaid Expenses account does not have a balance.
   - There are three Fixed Assets accounts that have *Truck* in the account name: Truck, Truck:Depreciation, and Truck:Original Cost.
   - Both the Truck account and the Truck:Original Cost account have a balance of $13,495.
   - There is an Other Current Liabilities account called *Loan Payable* with a balance of $4,000.
   - There is a Long Term Liabilities account called *Notes Payable* with a balance of $25,000.
   - There is no Interest Payable account.
   - There is no Interest Expense account.

In QuickBooks Online, the account balances that flow into the financial statements are based on the account type and detail types. If you want to subtotal two or more accounts on the financial statements, you can identify an account as a subaccount. Subaccounts show a subtotal amount on the financial statements in addition to the regular account balances. A parent account is an account that has a subaccount.

In the Craig's Design and Landscaping Services Chart of Accounts List, the Fixed Assets account called *Truck* is a parent account. The Fixed Assets accounts called *Truck:Depreciation* and *Truck:Original Cost* are subaccounts of the Truck account. This was set up so that when the accumulated depreciation is added to the Truck:Depreciation account, the accumulated depreciation will be deducted from the Truck:Original Cost account, and the net amount will be displayed on the financial statements.

On the Account List Report, when parent and subaccounts are used, subaccount names by default display the parent account name left aligned, followed by a colon and the subaccount name all on one line. The name appears as Parent:Subaccount. Review the Account List Report in Figure 5–A for the Truck accounts. Truck is the parent account, and the first subaccount is Depreciation, so the name appears as Truck:Depreciation. Similarly, the second subaccount is Original Cost, so on the Account List Report, you see Truck:Original Cost.

To view the Truck accounts:
1. With the Account List Report open, click the Truck account. The Account window for the Truck account appears.
2. In the *Detail Type* drop-down list, scroll down until you see *Vehicles* highlighted. See Figure 5–B.

FIGURE 5–B

Account Window—Truck
Parent Account

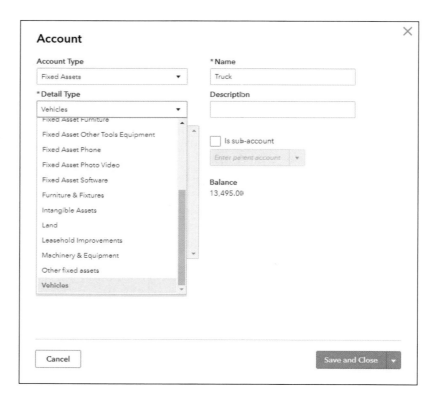

3. Close the Account window by clicking the X. You return to the Account List Report.
4. At the Account List Report, click *Truck:Depreciation*. The Account window for the Depreciation subaccount displays.
5. In the *Detail Type* drop-down list, notice *Accumulated Depreciation* is highlighted. See Figure 5–C.

FIGURE 5–C

Account Window—
Depreciation Subaccount

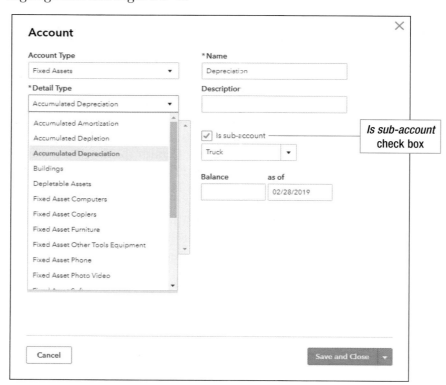

6. Close the Account window for Depreciation by clicking the X. You return to the Account List Report.
7. At the Account List Report, click *Truck:Original Cost.* The Account window for the Original Cost subaccount displays.
8. In the *Detail Type* drop-down list, scroll down until you see *Vehicles* highlighted. See Figure 5–D.

FIGURE 5–D
Account Window—
Original Cost Subaccount

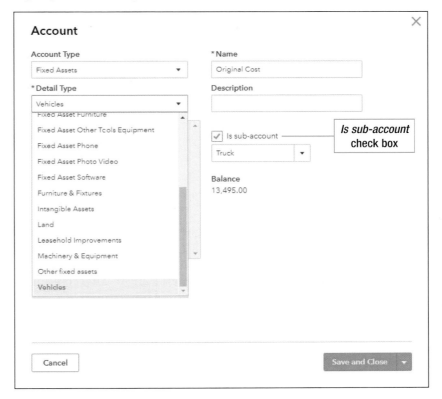

9. Close the Account window for Original Cost. You return to the Account List Report.
10. Return to the Dashboard.

Updating the Chart of Accounts List

To prepare for recording adjusting journal entries, you may need to update the Chart of Accounts List. Recall that you can view the Chart of Accounts List as a report, or you can view it as a list by clicking Accounting on the Navigation bar.

HINT
An alternative to using the Navigation bar to access the Chart of Accounts List is to click the Gear icon. Then, in the *Lists* column, click *All Lists.* At the Lists window, click *Chart of Accounts,* and the Chart of Accounts window appears.

To review the Chart of Accounts List using Accounting on the Navigation bar:
1. On the Navigation bar, click Accounting. If necessary, click the See your Chart of Accounts button. The Chart of Accounts window appears. See Figure 5–E.
2. Keep the Chart of Accounts window open for the next activity.

FIGURE 5–E Chart of Accounts Window—Partial

NAME	TYPE	DETAIL TYPE	QUICKBOOKS BALANCE	BANK BALANCE	ACTION
Checking	Bank	Checking	1,201.00	-3,621.93	View register ▾
Savings	Bank	Savings	800.00	200.00	View register ▾
Accounts Receivable (A/R)	Accounts receivable (A/R)	Accounts Receivable (A/R)	5,281.52		View register ▾
Inventory Asset	Other Current Assets	Inventory	596.25		View register ▾
Prepaid Expenses	Other Current Assets	Prepaid Expenses	0.00		View register ▾
Uncategorized Asset	Other Current Assets	Other Current Assets	0.00		View register ▾
Undeposited Funds	Other Current Assets	Undeposited Funds	2,062.52		View register ▾
Truck	Fixed Assets	Vehicles	13,495.00		View register ▾
Depreciation	Fixed Assets	Accumulated Depreciation	0.00		View register ▾
Original Cost	Fixed Assets	Vehicles	13,495.00		View register ▾
Accounts Payable (A/P)	Accounts payable (A/P)	Accounts Payable (A/P)	1,602.67		View register ▾
Mastercard	Credit Card	Credit Card	157.72	-304.96	View register ▾
Visa	Credit Card	Credit Card	0.00		View register ▾

Notice the column headings are similar to those in the Account List Report: *NAME, TYPE, DETAIL TYPE*, and *QUICKBOOKS BALANCE*. In the Chart of Accounts List, there is also a *BANK BALANCE* column and an *ACTION* column.

Notice the section where the Truck accounts are listed. The two subaccounts—Depreciation and Original Cost—are indented under the Truck parent account. Compare this to the Account List Report in Figure 5–A on page 130. On the Account List Report, the subaccounts are not indented under the parent account Truck, but rather the parent account Truck is listed to the left of each of the subaccounts: Depreciation and Original Cost.

Adding an Account

In preparation for recording month-end adjusting journal entries, it has been determined that Craig's Design and Landscaping Services needs to add a Prepaid Advertising account to the Chart of Accounts List.

To add a new account:
1. In the Chart of Accounts window in the upper right corner, click the New button. The Account window appears.
2. At the Account window, click the drop-down button in the *Account Type* field and then click *Other Current Assets*.
3. In the *Detail Type* drop-down list, click *Prepaid Expenses*.
4. In the *Name* field, key Prepaid Advertising. See Figure 5–F.

FIGURE 5–F

Account Window—New
Account—Prepaid
Advertising

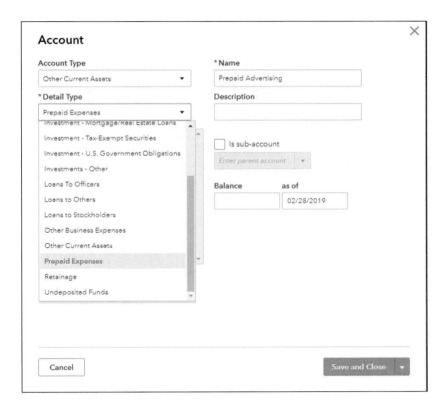

5. Confirm the information is correct and then click the Save and Close button. You return to the Chart of Accounts window with the new account added to the Chart of Accounts List.

6. Keep the Chart of Accounts window open for the next activity.

Editing an Account

It has been determined that the name of the Depreciation subaccount of the Truck parent account should be changed to Accumulated Depreciation.

To edit an account:

1. At the Chart of Accounts window, scroll to the subaccount Depreciation under the Truck parent account.

2. In the *ACTION* column for the Depreciation subaccount, click the drop-down arrow to the right of *View register*. The drop-down menu appears.

3. At the drop-down menu, click *Edit*. The Account window appears, and you can edit the account name.

4. In the *Name* field, delete *Depreciation* and key Accumulated Depreciation. See Figure 5–G.

5. Confirm the information is correct and then click the Save and Close button. You return to the Chart of Accounts window, and the account name has been updated.

6. Return to the Dashboard.

FIGURE 5–G
Account Window—Edit
Completed

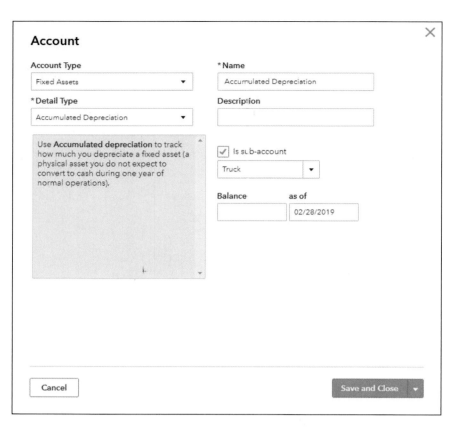

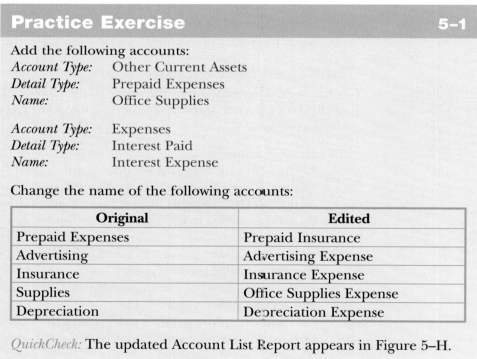

Practice Exercise 5–1

Add the following accounts:

Account Type:	Other Current Assets
Detail Type:	Prepaid Expenses
Name:	Office Supplies

Account Type:	Expenses
Detail Type:	Interest Paid
Name:	Interest Expense

Change the name of the following accounts:

Original	Edited
Prepaid Expenses	Prepaid Insurance
Advertising	Advertising Expense
Insurance	Insurance Expense
Supplies	Office Supplies Expense
Depreciation	Depreciation Expense

QuickCheck: The updated Account List Report appears in Figure 5–H.

FIGURE 5–H

Updated Account List
Report

ACCOUNT	TYPE	DETAIL TYPE	DESCRIPTION	BALANCE
Checking	Bank	Checking		1,201.00
Savings	Bank	Savings		800.00
Accounts Receivable (A/R)	Accounts receivable (A/R)	Accounts Receivable (A/R)		5,281.52
Inventory Asset	Other Current Assets	Inventory		596.25
Office Supplies	Other Current Assets	Prepaid Expenses		0.00
Prepaid Advertising	Other Current Assets	Prepaid Expenses		0.00
Prepaid Insurance	Other Current Assets	Prepaid Expenses		0.00
Uncategorized Asset	Other Current Assets	Other Current Assets		0.00
Undeposited Funds	Other Current Assets	Undeposited Funds		2,062.52
Truck	Fixed Assets	Vehicles		13,495.00
Truck:Accumulated Depreciation	Fixed Assets	Accumulated Depreciation		0.00
Truck:Original Cost	Fixed Assets	Vehicles		13,495.00
Accounts Payable (A/P)	Accounts payable (A/P)	Accounts Payable (A/P)		-1,602.67
Mastercard	Credit Card	Credit Card		-157.72
Visa	Credit Card	Credit Card		0.00
Arizona Dept. of Revenue Payable	Other Current Liabilities	Sales Tax Payable		0.00
Board of Equalization Payable	Other Current Liabilities	Sales Tax Payable		-370.94
Loan Payable	Other Current Liabilities	Other Current Liabilities		-4,000.00
Notes Payable	Long Term Liabilities	Other Long Term Liabilities		-25,000.00
Opening Balance Equity	Equity	Opening Balance Equity		9,337.50
Retained Earnings	Equity	Retained Earnings		0.00
Billable Expense Income	Income	Service/Fee Income		
Design income	Income	Other Primary Income		
Discounts given	Income	Discounts/Refunds Given		
Fees Billed	Income	Service/Fee Income		
Landscaping Services	Income	Other Primary Income		
Landscaping Services:Job Materials	Income	Other Primary Income		
Landscaping Services:Job Materials:Deck...	Income	Other Primary Income		
Landscaping Services:Job Materials:Foun...	Income	Other Primary Income		
Landscaping Services:Job Materials:Plant...	Income	Other Primary Income		
Landscaping Services:Job Materials:Sprin...	Income	Other Primary Income		
Landscaping Services:Labor	Income	Other Primary Income		
Landscaping Services:Labor:Installation	Income	Other Primary Income		
Landscaping Services:Labor:Maintenance...	Income	Other Primary Income		
Other Income	Income	Other Primary Income		
Pest Control Services	Income	Other Primary Income		
Refunds-Allowances	Income	Discounts/Refunds Given		
Sales of Product Income	Income	Sales of Product Income		
Services	Income	Service/Fee Income		
Unapplied Cash Payment Income	Income	Unapplied Cash Payment Income		
Uncategorized Income	Income	Service/Fee Income		
Cost of Goods Sold	Cost of Goods Sold	Supplies & Materials - COGS		
Advertising Expense	Expenses	Advertising/Promotional		
Automobile	Expenses	Auto		
Automobile:Fuel	Expenses	Auto		
Bank Charges	Expenses	Bank Charges		
Commissions & fees	Expenses	Other Miscellaneous Service Cost		
Disposal Fees	Expenses	Other Miscellaneous Service Cost		
Dues & Subscriptions	Expenses	Dues & subscriptions		
Equipment Rental	Expenses	Equipment Rental		
Insurance Expense	Expenses	Insurance		
Insurance Expense:Workers Compensation	Expenses	Insurance		
Interest Expense	Expenses	Interest Paid		
Job Expenses	Expenses	Other Miscellaneous Service Cost		
Job Expenses:Cost of Labor	Expenses	Other Miscellaneous Service Cost		
Job Expenses:Cost of Labor:Installation	Expenses	Other Miscellaneous Service Cost		
Job Expenses:Cost of Labor:Maintenance...	Expenses	Other Miscellaneous Service Cost		
Job Expenses:Equipment Rental	Expenses	Equipment Rental		
Job Expenses:Job Materials	Expenses	Supplies & Materials		
Job Expenses:Job Materials:Decks and P...	Expenses	Supplies & Materials		
Job Expenses:Job Materials:Fountain and...	Expenses	Supplies & Materials		
Job Expenses:Job Materials:Plants and Soil	Expenses	Supplies & Materials		
Job Expenses:Job Materials:Sprinklers an...	Expenses	Supplies & Materials		
Job Expenses:Permits	Expenses	Other Miscellaneous Service Cost		
Legal & Professional Fees	Expenses	Legal & Professional Fees		
Legal & Professional Fees:Accounting	Expenses	Legal & Professional Fees		
Legal & Professional Fees:Bookkeeper	Expenses	Legal & Professional Fees		
Legal & Professional Fees:Lawyer	Expenses	Legal & Professional Fees		
Maintenance and Repair	Expenses	Repair & Maintenance		
Maintenance and Repair:Building Repairs	Expenses	Repair & Maintenance		
Maintenance and Repair:Computer Repairs	Expenses	Repair & Maintenance		
Maintenance and Repair:Equipment Repairs	Expenses	Repair & Maintenance		
Meals and Entertainment	Expenses	Entertainment Meals		
Office Expenses	Expenses	Office/General Administrative Expenses		
Office Supplies Expense	Expenses	Supplies & Materials		
Promotional	Expenses	Advertising/Promotional		
Purchases	Expenses	Supplies & Materials		
Rent or Lease	Expenses	Rent or Lease of Buildings		
Stationery & Printing	Expenses	Office/General Administrative Expenses		
Taxes & Licenses	Expenses	Taxes Paid		
Travel	Expenses	Travel		
Travel Meals	Expenses	Travel Meals		
Unapplied Cash Bill Payment Expense	Expenses	Unapplied Cash Bill Payment Expense		
Uncategorized Expense	Expenses	Other Miscellaneous Service Cost		
Utilities	Expenses	Utilities		
Utilities:Gas and Electric	Expenses	Utilities		
Utilities:Telephone	Expenses	Utilities		
Interest Earned	Other Income	Interest Earned		
Other Portfolio Income	Other Income	Other Miscellaneous Income		
Depreciation Expense	Other Expense	Depreciation		
Miscellaneous	Other Expense	Other Miscellaneous Expense		
Penalties & Settlements	Other Expense	Penalties & Settlements		

EX5 [Your Name] Craig's Design and Landscaping Services

ACCOUNT LIST

Entering Original Activities Transactions

In Chapter 3, you learned to record transactions in the Bill window. Because we are using the Test Drive sample company file to demonstrate the activities in each chapter, the transactions are not saved when the file is closed. You will now enter transactions similar to those recorded in Chapter 3 so that you can learn how to record the related adjusting journal entries. When you complete the Case Problem at the end of the chapter, your transactions are saved, and you will not have to reenter the original transactions.

To enter a bill:

1. On the Navigation bar, click Expenses and then click the Vendors link.
2. Click *Lee Advertising*.
3. Click the New transaction button arrow and then click *Bill*. The Bill window opens with the background information for Lee Advertising filled.
4. In the *Terms* field, select *Net 30*, if necessary.
5. In the *Bill date* field, choose *02/02/2019*. The *Due date* field should fill based upon information in the vendor's file.
6. In the *Bill no.* field, key X-245.
7. Click the *Account details* section heading to expand it, if necessary, and then in the *ACCOUNT* column in the first line, click the drop-down list and click *Prepaid Advertising*.
8. In the *AMOUNT* column, key 600. See Figure 5–I.

FIGURE 5–I Bill Window—Completed

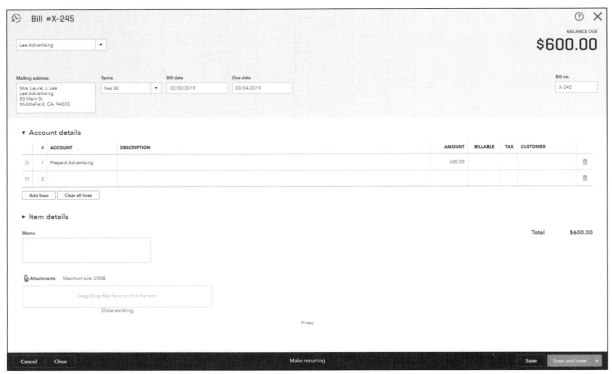

9. Confirm the information is correct and then click *Save and close* from the Save and new button list.
10. Return to the Dashboard.

Practice Exercise 5-2

Record the following transactions in the Bill window:

Feb. 6	Received bill from Computers by Jenni for purchase of office supplies, Bill no. K-222, $475, Net 30. Due date March 8, 2019 (charge to Office Supplies account).
Feb. 9	Received bill from Brosnahan Insurance Agency for one-year insurance policy, Bill no. 01-21, $2,400, Net 30. Due date March 11, 2019 (charge to Prepaid Insurance account).

Reports

The Trial Balance

In a manual accounting system, errors can occur when journal entries are recorded and posted to the general ledger or when doing mathematical computations. The trial balance is used to verify that the total debits equal the total credits, which means the general ledger is in balance. In a computerized system, on the other hand, there is less chance of the accounts being out of balance because the postings to the general ledger and mathematical computations occur automatically.

A trial balance is still useful, however. It allows you to view the accounts and their debit or credit balances without having to look at all the details in the general ledger. The trial balance should be printed before recording adjusting journal entries. After you record adjusting journal entries, you will not be able to retrieve preadjusted balances.

To view and print the trial balance:

1. On the Navigation bar, click Reports.
2. In the *For my accountant* section, click *Trial Balance.*
3. In the date fields, choose *01/01/2019* and *12/31/2019* (or the year you are using) and then click the Run report button. The Trial Balance Report displays. See Figure 5–J.
4. Print the report.
5. Return to the Dashboard.

HINT

Print the trial balance at this time. Once you record adjusting journal entries, you will no longer be able to view and print a preadjusted Trial Balance Report.

FIGURE 5–J

Trial Balance Report

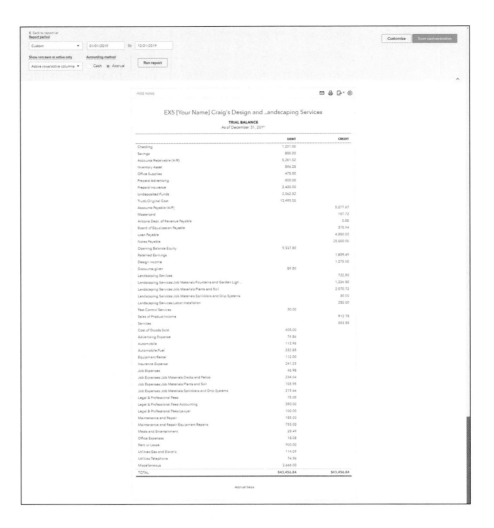

Activities

The Journal Entry Window

To adjust account balances based on accounting rules, you usually need to enter adjusting journal entries before preparing financial statements. In QuickBooks Online, adjusting journal entries are recorded in the Journal Entry window. As you have already seen, this window is set up similarly to what you would see in a manual accounting system. It lists the account and amount of the debit entry, the account and amount of the credit entry, and an explanation.

As you recall from Chapter 1, the third level of operation in QuickBooks is Activities. Activities identified as adjustments to account balances are entered in the Journal Entry window. There are no default accounts in this window because each adjusting journal entry is different. The account to debit and the account to credit must be indicated. Adjusting journal entries are usually dated the last day of the month.

The first adjusting journal entry Craig's Design and Landscaping Services makes on February 28, 2019, is to record (debit) Advertising Expense and reduce (credit) the Prepaid Advertising account for one month of service. The prepaid advertising was originally purchased on February 1 for $600 and represents a six-month prepayment. One month of Advertising Expense is $100 (or $600/6 months).

To record an adjusting journal entry:

1. On the title bar, click the Create icon and then click *Journal Entry* in the *Other* column.
2. In the *Journal date* field, choose *02/28/2019* (or the year you are using).
3. In the *Journal no.* field, key AJE1.

    QuickBooks Online allows you to assign journal entry numbers to each transaction. In this textbook, journal entry numbers are used for the adjusting journal entries. Once you start a sequence of numbers in the Journal Entry window, QuickBooks Online automatically assigns the next adjusting journal entry number in sequence; however, you can edit or delete the automatically assigned journal entry number.

4. In the first line of the *ACCOUNT* column, click the drop-down arrow and then click *Advertising Expense.*

HINT

Use the scroll arrow in the drop-down list to find the account.

5. In the *DEBITS* column, key 100.
6. Move to the second line in the *ACCOUNT* column, click the drop-down arrow, and then click *Prepaid Advertising.*
7. In the *CREDIT* column, *100* should appear; if it does not, key 100.
8. In the *DESCRIPTION* column, key To record one month of advertising expense. The *DESCRIPTION* column is optional; you do not have to enter an explanation. See Figure 5–K.

FIGURE 5–K

Journal Entry Window— Completed

Notice in the upper left corner of the window, to the left of Journal Entry #AJE1, the Recent Transactions icon ⟳. When you click the Recent Transactions icon, a list of the prior transactions appears. Click any prior transaction to view the prior journal entry.

HINT

Use the Save and new button when entering more than one journal entry.

9. Confirm the entry is correct and then click *Save and close* from the Save and new button list.
10. Return to the Dashboard.

In all journal entries, the total dollar value of debits must equal the total dollar value of credits. In the Journal Entry window, if you attempt to save an entry that is not in balance, a warning message appears that gives you the opportunity to correct the journal entry. If the journal entry is not corrected, you will not be able to save it.

Accounting Concept

For this adjusting journal entry, the general ledger posting is as follows:

Advertising Exp		Prepaid Advertising	
Dr	Cr	Dr	Cr
Adj 100		Bill 600	100 Adj
		Bal 500	

Practice Exercise   5-3

Record and save the following adjusting journal entries in the Journal Entry window separately. Notice the adjusting journal entry number automatically updates.

Feb. 28	Record one month of insurance expense. The insurance was purchased for $2,400 in February and recorded as Prepaid Insurance. It is a one-year policy effective February 1. *QuickCheck:* $200
Feb. 28	Record the depreciation expense on the Truck of $250 per month.
Feb. 28	Record one month of interest expense on the Loan Payable of $10 (credit Interest Payable). Add the new account *Interest Payable* while in the Journal Entry window by clicking *Add New* at the *ACCOUNT* field drop-down list. The account type and the detail type are both *Other Current Liabilities*.
Feb. 28	Record one month of interest expense on the Notes Payable of $57 (credit Interest Payable).
Feb. 28	The office supplies on hand totaled $300. Refer to the Office Supplies account on the Trial Balance to determine the amount of the adjustment. *QuickCheck:* $175

HINT

In the event a new account needs to be added while in the Journal Entry window, click *Add New* at the *ACCOUNT* field drop-down list. This opens the Account window and allows you to add the new account to the list without exiting the Journal Entry window.

Reports

Period-End Accounting Reports and Financial Statements

Reports, the fourth level of operation in QuickBooks, reflects the activities and adjustments recorded in the windows as well as the information compiled in the Lists. When you complete the adjusting journal entries, you should display and print the period-end accounting reports and the financial statements.

Accounting Reports

The period-end accounting reports consist of the Journal, General Ledger, and Adjusted Trial Balance Reports. These reports should be printed at the end of each month.

Journal Report

In the previous chapters, the Journal Report was printed for the entire month. However, it is not necessary to reprint all the journal entries when you wish to view only the adjusting journal entries. All reports can be customized to modify the appearance of the report or the fields of information to be displayed. In this case, we will customize the report using the Filter feature to display only the adjusting journal entries in the Journal Report.

To view, filter, correct, and print only the adjusting journal entries in the Journal Report:

1. On the Navigation bar, click Reports.
2. In the *For my accountant* section, click *Journal*.
3. By default, QuickBooks Online displays the current month's dates. In the date fields, choose *02/01/2019* and *02/28/2019* (or the year you are using) and press the Tab key. The Journal Report displays.

    All transactions for February, from all windows, display. Scroll to the bottom of the entries. Notice the transaction type *Journal Entry* on the last six journal entries. These are the adjusting journal entries entered in the Journal Entry window.

4. Click the Customize button at the top of the report. The Customize report window appears.
5. Click *Filter* to expand the section and display the various filter choices.
6. Click to insert a check mark next to *Transaction Type*.
7. Click the drop-down arrow in the box to the right of *Transaction Type*. A list of transaction types appears.
8. Scroll through the list and click to insert a check mark to the left of *Journal Entry. Journal Entry* appears in the box to the right of *Transaction Type*. See Figure 5–L.

HINT

If journal entries other than the adjusting journal entries are displayed, change the dates to 02/28/2019–02/28/2019 (or the year you are using).

FIGURE 5–L

Customize Report Window—Journal Entry Transaction Type Selected

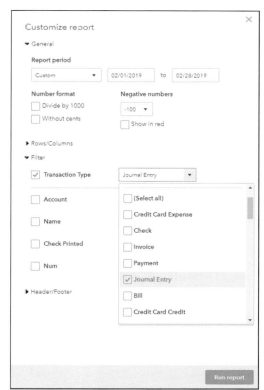

9. Confirm the information is correct and then click the Run report button at the bottom of the Customize report window. The Journal Report displays only journal entries with the Journal Entry transaction type. See Figure 5–M.

FIGURE 5–M Journal Report—Adjusting Journal Entries

Recall that on most reports in QuickBooks Online, you can drill down to the original window where an activity was recorded and make any necessary changes. This can also be done in the Journal Report.

Assume you realize the interest expense credited to the Interest Payable account (AJE5) for the Interest Expense related to the Notes Payable should have been $75, not $57 as noted in Practice Exercise 5–3.

10. In the *TRANSACTION TYPE* column for journal entry number AJE5, click *Journal Entry*. This opens the Journal Entry window for Journal Entry #AJE5.

11. In the Journal Entry #AJE5 window, in both the *DEBITS* and *CREDITS* columns, delete the amount and key 75. See Figure 5–N.

FIGURE 5–N Journal Entry Window—AJE5 Amount Corrected

12. Confirm the information is correct and then click the Save and close button. The correction to the journal entry is saved, and you return to the Journal Report with AJE5 updated to $75. See Figure 5–O.

FIGURE 5–O Journal Report—Adjusting Journal Entries—Updated AJE5

13. Print the report.
14. Return to the Dashboard.

General Ledger Report

All transactions recorded in any of the windows are posted to the general ledger. The General Ledger Report displays all activity in each account and lists the balance after each activity.

HINT

Depending on the time of year that you prepare this report, some of the amounts may be different.

To view the General Ledger Report:

1. On the Navigation bar, click Reports.
2. In the *For my accountant* section, click *General Ledger.*
3. By default, QuickBooks Online displays the current month dates. In the date fields, choose *01/01/2019* and *12/31/2019* (or the year you are using) and then click the Run report button. The General Ledger Report displays. See Figure 5–P.

FIGURE 5–P General Ledger Report—Partial

Notice there is an *AMOUNT* column and a *BALANCE* column but no *DEBIT* or *CREDIT* columns. Debit amounts are listed as positive numbers; credit amounts are preceded with a minus sign.

4. Return to the Dashboard.

Adjusted Trial Balance Report

HINT

Once you record the adjusting journal entries, you can no longer create a preadjusted trial balance.

The trial balance of December 31, 2019, (see Figure 5–J on page 140) was reviewed before preparing the adjusting journal entries. Typically, the trial balance is printed again after the adjusting journal entries have been recorded. The second printed trial balance is referred to as the *Adjusted Trial Balance Report.* To distinguish between the two printed trial balances, you will modify the report by changing the name in the heading of the second trial balance to *Adjusted Trial Balance.*

To view, customize the heading of, and print the Adjusted Trial Balance Report:

1. On the Navigation bar, click Reports.
2. In the *For my accountant* section, click *Trial Balance*.
3. In the date fields, choose *01/01/2019* and *12/31/2019* (or the year you are using) and then click the Run report button. The trial balance displays.
4. Click the Customize button at the top of the report. The Customize report window appears.
5. Click *Header/Footer* to display several header, footer, and alignment options.
6. In the *Header* section, confirm the check box to the left of *Report title* contains a check mark with *Trial Balance* displayed in the field at the right.
7. Key the word Adjusted before *Trial Balance* in the *Report title* field. See Figure 5–Q.

FIGURE 5–Q

Customize Report Window—Header Section—Report Title Updated

8. Confirm the information is correct and then click the Run report button at the bottom of the Customize report window. The report heading now displays the report title as *Adjusted Trial Balance*. See Figure 5–R.

FIGURE 5–R Trial
Balance Report—
Renamed Adjusted Trial
Balance

EX5 [Your Name] Craig's Design and Landscaping Services

ADJUSTED TRIAL EALANCE
As of December 31 , 2019

	DEBIT	CREDIT
Checking	1,201.00	
Savings	800.00	
Accounts Receivable (A/R)	5,281.52	
Inventory Asset	596.25	
Office Supplies	300.00	
Prepaid Advertising	500.00	
Prepaid Insurance	2,200.00	
Undeposited Funds	2,062.52	
Truck:Accumulated Depreciation		250.00
Truck:Original Cost	13,495.00	
Accounts Payable (A/P)		5,077.67
Mastercard		157.72
Arizona Dept. of Revenue Payable		0.00
Board of Equalization Payable		370.94
Interest Payable		85.00
Loan Payable		4,000.00
Notes Payable		25,000.00
Opening Balance Equity	9,337.50	
Retained Earnings		1,859.49
Design income		1,275.00
Discounts given	89.50	
Landscaping Services		722.50
Landscaping Services:Job Materials:Fountains and Garden Lighting		1,226.50
Landscaping Services:Job Materials:Plants and Soil		2,070.72
Landscaping Services:Job Materials:Sprinklers and Drip Systems		30.00
Landscaping Services:Labor:Installation		250.00
Pest Control Services	30.00	
Sales of Product Income		912.75
Services		503.55
Cost of Goods Sold	405.00	
Advertising Expense	174.86	
Automobile	113.96	
Automobile:Fuel	232.85	
Equipment Rental	112.00	
Insurance Expense	441.23	
Interest Expense	85.00	
Job Expenses	46.98	
Job Expenses:Job Materials:Decks and Patios	234.04	
Job Expenses:Job Materials:Plants and Soil	105.95	
Job Expenses:Job Materials:Sprinklers and Drip Systems	215.66	
Legal & Professional Fees	75.00	
Legal & Professional Fees:Accounting	390.00	
Legal & Professional Fees:Lawyer	100.00	
Maintenance and Repair	185.00	
Maintenance and Repair:Equipment Repairs	755.00	
Meals and Entertainment	28.49	
Office Expenses	18.08	
Office Supplies Expense	175.00	
Rent or Lease	900.00	
Utilities:Gas and Electric	114.09	
Utilities:Telephone	74.36	
Depreciation Expense	250.00	
Miscellaneous	2,666.00	
TOTAL	$43,791.84	$43,791.84

HINT

HINT: While some of
the balances may not
match, you should have
the following balances:

Office Supplies $300.00
Prepaid
Advertising   500.00
Prepaid
Insurance   2,200.00
Truck: Accumulated
Depreciation   250.00
Interest Payable   85.00
Depreciation
Expense   250.00
Interest Expense   85.00

You may also have the
following balances:
Advertising
Expense $174.86
Insurance
Expense   441.23

9. Print the report.
10. Return to the Dashboard.

HINT

Depending on the time of year that you prepare this report, some of the balances may be different, but your balance in the Adjusted Trial Balance Report should be $335 more than your balance in the Trial Balance Report.

Compare the effect of the adjusting journal entries on the account balances by comparing the trial balance (see Figure 5–J on page 140) to the adjusted trial balance (see Figure 5–R on page 148). *Note: The earlier amount showed $43,456.84, while the adjusted trial balance shows $43,791.84.*

Financial Statements

The financial statements include the income statement and the balance sheet. Companies must prepare financial statements at least once a year, but they can be prepared more frequently, such as quarterly or even monthly.

Profit and Loss Report (Income Statement)

The income statement is known as the *Profit and Loss Report* in QuickBooks Online. The Profit and Loss Report displays revenue and expenses for a specified period of time. This report can be displayed in a standard format, which displays the balances for the current year, or a comparative format, which displays the balances for both the current year and the prior year. In addition, a detailed Profit and Loss Report that lists all transactions affecting a particular item on the report can also be produced.

HINT

Depending on the time of year that you prepare this report, some of the balances may be different.

To view and print a year-to-date Profit and Loss Report:
1. On the Navigation bar, click Reports.
2. In the *Business overview* section, click *Profit and Loss*. This report can also be accessed in the *For my accountant* section of the Reports window.
3. By default, QuickBooks Online displays the current year dates. At the date fields, choose *01/01/2019* and *12/31/2019* (or the year you are using), if necessary, and then click the Run report button. The Profit and Loss Report displays.
4. Print the report. See Figure 5–S.
5. Return to the Dashboard.

FIGURE 5–S

Profit and Loss Report

EX5 [Your Name] Craig's Design and Landscaping Services

PROFIT AND LOSS
January - December 2019

	TOTAL
▼ Income	
Design income	1,275.00
Discounts given	-89.50
▼ Landscaping Services	722.50
▼ Job Materials	
Fountains and Garden Lighting	1,226.50
Plants and Soil	2,070.72
Sprinklers and Drip Systems	30.00
Total Job Materials	3,327.22
▼ Labor	
Installation	250.00
Total Labor	250.00
Total Landscaping Services	4,299.72
Pest Control Services	-30.00
Sales of Product Income	912.75
Services	503.55
Total Income	$6,871.52
▼ Cost of Goods Sold	
Cost of Goods Sold	405.00
Total Cost of Goods Sold	$405.00
GROSS PROFIT	$6,466.52
▼ Expenses	
Advertising Expense	174.86
▼ Automobile	113.96
Fuel	232.85
Total Automobile	346.81
Equipment Rental	112.00
Insurance Expense	441.23
Interest Expense	85.00
▼ Job Expenses	46.98
▼ Job Materials	
Decks and Patios	234.04
Plants and Soil	105.95
Sprinklers and Drip Systems	215.66
Total Job Materials	555.65
Total Job Expenses	602.63
▼ Legal & Professional Fees	75.00
Accounting	390.00
Lawyer	100.00
Total Legal & Professional Fees	565.00
▼ Maintenance and Repair	185.00
Equipment Repairs	755.00
Total Maintenance and Repair	940.00
Meals and Entertainment	28.49
Office Expenses	18.08
Office Supplies Expense	175.00
Rent or Lease	900.00
▼ Utilities	
Gas and Electric	114.09
Telephone	74.36
Total Utilities	188.45
Total Expenses	$4,577.55
NET OPERATING INCOME	$1,888.97
▼ Other Expenses	
Depreciation Expense	250.00
Miscellaneous	2,666.00
Total Other Expenses	$2,916.00
NET OTHER INCOME	$ -2,916.00
NET INCOME	$ -1,027.03

Accrual basis

Balance Sheet Report

In QuickBooks Online, the Balance Sheet Report, which shows the assets, liabilities, and equity balances as of a certain date, may be displayed in a standard, summary, or comparative format. In addition, a detailed report, showing all transactions affecting balance sheet accounts, can be produced.

HINT

Depending on the time of year that you prepare this report, some of the balances may be different.

To view and print a Balance Sheet Report:

1. On the Navigation bar, click Reports.
2. In the *Business overview* section, click *Balance Sheet*. This report can also be accessed in the *For my accountant* section of the Reports window.
3. By default, QuickBooks Online displays the current year dates. At the date fields, choose *01/01/2019* and *12/31/2019* (or the year you are using), if necessary, and then click the Run report button. The Balance Sheet Report displays.
4. Print the report. See Figure 5–T.

FIGURE 5–T
Balance Sheet Report

EX5 [Your Name] Craig's Design and Landscaping Services

BALANCE SHEET
As of December 31, 2019

	TOTAL
▾ ASSETS	
▾ Current Assets	
▾ Bank Accounts	
Checking	1,201.00
Savings	800.00
Total Bank Accounts	**$2,001.00**
▾ Accounts Receivable	
Accounts Receivable (A/R)	5,281.52
Total Accounts Receivable	**$5,281.52**
▾ Other Current Assets	
Inventory Asset	596.25
Office Supplies	300.00
Prepaid Advertising	500.00
Prepaid Insurance	2,200.00
Undeposited Funds	2,062.52
Total Other Current Assets	**$5,658.77**
Total Current Assets	**$12,941.29**
▾ Fixed Assets	
▾ Truck	
Accumulated Depreciation	-250.00
Original Cost	13,495.00
Total Truck	**13,245.00**
Total Fixed Assets	**$13,245.00**
TOTAL ASSETS	**$26,186.29**
▾ LIABILITIES AND EQUITY	
▾ Liabilities	
▾ Current Liabilities	
▾ Accounts Payable	
Accounts Payable (A/P)	5,077.67
Total Accounts Payable	**$5,077.67**
▾ Credit Cards	
Mastercard	157.72
Total Credit Cards	**$157.72**
▾ Other Current Liabilities	
Arizona Dept. of Revenue Payable	0.00
Board of Equalization Payable	370.94
Interest Payable	85.00
Loan Payable	4,000.00
Total Other Current Liabilities	**$4,455.94**
Total Current Liabilities	**$9,691.33**
▾ Long-Term Liabilities	
Notes Payable	25,000.00
Total Long-Term Liabilities	**$25,000.00**
Total Liabilities	**$34,691.33**
▾ Equity	
Opening Balance Equity	-9,337.50
Retained Earnings	1,859.49
Net Income	-1,027.03
Total Equity	**$ -8,505.04**
TOTAL LIABILITIES AND EQUITY	**$26,186.29**

Look at the *Fixed Assets* section on the printout of the Balance Sheet Report. Recall that in the Chart of Accounts List, parent and subaccounts were used for the fixed assets. When parent and subaccounts flow into the financial statements, the parent account name becomes a "heading" and a "total" for the related subaccounts. The account balances for the subaccounts are displayed and subtotaled and then added together to create the total for the parent account. For example, the parent account Truck is a heading, the subaccounts Accumulated Depreciation and Original Cost are displayed under the parent account, and then the parent account Truck is again displayed, this time as the total for the subaccounts. On the printout of the report, the balances of the subaccounts (-250 and 13,495) are displayed below the heading Truck, and the subtotal of these subaccounts (13,245) is displayed and labeled as the total for the parent Truck account.

5. Return to the Dashboard.

Registers

Because QuickBooks Online is designed for the non-accountant, it includes an alternative method for reviewing daily activity by using registers. Registers are available for any balance sheet account—that is, any asset, liability, or equity account. They are not available for income or expense accounts.

The register format is similar to that of a personal checkbook, but the information displayed in the registers is also similar to the information displayed in the general ledger.

HINT

Depending on the time of year that you prepare this report, some of the dates or balances may be different.

To view a register:
1. On the Navigation bar, click Accounting.
2. At the Chart of Accounts window, in the *ACTION* column in the *Checking* account line, click *View register*. The Bank Register window for the Checking account appears. See Figure 5–U.

FIGURE 5–U

Bank Register Window— Checking Account

Transactions that were entered in any of the other windows that affected the Checking account are also displayed here in the register. Scroll through the transactions and compare them with the Checking account in the general ledger (see Figure 5–P on page 146). Notice the date order of each: the register shows the most recent dates first, and the general ledger shows the older dates first. You can use the register to correct any activity already recorded by drilling down to the source of the activity.

To drill down to an Activity window using the register:

1. At the Bank Register for the Checking account, scroll to the transaction for *Pam Seitz - Legal & Professional Fees* and then click the transaction. The transaction expands, and you can now edit the information. See Figure 5–V.

FIGURE 5–V
Bank Register Window—
Checking Account—
Transaction Expanded

2. Click the Edit button. The Expense window appears, which is the window where the transaction was originally recorded. See Figure 5–W. Any corrections can be made in this window and then saved.

FIGURE 5–W Expense Window

3. Close the Expense window by clicking the X. You return to the Bank Register for the Checking account.
4. At the Bank Register window, click the Back to Chart of Accounts link in the upper left corner. You return to the Chart of Accounts window.

Registers are available only for balance sheet accounts. For income statement accounts (income and expenses), a register is not available, but an Account QuickReport is available. The Account QuickReport displays all the activity to the account, again similar to the general ledger information.

To view an income Account QuickReport:

1. At the Chart of Accounts window, scroll down to the Design income account and click *Run report* in the *ACTION* column. By default, the report displays activity for the past 90 days.
2. In the date field, key 01/01/2019 (or the current year) and press the Tab key. The *Report period* field updates from *Since 90 Days Ago* to *Custom*, and a blank field appears for the end date.
3. In the blank field, key 12/31/2019 (or the current year). The Account QuickReport displays, listing all the activity to this account during the time period chosen. See Figure 5–X.

FIGURE 5–X Account QuickReport

From this report, as with others, you can click any transaction listed and drill down to the window where the original activity was recorded.

4. Return to the Dashboard.

Exiting QuickBooks Online

At the end of each session, you should exit QuickBooks Online and close the browser.

To exit QuickBooks Online and close the browser:

1. On the title bar, click the Gear icon.
2. At the Company window, click *Sign Out* in the *Profile* column. This closes the company file and exits QuickBooks Online.
3. Close your browser.

Chapter Review and Assessment

 Study Tools include a presentation and a glossary. Use these resources, available from the links menu in the student ebook, to further develop and review skills learned in this chapter.

Procedure Review

To review the Chart of Accounts List as a report:
1. On the Navigation bar, click Accounting.
2. In the *For my accountant* section, click *Account List*. Recall the Chart of Accounts List is called *Account List* in the report format. If the *Customize reports instantly* message appears, close it. The Account List Report displays.

To view an account in the Account window:
1. Open the Account List Report.
2. Click an account. The Account window for the selected account opens.

To review the Chart of Accounts using Accounting on the Navigation bar:
1. On the Navigation bar, click Accounting. The Chart of Accounts window appears.

To add a new account:
1. On the Navigation bar, click Accounting. The Chart of Accounts window appears.
2. In the Chart of Accounts window in the upper right corner, click the New button.
3. At the Account window, click the drop-down arrow at the *Account Type* field and select the account type.
4. In the *Detail Type* drop-down list, select the detail type.
5. In the *Name* field, key the account name.
6. In the *Number* field, key the account number (if the account numbers feature is enabled).
7. Click the Save and Close button.

To edit an account:
1. On the Navigation bar, click Accounting. The Chart of Accounts window appears.
2. In the *ACTION* column for the account you wish to edit, click the drop-down arrow to the right of *View register* or *Run report*.
3. At the drop-down menu, click *Edit*. The Account window appears.
4. Make the appropriate edits.
5. Click the Save and Close button.

To record an adjusting journal entry:
1. On the title bar, click the Create icon and then click *Journal Entry* in the *Other* column.
2. In the *Journal date* field, choose the date.
3. In the *Journal no.* field, key a number such as AJE1.

4. In the first line of the *ACCOUNT* column, click the drop-down arrow and then click the account to be debited.
5. In the *DEBITS* column, key the amount.
6. Move to the second line in the *ACCOUNT* column, click the drop-down arrow, and then click the account to be credited.
7. In the *CREDIT* column, the amount should appear; if it does not, key the amount.
8. In the *DESCRIPTION* column, key an explanation if desired.
9. Click the Save and close button.

To view and print an accounting report or financial statement:
1. On the Navigation bar, click Reports.
2. In the *For my accountant* section or the *Business overview* section, click the desired report.
3. If necessary, in the date fields, choose the correct dates and then click the Run report button or press the Tab key.
4. Print the report.

To filter the information displayed in an accounting report or financial statement:
1. Open an accounting report or financial statement, enter the correct dates if necessary, and then click the Run report button or press the Tab key.
2. Click the Customize button at the top of the report. The Customize report window appears.
3. At the Customize report window, click *Filter* to expand the section for editing.
4. In the *Filter* section, select the category of information you wish to filter. For example, click the check box to the left of *Transaction Type* to insert a check mark.
5. Click the drop-down arrow in the box to the right of the *Transaction Type* field (displays *All*). A list of transaction types appears.
6. Scroll through the list and click the check box to the left of *Journal Entry* to insert a check mark. *Journal Entry* appears in the field to the right of *Transaction Type*.
7. Click the Run report button at the bottom of the Customize report window.

To customize the heading in a report or financial statement:
1. Open a report or financial statement, enter the correct dates, if necessary, and then click the Run report button or press the Tab key.
2. Click the Customize button at the top of the report. The Customize report window appears.
3. Click *Header/Footer* to expand the section for editing. Several header, footer, and alignment choices are displayed.
4. In the *Header* section, the check box to the left of *Report title* should be checked and the title of the report displayed in the field at the right.
5. In the *Report title* field, key the desired report title.
6. Click the Run report button. The report now displays the new title.

To view a register or Account QuickReport:
1. On the Navigation bar, click Accounting.
2. In the *ACTION* column for the account, click *View register* or *Run report*.

    Registers are used for assets, liabilities, and equity accounts; Account QuickReports are used for revenues and expenses accounts.
3. At the Account QuickReport, select the dates and then click the Run report button. The Account QuickReport displays.

Key Concepts

Select the letter of the item that best matches each definition.

a. Journal Entry window   f. Register
b. Filter   g. Header/Footer
c. Profit and Loss Report   h. Trial Balance Report
d. General Ledger Report   i. adjusting journal entries
e. Chart of Accounts   j. Balance Sheet Report

_____ 1. Recorded periodically so financial statements can be prepared according to accounting rules.
_____ 2. The report that shows assets, liabilities, and equity balances at a specified date.
_____ 3. The list of accounts a company uses in business.
_____ 4. The section in the Customize report window that is used to identify categories of information to be displayed in a report.
_____ 5. The report that lists the activity increases, decreases, and balances for each account.
_____ 6. Similar to a manual accounting system, this allows for the recording of a debit entry, a credit entry, and an explanation.
_____ 7. The report that displays the revenue and expenses for a specified period of time.
_____ 8. The section in the Customize report window that is used to change the heading on a report.
_____ 9. The format is similar to that of a checkbook and can be used to view the activities for any balance sheet account.
_____ 10. A report that displays all accounts and their debit or credit balance.

Procedure Check

Write a response for each of the following prompts.
1. The manager has requested a list of all accounts the company uses. Which is the best report to print to provide this information, and how would you obtain it?
2. The manager wants to know the balance in each of the company's accounts. Which is the best report to print to provide this information, and how would you obtain it?
3. You have been asked to review the adjusting journal entries and have located an error. How would you correct the error in the adjusting journal entry?

4. Describe what is included in the Journal Report and how you would display only the adjusting journal entries.
5. Your manager has a Trial Balance Report and an Adjusted Trial Balance Report, both with the same date, and she asks you to provide a description of each report. Include in your explanation the steps to change the name of the Trial Balance Report to *Adjusted Trial Balance*.
6. Explain the purpose of adjusting journal entries. Compare and contrast the process of recording adjusting journal entries in a manual accounting system and QuickBooks Online, and explain why there are no default accounts in the Journal Entry window.

 Case Problem

Demonstrate your knowledge of the QuickBooks Online features discussed in this chapter by completing the following case problem.

On June 1, 2019, Olivia Chen began her business, Olivia's Web Solutions. All daily activities for the month of June, including entering and paying bills, writing checks, recording sales (both cash and on account), collecting receivables, and depositing receipts, have been recorded. It is the end of the first month of business; the adjusting journal entries need to be recorded, and financial statements need to be printed. You will record the adjusting journal entries for June 30 using the information provided below. Your company file should include the account balances for Olivia's Web Solutions based on the transactions you recorded in Chapters 3 and 4.

1. Sign in to QuickBooks Online.
2. Change the company name to **OWS5 [*Your Name*] Olivia's Web Solutions**.
3. Add the following accounts to the Chart of Accounts List:

Account Type:	Fixed Assets
Detail Type:	Fixed Asset Computers
Name:	Computers
Number:	1700

Account Type:	Fixed Assets
Detail Type:	Accumulated Depreciation
Name:	Accum. Dep., Computers
Number:	1750
Is sub-account:	1700

Account Type:	Fixed Assets
Detail Type:	Fixed Asset Furniture
Name:	Furniture
Number:	1800

Account Type:	Fixed Assets
Detail Type:	Accumulated Depreciation
Name:	Accum. Dep., Furniture
Number:	1850
Is sub-account:	1800

Account Type:	Fixed Assets
Detail Type:	Fixed Asset Software
Name:	Software
Number:	1900

Account Type:	Fixed Assets
Detail Type:	Accumulated Depreciation
Name:	Accum. Dep., Software
Number:	1950
Is sub-account:	1900

Account Type:	Other Expense
Detail Type:	Depreciation
Name:	Dep. Exp., Computers
Number:	6075

Account Type:	Other Expense
Detail Type:	Depreciation
Name:	Dep. Exp., Furniture
Number:	6085

Account Type:	Other Expense
Detail Type:	Depreciation
Name:	Dep. Exp., Software
Number:	6095

Edit the following accounts:

1725 Computers - Cost	_Is sub-account:_	1700
1825 Furniture - Cost	_Is sub-account:_	1800
1925 Software - Cost	_Is sub-account:_	1900

Delete the following account:
6425 Repair Expense

4. Display and print the Trial Balance Report before preparing the adjusting journal entries (June 1, 2019–June 30, 2019).
5. Use the information below to prepare adjusting journal entries. Record each adjusting journal entry separately, and use June 30, 2019, for the date.
   a. The prepaid insurance represents a one-year policy. Record insurance expense for one month. Refer to the trial balance to determine the amount in the Prepaid Insurance account. For Journal no., use _AJE1._
   b. The prepaid advertising represents a six-month contract. Record the advertising expense for one month.
   c. Monthly depreciation on the assets: $75 for Computer, $50 for Furniture, and $100 for Software. Record each depreciation expense as a separate adjusting journal entry.
   d. The computer supplies on hand total $350. Compare with the amount in the Computer Supplies account to determine how much of the account has been used and then record the expense.

e. The office supplies on hand total $325. Compare with the amount in the Office Supplies account to determine how much of the account has been used and then record the expense.

f. The interest on the note payable for one month is $25. Record the interest expense. Add to the Chart of Accounts List the Interest Payable account, Other Current Liabilities, number 2030.

6. Display and print the following reports for June 30, 2019:

a. Journal: Only the adjusting journal entries (June 30, 2019– June 30, 2019)

b. Trial Balance: Change name in header of the report to *Adjusted Trial Balance* (June 1, 2019–June 30, 2019)

c. Profit and Loss (June 1, 2019–June 30, 2019)

d. Balance Sheet (June 1, 2019–June 30, 2019)

CHAPTER 6

Inventory

Managing Inventory and Paying Sales Tax

Objectives

- Identify the two inventory systems
- Update the Products and Services List
- Record purchases of products in the Bill and Check windows
- Identify transactions requiring sales tax
- Record adjustment to product inventory in the Inventory Quantity Adjustment window
- Record payment of sales tax in the Sales Tax Center window
- Display and print inventory-related reports

QuickBooks Online allows you to track inventory transactions. **Inventory** is ready-made merchandise that is sold to customers for a profit. Before you can enter inventory transactions, you must establish a file for each inventory item. Inventory item files are included in the Products and Services List.

Once you establish an inventory item file, transactions for the item can be entered in the Bill, Check, Invoice, Sales Receipt, and Inventory Quantity Adjustment activity windows in much the same manner as was done in earlier chapters. Every time the company receives merchandise for resale, sells merchandise, or adjusts the inventory because of loss or damage, QuickBooks Online records that information in the Products and Services List. This allows you to accurately determine inventory quantity, value, and profit on sales. In addition, QuickBooks Online automatically changes balance sheet and income statement accounts based on the inventory information on the Products and Services List.

In this chapter, our sample company, Craig's Design and Landscaping Services, will purchase and sell garden and landscaping products to clients in addition to providing design and landscaping services. This means that the company must now be concerned with tracking inventory.

QuickBooks Online versus Manual Accounting: Inventory Transactions

As discussed in previous chapters, in a manual accounting system, purchases on account are recorded in a purchases journal while sales on account are recorded in a sales journal. This is true whether the purchase or sale is for services or for merchandise. Cash transactions are recorded in the cash receipts or cash payments journals, again for both inventory and non-inventory items.

In QuickBooks Online, the Products and Services List serves as an inventory subsidiary ledger for the company. The list includes all items the company sells, both inventory and service items. Relevant information for each inventory item, such as name/number, type, description, cost, sales price, and related general ledger accounts, is entered at the time the item file is created and is updated as necessary.

When the company purchases an inventory item from a vendor on account, the transaction is recorded in the Bill activity window in much the same manner as non-inventory purchases were recorded. When the inventory items are sold on account, the invoice is recorded in the Invoice activity window in a manner similar to that done for other revenues. When you enter these transactions, QuickBooks Online updates the Chart of Accounts List (general ledger) and at the same time updates each vendor and customer file. In addition, it updates the Products and Services List to reflect the purchase and sale of the inventory items. Cash purchases of inventory items are recorded in the Check activity window, while cash sales of inventory are recorded in the Sales Receipt activity window. Changes in inventory that are not a result of a sale or purchase are recorded in the Inventory Quantity Adjustment activity window. In all instances in which inventory items are purchased, sold, or adjusted, the Products and Services List is updated to reflect the new inventory quantity and value.

Accounting for Inventory Transactions

There are two types of inventory systems: periodic and perpetual. Under the **periodic inventory system**, separate records are *not* maintained for inventory items, and no attempt is made to adjust the inventory account for purchases and sales. Instead, inventory is counted periodically to determine inventory quantity, value, cost of goods sold, and gross profit. In the past, the periodic system was often used by businesses that sold high-volume, low-cost goods, for which keeping individual inventory records was not practical.

Under the **perpetual inventory system**, accounting records that continuously show the current inventory quantity and value are maintained. When inventory is purchased, the inventory (asset) account is increased. When inventory is sold, the inventory account is reduced. In addition, the cost of goods sold is simultaneously computed to arrive at gross profit. Before the availability of low-cost computer hardware and software, only businesses with low-volume, high-cost goods used the perpetual system. Now, with computers pervasive in business, most companies are able to use a perpetual inventory system.

QuickBooks Online, like almost all general ledger accounting software programs, uses the perpetual system because it not only allows the user to know the current inventory quantity and value at any given moment, but it also calculates the cost of goods sold and gross profit after each sale without the need for a periodic physical inventory count.

Chapter Problem

In this chapter, you will track inventory transactions for Craig's Design and Landscaping Services, the QuickBooks Online Test Drive sample company. The company will begin selling decorative garden items, such as fountains, pumps, and outdoor furniture, in addition to providing design and landscaping services. Information for several inventory products has been entered in the Products and Services List. This information is contained in the QuickBooks Online Test Drive sample company file.

To begin, open the Test Drive sample company file for Craig's Design and Landscaping Services. Change the company name in the file to **EX6 [*Your Name*] Craig's Design and Landscaping Services** and key 12-3456788 in the *EIN* field. You may also want to extend the time-out period to three hours. Finally, customize the Invoice and Sales Receipts windows to display the invoice number and remove the *SERVICE DATE* column as described in Chapter 4.

Lists

The Products and Services List

Recall from Chapter 1 that the second level of operation in QuickBooks Online is to record information in Lists. The Products and Services List contains a file for each type of service or inventory item sold by the company. If the item sold is an inventory product, QuickBooks Online calls this an inventory item as opposed to a service item. You should enter the information for each inventory item in the Products and Services List before recording transactions. This will make the Activities function run more smoothly. However, if you inadvertently omit an item, you can add that item during the Activities level of operation with minimal disruption.

HINT

As mentioned in Chapter 4, the Products and Services List can also be accessed by clicking Sales on the Navigation bar.

The Products and Services List contains important information on each product, such as type of item; stock keeping unit (SKU) number; category; description; cost; general ledger posting accounts for inventory asset, cost of goods sold, and sales; and sales tax status. All products or services sold by the company should be included in the Products and Services List. Periodically, these files need to be updated as products are added or discontinued or as background information changes.

Craig's Design has entered information for various inventory items in the Products and Services List.

To review the Products and Services List:

1. On the title bar, click the Gear icon and then click *Products and Services* in the *Lists* column. The Products and Services window displays. See Figure 6–A.

FIGURE 6–A Products and Services Window

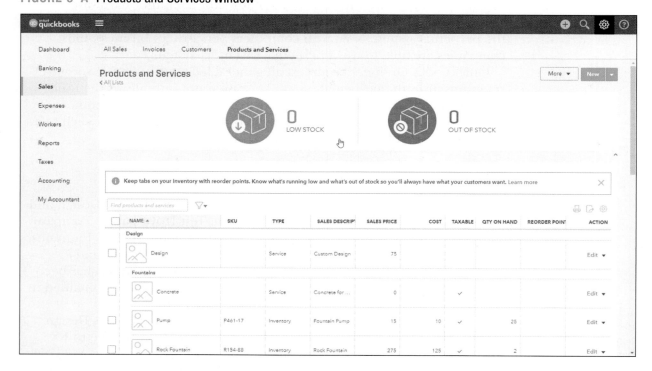

To view a specific inventory item file:

1. Place the mouse pointer over the item name *Rock Fountain* and double-click. The Product/Service information—Inventory window appears. See Figure 6–B.

FIGURE 6–B
Product/Service Information—Inventory Window

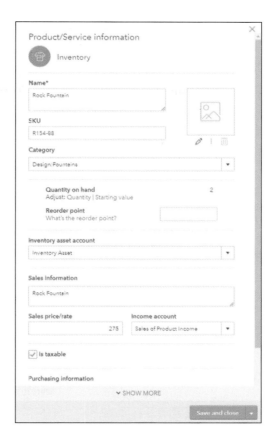

Note the following fields in this window:

Name field	Used to assign an identifying name to each item.
SKU field	Used to assign a stock keeping unit number for each product.
Category field	Allows you to group products by broad categories with individual products in sub-categories.
Inventory asset account field	This is the default general ledger posting account for the inventory balance sheet account when items are purchased. Override this entry as needed.
Sales Information field	Used to enter a description of the item for purchase or sales activity windows.
Sales price/rate field	This is the default unit-selling price or rate that appears in sales activity windows (e.g., Invoice and Sales Receipt windows). Override this entry as needed.
Income account field	This is the default general ledger posting account for revenue when the product is sold. Override this account as needed.
Is taxable field	Used to indicate if the item is taxable or non-taxable for sales tax purposes.
Cost field	Used to enter the typical unit cost for the item. This amount will appear in the purchase activity windows (e.g., Bill and Check windows) as the default cost amount. Override as needed.
Expense account field	Lists the default general ledger posting account for cost of goods sold when the item is sold. Override as needed.

2. Close the Product/Service information—Inventory window.
3. Return to the Dashboard.

The Products and Services List is updated periodically when new inventory items are added, unused items are deleted, or modifications are made to inventory items.

Adding a Product

The company has decided to sell a category of outdoor furniture to its clients. The first product will be chairs. Craig's Design will need to add this product to the Products and Services List.

To add a product:
1. On the title bar, click the Gear icon and then click *Products and Services* in the *Lists* column.
2. At the Products and Services window, click the New button. The Product/Service information—Select a type window appears. See Figure 6–C.
3. At the Product/Service information—Select a type window, click *Inventory*. The Product/Service information—Inventory window appears. See Figure 6–D.

FIGURE 6–C Product/Service Information— Select a Type Window

FIGURE 6–D Product/Service Information— Inventory Window

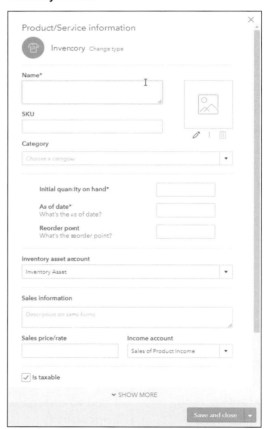

4. Complete the window with the information below. Your screen should look like Figure 6–E.

Name:	Outdoor Chairs
SKU:	C101
Category:	

   a. At the drop-down list, click *Add new.*
   b. In the *Name* field, key Outdoor Furniture and click the Save button.

Initial quantity on hand:	0
As of date:	03/01/2019
Inventory asset account:	Inventory Asset
Sales/Purchasing information:	Outdoor Chairs
Sales price/rate:	200
Income account:	Sales of Product Income
Is taxable:	(Insert a check mark, if necessary.)
Cost:	100
Expense Account:	Cost of Goods Sold

HINT

Remember to use the current year.

FIGURE 6–E

Product/Service Information—Inventory Window—Completed

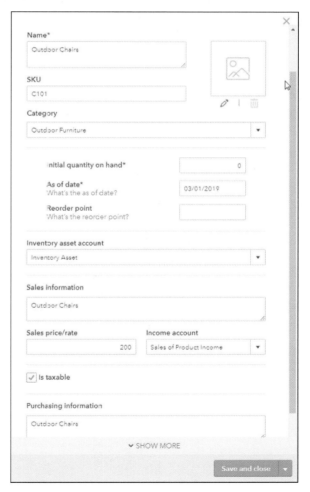

5. Confirm the information is correct and then click the Save and close button.
6. Keep the Products and Services window open for the next activity.

Making a Product Inactive

Craig's Design wishes to make the Sprinkler Pipes product file inactive because the company has decided not to sell this product.

To make a product inactive:

1. At the Products and Services window, in the *ACTION* column drop-down list for *Sprinkler Pipes*, click *Make inactive*.
2. At the warning message, *Are you sure you want to make Landscaping:Sprinklers:Sprinkler Pipes inactive?*, click the Yes button to remove the product file from the Products and Services List.
3. Keep the Products and Services window open for the next activity.

Editing a Product

Craig's Design needs to edit the product file for Fountains:Pumps because the unit cost has increased to $20 and the sales price to $30.

To edit a product file:

1. At the Products and Services window, click *Edit* in the *ACTION* column for the *Pump* product file. This opens the Product/Service information—Inventory window.
2. In the *Sales price/rate* and *Cost* fields, delete the current information and then key the new amounts shown in Figure 6–F.

FIGURE 6–F

Product/Service Information—Inventory Window—Updated

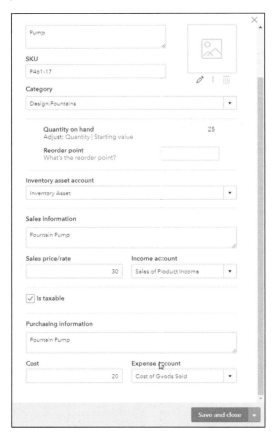

3. Confirm the information is correct and then click the Save and close button.
4. Return to the Dashboard.

FIGURE 6–G Updated Products and Services List

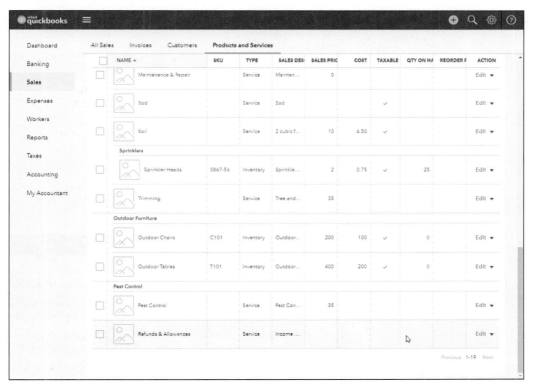

Activities • **Purchasing Inventory**

Recall from Chapter 1 that the third level of operation in QuickBooks Online is Activities, in which you record the daily business activities. Activities identified as purchases of inventory items on account are recorded in the Bill window. Activities identified as purchases of inventory items for cash are recorded in the Check window.

Recording Inventory Purchases Using the Bill Window

In Chapter 3, you used the Bill activity window when goods and services were purchased on account from a vendor. There are two details sections in the Bill window: *Account* and *Item*. When you opened the Bill window from the Create icon, you used the *Account details* section to record your non-inventory purchases. When a company wishes to use the inventory preference, the *Item details* section will be used to record the purchase of inventory products. In the Bill window, the *Item details* section is similar to the *Account details* section but provides additional fields that relate to inventory. The Bill window with the *Item details* section expanded is shown in Figure 6–H.

FIGURE 6–H Bill Window—Item Details Section Expanded

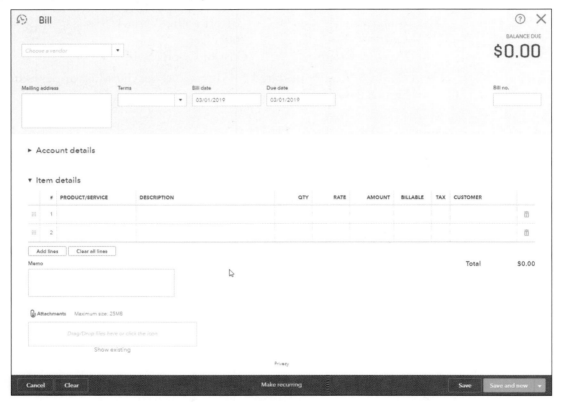

The *Item details* section of the Bill window contains the following columns:

PRODUCT/SERVICE column	Click the inventory product purchased at the drop-down list. Once an item is chosen, the *DESCRIPTION, RATE,* and *AMOUNT* columns are automatically filled based on information in the product file.
QTY column	Enter the quantity purchased. QuickBooks Online multiplies the quantity purchased by the *RATE* (unit cost) to arrive at the *AMOUNT* figure. In the *QTY* column, once you enter a figure, a pop-up will display the current quantity on hand. You can enter the quantity in the field while this pop-up is displayed.

Notice that a field for the general ledger accounts is not displayed. Recall that when you entered items in the Products and Services List, the general ledger accounts for the purchase (inventory asset account) and sale (income account and expense account) of inventory items were indicated. QuickBooks Online uses the information in the Products and Services List and the information entered in the Bill window to adjust the correct accounts automatically.

The *Item details* section of the Bill window is designed for purchases of inventory items on account. The default accounts are the Inventory asset account and the Accounts Payable account. QuickBooks Online uses the information in the Products and Services List to correctly record the amount and account for the inventory asset. The transaction is recorded as follows:

			Inventory		XXX			
			Accounts Payable				XXX	

Craig's Design and Landscaping Services has decided to sell a line of outdoor furniture along with the existing products. The vendor for these products needs to be added to the Vendor List. Follow the procedure presented in Chapter 3 to add this vendor:

First name:	Jeffrey
Last name:	Greene
Company:	Greene Grove Furniture Co.
Display name as:	Greene Grove Furniture Co.
Address:	889 Main Street
	Middlefield CA 94303
Phone:	650-555-4112
Mobile:	650-555-4113
Terms:	Net 30
Opening balance:	0
as of:	March 1, 2019
Account no.:	CDL-656

Close the Vendors window by clicking Dashboard on the Navigation bar.

Recording a Purchase of an Inventory Item on Account

On March 1, 2019, Craig's Design purchases 10 outdoor chairs from Greene Grove Furniture Co. at a cost of $100 each, its Bill no. C-588. The bill is due March 31, 2019, Net 30.

To record a purchase of an inventory item on account:
1. On the title bar, click the Create icon and then click *Bill* in the *Vendors* column.
2. At the *Choose a vendor* drop-down list, click *Greene Grove Furniture Co.*
3. Confirm that the *Terms* field reads *Net 30.*
4. Complete the *Bill date, Due date,* and *Bill no.* fields in the same way you would for non-inventory purchases. See Figure 6–I.

FIGURE 6–I

Bill Window—Partially
Completed

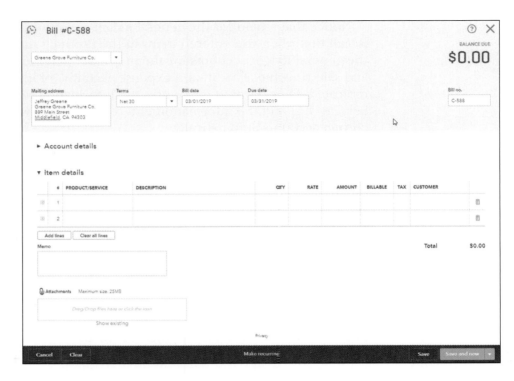

5. Click the *Item details* section heading if it is not already active. In the *PRODUCT/SERVICE* column, select *Outdoor Chairs*. The *DESCRIPTION* and *RATE* columns fill in automatically.
6. In the *QTY* column, key 10 and then move to the next field. The *AMOUNT* column is completed automatically. See Figure 6–J.

FIGURE 6–J

Bill Window—
Completed

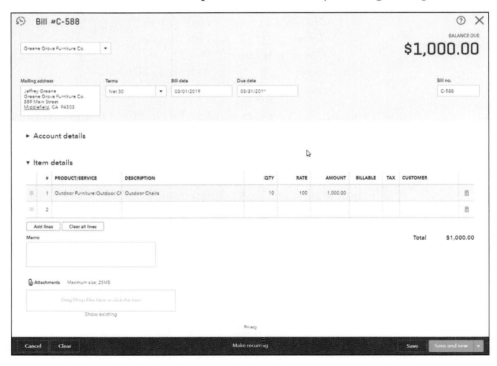

7. Confirm the data is correct and then click *Save and close* from the Save and new button list to return to the Dashboard.

In addition to the general ledger and vendor file changes, this transaction updates the product file for Outdoor Chairs to reflect a quantity of 10 on hand with an inventory value of $1,000.

Accounting Concept

For a purchase of inventory on account, the general ledger posting is as follows:

In addition, the vendor file (subledger) for Greene Grove Furniture Co. reflects the new liability:

Inventory Asset		Accts Payable		Greene Grove	
Dr	Cr	Dr	Cr	Dr	Cr
1,000			1,000		1,000

Recording Inventory Purchases Using the Check Window

Like the Bill window, the Check window has an *Account details* section and an *Item details* section. For purchase of inventory items for cash, you switch to the *Item details* section after opening the Check window. The fields to enter information for inventory items in the *Item details* section of the Check window are similar to those in the Bill window.

The *Item details* section of the Check window is designed for purchases of inventory items for cash. The default accounts are the Inventory asset account and the Cash account. QuickBooks Online uses the information on the Products and Services List to correctly record the amount and account for the inventory asset. The transaction is recorded as follows:

Inventory		XXX		
Cash			XXX	

Recording Inventory Purchases for Cash

On March 2, 2019, Craig's Design purchases and receives two rock fountains from Norton Lumber and Building Materials at a cost of $125 each, its Bill no. 6844, paid with Check no. 71.

To record a purchase and receipt of inventory items for cash:
1. On the title bar, click the Create icon and then click *Check* in the *Vendors* column.
2. At the *Choose a payee* drop-down list, click *Norton Lumber and Building Materials*.
3. Confirm the *Checking* bank account displays in the *Bank Account* field, the *Payment date* field is *03/02/2019*, and the *Check no.* field reads *71*.
4. Click the *Item details* section heading if it is not already active.
5. In the *PRODUCT/SERVICE* column, click *Rock Fountain*.
6. In the *QTY* column, key 2 and then move to the next column. QuickBooks Online completes the *AMOUNT* column. See Figure 6–K.
7. Click *Save and close* from the Save and new button list.

FIGURE 6–K Check Window—Completed

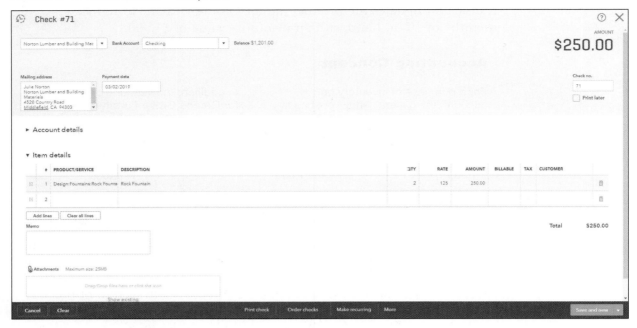

Accounting Concept

For a cash payment for the purchase of inventory, the general ledger posting is as follows:

Inventory Asset		Cash - Checking	
Dr	Cr	Dr	Cr
250			250

In addition, the product file for Rock Fountains is updated to reflect the new purchase.

Practice Exercise   6–2

HINT

When you open the Check window for either of these vendors in the Test Drive, you may see the information from the previous transaction with the company. Use the trash can icon at the right of each line to remove each transaction one at a time.

Record the following transactions in the Bill or Check window:

Mar. 6	Purchased and received four outdoor tables from Greene Grove Furniture Co. at a cost of $200 each, its Bill no. C-610. The bill is due April 5, 2019. *QuickCheck:* $800
Mar. 13	Purchased and received five pumps from Hicks Hardware at a cost of $20 each. Pay immediately with Check no. 72. *QuickCheck:* $100

Sales Tax

When it sells a product to a customer, a company is usually required to collect **sales tax** on the sale. The sales tax amount charged is added to the invoice price of the product. For example, a customer purchases an item with a retail price of $1,000, and the applicable sales tax rate is 6%. The retailer adds $60 to the invoice and collects $1,060 from the customer. At a later date, the retailer remits the tax collected from customers to the appropriate state sales tax collection agency. Rules for applying and collecting sales tax are complex and beyond the scope of this textbook. For examples and cases in this textbook, assume every customer pays sales tax. QuickBooks Online, like most general ledger software programs, is equipped to track sales-taxable transactions and to facilitate the collection and payment of taxes due.

In this chapter, Craig's Design and Landscaping Services will sell garden products to its customers. All sales of these products are subject to a sales tax charge of 8%, which is added to the invoice total. The tax will be payable to the Board of Equalization, State of California at the end of each month. Sales tax will not be collected on services (design and landscaping) in this textbook, because services generally are not subject to sales tax. Note, however, that is not the case in all localities.

As you know from Chapter 4, a sale on account is recorded in the Invoice window, and a sale for cash is recorded in the Sales Receipt window. The default account in the Invoice window is a debit to Accounts Receivable, and the default account in the Sales Receipt window is a debit to Cash or Undeposited Funds. When sales tax is charged on the sale of an item, a default Sales Tax Payable account is credited in both the Invoice and Sales Receipt windows. The sale of taxable products either for cash or on account results in the following general ledger posting:

Accounts Receivable/Cash (or Undeposited Funds)	XXX		
Sales			XXX
Sales Tax Payable			XXX

Sale of Inventory

Activities identified as sales of inventory items on account are recorded in the Invoice window. Activities identified as sales of inventory items for cash are recorded in the Sales Receipt window. Activities recorded in these windows are similar to those in Chapter 4, but additional fields in the window are used that relate to inventory.

Inventory Sales on Account in the Invoice Window

The Invoice window is designed for the sale of services, as in Chapter 4, and the sale of inventory items on account. The default accounts are Accounts Receivable, Cost of Goods Sold, Inventory, Sales Tax Payable, and Sales. QuickBooks Online uses the Products and Services List to determine the correct amount and account for the Cost of Goods Sold, Inventory, and Sales accounts. If an item is marked as taxable, QuickBooks Online uses the Products and Services List to determine the correct amount of sales tax to be recorded in the Sales Tax Payable account. The transaction is recorded as follows:

Accounts Receivable		XXX		
Cost of Goods Sold		XXX		
Inventory			XXX	
Sales Tax Payable			XXX	
Sales			XXX	

Recording a Sale of Products and Services on Account

On March 15, 2019, Craig's Design sells the following items to Kookies by Kathy on account, Invoice no. 1038, Net 30:

4 outdoor chairs	$ 800.00
1 outdoor table	400.00
Total sale of merchandise	$ 1,200.00
Sales tax (0.08 × $1,200)	96.00
Design services (4 hours)	300.00
Total sale on account	$ 1,596.00

To record a sale of products and services on account:

1. On the title bar, click the Create icon and then click *Invoice* in the *Customers* column.
2. At the *Choose a customer* drop-down list, click *Kookies by Kathy*.
3. Confirm that the *Terms* field reads *Net 30*.
4. Enter the information listed above in the *Invoice date* and *Invoice no.* fields.
5. In the *PRODUCT/SERVICE* column for the first line, click *Outdoor Chairs*. The *DESCRIPTION*, *RATE*, and *TAX* columns will fill in automatically. Note that a check mark should appear in the *TAX* column for taxable items. The box will be blank for non-taxable service items.
6. In the *QTY* column, key 4 and then move to the next column. See Figure 6–L.

HINT

Remember, you can also access the Invoice window from the *ACTION* column for this customer.

FIGURE 6–L
Invoice Window—Partially Completed

HINT

You may need to press the Tab key to move to additional lines in the Invoice window, or you can enlarge the window.

7. Move to the second line. In the *PRODUCT/SERVICE* column, click *Outdoor Tables.* QuickBooks Online fills the *DESCRIPTION, RATE,* and *TAX* columns.
8. In the *QTY* column, key 1 and then move to the third line.
9. In the *PRODUCT/SERVICE* column, click *Custom Design.* QuickBooks Online fills the remaining fields.
10. In the *QTY* column, key 4.
11. At the *Select a sales tax rate* drop-down list, click *California (8%).* The sales tax will be calculated on the taxable items only. See Figure 6–M.

FIGURE 6–M Invoice Window—Completed

HINT

If you miss an item, click the Add lines button; if you wish to erase all the lines, click the Clear all lines button.

12. Confirm the information is correct and then click *Save and close* from the Save and send button list to return to the Dashboard.

Accounting Concept

For a sale of inventory products on account, the general ledger posting is as follows:

Accts Receivable		Sale of Inventory			
Dr	Cr	Dr	Cr	4 chairs @ 200 =	800
1,596			1,200	1 table @ 400 =	400
					1,200

Sales Tax Payable		Service Revenue	
Dr	Cr	Dr	Cr
	96		300

The cost of the inventory sold and resulting decline in the inventory is recorded as follows:

Cost of Goods Sold		Inventory			
Dr	Cr	Dr	Cr	4 chairs @ 100 =	400
600			600	1 table @ 200 =	200
					600

Inventory Sales for Cash in the Sales Receipt Window

The Sales Receipt window is designed for cash received for both the sale of services and the sale of inventory items for cash. Once an inventory item is chosen, QuickBooks Online uses the information from the Products and Services List to correctly record the Cost of Goods Sold, Inventory, and Sales accounts. If an item is marked as taxable, QuickBooks Online uses the Products and Services List to determine the correct amount of sales tax to be recorded in the Sales Tax Payable account. The transaction is recorded as follows:

Cash (or Undeposited Funds)		XXX	
Cost of Goods Sold		XXX	
Inventory			XXX
Sales Tax Payable			XXX
Sales			XXX

Companies that have cash sales of numerous low-cost items use the Sales Receipt window to enter these sales in batches on a periodic basis, such as weekly or semimonthly.

Recording a Sale of an Inventory Item for Cash

On March 22, 2019, Craig's Design sells the following items to Kate Whelan, Sales Receipt no. 1039, receiving payment immediately, her Check no. 5477. Deposit to Undeposited Funds.

1 rock fountain	$ 275.00
2 pumps	60.00
Total sale of merchandise	$ 335.00
Sales tax (0.08 × $335)	26.80
Custom design services (4 hrs)	300.00
Total sale for cash	$ 661.80

To record a cash sale of inventory:

1. On the title bar, click the Create icon and then click *Sales Receipt* in the *Customers* column.
2. At the *Choose a customer* drop-down list, click *Kate Whelan*.
3. In the *Sales Receipt date* field, select *03/22/2019*.
4. In the *Sales Receipt no.* field, key 1039, if necessary.
5. At the *Payment method* drop-down list, click *Check*.
6. In the *Reference no.* field, key 5477.
7. Confirm the *Deposit to* field displays *Undeposited Funds*.
8. Complete the rest of the fields for each item in the same manner as you would in the Invoice window. See Figure 6–N.

FIGURE 6–N Sales Receipt Window—Completed

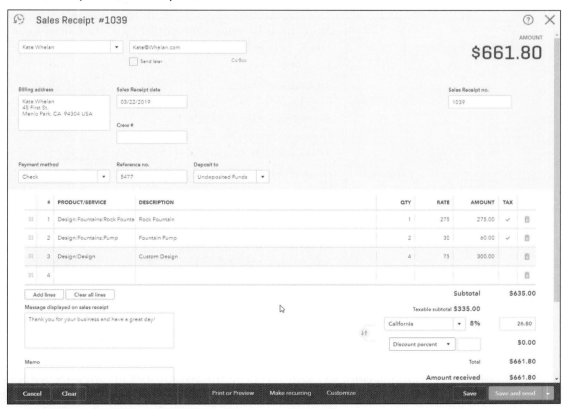

9. Confirm the information is correct and then click *Save and close* from the Save and send button list to return to the Dashboard.

Accounting Concept

For a sale of inventory products for cash, the general ledger posting is as follows:

Undeposited Funds			Sale of Inventory			1 fount. @ 275 = 275
Dr	Cr		Dr	Cr		2 pumps @ 30 = 60
661.80				335		335

Sales Tax Payable			Service Revenue	
Dr	Cr		Dr	Cr
	26.80			300

The cost of the inventory sold and resulting decline in the inventory is recorded as follows:

Cost of Goods Sold			Inventory			1 fount. @ 125 = 125
Dr	Cr		Dr	Cr		2 pumps @ 20 = 40
165				165		165

Practice Exercise   6–3

Record the following transactions in the Invoice or Sales Receipt window:

Mar. 27	Sold the following on account to Mark Cho, Invoice no. 1040, Terms Net 30 Days:	
	1 outdoor table	$ 400.00
	4 outdoor chairs	800.00
	Total sale of merchandise	$ 1,200.00
	Sales tax (0.08 × $1,200)	96.00
	Custom design services (6 hrs)	450.00
	Total sale on account	$ 1,746.00
Mar. 29	Sold the following for cash to Wedding Planning by Whitney, Sales Receipt no. 1041, her Check no. 1361:	
	1 rock fountain	$ 275.00
	2 pumps	60.00
	Total sale of merchandise	$ 335.00
	Sales tax (0.08 × $335)	26.80
	Custom design services (6 hrs)	450.00
	Total sale for cash	$ 811.80

The Inventory Quantity Adjustment Window

In QuickBooks Online, you use the Inventory Quantity Adjustment activity window to record changes in the inventory from events other than a purchase or sale. If inventory items are lost, stolen, damaged, or spoiled, the resulting change in the inventory quantity and/or value is recorded in this window as an **inventory adjustment**. The reduction is considered a loss or expense with a corresponding reduction of the inventory asset account. The account used to record the reduction to inventory is the Inventory Adjustment or Shrinkage account. This is a Cost of Goods Sold account, and it will be included in the *Cost of Goods Sold* section of the income statement.

Activities identified as adjustments to inventory are recorded in the Inventory Quantity Adjustment window. All transactions entered in this window result in a debit to the Inventory Adjustment or Shrinkage account and a credit to the appropriate inventory asset account. QuickBooks Online records the transaction as follows:

	Inventory Adjustment (Loss/Expense)	XXX	
	Inventory (Asset)		XXX

On March 31, 2019, Craig's Design discovers that a pump is damaged and cannot be returned to the manufacturer.

To record an inventory adjustment:

1. On the title bar, click the Create icon and then click *Inventory Qty Adjustment* in the *Other* column.
2. In the *Adjustment date* field, choose *03/31/2019*.
3. At the *Inventory adjustment account* drop-down list, choose *Inventory Shrinkage*, if necessary.
4. In the *Reference no.* field, key Inv. Adj. 1.
5. In the *PRODUCT* column, choose *Pump*. The *QTY ON HAND* column should display *26*.
6. In the *NEW QTY* column, key 25 and then move to the next field. The *CHANGE IN QTY* column should read *-1*. See Figure 6–O.
7. Confirm the information is correct and then click the Save and close button to return to the Dashboard.

FIGURE 6–O
Inventory Quantity Adjustment Window— Complete

Activities

The Sales Tax Center Window

In QuickBooks Online, the Sales Tax Center window is used to record the remittance of sales tax charged to customers to the proper tax agency. QuickBooks Online uses the default accounts Sales Tax Payable and Cash.

QuickBooks Online records the transaction as follows:

		Sales Tax Payable		XXX	
		Cash			XXX

At the conclusion of each month, Craig's Design remits the sales tax collected from customers to the appropriate state agency. In this chapter, we will use the sales tax data previously entered by QuickBooks Online in the Test Drive sample company file. Since the sales that you have entered may be outside the date range for the sales tax remittance, we will use the data residing in the Test Drive sample company file.

HINT

The Balance amount may vary depending on when you access the Test Drive.

To pay the sales tax collected:
1. On the Navigation bar, click Taxes. The Sales Tax Center window opens with the Test Drive data for sales tax displayed. See Figure 6–P.

FIGURE 6–P Sales Tax Center Window

2. Click the Record Tax Payment button. The Record Sales Tax Payment window appears. See Figure 6–Q.

FIGURE 6–Q
Record Sales Tax Payment Window

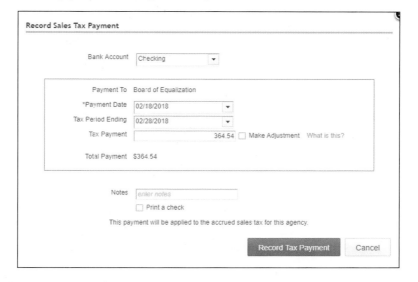

3. Confirm the *Bank Account* field displays *Checking*.
4. In the *Payment Date* and *Tax Period Ending* fields, accept the default dates.
5. Accept the amount in the *Tax Payment* field. Your amount may differ as the Test Drive transactions are updated periodically by QuickBooks Online.
6. Confirm the information is correct and then click the Record Tax Payment button. You return to the Sales Tax Center window with the payment recorded. Note the balance for Board of Equalization is $0. The liability is now paid. See Figure 6–R.

FIGURE 6–R Record Sales Tax Payment Window—Completed

7. Return to the Dashboard.

Accounting Concept

For a payment of sales tax, the general ledger posting is as follows:

Cash - Checking			Sales Tax Payable		
Dr	Cr		Dr	Cr	
	Pay	324.54	Pay	324.54	324.54
				Bal	0

Activities

Make Deposits

Recall from Chapter 4 that Craig's Design deposits all funds collected from customers at the end of the month. Before reviewing the reports for the month, the deposits should be recorded.

Practice Exercise 6–4

Record the following transaction in the Deposits window:

Mar. 31	Deposit all undeposited funds to the Cash - Checking account. *QuickCheck:* $3,536.12

Reports

Inventory Reports, Accounting Reports, and Financial Statements

Recall from Chapter 1 that Reports, the fourth level of operation, reflect the activities recorded in the various Lists and Activities windows. Inventory activities entered in the various windows flow into the reports, many of which should be reviewed and printed at the end of the month.

Inventory Reports from the Reports Menu

Inventory reports, such as the Inventory Valuation Detail Report, Purchases by Product/Service Detail Report, and Sales by Product/Service Detail Report, help the company track and manage its inventory.

Inventory Valuation Detail Report

The Inventory Valuation Detail Report displays the transactions affecting each inventory item along with the quantity and value on hand for each.

To view and print the Inventory Valuation Detail Report:
1. On the Navigation bar, click Reports and then click the All link, if necessary.
2. In the *Sales and Customers* section, click *Inventory Valuation Detail.*
3. In the date fields, choose *03/01/2019* and *03/31/2019* and then click the Run report button.
4. Print the report. See Figure 6–S.
5. Return to the Dashboard.

FIGURE 6–S Inventory Valuation Detail Report

EX6 [Your Name] Craig's Design and Landscaping Services
INVENTORY VALUATION DETAIL
March 2019

DATE	TRANSACTION TYPE	NUM	NAME	QTY	RATE	FIFO COST	QTY ON HAND	ASSET VALUE
Design								
Fountains								
Pump								
Beginning Balance							25.00	250.00
03/13/2019	Check	72	Hicks Hardware	5.00	20.00	100.00	30.00	350.00
03/22/2019	Sales Receipt	1039	Kate Whelan	-2.00	20.00	-40.00	28.00	310.00
03/29/2019	Sales Receipt	1041	Wedding Planning by Whitney	-2.00	20.00	-40.00	26.00	270.00
03/31/2019	Inventory Qty Adjust	Inv. Adj.1		-1.00	20.00	-20.00	25.00	250.00
Total for Pump				0.00		$0.00	25.00	$250.00
Rock Fountain								
Beginning Balance							2.00	250.00
03/01/2019	Check	71	Norton Lumber and Building Materials	2.00	125.00	250.00	4.00	500.00
03/22/2019	Sales Receipt	1039	Kate Whelan	-1.00	125.00	-125.00	3.00	375.00
03/29/2019	Sales Receipt	1041	Wedding Planning by Whitney	-1.00	125.00	-125.00	2.00	250.00
Total for Rock Fountain				0.00		$0.00	2.00	$250.00
Total for Fountains				0.00		$0.00	27.00	$500.00
Total for Design				0.00		$0.00	27.00	$500.00
Landscaping								
Sprinklers								
Sprinkler Heads								
Beginning Balance							25.00	18.75
Total for Sprinkler Heads							25.00	$18.75
Total for Sprinklers							25.00	$18.75
Total for Landscaping							25.00	$18.75
Outdoor Furniture								
Outdoor Chairs								
03/01/2019	Inventory Starting Value	START		0.00	100.00	0.00	0.00	0.00
03/01/2019	Bill	C-588	Greene Grove Furniture Co.	10.00	100.00	1,000.00	10.00	1,000.00
03/15/2019	Invoice	1038	Kookies by Kathy	-4.00	100.00	-400.00	6.00	600.00
03/27/2019	Invoice	1040	Mark Cho	-4.00	100.00	-400.00	2.00	200.00
Total for Outdoor Chairs				2.00		$200.00	2.00	$200.00
Outdoor Tables								
03/01/2019	Inventory Starting Value	START		0.00	200.00	0.00	0.00	0.00
03/06/2019	Bill	C-610	Greene Grove Furniture Co.	4.00	200.00	800.00	4.00	800.00
03/15/2019	Invoice	1038	Kookies by Kathy	-1.00	200.00	-200.00	3.00	600.00
03/27/2019	Invoice	1040	Mark Cho	-1.00	200.00	-200.00	2.00	400.00
Total for Outdoor Tables				2.00		$400.00	2.00	$400.00
Total for Outdoor Furniture				4.00		$600.00	4.00	$600.00

Purchases by Product/Service Detail Report

The Purchases by Product/Service Detail Report displays all purchases of inventory items grouped by category and product. The report shows the dates products were purchased, the quantity acquired, and the rate paid.

To view and print the Purchases by Product/Service Detail Report:
1. On the Navigation bar, click Reports.
2. In the *Expenses and Vendors* section, click *Purchases by Product/Service Detail.*
3. In the date fields, choose *03/01/2019* and *03/31/2019* and then click the Run report button.
4. Print the report. See Figure 6–T.
5. Return to the Dashboard.

FIGURE 6–T Purchases by Product/Service Detail Report

EX6 [Your Name] Craig's Design and Landscaping Services

PURCHASES BY PRODUCT/SERVICE DETAIL

March 2019

DATE	TRANSACTION TYPE	NUM	VENDOR	MEMO/DESCRIPTION	QTY	RATE	AMOUNT	BALANCE
Design								
Fountains								
Pump								
03/13/2019	Check	72	Hicks Hardware	Fountain Pump	5.00	20.00	100.00	100.00
03/31/2019	Inventory Qty Adjust	Inv. Adj.1			1.00	20.00	20.00	120.00
03/31/2019	Inventory Qty Adjust	Inv. Adj.1			-1.00	20.00	-20.00	100.00
03/31/2019	Inventory Qty Adjust	Inv. Adj.1			-1.00			100.00
Total for Pump					4.00		$100.00	
Rock Fountain								
03/01/2019	Check	71	Norton Lumber and Building Materials	Rock Fountain	2.00	125.00	250.00	250.00
Total for Rock Fountain					2.00		$250.00	
Total for Fountains					6.00		$350.00	
Total for Design					6.00		$350.00	
Outdoor Furniture								
Outdoor Chairs								
03/01/2019	Inventory Starting Value	START		Outdoor Chairs - Opening inventory and value	0.00	100.00	0.00	0.00
03/01/2019	Bill	C-588	Greene Grove Furniture Co.	Outdoor Chairs	10.00	100.00	1,000.00	1,000.00
Total for Outdoor Chairs					10.00		$1,000.00	
Outdoor Tables								
03/01/2019	Inventory Starting Value	START		Outdoor Tables - Opening inventory and value	0.00	200.00	0.00	0.00
03/06/2019	Bill	C-610	Greene Grove Furniture Co.	Outdoor Tables	4.00	200.00	800.00	800.00
Total for Outdoor Tables					4.00		$800.00	
Total for Outdoor Furniture					14.00		$1,800.00	
TOTAL					20.00		$2,150.00	

Sales By Product/Service Detail Report

The Sales by Product/Service Detail Report displays all sales information for each product. The report shows customer name, sales price per unit, quantity sold, and total sales.

To view and print the Sales by Product/Service Detail Report:
1. On the Navigation bar, click Reports.
2. In the *Sales and Customers* section, click *Sales by Product/Service Detail.*
3. In the date fields, choose *03/01/2019* and *03/31/2019* and then click the Run report button. See Figure 6–U.
4. Print the report.
5. Keep the Sales by Product/Service Detail Report open for the next activity.

The Sales by Product/Service Detail Report, like several reports reviewed in prior chapters, allows you to drill down to view the source transaction. Craig's Design wishes to see the detail of the sale to Kookies by Kathy on March 15, 2019, Invoice no. 1038.

FIGURE 6–U Sales by Product/Service Detail Report

To drill down to a specific sale transaction:

1. Place the mouse pointer over *Kookies by Kathy* for the transaction on 03/15/2019 until the name becomes a link.
2. Click the name link. The Invoice window for this transaction appears. See Figure 6–V.
3. Close the Invoice window and click Dashboard on the Navigation bar to return to the Dashboard.

FIGURE 6–V Invoice Window

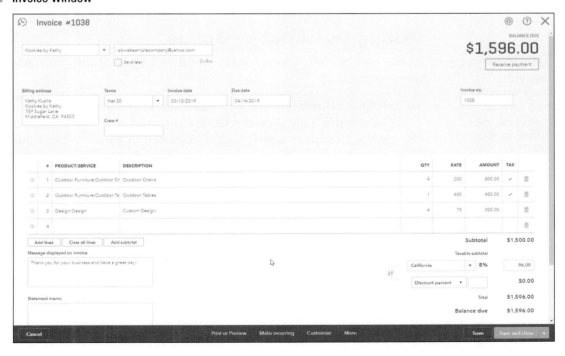

Accounting Reports and Financial Statements

At the end of each month, the Journal Report should be viewed and printed. Your printout should look like Figure 6–W.

FIGURE 6–W Journal Report—Partial

EX6 [Your Name] Craig's Design and Landscaping Services
JOURNAL
March 2019

DATE	TRANSACTION TYPE	NUM	NAME	MEMO/DESCRIPTION	ACCOUNT	DEBIT	CREDIT
03/01/2019	Inventory Starting Value	START		Outdoor Chairs - Opening inventory and value	Opening Balance Equity	$0.00	
				Outdoor Chairs - Opening inventory and value	Inventory Asset	$0.00	
						$0.00	
03/01/2019	Inventory Starting Value	START		Outdoor Tables - Opening inventory and value	Opening Balance Equity	$0.00	
				Outdoor Tables - Opening inventory and value	Inventory Asset	$0.00	
						$0.00	
03/01/2019	Bill	C-588	Greene Grove Furniture Co.		Accounts Payable (A/P)		$1,000.00
				Outdoor Chairs	Inventory Asset	$1,000.00	
						$1,000.00	**$1,000.00**
03/01/2019	Check	71	Norton Lumber and Building Materials		Checking		$250.00
				Rock Fountain	Inventory Asset	$250.00	
						$250.00	**$250.00**
03/06/2019	Bill	C-610	Greene Grove Furniture Co.		Accounts Payable (A/P)		$800.00
				Outdoor Tables	Inventory Asset	$800.00	
						$800.00	**$800.00**
03/13/2019	Check	72	Hicks Hardware		Checking		$100.00
				Fountain Pump	Inventory Asset	$100.00	
						$100.00	**$100.00**
03/15/2019	Invoice	1038	Kookies by Kathy		Accounts Receivable (A/R)	$1,596.00	
				Outdoor Chairs	Inventory Asset		$400.00
				Outdoor Chairs	Cost of Goods Sold	$400.00	

Exiting QuickBooks Online

HINT

Any work you do in the Test Drive sample company file is not saved when you exit out of the company file.

At the end of each session, you should exit QuickBooks Online and close the browser.

To exit QuickBooks Online and close the browser:
1. On the title bar, click the Gear icon.
2. At the Company window, click *Sign Out* in the *Profile* column. This closes the company file and exits QuickBooks Online.
3. Close your browser.

To view and print inventory reports:
1. On the Navigation bar, click Reports.
2. In either the *Sales and Customers* or *Expenses and Vendors* sections, click the appropriate report.
3. Select the appropriate dates in the date fields.
4. Click the Run report button.
5. Print the report.

Key Concepts

Select the letter of the item that best matches each definition.

a. Bill window *Items details* section
b. Inventory Quantity Adjustment
c. Products and Services List
d. Inventory category
e. Purchases by Product/Service Detail

f. sales tax
g. Sales Tax Center
h. Inventory Valuation Detail
i. Sales by Product/Service Detail
j. Record Sales Tax Payment

_____ 1. Report that displays all transactions affecting each inventory item.

_____ 2. A way of grouping similar inventory products in the Products and Services List.

_____ 3. Window used to record purchases of inventory items on account.

_____ 4. Window used to adjust quantity of inventory as a result of damage or loss.

_____ 5. Contains a file of all inventory items.

_____ 6. Window used to remit sales tax collected from customers to the appropriate state tax agency.

_____ 7. Report that displays each purchase transaction for inventory items.

_____ 8. Window in the Sales Tax Center used to enter the amount of the payment.

_____ 9. Report that shows sales information for each inventory item.

_____ 10. Tax collected by a retailer from a customer on sales of goods.

Procedure Check

Write a response for each of the following prompts.
1. Your company will be selling a new product. Describe the steps that must be taken to add the new product to the system.
2. Explain the difference between using the *Account details* section versus the *Item details* section of the Bill window.
3. Your company wishes to determine which inventory items generate the most revenue. How could you use QuickBooks Online to develop this information?
4. At year-end, you wish to confirm the quantity on hand for each inventory item. How would you use QuickBooks Online reports to determine the quantity and value of the ending inventory?

5. Discuss the advantages of using a computerized accounting system to maintain a perpetual inventory system.

Case Problem

Demonstrate your knowledge of the QuickBooks Online features discussed in this chapter by completing the following case problem.

On June 1, 2019, Olivia Chen began her business, Olivia's Web Solutions. In the first month of business, Olivia set up the office, provided web page design and internet consulting services, and recorded month-end activity. In July, the second month of business, Olivia will purchase and sell inventory items of computer hardware and software. For customers who purchase merchandise inventory, the terms of payment are Net 30 days. Quickbooks Online will use the New York address of the company to determine the sales tax rate of 8.625%. The company file includes the information for Olivia's Web Solutions as of July 1, 2019.

1. Sign in to QuickBooks Online.
2. Change the name to **OWS6 [*Your Name*] Olivia's Web Solutions**.
3. Unlike the Test Drive sample company, you will need to activate the Sales Tax Center to track sales tax by following these steps:
    a. On the Navigation bar, click Taxes. The Sales Tax Center window displays.
    b. Click the Set up sales tax button
    c. At the Set up sales tax window, confirm the address, click the Looks good button, and then click Next. (QuickBooks Online will use the address to determine the sales tax rate.)
    d. Check *No* at the *Do you need to collect sales tax outside of New York?* question. You will then move to the Can you tell us about who you pay? window.
    e. In the *When did your current tax period start?* drop-down list, choose *June*.
    f. In the *How often do you have to file a tax return for this agency?* drop-down list, choose *Quarterly*.
    g. In the *When did you start collecting sales tax for this agency?* field, key 07/01/2019 and then click Next.
    h. At the Sales tax is set up! window, click the Got it button.
    i. Return to the Dashboard.
4. Add the following products to the Products and Services List:
Name:	Scanners
SKU:	H101
Category:	Hardware (add new)
Initial quantity on hand:	0
As of date:	06/01/2019
Inventory asset account:	1265 Inventory of Scanners

Sales/Purchasing	
information:	Scanners
Sales price/rate:	600
Income account:	4065 Sale of Scanners
Is taxable:	(Insert a check mark.)
Sales tax category:	Professional Services
What you sell:	Computer scanner
Cost:	300
Expense account:	5065 Cost of Scanners Sold

Name:	Desktop Publishing Software
SKU:	S101
Category:	Software Products (add new)
Initial quantity on hand:	0
As of date:	06/01/2019
Inventory asset account:	1275 Inventory of Desktop Pub. Software

Sales/Purchasing	
information:	Desktop Publishing Software
Sales price/rate:	200
Income account:	4075 Sale of Desktop Pub. Software
Is taxable:	(Insert a check mark.)
Sales tax category:	Professional Services
What you sell:	Tangible canned software
Cost:	100
Expense account:	5075 Cost of Desktop Pub. Software Sold

Name:	Computers
SKU:	H102
Category:	Hardware
Initial quantity on hand:	0
As of date:	June 1, 2019
Inventory asset account:	1260 Inventory of Computers
Sales/Purchasing	
information:	Computer System
Sales price/rate:	2000
Income account:	4060 Sale of Computers
Is taxable:	(Insert a check mark.)
Sales tax category:	Professional Services
What you sell:	Computer hardware
Cost:	1000
Expense account:	5060 Cost of Computers Sold

Name:	HTML Software
SKU:	S102
Category:	Software Products
Initial quantity on hand:	0
As of date:	06/01/2019
Inventory asset account:	1270 Inventory of HTML Software

Sales information:	HTML Software
Sales price/rate:	150
Income account:	4070 Sale of HTML Software
Is taxable:	(Insert a check mark.)
Sales tax category:	Professional Services
What you sell:	Tangible canned software
Cost:	75
Expense account:	5070 Cost of HTML Software Sold

5. Add the following vendors to the Vendor List:

First name:	Customer
Last name:	Service
Company:	Computec Computers
Display name as:	Computec Computers
Address:	3631 Gate Blvd.
	Greenboro NC 27407
Phone:	702-555-6564
Mobile:	702-555-6563
Terms:	Net 30
Opening balance:	0
as of:	July 1, 2019

First name:	Customer
Last name:	Service
Company:	InterSoft Development Co.
Display name as:	InterSoft Development Co.
Address:	556 Route 347
	Hauppauge NY 11654
Phone:	631-555-3634
Mobile:	631-555-3635
Terms:	Net 30
Opening balance:	0
as of:	July 1, 2019

First name:	Customer
Last name:	Service
Company:	Scanntronix
Display name as:	Scanntronix
Address:	2554 Bedford Rd.
	Boston MA 02164
Phone:	617-555-8778
Mobile:	617-555-8776
Terms:	Net 30
Opening balance:	0
as of:	July 1, 2019

First name:	Customer
Last name:	Service
Company:	Textpro Software
Display name as:	Textpro Software
Address:	877 Route 5
	Ft. Lauderdale FL 70089

Phone:	615-555-4545
Mobile:	615-555-4546
Terms:	Net 30
Opening balance:	0
as of:	July 1, 2019

6. Using the appropriate window, record the following transactions for July:

Jul. 2   Purchased 10 computers on account from Computec Computers at $1,000 each, its Bill no. 068788.

Jul. 2   Purchased 20 scanners on account from Scanntronix at $300 each, its Bill no. 10089-30.

Jul. 2   Purchased 10 desktop publishing software packages from Textpro Software at $100 each, paid immediately, Check no. 9. Do not print check.

Jul. 2   Purchased 20 HTML software packages from InterSoft Development Co. at $75 each, paid immediately, Check no. 10. Do not print check.

HINT

The New York state sales tax rate is 8.625%.

Jul. 5   Sold 3 computers for $2,000 each, 2 scanners for $600 each, and 1 desktop publishing software package for $200 on account to Long Island Water Works, Invoice no. 1011, Net 30. In addition, provided 10 hours of internet consulting services.

Jul. 6   Sold 2 computers on account to Miguel's Restaurant, Invoice no. 1012, Net 30. In addition, provided 8 hours of web page design services.

Jul. 9   Sold 1 scanner for $600 and 1 desktop publishing software package for $200 to the Singh Family, Sales Receipt no. 1013. Received payment immediately, their Check no. 901.

Jul. 12   Sold 1 computer for $2,000, 2 scanners for $600 each, and 1 HTML software package for $150 on account to Breathe Easy, Invoice no. 1014, Net 30. In addition, provided 12 hours of internet consulting services.

Jul. 13   Received full payment from Long Island Water Works for Invoice no. 1011, Check no. 125671.

Jul. 16   Purchased 5 computers on account from Computec Computers at $1,000 each, its Bill no. 072445.

Jul. 16   Purchased 5 desktop publishing software packages from Textpro Software at $100 each, paid immediately, Check no. 11. Do not print check.

Jul. 19   Sold 1 computer for $2,000 and 1 desktop publishing software package for $200 to the Schneider Family, Sales Receipt no. 1015. Received payment immediately, their Check no. 899.

Jul. 20   Sold 3 computers for $2,000 each, 3 scanners for $600 each, and 2 desktop publishing software packages for $200 each on account to South Shore School District, Invoice no. 1016, terms Net 30. In addition, provided 16 hours of web page design services.

Jul. 26	Received full payment from Miguel's Restaurant for Invoice no. 1012, Check no. 4110.
Jul. 27	Received full payment from Breathe Easy for Invoice nos. 1006 (remaining balance) and 1014, Check no. 1874.
Jul. 30	Purchased 5 computers on account from Computec Computers at $1,000 each, its Bill no. 073111.
Jul. 30	Paid in full Computec Computers, Bill no. 068788 (Check no. 12). Do not print check.
Jul. 30	Paid in full Scanntronix, Bill no. 10089-30 (Check no. 13). Do not print check.
Jul. 30	Upon reviewing the inventory, Olivia discovers 1 HTML software package was damaged, through no fault of the manufacturer, and cannot be sold. Adjust the inventory on hand to remove 1 HTML software package from the inventory. Inv. Adj. 1. Use the Inventory Adjustment account.
Jul. 31	Deposit all undeposited funds to the Cash - Checking account.

7. Display and print the following reports for July 1, 2019, to July 31, 2019:
   a. Inventory Valuation Detail
   b. Sales by Product/Service Detail
   c. Purchases by Product/Service Detail
   d. Journal
   e. Profit and Loss (June 1, 2019–July 31, 2019)
   f. Balance Sheet (June 1, 2019–July 31, 2019)

CHAPTER 7

Banking

Transferring Funds, Reconciling Cash Accounts, and Managing Credit Card Charges

Objectives

- Transfer funds between accounts using the Transfer window
- Reconcile cash accounts using the Reconcile windows
- Enter credit card charges using the Expense window
- Pay credit card charges using the Credit Card Credit window
- Display and print banking-related reports and accounting reports

An integral part of operating any business is effectively managing cash. This usually involves maintaining cash in one or more bank accounts. In addition, it involves transferring funds among the bank accounts, reconciling account balances, using credit cards for business purchases, and making credit card payments. QuickBooks Online allows you to transfer funds from one bank account to another, process the month-end bank reconciliation, and enter and pay credit card charges.

Many companies have more than one checking account. The regular bank account, commonly known as the *operating account*, is used to pay bills and collect and deposit receivables and other funds. Usually, a company maintains a separate account for savings. Funds will be transferred periodically to and from each account.

As a business grows in complexity, the need for special-purpose accounts grows correspondingly. For example, many companies have interest-bearing money market accounts that are designed to hold excess funds temporarily. These funds earn interest until they are needed for an operating activity, at which time they are transferred to a checking account.

transfer funds The movement of money from one account to another account.

Companies can **transfer funds** as needed among the different accounts, often via online banking connections. With QuickBooks Online, you can use the Transfer window to record and monitor the transfer of funds between accounts.

Companies typically receive a statement from the bank at the end of the month detailing the activity the bank has recorded in the company's checking account, along with a month-end balance. Often, this balance does not agree with the company's records. Differences in the account balance usually occur because the bank has recorded transactions that the company does not know about. **Bank reconciliation** is a procedure used to determine the correct cash balance by accounting for these differences and ensuring that they are not a result of errors, either by the bank or the company, or from theft of funds. In addition, if the bank makes changes to the company's account, the company will have to record transactions in the general ledger accounts to reflect these changes. In QuickBooks Online, the Reconcile windows are used to reconcile the balance per the bank statement to the balance per the accounting records.

bank reconciliation The procedure used to determine the correct cash balance in an account by comparing the activity recorded in the account with the activity recorded on the bank statement.

credit card charge Expenditure charged to a credit card to be paid at a later date.

Many companies use credit cards to pay bills. These **credit card charges** allow the company to track expenses of a specific nature, such as travel and entertainment expenses, and to defer payment of expenses as needed. In QuickBooks Online, the Expense window is used to record credit card expenditures. The Credit Card Credit window is used to pay the credit card balance.

In this chapter, our sample company, Craig's Design and Landscaping Services, will transfer funds between accounts, process bank reconciliations, and use a credit card to pay for expenses

QuickBooks Online versus Manual Accounting: Banking

Banking activities in both manual and computerized accounting systems require a company to record transfers of funds among bank accounts, reconcile each bank account balance to the company's balances, and track charges and payments by credit card.

Funds Transfer

In a manual accounting system, when funds are transferred to or from one cash account to another, the transaction can be handled in several ways. Transfers from the company's operating account can be recorded in the cash payments journal or the general journal. If the cash payments journal is used for transfers out of the cash accounts, the cash receipts journal will be used for transfers into the cash accounts. Similarly, if the general journal is used to record the transfer out of the cash accounts, it also will be used to record the transfers into the cash accounts. A cash payments journal procedure is used when a check is drawn from a cash account to accomplish the transfer. If the transfer is accomplished via a bank credit and debit memo, electronic transfer, or phone transfer, the general journal procedure is used.

In QuickBooks Online, transfers among bank accounts, if not done by check, are recorded in the Transfer activity window. This window indicates the cash accounts involved in the transfer and the amount of the transfer.

Bank Reconciliation

The steps to complete a bank reconciliation in QuickBooks Online are similar to those in a manual accounting system. The company receives a statement from the bank detailing the activity in the account for the month. The statement shows the deposits (or other additions) to the account along with the checks that have cleared (were paid by) the bank. If the account has earned interest, it is added to the balance by the bank. If the bank has charged any fees, called *service* or *bank charges*, they will be deducted from the account. Other items that may appear are non-sufficient funds (NSF) checks, credit memos (additions), or debit memos (subtractions). The bank statement is compared with the company's accounting records, and any differences are identified. These differences are called **reconciling items**, and they generally fall into three categories: timing differences, such as a **deposit in transit** or an **outstanding check**; omissions, such as the interest recorded by the bank not yet recorded by the company; or errors by either party. The first two are normal differences that are expected as part of the reconciliation process. If all timing differences and omissions are accounted for and there are no errors, the adjusted bank balances will agree with the adjusted balance for the company's books. The account is then said to be reconciled. However, if there is an error, a difference will remain until the source of the mistake is found.

In QuickBooks Online, the bank reconciliation procedure is carried out using the Reconcile windows. Once a cash account is identified, the windows display all activity to the account, including deposits or other additions (debits) and checks or other reductions (credits). This information is compared with the bank statement to reconcile the account.

Credit Card Charges

In a manual accounting system, a credit card charge is usually recorded when the bill is paid by the company or tracked as part of accounts payable. This often results in expenses being recorded in periods after they are actually incurred. In QuickBooks Online, a credit card charge can be recorded immediately when it is incurred by using the Expense window. The program also tracks the resulting credit card liability, which will be paid at a later date and separate from accounts payable using the Credit Card Credit window.

reconciling items
Differences between the bank statement and the company's records that have to be reconciled so that the cash balance in the company's accounting records agrees with the balance in its bank statement.

deposit in transit
A deposit recorded on the company's books, usually at the end of the month, yet deposited too late to be on the current month's bank statement.

outstanding check
A check written and recorded by a company that has not yet been paid by the bank.

This method ensures that assets and/or expenses are recorded in the proper time period and that the credit card liability is tracked.

Chapter Problem

In this chapter, Craig's Design and Landscaping Services will transfer funds among the company's bank accounts, prepare a reconciliation of the cash accounts, and enter credit card transactions. This information, along with beginning balances, is contained in the QuickBooks Online Test Drive sample company file.

To begin, open the Test Drive sample company file for Craig's Design and Landscaping Services. Change the company name in the file to **EX7** [*Your Name*] **Craig's Design and Landscaping Services** and key 12-3456788 in the *EIN* field. You may also want to extend the time-out period to three hours.

Activities

The Transfer Window

As you know, the third level of operations in QuickBooks Online is Activities, or recording the daily transactions of the business. In QuickBooks Online, you use the Transfer window to record the movement of funds among the cash accounts of the business. If you transfer funds by writing a check from one cash account to be deposited into another cash account, you can use the Check window. However, when you transfer funds via bank memo, telephone, ATM, or online services, you use the Transfer window to record the transaction. In the Transfer window, since there are no default accounts, you identify the source (transferor) cash account, the receiving (transferee) account, and the amount to be transferred. The transaction is recorded as follows:

		Transferee Cash Account	XXX	
		Transferor Cash Account		XXX

The QuickBooks Online Transfer window appears in Figure 7–A.

FIGURE 7–A
Transfer Window

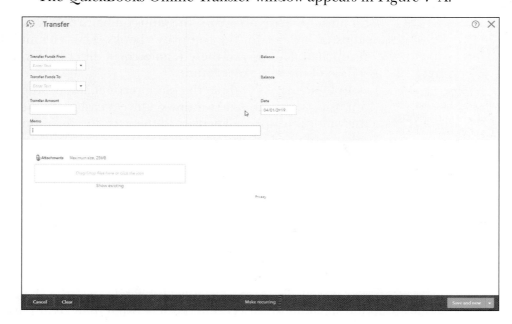

The Transfer window also displays the current balance of the source account, thus preventing you from overdrawing it.

On April 30, 2019, Craig's Design wants you to transfer $500 from the company's Cash - Savings account to its Cash - Checking account so there are sufficient funds in that account to pay May's operating expenses.

To transfer funds:

1. On the title bar, click the Create icon and then click *Transfer* in the *Other* column.
2. At the *Transfer Funds From* drop-down list, click *Savings*. The balance in the account displays.
3. At the *Transfer Funds To* drop-down list, click *Checking*.
4. In the *Transfer Amount* field, key 500.
5. In the *Date* field, choose *04/30/2019*.
6. In the *Memo* field, key Funds Transfer. See Figure 7–B.
7. Confirm the information is correct and then click *Save and close* from the Save and new button list to return to the Dashboard.

FIGURE 7–B Transfer Window—Completed

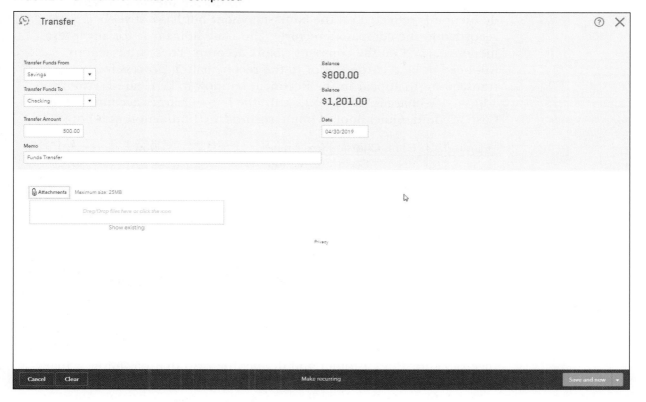

Accounting Concept

For a transfer of funds between accounts, the general ledger posting is as follows:

Cash - Savings				Cash - Checking			
Dr		**Cr**		**Dr**		**Cr**	
Bal	800.00	Trf	500.00	Bal	1.201.00		
				Trf	500.00		
Bal	300.00			Bal	1,701.00		

The Reconcile Windows

In QuickBooks Online, Activities identified as bank reconciliation are processed in the Reconcile windows. The reconciliation procedure in QuickBooks Online accomplishes two purposes. First, it ensures that the company's cash records are correct and agree with that of the bank. Second, transactions missing from the company's records that are discovered during the reconciling process can be recorded at this time.

The Reconcile windows display all additions to a given account, such as deposits and transfers in, and all reductions to the account, such as checks written and transfers out. Using the Reconcile windows, you can compare the information for each account with the bank statement for that account. You can indicate the transactions that have cleared or have been paid by the bank by placing a check mark next to the transaction, and you can add transactions recorded on the bank statement that are not yet on the company's books.

As part of the reconciling process, you may need to make adjustments to the cash account. For example, the bank may have deducted service charges from the company's bank account during the month. This deduction is reflected on the bank statement but has not yet been recorded in the company's records. The same holds true for any interest income earned on the company's bank account. These transactions will need to be recorded prior to the reconciliation process for the transactions to appear in the Reconcile window to be cleared. When you add service charges, the accounts are the Bank Charges account and the Cash account. QuickBooks Online records the transaction as follows:

		Bank Charges (expense)		XXX	
		Cash - Checking			XXX

When you record interest income, the accounts are the Cash - Checking account and the Interest Earned account. QuickBooks Online records the transaction as follows:

		Cash - Checking		XXX	
		Interest Earned			XXX

If the bank records an NSF check from a customer, QuickBooks Online does not automatically record the transaction. Instead, you must record the transaction in the Journal window to reestablish the accounts receivable for this customer and deduct the cash that was never actually collected.

QuickBooks Online contains two separate, sequential Reconcile windows. The first time you reconcile an account, the Find your balance window appears. Bypass that by clicking the Reconcile your account button and then bypass the Reconcile like a pro window. The first reconcile window, titled Reconcile an account, appears. This window allows you to select a bank account to reconcile, enter the ending statement balance and statement date, and view reconciliation history and reports. See Figure 7–C.

FIGURE 7–C
Reconcile an Account
Window

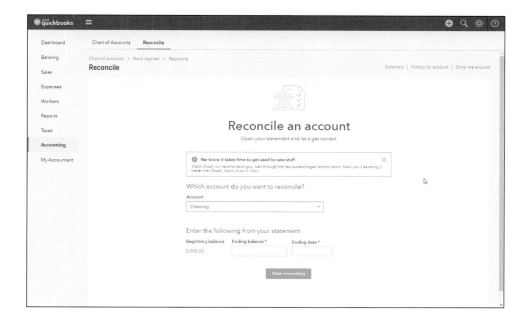

Once you click the Start reconciling button at the first window, the second Reconcile window appears, displaying all checks and other payments and all deposits and other credits to this account. You will then select the transactions that have cleared. See Figure 7–D.

FIGURE 7–D
Start Reconciling
Window

This window contains the following links:

Payments link	Select this link to display all checks and other payments from the account.
Deposits link	Select this link to display all deposits and other additions to the accounts.
All link	Select this link to display all activity in the account.

If all reconciling items are accounted for, the difference will be zero. If after completing the reconciliation process a difference remains, it is probably due to an error by either the bank or the company. You must identify the error and correct it before completing the reconciliation. When the difference amount is zero, click the Finish Now button. The account is now reconciled, and a reconciliation report can be printed.

Interest Earned and Bank Charges

Unlike the complete QuickBooks Online version, the Test Drive does not provide data input fields for interest earned and bank charges as part of the Reconciliation windows. Both will need to be entered prior to beginning the reconciliation process. The interest earned and the bank charges will be entered via the Journal window as a journal entry in the manner covered in Chapter 5. These are not adjusting entries.

For the Olivia's Web Solutions file you have built with this textbook, the Reconcile an account window will contain input fields for both bank service charges and interest income. See Figure 7–E.

FIGURE 7–E

Reconcile an Account Window

For the Case Problem at the end of the chapter, it will not be necessary to enter these amounts in the Journal window prior to the reconciliation process. During the reconciliation process, you will enter the amount of the service charges and interest earned at the date of the reconciliation in the Reconcile an account window. However, for the chapter problem, you will enter these amounts via journal entries.

Reconciling Using the Test Drive Data

As you recall from preceding chapters, the QuickBooks Online Test Drive sample company file comes with previously entered transactions. The dates of these transactions adjust depending upon when you access the program. For example, if you access the file in October 2018, the current month will be October 2018, and transaction dates may go as far back as May 2018. If you access the program in January 2019, transaction dates will go back to August 2018, and so on.

This text was written in February 2018. Therefore, while the chapter problems will be reconciling the account during April 2019, you will be clearing transactions that were recorded a number of months earlier.

On April 30, 2019, Craig's Design receives the bank statement for the Cash - Checking account from the bank. After a review of the bank statement, you determine the following:

- The cash balance per the bank statement is $998.60.
- The cash balance per the company's books is $1,671.00.
- The bank charged the account $35 for bank service charges.
- The bank credited the account for $5 of interest income.
- All deposits, except the deposit of $868.15, have cleared the bank.
- All checks and payments, except Check nos. 75 and 76, have cleared the bank.
- A check for $108 from Amy's Bird Sanctuary included in the deposit of $408 was returned as NSF. The bank deducted the amount from the statement.

To record interest earned:
1. On the title bar, click the Create icon and then click *Journal Entry* in the *Other* column.
2. In the *Journal date* field, choose *04/30/2019.*
3. In the *Journal no.* field, accept *1.*
4. In the first line of the *ACCOUNT* column, click *Checking* at the drop-down list.
5. In the *DEBITS* column, key *5.*
6. Move to the second line of the *ACCOUNT* column and then click *Interest Earned* at the drop-down list.
7. If *5* does not automatically display in the *CREDITS* column, key *5.*
8. In the *DESCRIPTION* column, key Bank Interest - April 2019. See Figure 7–F.
9. Confirm the information is correct and then click the Save and new button.

FIGURE 7–F Journal Window—Completed

To record bank charges:

1. In the *Journal date* field, choose *04/30/2019*, if necessary.
2. In the *Journal no.* field, accept *2*.
3. In the first line of the *ACCOUNT* column, click *Bank Charges* at the drop-down list.
4. In the *DEBITS* column, key 35.
5. Move to the second line of the *ACCOUNT* column and then click *Checking* at the drop-down list.
6. If *35* does not automatically display in the *CREDITS* column, key 35.
7. In the *DESCRIPTION* column, key Bank Charges - April 2019. See Figure 7–G.

FIGURE 7–G Journal Window—Completed

8. Confirm the information is correct and then click *Save and close* from the Save and new button list to return to the Dashboard.

When you access the Reconcile window, the foregoing transactions will appear and will need to be cleared.

To reconcile the Cash - Checking account with the bank statement:

1. On the title bar, click the Gear icon and then click *Reconcile* in the *Tools* column. If this is your first time accessing the Reconcile window, bypass the Find your balance and Reconcile like a pro windows. The Reconcile an account window appears.
2. At the *Account* drop-down list, accept *Checking*. Close the *Welcome! Grab your statement and we'll get started* pop-up window.
3. In the *Ending balance* field, key 998.60.
4. In the *Ending date* field, choose *04/30/2019*. See Figure 7–H.

> **HINT**
> You cannot edit the Beginning Balance figure.

FIGURE 7–H Reconcile an Account Window

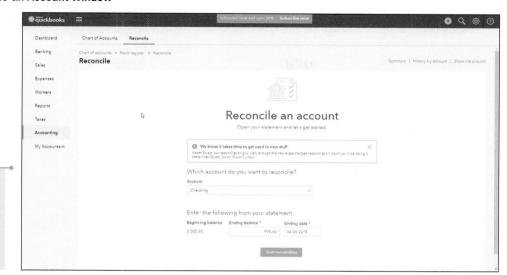

HINT

Remember that the window for the Case Problem file will have an input field for bank service charges and interest earned.

5. Confirm the information is correct and then click the Start reconciling button. The Reconcile - Checking window appears displaying the activity for that account.
6. Click the Deposits link to display all additions to the account. Insert a check mark next to all deposits, except the deposit of $868.15, which has not cleared the bank, to indicate that all have cleared. See Figure 7–I.

FIGURE 7–I Reconcile - Checking Window with Cleared Deposits Selected

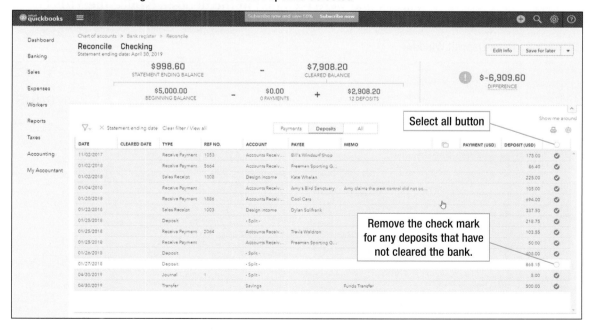

7. Click the Payments link to display all withdrawals from the account. Insert a check mark next to all checks and payments except Check nos. 75 and 76, as they have not cleared the bank. The difference is now *-108.00*, which matches the amount of the NSF check from Amy's Bird Sanctuary. See Figure 7–J.

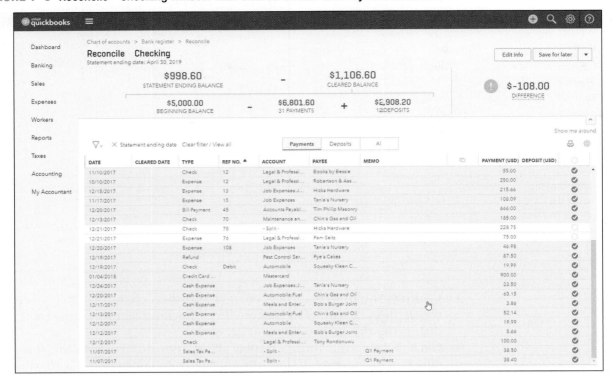

8. Click the Deposits link, click the deposit of $408, and then click the
    Edit button to select it. The Bank Deposit window appears, listing the
    checks that were included in the deposit. Notice the $108 check from
    Amy's Bird Sanctuary is included in the deposit. See Figure 7–K.

FIGURE 7–K Bank Deposit Window

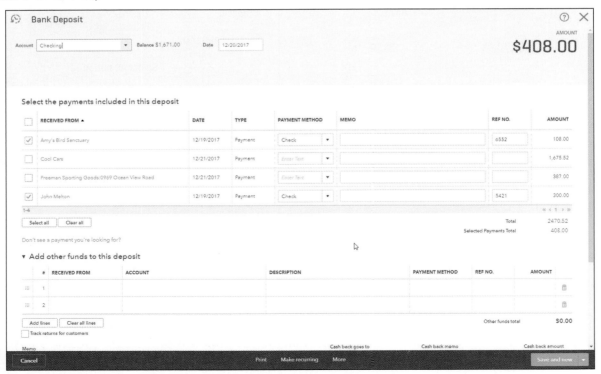

HINT

If you leave the Reconcile window at this point, the items checked off will be saved.

When this deposit was made, the bank recorded the total deposit and increased the bank balance by $408. When the Amy's Bird Sanctuary check was returned due to NSF, the bank then deducted the $108 from the bank balance. To reconcile with the bank account, the $108 must be deducted from the Cash - Checking account.

9. If the check mark was removed from the deposit, click the deposit to replace the check mark. Close the Bank Deposit window.

10. With the Reconcile window open, click the Create icon and then click *Journal Entry*.

11. In the *Journal date* field, choose *04/30/2019*.

12. In the *Journal no.* field, key *3*, if necessary.

13. Enter the following journal entry in the manner covered in Chapter 5:

ACCOUNT:	Accounts Receivable
DEBITS:	108
NAME:	Amy's Bird Sanctuary

ACCOUNT:	Cash - Checking
CREDITS:	108
DESCRIPTION:	NSF check

See Figure 7–L.

FIGURE 7–L Journal Entry Window

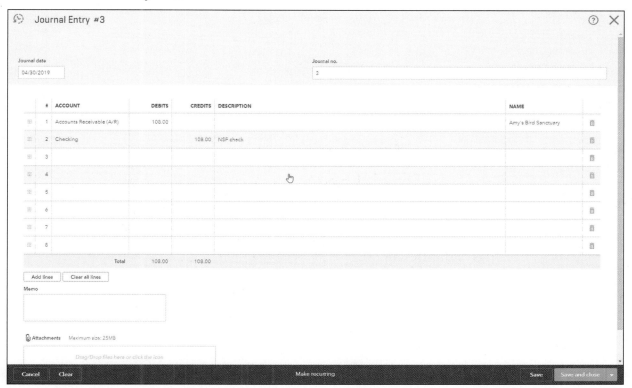

14. Confirm the information is correct and then click *Save and close* from the Save and new button list. You return to the Reconcile - Checking window.

15. Click the Payments link and scroll down until you locate the $108 adjustment to the Cash account for the NSF check. Click to insert a check mark next to the entry. The *DIFFERENCE* is now zero. See Figure 7–M.

FIGURE 7–M Reconcile - Checking Window—Completed

16. Confirm the information is correct and then click the Finish now button. The Success! You reconciled your account window appears. Click the View report button. The Reconciliation Report for April 30, 2019, appears. See Figure 7–N.

17. Print the report.

18. Return to the Dashboard.

You should print the report immediately. The Reconciliation Report is also available from the Reports window. However, this option is available only until you complete the next reconciliation.

FIGURE 7–N
Reconciliation Report—Cash - Checking Account

1/16/2018

EX7 [Your Name] Craig's Design and Landscaping Services

Checking, Period Ending 04/30/2019

RECONCILIATION REPORT

Reconciled on: 01/16/2018

Reconciled by: Craig Carlson

Any changes made to transactions after this date aren't included in this report.

Summary	USD
Statement beginning balance	5,000.00
Checks and payments cleared (32)	-6,909.60
Deposits and other credits cleared (12)	2,908.20
Statement ending balance	998.60
Uncleared transactions as of 04/30/2019	564.40
Register balance as of 04/30/2019	1,563.00

Details

Checks and payments cleared (32)

DATE	TYPE	REF NO.	PAYEE	AMOUNT (USD)
09/18/2017	Bill Payment	10	Robertson & Associates	-300.00
10/10/2017	Expense	12	Robertson & Associates	-250.00
11/01/2017	Check	4	Chin's Gas and Oil	-54.55
11/07/2017	Sales Tax Payment			-38.50
11/07/2017	Sales Tax Payment			-38.40
11/10/2017	Expense	9	Tania's Nursery	-89.09
11/10/2017	Check	12	Books by Bessie	-55.00
11/16/2017	Check	5	Chin's Gas and Oil	-62.01
11/17/2017	Expense	15	Tania's Nursery	-108.09
11/30/2017	Bill Payment	7	Hicks Hardware	-250.00
12/03/2017	Expense	8	Hicks Hardware	-24.36
12/12/2017	Cash Expense		Squeaky Kleen Car Wash	-19.99
12/12/2017	Cash Expense		Bob's Burger Joint	-5.66
12/12/2017	Check		Tony Rondonuwu	-100.00
12/13/2017	Check	70	Chin's Gas and Oil	-185.00
12/13/2017	Cash Expense		Chin's Gas and Oil	-52.14
12/14/2017	Bill Payment	11	Hall Properties	-900.00
12/15/2017	Check	2	Mahoney Mugs	-18.08
12/15/2017	Expense	13	Hicks Hardware	-215.66
12/17/2017	Cash Expense		Bob's Burger Joint	-3.86
12/18/2017	Bill Payment	1	Brosnahan Insurance Agency	-2,000.00
12/19/2017	Bill Payment	3	Books by Bessie	-75.00
12/19/2017	Refund	1020	Pye's Cakes	-87.50
12/19/2017	Check	Debit	Squeaky Kleen Car Wash	-19.99
12/20/2017	Bill Payment	6	PG&E	-114.09
12/20/2017	Cash Expense		Chin's Gas and Oil	-63.15
12/20/2017	Expense	108	Tania's Nursery	-46.98
12/20/2017	Bill Payment	45	Tim Philip Masonry	-666.00
12/24/2017	Cash Expense		Tania's Nursery	-23.50
01/04/2018	Credit Card Credit			-900.00
04/30/2019	Journal	2		-35.00
04/30/2019	Journal	3		-108.00
Total				-6,909.60

Deposits and other credits cleared (12)

DATE	TYPE	REF NO.	PAYEE	AMOUNT (USD)
09/26/2017	Receive Payment	1053	Bill's Windsurf Shop	175.00
11/26/2017	Receive Payment	5664	Freeman Sporting Goods:55 T…	86.40
11/26/2017	Sales Receipt	1008	Kate Whelan	225.00
11/28/2017	Receive Payment		Amy's Bird Sanctuary	105.00
12/14/2017	Receive Payment	1886	Cool Cars	694.00
12/16/2017	Sales Receipt	10264	Dylan Sollfrank	337.50
12/19/2017	Receive Payment		Freeman Sporting Goods:55 T…	50.00
12/19/2017	Receive Payment	2064	Travis Waldron	103.55
12/19/2017	Deposit			218.75
12/20/2017	Deposit			408.00
04/30/2019	Transfer			500.00
04/30/2019	Journal	1		5.00
Total				2,908.20

Additional Information

Uncleared checks and payments as of 04/30/2019

DATE	TYPE	REF NO.	PAYEE	AMOUNT (USD)
12/21/2017	Check	75	Hicks Hardware	-228.75
12/21/2017	Expense	76	Pam Seitz	-75.00
Total				-303.75

Uncleared deposits and other credits as of 04/30/2019

DATE	TYPE	REF NO.	PAYEE	AMOUNT (USD)
12/21/2017	Deposit			868.15
Total				868.15

Accounting Concept

For a bank reconciliation, the postings to the general ledger are as follows:

Cash - Checking				Accts Rec	
Dr		Cr		Dr	Cr
	1,701.00	108.00 NSF		108.00 NSF	
Int Inc	5.00	35.00 SC			
Bal	1,563				

Bank Service Charges			Interest Income	
Dr	Cr		Dr	Cr
35.00				5.00

Adjusted Bank Statement Balance:

Ending Balance		$998.60
Deposit-in-transit		868.15
Outstanding Checks:		
No. 75	228.75	
No. 76	75.00	(303.75)
		$1,563.00

In addition, the customer file for Amy's Bird Sanctuary reflects the increased receivable amount:

Amy's Bird Sanctuary	
Dr	Cr
108	

Activities

The Expense Window

Activities identified as credit card charges for goods or services are recorded in the Expense window. When a credit card is used to purchase goods from a vendor, the asset purchased or expense incurred is recorded as if the goods were purchased with cash or on account. The purchase creates a liability in the form of a credit card balance that will be paid at a later date. The default account is a Credit Card Liability account. Since the liability is not posted to the Accounts Payable account, Accounts Payable is not used to track the credit card liability. The transaction is recorded as follows:

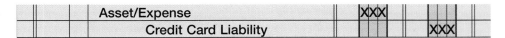

When the credit card bill is paid, the credit card liability is reduced by a cash payment. The default accounts are the Credit Card Liability account and the Cash account. The journal entry is as follows:

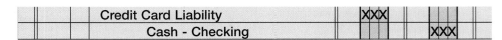

The QuickBooks Online Expense window appears in Figure 7–O.

FIGURE 7–O Expense Window

The procedures for the Expense window are similar to those of the Bill and Check windows. QuickBooks Online allows you to track the activity of more than one credit card. Choose the credit card for the current transaction from the drop-down list.

Entering a Credit Card Charge

On May 1, 2019, Craig's Design charged $100 using its Mastercard for equipment rental purchased from Ellis Equipment Rental, its Ref no. 546.

To enter a credit card charge:
1. Click the Create icon and then click *Expense* in the *Vendors* column. The Expense window appears.
2. At the *Choose a payee* drop-down list, click *Ellis Equipment Rental.* Click the Yes button at the pop-up window, if necessary.
3. Select *Mastercard* for the credit card, if necessary.
4. In the *Payment date* field, choose *05/01/2019.*
5. At the *Payment method* drop-down list, click *MasterCard.*
6. In the *Ref no.* field, key 546.
7. In the *ACCOUNT* column in the *Account details* section, click *Equipment Rental,* if necessary.
8. Select the number in the *AMOUNT* column and accept 112. See Figure 7–P.
9. Confirm the information is correct and then click the Save and new button.

FIGURE 7–P Expense Window—Completed

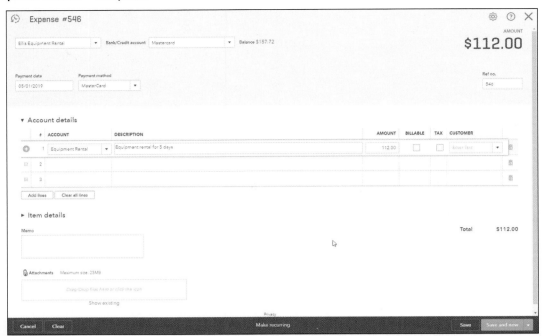

Accounting Concept

For a credit card charge for an equipment rental expense, the general journal posting is as follows:

Equipment Rental		Mastercard Liability	
Dr	Cr	Dr	Cr
112			112

Practice Exercise 7–1

Record the following purchase:

On May 18, 2019, Craig's Design used the Mastercard to purchase advertising from Lee Advertising, $350, Ref no. 84441.

Paying a Credit Card Using the Credit Card Credit Window

On May 22, 2019, Craig's Design wishes to pay the balance of the Mastercard, Check no. 100.

To pay a credit card balance:
1. On the title bar, click the Create icon and then click *Credit Card Credit* in the *Vendors* column.
2. Notice that *Mastercard* is the default credit card and the balance is $619.72. Leave the *Choose a payee* field blank.
3. In the *Payment date* field, choose *05/22/2019*.
4. In the *Ref no.* field, key *100*.
5. In the *ACCOUNT* column in the *Account details* section, click *Checking*.
6. In the *AMOUNT* column, key 619.72. See Figure 7–Q.

HINT

If there is a previous transaction for the selected vendor, QuickBooks Online will automatically fill data from that transaction. You should delete that data before completing this Practice Exercise.

HINT

Remember that since the vendor was paid via a credit card, the liability for the charge is now with the credit card company.

FIGURE 7–Q Credit Card Credit Window—Completed

7. Confirm the information is correct and then click *Save and close* from the Save and new button list to return to the Dashboard.

Accounting Concept

For a payment of a credit card charge, the general ledger posting is as follows:

Mastercard Liability		Cash - Checking	
Dr	Cr	Dr	Cr
Pmt 619.72	619.72		619.72
	Bal 0		

Reports

Banking Reports and Accounting Reports

As you know, in QuickBooks Online, the fourth level of operation is to view and print reports. As we reviewed in prior chapters, reports for an activity can be accessed from the Reports window.

Banking Reports

The reconciliation detail reports are printed as part of the reconciliation process. In addition to the reconciliation reports, the company also uses the following reports:

Deposit Detail Report

The Deposit Detail Report displays the components of all deposits to each cash account for a specified period of time. The report will show the payee's name, amount of each payment, nature of payment, and date of payment and deposit. This report is helpful in tracing a collection from a customer to the actual bank deposit.

To view and print the Deposit Detail Report:
1. On the Navigation bar, click Reports and then click the All link, if necessary.
2. In the *Sales and Customers* section, click *Deposit Detail.*
3. At the *Report period* drop-down list, click *Since 365 Days Ago.*
4. Click the Run report button. The report for the period displays. See Figure 7–R.

FIGURE 7–R

Deposit Detail Report

EX7 [Your Name] Craig's Design and Landscaping Services

DEPOSIT DETAIL

Since January 16, 2017

DATE	TRANSACTION TYPE	NUM	CUSTOMER	VENDOR	MEMO/DESCRIPTION	CLR	AMOUNT
Checking							
08/07/2017	Deposit				Opening Balance	R	5,000.00
							5,000.00
09/26/2017	Payment	1053	Bill's Windsurf Shop			R	175.00
			Bill's Windsurf Shop				-175.00
11/26/2017	Payment	5664	Freeman Sporting Goods:55 Twin Lane			R	86.40
			Freeman Sporting Goods:55 Twin Lane				-86.40
11/26/2017	Sales Receipt		Kate Whelan			R	225.00
			Kate Whelan		Custom Design		225.00
11/28/2017	Payment		Amy's Bird Sanctuary		Amy claims the pest control did not occur	R	105.00
			Amy's Bird Sanctuary				-105.00
12/14/2017	Payment	1886	Cool Cars			R	694.00
			Cool Cars				-694.00
12/16/2017	Sales Receipt	10264	Dylan Sollfrank			R	337.50
			Dylan Sollfrank		Custom Design		337.50
12/19/2017	Payment		Freeman Sporting Goods:55 Twin Lane			R	50.00
			Freeman Sporting Goods:55 Twin Lane				-50.00
12/19/2017	Payment	2064	Travis Waldron			R	103.55
			Travis Waldron				-103.55
12/19/2017	Deposit					R	218.75
			Diego Rodriguez				-140.00
			Pye's Cakes				-78.75
12/20/2017	Deposit					R	408.00
		6552	Amy's Bird Sanctuary				-108.00
		5421	John Melton				-300.00
12/21/2017	Deposit						868.15
			Freeman Sporting Goods:0969 Ocean View Road				-226.75
			Dukes Basketball Camp				-460.40
			Sushi by Katsuyuki				-80.00
			Travis Waldron				-81.00
			Amy's Bird Sanctuary				-220.00
					Money to savings		200.00
Savings							
12/17/2017	Deposit				Opening Balance	R	600.00
							600.00

5. Print the report.
6. Return to the Dashboard.

Check Detail Report

The Check Detail Report displays detailed information for all checks written from a specified cash account. The report includes the check number, date written, payee, and purpose (type) of check. Since it lists each check, the report is helpful in finding missing or duplicate checks.

To view and print the Check Detail Report:
1. On the Navigation bar, click Reports.
2. In the *Expenses and Vendors* section, click *Check Detail.*
3. At the *Report period* drop-down list, click *Since 365 Days Ago.*
4. Click the Run report button. See Figure 7–S.
5. Print the report.
6. Return to the Dashboard.

FIGURE 7–S
Check Detail Report

EX7 [Your Name] Craig's Design and Landscaping Services
CHECK DETAIL
Since January 16, 2017

DATE	TRANSACTION TYPE	NUM	NAME	MEMO/DESCRIPTION	CLR	AMOUNT
Checking						
09/18/2017	Bill Payment (Check)	10	Robertson & Associates		R	-300.00
						-300.00
10/10/2017	Expense	12	Robertson & Associates		R	-250.00
						250.00
11/01/2017	Check	4	Chin's Gas and Oil		R	-54.55
						54.55
11/07/2017	Sales Tax Payment			Q1 Payment	R	-38.40
				Q1 Payment		-38.40
11/07/2017	Sales Tax Payment			Q1 Payment	R	-38.50
				Q1 Payment		-38.50
11/10/2017	Expense	9	Tania's Nursery		R	-89.09
				Morning Glories and Sod		89.09
11/10/2017	Check	12	Books by Bessie		R	-55.00
						55.00
11/16/2017	Check	5	Chin's Gas and Oil		R	-62.01
						62.01
11/17/2017	Expense	15	Tania's Nursery		R	-108.09
						108.09
11/30/2017	Bill Payment (Check)	7	Hicks Hardware		R	-250.00
						-250.00
12/03/2017	Expense	8	Hicks Hardware		R	-24.36
						-24.36
12/12/2017	Check		Tony Rondonuwu		R	-100.00
				Consulting		100.00
12/13/2017	Check	70	Chin's Gas and Oil		R	-185.00
						185.00
12/14/2017	Bill Payment (Check)	11	Hall Properties		R	-900.00
						-900.00
12/15/2017	Check	2	Mahoney Mugs		R	-18.08
				Office Supplies		18.08
12/15/2017	Expense	13	Hicks Hardware		R	-215.66
						215.66
12/18/2017	Bill Payment (Check)	1	Brosnahan Insurance Agency		R	-2,000.00
						-2,000.00
12/19/2017	Bill Payment (Check)	3	Books by Bessie		R	-75.00
						-75.00
12/19/2017	Check	Debit	Squeaky Kleen Car Wash		R	-19.99
						19.99
12/20/2017	Bill Payment (Check)	6	PG&E		R	-114.09
						-114.09
12/20/2017	Bill Payment (Check)	45	Tim Philip Masonry		R	-666.00
						-666.00
12/20/2017	Expense	108	Tania's Nursery		R	-46.98
						46.98
12/21/2017	Check	75	Hicks Hardware			-228.75
				Rock Fountain		125.00
				Sprinkler Heads		11.25
				Sprinkler Pipes		62.50
				Fountain Pump		30.00
12/21/2017	Expense	76	Pam Seitz			-75.00
				Counsel		75.00

Accounting Reports

In addition to the banking reports, there are other reports related to the company's banking that can be viewed and printed at the end of the month.

Transaction Detail by Account Report

An additional report that can be helpful in the reconciliation process is the Transaction Detail by Account Report. This report will display, for the cash accounts, all checks written by the company. It will also indicate if the checks have cleared the bank. This report is similar to the General Ledger Report.

To view the Transaction Detail by Account Report:
1. On the Navigation bar, click Reports.
2. In the *For my accountant* section, click *Transaction Detail by Account*.
3. At the *Report period* drop-down list, click *Since 365 Days Ago*.

4. Click the Run report button. The report for the period displays. See Figure 7–T for a partial listing.

5. Return to the Dashboard.

Journal Report

At the end of each month, the Journal Report should be viewed and printed. See Figure 7–U.

FIGURE 7–U Journal Report

EX7 [Your Name] Craig's Design and Landscaping Services

JOURNAL

April - May, 2019

DATE	TRANSACTION TYPE	NUM	NAME	MEMO/DESCRIPTION	ACCOUNT	DEBIT	CREDIT
04/30/2019	Transfer			Funds Transfer	Savings		$500.00
				Funds Transfer	Checking	$500.00	
						$500.00	**$500.00**
04/30/2019	Journal Entry	1			Checking	$5.00	
				Bank Interest - April 2019	Interest Earned		$5.00
						$5.00	**$5.00**
04/30/2019	Journal Entry	2			Bank Charges	$35.00	
				Bank Charges - April 2019	Checking		$35.00
						$35.00	**$35.00**
04/30/2019	Journal Entry	3			Accounts Receivable (A/R)	$108.00	
				NSF check	Checking		$108.00
						$108.00	**$108.00**
05/01/2019	Expense	546	Ellis Equipment Rental		Mastercard		$112.00
				Equipment rental for 5 days	Equipment Rental	$112.00	
						$112.00	**$112.00**
05/18/2019	Expense	84441	Lee Advertising		Mastercard		$350.00
					Advertising	$350.00	
						$350.00	**$350.00**
05/22/2019	Credit Card Credit	100			Mastercard	$619.72	
					Checking		$619.72
						$619.72	**$619.72**
TOTAL						**$1,729.72**	**$1,729.72**

Exiting QuickBooks Online

HINT

Any work you do in the Test Drive sample company file is not saved when you exit out of the company file.

At the end of each session, you should exit QuickBooks Online and close the browser.

To exit QuickBooks Online and close the browser:
1. On the title bar, click the Gear icon.
2. At the Company window, click *Sign Out* in the *Profile* column. This closes the company file and exits QuickBooks Online.

3. Close your browser.

Chapter Review and Assessment

 Study Tools include a presentation and a glossary. Use these resources, available from the links menu in the student ebook, to further develop and review skills learned in this chapter.

Procedure Review

To transfer funds between accounts:
1. On the title bar, click the Create icon and then click *Transfer* in the *Other* column.
2. At the *Transfer Funds From* drop-down list, click the cash account from which the funds are being transferred.
3. At the *Transfer Funds To* drop-down list, click the cash account to which the funds are being transferred.
4. Key the transfer amount in the *Transfer Amount* field.
5. In the *Date* field, select the transfer date.
6. Click the Save and close button.

To record interest earned (if not able to enter in the Reconcile windows):
1. On the title bar, click the Create icon and then click *Journal Entry* in the *Other* column.
2. Select the date in the *Journal date* field.
3. In the *Journal no.* field, enter the number of the journal entry.
4. In the first line of the *ACCOUNT* column, click the appropriate bank account from the drop-down list.
5. Key the amount in the *DEBITS* column.
6. Move to the second line of the *ACCOUNT* column and then click *Interest Revenue* at the drop-down list.
7. Key the amount in the *CREDITS* column, if necessary.
8. In the *DESCRIPTION* column, key a brief explanation.
9. Click the Save and close button.

To record bank charges (if not able to enter in the Reconcile windows):
1. On the title bar, click the Create icon and then click *Journal Entry* in the *Other* column.
2. Select the date in the *Journal date* field.
3. In the *Journal no.* field, enter the number of the journal entry.
4. In the first line of the *ACCOUNT* column, click the appropriate bank charges expense account at the drop-down list.
5. Key the amount in the *DEBITS* column.
6. Move to the second line of the *ACCOUNT* column and then click the appropriate bank account at the drop-down list.
7. Key the amount in the *CREDITS* column, if necessary.
8. In the *DESCRIPTION* column, key a brief explanation.
9. Click the Save and close button.

To reconcile a cash account:
1. On the title bar, click the Gear icon and then click *Reconcile* in the *Tools* column.
2. At the *Account* drop-down list, select the account to be reconciled, enter the balance and date, and then click the Start reconciling button. (If the window contains fields for service charges and interest earned, enter them here, rather than as journal entries.)
3. At the Reconcile window, click the Deposits link and enter a check mark next to all deposits that have cleared the bank.
4. Click the Payments link and insert a check mark next to checks and payments that have cleared the bank.
5. If there are any NSF checks, record them in the Journal window while the Reconcile window is open.
6. At the Journal window, click the Save and close button and then return to the Reconcile window.
7. Insert a check mark next to any NSF amounts in the *Payments* section.
8. Confirm the *DIFFERENCE* field displays *$0.00.*
9. Click the Finish Now button.

To enter a credit card charge:
1. On the title bar, click the Create icon and then click *Expense* in the *Vendors* column.
2. At the *Choose a payee* drop-down list, click the vendor name.
3. At the *Credit card* drop-down list, click the appropriate credit card.
4. Select the charge date at the *Payment date* field.
5. In the *Payment method* field, select the appropriate credit card.
6. Key the vendor reference number in the *Ref no.* field.
7. In the *ACCOUNT* column in the *Account details* section, click the appropriate expense/asset account.
8. Key the charge amount in the *AMOUNT* column.
9. Click the Save and close button.

To pay a credit card balance:
1. On the title bar, click the Create icon and then click *Credit Card Credit.*
2. Select the appropriate credit card to pay and leave the *Choose a payee* field blank.
3. Select the check date in the *Payment date* field.
4. Key the reference number in the *Ref no.* field.
5. In the *ACCOUNT* column in the *Account details* section, click the appropriate bank account.
6. In the *AMOUNT* column, key the amount of the check.
7. Click the Save and close button.

To view banking reports:
1. On the Navigation bar, click Reports and then scroll to the *Sales and Customers* or *Expenses and Vendors* sections.
2. Select a report.
3. Indicate the appropriate dates of the report.
4. Click the Run report button.

Key Concepts

Select the letter of the item that best matches each definition.

a. bank reconciliation
b. Reconciliation Report
c. Reconcile windows
d. Reconciling items
e. Credit Card Credit window

f. Transfer window
g. deposit in transit
h. Expense window
i. cleared checks
j. NSF check

_____ 1. A deposit made by the company too late to appear on the current bank statement.

_____ 2. The procedure to account for all differences between the company's cash account record and the bank statement.

_____ 3. A check that has been received but returned by the bank for non-sufficient funds.

_____ 4. Activity windows used to reconcile a cash account.

_____ 5. Activity window used to transfer funds among cash accounts.

_____ 6. Report that displays detailed information for that month's bank reconciliation.

_____ 7. Activity window used to enter credit card charges.

_____ 8. Window used to pay the credit card balance.

_____ 9. Items, such as deposits in transit, outstanding checks, bank charges, and interest income, that account for differences in cash between the company's books and the bank statement.

_____ 10. Checks written by the company that have cleared the bank.

Procedure Check

Write a response for each of the following prompts.

1. Your company has four cash accounts. How would you use QuickBooks Online to move funds from one account to another without having to write a check?

2. Your company wishes to verify the accuracy of the accounting records concerning its cash accounts. How would you use QuickBooks Online to accomplish this?

3. What is an NSF check, and how is it treated?

4. Your company has given all sales personnel a company credit card for travel and entertainment expenses. How would you use QuickBooks Online to record the sales force's expenses?

5. Describe the steps to prepare a bank reconciliation that are common to both a manual accounting system and QuickBooks Online.

 ## Case Problem

Demonstrate your knowledge of the QuickBooks Online features discussed in this chapter by completing the following case problem.

On August 31, 2019, Olivia's Web Solutions will open a new bank account and transfer funds among the various cash accounts. At the end of August, after receiving the bank statement for the company's Cash - Checking account, Olivia Chen will prepare a bank reconciliation. In addition, during the month of September, Olivia Chen will begin using a credit card for travel and entertainment expenses. The company file includes the information for Olivia's Web Solutions as of August 31, 2019.

1. Sign in to QuickBooks Online.
2. Change the company name to **OWS7 [*Your Name*] Olivia's Web Solutions**.
3. Add the following accounts:

Type	Number and Name
Bank	1050 Cash - Money Market
Credit Card	2015 Travelers Express Card

4. Add the following vendor:

   Reliable Business Travel

5. Using the Transfer window, record the following transaction:

   Aug. 31   Transfer $4,000 from the Cash - Checking account to the Cash - Money Market account.

6. Using the Reconcile windows, prepare a bank reconciliation for the Cash - Checking account as of August 31, 2019, based on the information below. Since your Reconcile an account window has fields for *Service charge* and *Interest earned*, you can enter amounts there rather than via a journal entry.
   a. The cash figure per the bank statement was $27,257 as of August 31.
   b. The cash balance per the company's books was $22,855.94.
   c. The bank charged the account $30 for bank service charges.
   d. The bank credited the account $20 for interest income.
   e. All deposits cleared the bank.
   f. Check no. 12 did not clear the bank.
   g. A check from Breathe Easy from the July 31 deposit was returned NSF (Journal no. NSF).

7. Print the Reconciliation Report. The statement closing date is August 31, 2019.
8. Using the Expense window, enter the following transaction:

   Sep. 15   Travel and entertainment expenses of $750 to attend a sales convention in Florida were paid to Reliable Business Travel with the Travelers Express credit card, Reference no. 6554.

9. Using the Credit Card Credit window, enter the following transaction:

   Sep. 28   Paid $400 toward the Travelers Express credit card charge incurred on September 15, Check no. 14.

10. Display and print the following reports:
    a. Deposit Detail (June 1, 2019, to August 31, 2019)
    b. Check Detail (June 1, 2019, to August 31, 2019) for the Cash - Checking account
    c. Journal (August 31, 2019, to September 30, 2019)

CHAPTER 8

Customization of Your Company File

Customizing Windows, Lists, and Reports; and Processing Fiscal Year Closing

Objectives

- Customize the Dashboard
- Customize Lists
- Customize Activities windows and documents
- Set up recurring transactions
- Customize the appearance of reports
- Process Fiscal Year Closing

At this point, you should have a good understanding of operating QuickBooks Online and be able to create and set up a new company file, update the Lists, record transactions in the Activities windows, and view and print a variety of Reports, such as management reports, accounting reports, and financial statements.

In this chapter, you will learn how to customize the Dashboard, customize Lists by merging entries, customize Activities by personalizing the Invoice window and related printed invoices, and record recurring transactions. Next you will learn how to customize Reports and save the settings, view and print graphs, and export a report to Microsoft® Excel®. Finally, you will conclude the accounting cycle in QuickBooks Online by viewing fiscal year closing and setting the closing date.

Chapter Problem

To begin, open the Test Drive sample company file for Craig's Design and Landscaping Services. Change the company name in the file to **EX8 [*Your Name*] Craig's Design and Landscaping Services** and key 12-3456788 in the *EIN* field. You may also want to extend the time-out period to three hours.

Customizing the Dashboard

As you know, when you open the Test Drive sample company file, the Dashboard appears. Along the top of the Dashboard is the title bar with the icons at the right. Below the title bar is the company name, and at the left is the Navigation bar. Most of the window consists of the Dashboard, which provides a company snapshot of Invoices, Expenses, Profit and Loss, Sales, and Bank accounts. See Figure 8–A.

FIGURE 8–A
Dashboard

Navigation Bar

As was seen in Chapter 1, along the left of the Dashboard is the Navigation bar. The Navigation bar is used in this textbook to access the Lists, Activities windows, and Reports. The Navigation bar can be hidden to allow more space in the Activities and Reports windows.

To hide the Navigation bar:

1. On the title bar, click the company name. If the sample company name is not displayed, click the button containing three lines ☰ to the right of Intuit QuickBooks. The Navigation bar is hidden.

To display the Navigation bar:

1. On the title bar, click the button containing three lines. The Navigation bar displays on the left.

HINT

The company name may not appear on the title bar for the Test Drive sample company at this time, but it will be displayed in your subscription account company file.

Dashboard

The Dashboard consists of several panels: Setup guide, Invoices, Expenses, Profit and Loss, Sales, Bank Accounts, and Discover.

Setup Guide Panel

The first panel of the Dashboard is the Setup guide, which consists of five sections: *Start invoicing*, *See how much you're making*, *Pay your employees*, *Start tracking time*, and *Connect with an accountant*. (These sections are periodically changed in QuickBooks Online. You may see different section titles.) As you click each of these section headings on the left, the information and shortcuts on the right change accordingly. See Figure 8–B.

FIGURE 8–B
Setup Guide Panel

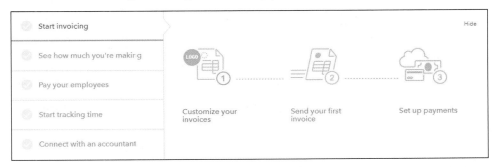

Invoices, Expenses, Profit and Loss, Sales, Bank Accounts, and Discover Panels

HINT

The order of the Panels may be different in your subscription account.

The Invoices panel displays the overdue and not yet due invoices for the past year and the past month. In addition, it displays the invoices collected and deposited and the invoices collected and not yet deposited. Click the Invoice panel and you are moved to the Invoices list, which can also be accessed by clicking Sales on the Navigation bar.

The Expenses, Profit and Loss, and Sales panels display the dollar amounts for the past month. In each of these panels, you can click the drop-down arrow next to *Last month* and choose a variety of other time periods to display. Click the Expenses panel and you are moved to the Expenses Transaction report for the past month.

The Bank accounts panel lists bank accounts and credit card accounts. These accounts can be connected and disconnected to the appropriate banking centers, but this function is beyond the scope of this textbook. If you click any of the accounts in the Bank accounts panel, you are moved to the list of the transactions for that account.

At the bottom of the Dashboard (you may have to scroll), the Discover panel provides several business tips. If you click *Hide*, you are moved to the next tip. When the next tip is displayed, you will see left and right arrows in the window where you can select the next or previous tip.

HINT

If the Discover panel does not appear in the Test Drive, it will appear in your subscription account.

Privacy

As noted in Chapter 1, a company file can be set up so several users can access a company file. This would be done in a business in which you may have several bookkeepers, or other financial team members or managers, who would need to access the company file in QuickBooks Online. The main user of the QuickBooks Online company file is identified as the Master Administrator of the company file. When the Master Administrator of the company file authorizes users to have access to the company file, the Master Administrator indicates which parts of the company file each user can access. When the company file is opened by users other than the Master Administrator of the company file, it may not be appropriate for the other users to see the dollar values in the Invoices, Expenses, Profit and Loss, Sales, and Bank accounts panels.

HINT

Master Administrators have additional authority such as the ability to undo a bank reconciliation.

Near the top right of the Dashboard is a PRIVACY toggle. The Master Administrator controls the PRIVACY toggle. However, the Master Administrator can designate other users as Company Administrators who will also be able to manipulate the PRIVACY toggle. See Figure 8–C.

FIGURE 8–C
PRIVACY Toggle

The PRIVACY toggle has two settings: off and on. By default, the PRIVACY toggle is turned off.

To turn on (enable) the PRIVACY option:
1. Click in the blank space in the PRIVACY toggle. The PRIVACY toggle turns green. The Dashboard panels no longer display. A message displays stating *See your financial info by turning privacy off.*

To turn off (disable) the PRIVACY option:
1. Click in the blank space in the PRIVACY toggle. The PRIVACY toggle dims. The Dashboard panels now display.

Customizing Lists

Lists

You have previously learned to add, edit, or delete (make inactive) vendors, customers, accounts, service items, and inventory part items in the appropriate lists. You can also combine or merge accounts, customers, vendors, service items, and inventory part items. To do so, you simply use a name or number already in use, and QuickBooks Online will inquire if you wish to merge the two items. For accounts, the Account Type and Detail Type must be the same for the accounts to be merged.

Certain accounts cannot be merged, such as the opening balance equity, retained earnings, undeposited funds, uncategorized income, and uncategorized expense accounts. The same merge process can be used to combine vendors, customers, service items, and inventory part items. QuickBooks Online will update all information based on the merge.

Craig's Design and Landscaping Services currently has a Commissions & fees account and a Disposal Fees account. Craig's Design decides to merge the two accounts into the Disposal Fees account.

To merge two accounts:
1. Open the Chart of Accounts List by clicking Accounting, then click the See your Chart of Accounts button, if necessary.
2. Scroll to the Expenses accounts and locate the two accounts: Commissions & fees and Disposal Fees. Notice that for both of these accounts, the Type is *Expenses* and the Detail Type is *Other Miscellaneous Service Cost.*
3. On the row that displays the account name Commissions & fees, in the *ACTION* column, click the drop-down arrow to the right of *Run report.* The drop-down menu appears.
4. At the drop-down menu, click *Edit.* The Account window appears, and you can edit the account name.
5. In the *Name* field, delete Commissions & fees and key Disposal Fees.
6. Click the Save and Close button. A message informs you that the account is already in use and asks if you wish to merge the accounts.
7. At the message, click the Yes button. Look at the Chart of Accounts List. Notice there is no longer a Commissions & fees account.
8. Return to the Dashboard.

Activities

Customizing Activities Windows and Documents

In all preceding chapters, the Activities windows displayed were based on default settings. QuickBooks Online allows you to change the default settings of a window as well as those of a document that can be printed as a result of data entered in a window.

To customize the Invoice window:
1. On the Navigation bar, click Sales and then click the Customers link. The list of all customers appears.
2. At the Customers window, click *Amy's Bird Sanctuary.* Information for Amy's Bird Sanctuary appears.
3. Click the Transaction List tab, if necessary, and then click *Invoice No. 1021.* The information originally recorded in Invoice no. 1021 displays. See Figure 8–D.

FIGURE 8–D Invoice Window—Invoice No. 1021

FIGURE 8–D Invoice Window—Invoice No. 1021

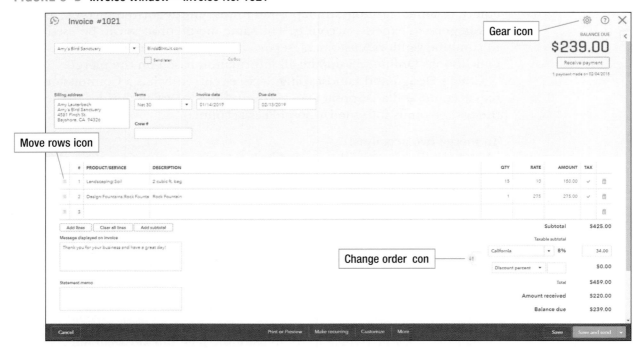

As in many other windows and reports in QuickBooks Online, when you place the mouse pointer over the dimmed line between the column titles, it becomes two parallel lines with arrows pointing left and right. Click and drag in either direction to make the columns wider or narrower.

4. In the first column of the row containing the product *Landscaping Soil* is the Move Rows icon ⊞. Hover the mouse pointer over the Move Rows icon, and it becomes a four-headed arrow. Click and drag the row down to change the order of appearance.

Use the Move Rows icon to reorder the rows. When you move the rows, a Revert button appears in the lower left corner of the window. Click the Revert button and then click the Yes button at the pop-up message to return to the original order of the invoice.

In the bottom right corner of the invoice, notice the up and down arrows icon ⬍ next to the *California* and *Discount percent* fields. Click the icon to change the order of appearance of these fields on the invoice. Click the icon once more to leave the *California sales tax* field above the *Discount percent* field.

5. In the upper right corner of the window, click the Gear icon. The Customize what you see here panel appears. This panel is used to customize the Invoice window.

6. Click the check box to the left of *Crew #* to remove the field from the Invoice window.

7. Click *Add your own field.* There can be a maximum of three custom fields. The *Crew #* field reappears.

8. Click *Add another field.* When the second field appears, remove the check mark from the *Crew #* field.

9. In the blank field, key Date ordered and then press the Tab key. A *Date ordered* field appears in the Invoice window. See Figure 8–E.

FIGURE 8–E Invoice Window—Customize What You See Here Panel—Updated

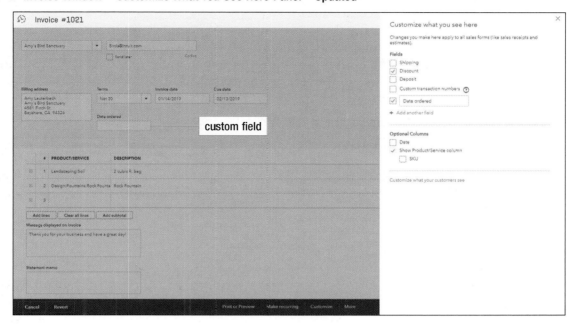

10. Confirm the information is correct and then click the X in the Customize what you see here panel to close it. You return to the Invoice window for Invoice 1021 with the fields updated.

11. Click the Save button to save the changes, but do not close the Invoice window. Click the Yes button at the warning message, if necessary.

To customize a document invoice:

1. At the Invoice window for Invoice no. 1021, click the Print or Preview button. A menu list appears.

2. At the Print or Preview menu list, click *Print or Preview*. The QuickBooks Online default (standard) document invoice appears for Invoice no. 1021. This invoice can be printed, saved as a PDF, or emailed to the customer when the account is set up for online transactions. See Figure 8–F.

FIGURE 8–F

Print Preview for Default (Standard) Document Invoice—Invoice No. 1021

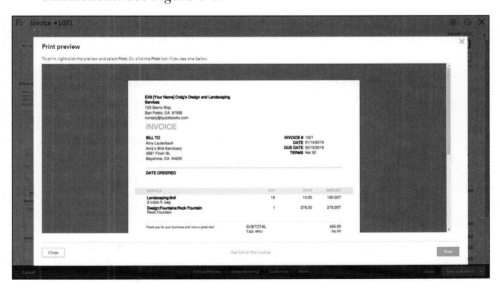

3. Close the Print preview window by clicking the X. You return to Invoice no. 1021.
4. Click the Customize button. A menu list appears.
5. At the Customize menu list, click *New style*. This opens the Create invoices that turn heads and open wallets window with tabs and options to the left and a preview of the document to the right. See Figure 8–G.

FIGURE 8–G   Create Invoices That Turn Heads and Open Wallets Window

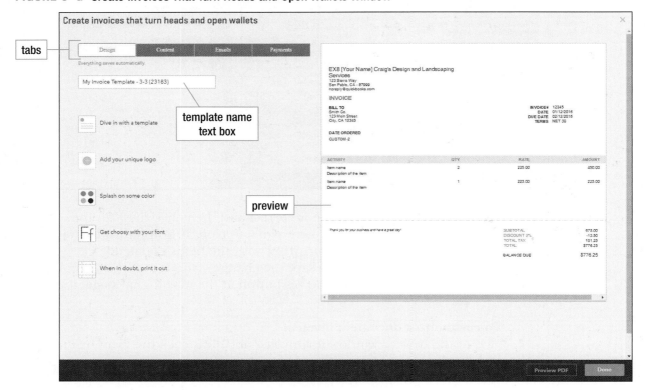

Customize the document using the following tabs:

Design tab	Use options on this tab to name the custom template, select a different style, add your company logo, choose a color scheme, change the font, and edit print settings. You can also specify paper and envelope options.
Content tab	Edit the fields and the information that appears on the document.
Emails tab	Create messages to be included when a document is sent to a customer via email.
Payments tab	Use options on this tab to allow a customer to pay directly from the bank or by credit card. The customer must be set up to accept electronic payments.

6. Click the Design tab, if necessary. A new template name is automatically assigned. Delete the name and number in the template name text box and then key Custom Invoice 1.

7. Click *Dive in with a template* or *Change up the template*. There are several document styles represented by different icons and labels.

8. Click each of the template icons, and as you do, the style displays on the right. Select one template. The example shown in Figure 8–H uses the Bold template.

9. Click *Try other colors* or *Splash on some color* and select a color. The example in Figure 8–H uses green.

10. Click *Select a different font* or *Get choosy with your font* and choose a font and font size. The example in Figure 8–H uses Helvetica 10pt.

11. Click the Content tab. The preview of the document to the right is segmented into three sections for easy editing.

12. Click the top section. When you click a section of the preview document, the corresponding check boxes and fields appear to the left for editing.

HINT

If the phone number does not appear in the heading of the preview document, make sure there is a check mark in the box to the left of *Phone* or key only the numbers without the hyphens.

13. Click the check box to the left of the *Phone* field and then key 510-555-1515 in the field. The phone number displays in the heading of the preview document.

14. Click the Done button to save the invoice template for future use. You are returned to the Invoice window for Invoice no. 1021.

15. Click the Customize button again. The menu list appears and now lists the new template, *Custom Invoice 1.* You have the choice to select the new style, select the standard template, create a new style, or edit the current template.

16. At the Customize menu list, *Custom Invoice 1* should be selected. If not, select the new template by clicking it.

17. Click the Print or Preview button and then click *Print or Preview* at the menu list. If a warning appears, click the Yes button. The Print preview window appears.

18. To print the invoice or save it as a PDF, click the Print button. You do not need to print the invoice in this activity. See Figure 8–H.

FIGURE 8–H Invoice No. 1021—Custom Invoice 1

HINT

Your invoice may look different depending on the choices you made.

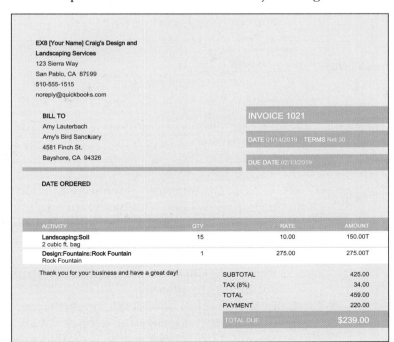

EX8 [Your Name] Craig's Design and
Landscaping Services
123 Sierra Way
San Pablo, CA 87599
510-555-1515
noreply@quickbooks.com

BILL TO
Amy Lauterbach
Amy's Bird Sanctuary
4581 Finch St.
Bayshore, CA 94326

INVOICE 1021

DATE 01/14/2019   TERMS Net 30

DUE DATE 02/13/2019

DATE ORDERED

ACTIVITY	QTY	RATE	AMOUNT
Landscaping:Soil 2 cubic ft. bag	15	10.00	150.00T
Design:Fountains:Rock Fountain Rock Fountain	1	275.00	275.00T

Thank you for your business and have a great day!

SUBTOTAL	425.00
TAX (8%)	34.00
TOTAL	459.00
PAYMENT	220.00
TOTAL DUE	$239.00

19. Close the Print preview window by clicking the X. You are returned to the Invoice window for Invoice no. 1021.
20. Close the Invoice window by clicking the X.
21. On the Navigation bar, click Sales and then click the Customers link.
22. At the Customers window, click *Freeman Sporting Goods*.
23. At the Transactions List for Freeman Sporting Goods, click *Invoice No. 1005*.
24. At the Invoice window for Invoice no. 1005, click the Customize button. At the Customize menu list, notice the default style is the *Standard* invoice, but *Custom Invoice 1* is also on the menu list. You can select your customized invoice for this customer or any other customer.
25. Close Invoice no. 1005. At the warning message, click the Yes button.
26. Return to the Dashboard.

Activities

Establishing Recurring Transactions

Many routine business activities are repeated, often at daily, weekly, and monthly intervals. QuickBooks Online allows you to set up repetitive transactions as recurring transactions. Once a recurring transaction is set up, you can recall the transaction at the appropriate time to record it, you can have QuickBooks Online automatically record the transaction on certain dates, or you can have QuickBooks Online send you a reminder to record the transaction.

On June 1, 2019, Craig's Design and Landscaping Services decides to run some advertisements every week and will pay Lee's Advertising $100 per month for the cost of the advertisements. Because this will be a routine bill, Craig's Design decides to set it up as a recurring transaction.

To set up a recurring transaction:

1. On the title bar, click the Gear icon and then click *Recurring Transactions* in the *Lists* column. The Recurring Transactions window appears. See Figure 8–I.

FIGURE 8–I
Recurring Transactions Window

Notice two items—Telephone Bill and Monthly Building Lease—have already been set up as recurring transactions.

2. Click the New button. The Select Transaction Type window appears.
3. At the Select Transaction Type window, click the *Transaction Type* drop-down arrow, select *Check*, and then click the OK button. The Recurring Check window appears with the next check number automatically filled.
4. In the *Template name* field, key Advertisement.
5. In the *Type* field, click the drop-down arrow. The three choices are *Scheduled* (the check will be recorded on the next scheduled date), *Reminder* (QuickBooks Online will send you a reminder to record the

recurring transactions), and *Unscheduled* (QuickBooks Online records the information for when you want to recall it).

6. Click the default option, *Scheduled*.
7. In the *Payee* field, select *Lee Advertising* from the drop-down list.
8. Confirm the *Checking* bank account displays in the *Account* field, the *Check no.* field displays *71*, and the *Print later* check box is unchecked. Notice the default interval of pay is the first day of each month. This interval can be customized using the different fields in the *Interval* section.
9. In the *Start date* field, choose *06/01/2019*.
10. In the *ACCOUNT* column, click *Advertising*.
11. In the *AMOUNT* column, key 100. See Figure 8–J.

FIGURE 8–J   Recurring Check Transaction Template Window—Completed

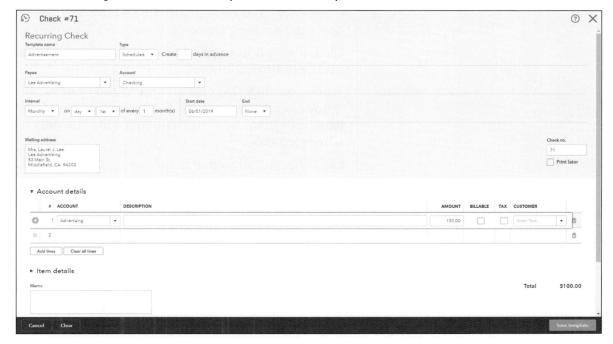

12. Confirm the information is correct and then click the Save template button. You are returned to the Recurring Transactions window with Advertisement for Lee Advertising recorded as a recurring transaction to be automatically recorded monthly starting June 1, 2019. See Figure 8–K.

FIGURE 8–K   Recurring Transaction Window—Updated

13. At the Recurring Transactions window, in the *ACTION* column for Lee Advertising, click the drop-down arrow. The drop-down menu appears.

The following options are available in the *ACTION* column drop-down menu:

Edit	Click this option to edit the template for this recurring transaction.
Use	This option opens the transaction with the current date and the current check number included. You can save the transaction if it was not automatically scheduled.
Duplicate	Click this option to open the Recurring Transaction window with all fields filled in based on the original transaction. You can update the window and then save the recurring transaction with a different name.
Pause	Click this option to postpone this recurring transaction until further notice.
Skip next date	When you click this option, QuickBooks Online will not record the transaction for the next scheduled date but will move to the date following the next scheduled date.
Delete	Click this option to delete the recurring transaction.

An alternative to recording recurring transactions in the Recurring Transactions window is to record the transaction in an Activity window (such as Bill, Check, Invoice, and so on). After entering the information in the Activity window, click the Make Recurring button and then edit the recurring activity at the window that displays.

14. Return to the Dashboard.

Customizing the Appearance of Reports

Reports

As you have seen, QuickBooks Online contains a large variety of pre-established management reports, accounting reports, and financial statements, many of which you have displayed and printed throughout this textbook.

As you have also seen, when you display a report, there is a Customize button that allows you to customize a report. There are general settings, rows/columns settings, and header/footer settings that can all be customized. In addition, you can customize the report by selecting certain fields of information for display (filters). After customizing a report, you can save the customized report for later recall. Also in every report are icons that allow you to email a report or export a report into an Excel spreadsheet. An emailed report is sent as a PDF file.

In prior chapters, you displayed and printed reports using the pre-established settings—except in Chapter 5, in which you modified the report using the *Filter* and *Header/Footer* sections of the Customize report window. In this chapter, you will see additional features used to customize a report, save and recall a customized report, export a report to Excel, and view graphs created by QuickBooks Online.

Reports Window

The Reports window is where you can access all of the reports provided by QuickBooks Online.

To view the Reports window:

1. On the Navigation bar, click Reports. The Reports window appears. See Figure 8–L.

FIGURE 8–L
Reports Window

2. Keep the Reports window open for the next activity.

Along the top of the Reports window are three links: All, Custom Reports, and Management Reports. So far in this text, the default is the All link, which is underlined. After using the other links, when you click Reports on the Navigation bar, the last link used will be the default. The links contain the following:

All link	All reports are listed in ten sections. The section headings are: *Favorites, Business overview, Who owes you, Sales and Customers, What you owe, Expenses and Vendors, Sales tax, Employees, For my accountant,* and *Payroll.* Listed below each of these section headings are the reports associated with the section heading.
Custom Reports link	When you customize a report and then save it, the saved report title will be listed here.
Management Reports link	QuickBooks Online provides easy access to the Company Overview, Sales Performance, and Expenses Performance reports here.

Customize Button

The Customize button is used to adjust the appearance of the report. Clicking the Customize button opens the Customize report window, which consists of up to four sections: *General, Rows/Columns, Filter,* and *Header/Footer.* Not all reports have all four sections in the Customize report window.

Customize Report Window—General Section

The *General* section of the Customize report window is used to customize the report period, the accounting method, the number format, and the presentation of negative numbers.

To customize the General Ledger Report:
1. At the Reports window, click the All link, and then in the *For my accountant section,* click *General Ledger.*
2. Since this is the Test Drive and the dates change each month, in the date fields, enter a one-year period of time ending with the current month. For example, if you are completing this exercise in January, enter February 1 to January 31; if you are completing the exercise in October, enter November 1 to October 31. For this example, the dates April 1, 2018 to March 31, 2019 were entered.
3. Click the Run report button. See Figure 8–M.

HINT

Depending on the time of year that you prepare this report, some of the dates may differ.

FIGURE 8–M General Ledger Report—Partial

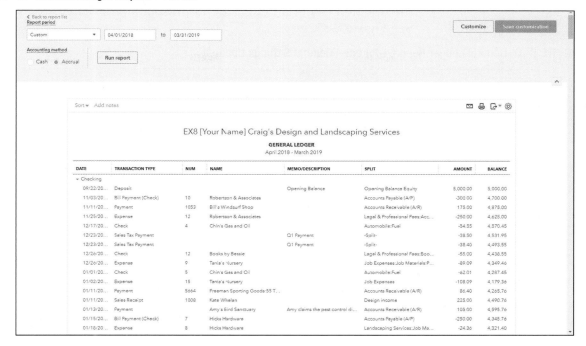

Notice when you entered the dates, the box to the left of the dates changed to *Custom*. Click the drop-down arrow next to *Custom* to see the different periods of time that can be used.

4. Click the Customize button. The Customize report window appears. The first section is the *General* section. You can change the dates here or in the Reports window as you just did. In this section, you can also change the accounting method and format the numbers.

5. In the Customize report window, in the *General* section, under Number format, click to insert a check mark in the check box to the left of *Without cents*.

6. Under Negative numbers, click to insert a check mark in the check box to the left of *Show in red*. See Figure 8–N.

FIGURE 8–N

Customize Report Window—
General Section—Updated

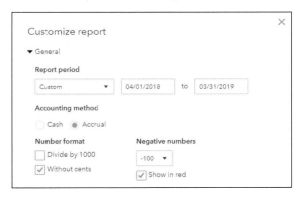

By default, QuickBooks Online does not show debits and credits in the Account List Report or in the General Ledger Report. Debit amounts are shown as positive numbers, and credit amounts are shown as negative amounts. By activating this option, the credit dollar values will be displayed in red.

7. Click the Run report button. The Customize report window closes, and the updated General Ledger Report displays with the custom settings. See Figure 8–O.

FIGURE 8–O General Ledger Report—Partial—General Settings Updated

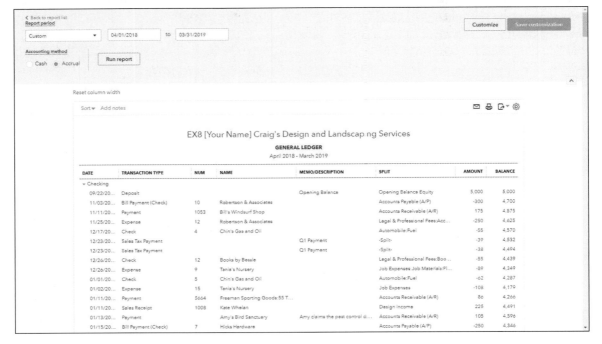

8. Keep the Reports window open for the next activity.

Save and Open Customized Reports

The changes you just made to the report remain in place as long as the report is displayed. However, as soon as you close the report, those changes are lost. When you reopen the report, the original default settings are again displayed. Instead of having to change the settings each time you open the report, you can save the changes to a report by using the Save customization button. After you have saved the customized report, you can then later recall the report with the customized settings.

To save the customized General Ledger Report:
1. At the updated General Ledger Report with the custom settings of *Without cents* and *Show in red* active, click the Save customization button.
2. In the *Custom report name* field, key General Ledger - Custom. See Figure 8–P.

FIGURE 8–P
Save Customization Button Menu

3. Confirm the information is correct and then click the Save button.
4. Return to the Dashboard.

The next time you open the General Ledger Report, it will display with the original settings. To view the General Ledger Report with the custom settings, you must open the custom report.

To open a saved customized report:
1. On the Navigation bar, click Reports and then click the Custom Reports link.
2. In the *ACTION* column for the General Ledger - Custom report, click the drop-down arrow next to *Edit.* See Figure 8–Q.

FIGURE 8–Q Custom Reports Window

Notice the choices in the *ACTION* column. If you click *Edit,* the Custom Report window appears. This is the same window that opens when you click the Save customization button. You can edit the name of the report from this window. The choices on the drop-down list in the *ACTION* column allow you to export the report as a PDF, export the report as a Microsoft Excel spreadsheet, or delete the report from the Custom Reports.

3. Click the report name *General Ledger - Custom.* The General Ledger - Custom Report opens with the custom settings intact.

If you make any changes to a saved customized report, they will be stored only while the report is displayed. If you wish to save the new changes, you must click the Save customization button again. If you do not change the name of the report at the Custom Report window, the customized report will be updated with the new settings. If you change the name of the report, a new customized report will be saved with the new name.

Customize Report Window—Rows/Columns Section

The *Rows/Columns* section is used to select and reorder the columns in the report.

To select, deselect, and reorder the columns in a report:
1. Open the General Ledger - Custom Report, if necessary.
2. Click the Customize button. The Customize report window displays.
3. Click *Rows/Columns* to expand the section.
4. Click *Change columns.* A list of column titles displays.

The list is separated into two sections by a light gray line. Above the line are all the column titles that display in the General Ledger Report. Below the line are all the additional column titles that can be displayed in the report. If you remove a check mark, the column title moves below the line. If you insert a check mark, the column title moves above the line to the bottom of the list of displayed column titles.

As noted earlier, by default, QuickBooks Online does not use debits and credits in the General Ledger Report or the Account List Report. Instead, it shows debit amounts as positive numbers and credit amounts as negative numbers in the *AMOUNT* column. At the Customize report window, you have the option to display debits and credits in the General Ledger Report.

5. Above the line, click to remove the check mark from the *Amount* option by clicking the check box to the left of *Amount*. The *Amount* option moves below the line to the bottom of the list.
6. Below the line, click to insert a check mark next to the *Debit* option. The *Debit* option moves above the line to the bottom of the list.
7. Below the line, click to insert a check mark next to the *Credit* option. The *Credit* option moves above the line to the bottom of the list. See Figure 8–R.

FIGURE 8–R

Customize Report Window—Rows/Columns Section—Updated with Selected and Deselected Columns

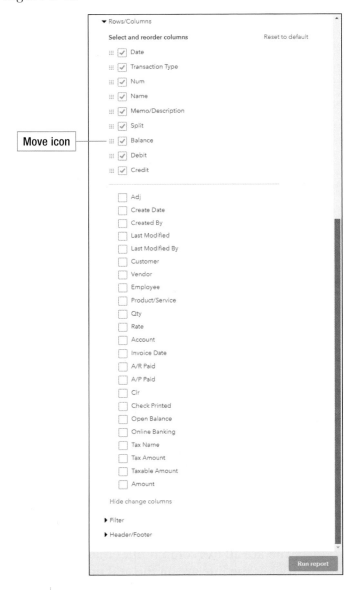

8. Confirm the information is correct and then click the Run report button. The Customize report window closes, and the General Ledger report displays with the *AMOUNT* column removed and the *DEBIT* and *CREDIT* columns added. Notice that while the *BALANCE* column does not show the cents, the *DEBIT* and *CREDIT* columns do. Totals for each account will remove the cents, but the detailed items will show cents for the debits and credits.

    The *BALANCE* column appears before the *DEBIT* and *CREDIT* columns on the report. The order of the columns can be changed at the Customize report window.

9. Click the Customize button.

10. At the Customize report window, in the *Rows/Columns* section, hover the mouse pointer over the Move icon to the left of the *Balance* check box. The mouse pointer becomes a four-headed arrow. Click and drag the *Balance* option below the *Credit* option and then release the mouse button. See Figure 8–S.

FIGURE 8–S

Customize Report Window—Rows/Columns Section—Updated with Balance Column Moved

11. Confirm the information is correct and then click the Run report button. The Customize report window closes, and the General Ledger Report displays with the *BALANCE* column positioned after the *DEBIT* and *CREDIT* columns. See Figure 8–T.

FIGURE 8–T General Ledger Report—Partial—Updated with Balance Column Moved

12. Confirm the report is correct and then click the Save customization button.

13. Accept the name *General Ledger - Custom* in the *Custom report name* field and then click the Save button.

   If you keep the name the same, the customized report is updated with the new settings. If you assign a different name—for example, General Ledger - Debits and Credits—a new customized report will be saved with the new name. The original customized report, General Ledger - Custom, will remain with only the original updated General settings.

14. Return to the Dashboard.

Customize Report Window—Filter Section

The *Filter* section is used to add or delete fields of information displayed in a report. In the *Filter* section of the Customize report window, you can filter existing fields created by QuickBooks Online. You used this section of the Customize report window in Chapter 5 when you displayed only transactions from the Journal window.

Customize Report Window—Header/Footer Section

The *Header/Footer* section is used to establish the presentation of the headers (including titles) and footers (including date prepared and time prepared) to be displayed in a report. You used this section of the Customize report window in Chapter 5 to change the name of the report in the header.

   You may have noticed that when reports are displayed, by default, the date and time the report is prepared are always displayed in the footer of the report. You can use the *Date prepared* and *Time prepared* check boxes to tell the software to display or hide the current date and time on each report. By default, both boxes are checked, which tells the software to display the current date and time as maintained by your computer.

   If you print reports often, it is useful to have the date and time you print a report listed to avoid confusion among the many printouts. But there may be times you do not want the date or time displayed on the report.

To disable the *Date prepared* and *Time prepared* options in a report:

1. Open the Account List Report. Scroll to the bottom of the report and notice that the date and time prepared are in the footer.

2. Click the Customize button at the top of the report. The Customize report window appears.

3. At the Customize report window, click the *Header/Footer* section to expand it.

4. To remove the display of the date prepared from the footer of the report, click the check box to the left of *Date prepared* to remove the check mark.

5. To remove the display of the time prepared from the footer of the report, click the check box to the left of *Time prepared* to remove the check mark. See Figure 8–U.

HINT

To open the Account List Report, on the Navigation bar, click Reports and then click the All link. In the *For my accountant* section, click Account List.

FIGURE 8–U

Customize Report
Window—Header/Footer
Section—Date Prepared
and Time Prepared
Disabled

6. Click the Run report button. The Account List Report displays without the date prepared and time prepared in the footer of the report.

To enable the *Date prepared* and *Time prepared* options in a report:
1. With the Account List Report still open, scroll to the bottom of the report and notice that the date and time prepared are not displayed in the footer of the report.
2. Click the Customize button at the top of the report. The Customize report window appears.
3. In the Customize report window, click the *Header/Footer* section to expand it, if necessary.
4. To display the date prepared in the footer of the report, click the check box to the left of *Date prepared* to insert a check mark.
5. To display the time prepared in the footer of the report, click the check box to the left of *Time prepared* to insert a check mark.
6. Click the Run report button. The Account List Report now displays the date and time prepared in the footer of the report.
7. Return to the Dashboard.

Export as Excel Icon

QuickBooks Online allows you to export all reports to a new Microsoft Excel worksheet. You can then use Excel to further customize the report. Excel must be installed on your computer to export the report.

To export a report to a new Microsoft Excel worksheet:
1. Open the Balance Sheet Report. Accept the default dates.
2. Click the Export icon ⬚▾ at the top of the report. A drop-down menu appears.
3. At the *Export* drop-down menu, click *Export to Excel*. In the lower left corner of the window, you will see part of the company name followed by *.xlsx*. This is the link to the downloaded Excel spreadsheet.

HINT
To open the Balance Sheet Report, on the Navigation bar, click Reports and then click the All link. In the *Business overview* section, click *Balance Sheet*.

4. Click the arrow at the right of the file name.
5. At the drop-down menu, click *Open.* Excel opens, and the Balance Sheet Report is exported into a worksheet. See Figure 8–V.

FIGURE 8–V Balance Sheet Report Exported to Microsoft Excel

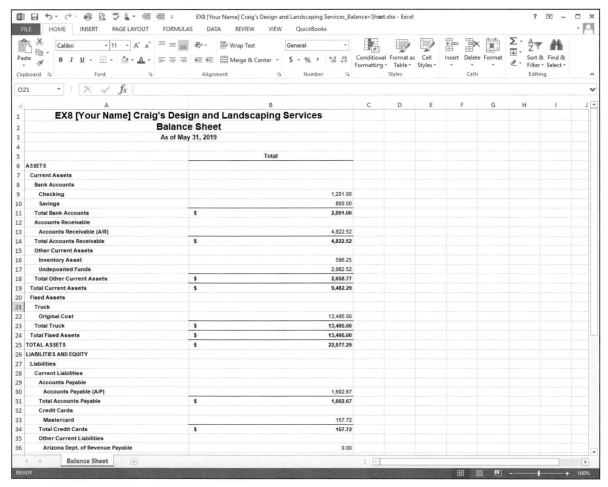

You can revise the report in Excel according to your preferences.
6. Close Excel by clicking the X in the upper right corner of the window.
7. At the *Do you want to save the changes* message, click the Don't save button. You return to QuickBooks Online.
8. Return to the Dashboard.

Graphs

QuickBooks Online allows you to display financial information in graph format. Graph presentations are available in the Business Snapshot, which is accessed from the Reports window.

To view the graphs in QuickBooks Online:
1. On the Navigation bar, click Reports and then click the All link.
2. In the *Business overview* section, click *Business Snapshot.* The My Income, My Expenses, Previous Year Income Comparison, and Previous Year Expense Comparison graphs appear. See Figure 8–W.

FIGURE 8–W Business Snapshot Graphs

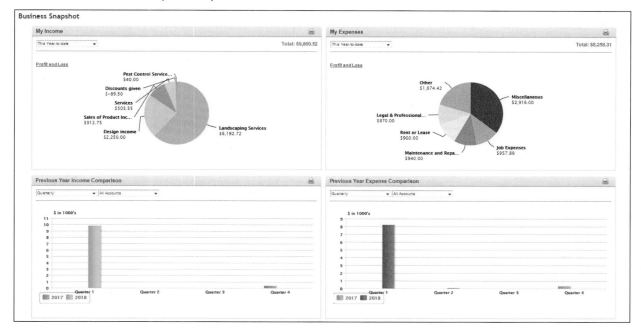

3. Return to the Dashboard.

Fiscal Year

fiscal year The 12-month financial reporting year of the company. It can be the calendar year or any other 12-month period.

Businesses must prepare their financial statements, including the Profit and Loss Report and the Balance Sheet Report, at least once per year. The year can be the calendar year or any other 12-month period. This 12-month financial reporting year for the company is called a **fiscal year**.

In QuickBooks Online, the start of the fiscal year is displayed in the Account and Settings window on the Advanced tab.

To view the fiscal year for Craig's Design and Landscaping Services:

HINT

Alternatively, open the Account and Settings window by clicking the company name on the Dashboard.

1. On the title bar, click the Gear icon and then click *Account and Settings* in the *Your Company* column. The Account and Settings window appears.
2. In the Account and Settings window, click the Advanced tab on the left. In the *Accounting* section of the Advanced tab, the first month of the fiscal year for this company is January. This means that the fiscal year for Craig's Design and Landscaping Services is January 1 through December 31.

HINT

To open the Profit and Loss Report, on the Navigation bar, click Reports and then click the All link. In the *Business overview* section, click *Profit and Loss*.

3. Close the Account and Settings window by clicking the X or by clicking the Done button.

Fiscal Year Closing

In a manual accounting system, and most other computerized accounting software packages, the books are closed on fiscal year end. When the books are closed, the temporary accounts—usually revenues, expenses, and some equity accounts—are brought to a zero balance, and the net income for the year is transferred into a capital or retained earnings

HINT

To view fiscal year closing, in the date fields enter January 1–December 31 for the current calendar year. The amount of net income may be different, but the amount on your Profit & Loss Statement should carry over to the Balance Sheet for the same period of time.

equity account for the next year. After the books are closed, preclosing balances in the temporary accounts are no longer accessible.

QuickBooks Online does not require you to close the books on fiscal year end. However, at the start of the fiscal year, QuickBooks Online automatically transfers the net income for the previous fiscal year into the Retained Earnings account. In addition, at the beginning of the new fiscal year, all revenue and expense accounts will begin with a zero balance so the net income for the new fiscal year can be accumulated.

To see the effect of fiscal year closing, first view the Profit and Loss Report for Craig's Design and Landscaping Services. There is a net income of $662.87. You may have a different net income. See Figure 8–X.

FIGURE 8–X
Profit and Loss Report—January 1, 2019–December 31, 2019—Net Income

NET OPERATING INCOME	$3,328.87
▾ Other Expenses	
Miscellaneous	2,666.00
Total Other Expenses	**$2,666.00**
NET OTHER INCOME	$ -2,666.00
NET INCOME	$662.87

The net income is carried over to the Balance Sheet Report. You may have a different net income, but the net income you have for Figure 8–X should be the same as the net income you have for Figure 8–Y. See Figure 8–Y.

FIGURE 8–Y
Balance Sheet Report—December 31, 2019—Equity Section

▾ Equity	
Opening Balance Equity	-9,337.50
Retained Earnings	554.59
Net Income	662.87
Total Equity	**$ -8,120.04**
TOTAL LIABILITIES AND EQUITY	$22,977.29

2019 Net Income

Assuming no other activity for the year 2019, now look at the Balance Sheet and Profit and Loss Reports for the first day of the new fiscal year, January 1, 2020. Notice on the Balance Sheet Report that there is no longer an amount for Net Income, but the $662.87 has been transferred into the Retained Earnings account (Previous Retained Earnings balance of $554.59 + 2019 Net Income of $662.87 = $1,217.46). See Figure 8–Z.

FIGURE 8–Z
Balance Sheet Report—January 1, 2020—Equity Section

▾ Equity	
Opening Balance Equity	-9,337.50
Retained Earnings	1,217.46
Net Income	
Total Equity	**$ -8,120.04**
TOTAL LIABILITIES AND EQUITY	$22,977.29

Retained Earnings account

In addition, the revenue and expenses all begin with a zero balance for the start of the new fiscal year. Since there are no revenues or expenses on January 1, 2020, there is no income. See Figure 8–AA.

FIGURE 8–AA
Profit and Loss
Report—
January 1, 2020

At this point, if you had a Drawings account and would like to close it, you would have to record an adjusting journal entry in the Journal Entry window. Return to the Dashboard.

Set Closing Date

Because QuickBooks Online does not actually close the books, you still have access to all records for prior years. As a precaution, however, you can protect the data for a fiscal year by restricting access to the records so no changes can be made after fiscal year end. This is accomplished when you set the closing date. This setting is in the same section of the Account and Settings window where you just viewed the fiscal year.

After setting a closing date, under the *Closing date* field, there is another field with the default message *Allow changes after viewing a warning*. This allows you to change transactions dated before the closing date, but you will receive a warning message that this transaction's date is prior to your company's closing date and it will affect your accounting. To further protect the company file from adding or editing transactions that occurred prior to the fiscal year end, you can password-protect the recording of transactions.

To set the closing date:
1. On the title bar, click the Gear icon and then click *Account and Settings* in the *Your Company* column.
2. In the Account and Settings window, click the Advanced tab.
3. Click the *Accounting* section heading to expand it for editing. Notice there is no check mark in the check box to the left of *Close the books* and *Off* displays to the right. This means the closing date is turned off and the books are open, and transactions before the fiscal year end can still be added and revised after the end of the fiscal year.
4. Click the check box to the left of *Close the books* to insert a check mark. A blank field appears to enter the closing date.
5. In the *Closing date* field, key 12/31/2019 or use the year prior to the one in which you are working.
6. Click the drop-down arrow to the right of *Allow changes after viewing a warning* and click *Allow changes after viewing a warning and entering password.* The *Password* and *Confirm Password* fields appear.
7. In the *Password* and *Confirm Password* fields, key QBOstudent or a password of your choosing. See Figure 8–BB.

FIGURE 8–BB
Account and Settings
Window—Advanced
Tab—Completed

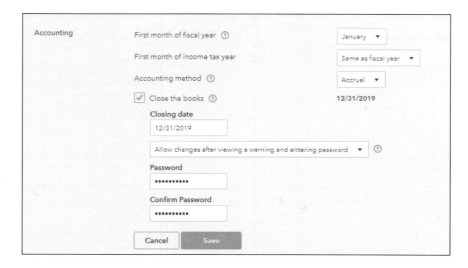

8. Confirm the information is correct and then click the Save button.
9. Close the Account and Settings window by clicking the X or by clicking the Done button.

If you need to make a change to a transaction in the company file after you set the closing date, you will receive a warning that the company file is closed, and you will need to enter the password to save any changes.

To enter updated information in a company file that is closed:
1. Open the Journal Report and enter the dates from *01/01/2019* to *12/31/2019*, or use the year prior to the one in which you are working.
2. Double-click the transaction for Robertson & Associates. The transaction appears in the Bill window.
3. Change the amount to $500 and then click the Save and close button.
4. At the transaction message, click the Yes button. The Closing date message appears, informing you that this transaction's date is prior to your company's closing date and it will affect your accounting and asking if you are sure you want to save it. There is also a blank field for you to enter the closing date password (QBOstudent).
5. Click the No button at the *Closing date* message to reject the change. You are returned to the Bill window.
6. Close the Bill window by clicking the X.
7. At the message asking if you want to leave without saving, click the Yes button. You return to the Journal Report.
8. Return to the Dashboard.

Exiting QuickBooks Online

At the end of each session, you should exit QuickBooks Online and close the browser.

To exit QuickBooks Online and close the browser:
1. On the title bar, click the Gear icon.
2. At the Company window, click *Sign Out* in the *Profile* column. This closes the company file and exits QuickBooks Online.
3. Close your browser.

> **HINT**
> To open the Journal Report, on the Navigation bar, click Reports and then click the All link. In the *For my accountant* section, click *Journal*.

> **HINT**
> Any work you do in the Test Drive sample company file is not saved when you exit out of the company file.

Chapter Review and Assessment

 Study Tools include a presentation and a glossary. Use these resources, available from the links menu in the student ebook, to further develop and review skills learned in this chapter.

Procedure Review

To hide the Navigation bar:
1. On the title bar, click the company name. If the company name is not displayed, click the button displaying three lines to the right of Intuit QuickBooks. The Navigation bar is hidden. If the company name was not displayed in the title bar, it will be displayed after clicking the button displaying three lines.

To display the Navigation bar:
1. On the title bar, click the button containing the three lines. The Navigation bar displays on the left.

To turn on (enable) the PRIVACY option:
1. Click in the blank space in the PRIVACY toggle. The PRIVACY toggle turns green. The Dashboard panels no longer display. A message displays stating *See your financial info by turning privacy off.*

To turn off (disable) the PRIVACY option:
1. Click in the blank space in the PRIVACY toggle. The PRIVACY toggle is dimmed. The Dashboard panels now display.

To merge two accounts:
1. Open the Chart of Accounts List by clicking Accounting. Click the See your Chart of Accounts button, if necessary.
2. Scroll to the Expenses accounts and locate the two accounts you would like to merge. Note that both accounts must have the same Account Type and Detail Type.
3. On the row of one of the accounts you want to merge, in the *ACTION* column, click the drop-down arrow to the right of *Run report*. The drop-down menu appears.
4. At the drop-down menu, click *Edit*. The Account window appears, and you can edit the account name.
5. In the *Name* field, delete the name and key the exact name of the account you wish to merge.
6. Click the Save and Close button. A message informs you that the account is already in use and asks if you wish to merge the accounts.
7. At the message, click the Yes button.
8. Return to the Dashboard.

To customize the Invoice window:
1. On the Navigation bar, click Sales and then click the Customers link. The list of all customers appears.
2. Click a customer name in the Customers List. The information for the company appears.

3. Click the Transaction List tab, if necessary, and then click an invoice. The information originally recorded in the Invoice window displays.

4. In the first column of each row of the list of products and services is the Move Rows icon. Click and hold the Move Rows icon, and the mouse pointer becomes a four-headed arrow. Drag the Move Rows icon to change the order of the rows. When you move the rows, a Revert button appears in the lower left corner of the window. Click the Revert button to return to the original order of the invoice.

5. In the upper right corner, click the Gear icon. The Customize what you see here panel appears. This panel is used to customize the Invoice window.

6. Add or delete fields. There can be up to three custom fields.

7. Close the Customize what you see here panel. You return to the Invoice window with the fields updated.

8. Click the Save button to save the changes. Click the Yes button at the warning message, if necessary.

To customize a document invoice:

1. With the Invoices window open and an invoice displayed, click the Print or Preview button. A menu list appears.

2. At the Print or Preview menu list, click *Print or Preview*. The QuickBooks Online default (standard) document invoice appears for the invoice. This invoice can be printed, saved as a PDF, or emailed to the customer when the account is set up for online transactions.

3. Close the Print Preview window by clicking the X. You return to the Invoice window.

4. In the Invoice window, click the Customize button. A menu list appears.

5. At the Customize menu list, click *New Style*. You are moved to the Create invoices that turn heads and open wallets window, where you can customize the invoice.

6. Use the different tabs and options to customize the invoice document.

7. Click the Done button. You are returned to the Invoice window.

8. Click *Save and close* from the Save and send button list.

9. Open another invoice.

10. Click the Customize button again. The menu list appears and now includes the new template name or number. You have the choice to select the new template, select the standard (default) style, create a new style, or edit the current template.

11. At the Customize menu list, the new template should be selected. If not, select the new template number by clicking it.

To set up a recurring transaction:

1. On the title bar, click the Gear icon and then click *Recurring Transactions* in the *Lists* column. The Recurring Transactions window appears.

2. Click the New button. The Select Transaction Type window appears.

3. At the Select Transaction Type window, click the *Transaction Type* drop-down arrow, click the desired transaction such as *Check*, and then click the OK button.
4. The appropriate window will appear. For example, the Recurring Check window appears with the next check number noted.
5. In the *Template name* field, key an identifying name for the recurring transaction.
6. In the *Type* field, choose either *Scheduled*, *Reminder*, or *Unscheduled*.
7. In the *Payee* drop-down list, click the company name.
8. At the Check window, the *Checking* bank account should be displayed in the *Account* field and the *Check no.* field should be filled. Confirm the *Print later* box is unchecked.
9. Complete the remaining fields to set up the recurring transaction.
10. Click the Save template button. You return to the Recurring Transactions window with the recurring transaction recorded.

To customize the General Ledger Report:
1. On the Navigation bar, click Reports, click the All link, and then in the *For my accountant* section, click *General Ledger*.
2. In the date fields, enter a one-year period of time.
3. Click the Run report button.
4. Click the Customize button. The Customize report window appears. The first section is the *General* section. You can change the dates here or in the Reports window as you just did. In this section, you can also change the accounting method and format the numbers using the *Without cents* and/or *Show in red* options.
5. Click the Run report button. The Customize report window closes, and the General Ledger Report is updated with the custom settings.

To save the customized General Ledger Report:
1. At the General Ledger Report with the custom settings active, click the Save customization button.
2. In the *Custom report name* field, key the desired report name.
3. Click the Save button.

To open a saved customized report:
1. On the Navigation bar, click Reports and then click the Custom Reports link. The Custom reports window appears with your custom report listed.
2. Click the report name. The report opens with the updated settings intact. If you make any changes to a saved customized report, you must save the new changes either with the same report name or a new report name.

To select, deselect, and reorder the columns on a report:
1. Open your custom report.
2. Click the Customize button. The Customize report window displays.
3. Click the *Rows/Columns* section to expand it.
4. Click *Change columns*. A list of column titles displays.

5. Above the light gray line, remove the check mark from the check box to the left of any column title you wish to exclude from the report. Unchecked column titles are moved below the line.

6. Below the line, insert a check mark in the check box to the left of any column title you wish to include in the report. Checked column titles are moved above the line.

7. At the Customize report window, in the *Rows/Columns* section, click and drag the Move icon next to a column title until the column title appears in the correct position, then release the mouse button.

8. Click the Run report button. The Customize report window closes, and the General Ledger Report displays with the columns appearing as specified.

9. Click the Save customization button.

10. In the *Custom report name* field, accept the name that displays and then click the Save button. The custom report displays with the new changes.

To disable the *Date prepared* and *Time prepared* options in a report:

1. Open a report. Scroll to the bottom of the report and notice that the date and time prepared are in the footer.

2. Click the Customize button at the top of the report. The Customize report window appears.

3. In the Customize report window, click the *Header/Footer* section to expand it.

4. To remove the date prepared from the footer of the report, click the check box to the left of *Date prepared* to remove the check mark.

5. To remove the time prepared from the footer of the report, click the check box to the left of *Time prepared* to remove the check mark.

6. Click the Run report button. The Account List Report displays with the date and time prepared removed from the footer of the report.

To enable the *Date prepared* and *Time prepared* options in a report:

1. Open a report. Scroll to the bottom of the report and notice that the date and time prepared are not displayed in the footer.

2. Click the Customize button at the top of the report. The Customize report window appears.

3. In the Customize report window, click the *Header/Footer* section to expand it.

4. To display the date prepared in the footer of the report, click the check box to the left of *Date prepared* to insert a check mark.

5. To display the time prepared in the footer of the report, click the check box to the left of *Time prepared* to insert a check mark.

6. Click the Run report button. The report is updated to display the date prepared and time prepared in the footer.

To export a report to a new Microsoft Excel worksheet:

1. Open a report. Accept the default dates.

2. Click the Export icon at the top of the report. A drop-down menu appears.

3. At the *Export* drop-down menu, click *Export to Excel.* In the lower left corner of the window, you will see part of the company name followed by *.xlsx.* This is the link to the downloaded Excel spreadsheet.

4. Click the drop-down arrow to the right of the file name.

5. At the drop-down menu, click *Open.* Excel opens, and the report is exported into a worksheet.

6. Close Excel by clicking the X in the upper right corner of the window.

7. At the message asking if you want to save changes, click the Don't Save button.

To view the graphs in QuickBooks Online:

1. On the Navigation bar, click Reports and then click the All link.

2. In the *Business overview* section, click *Business Snapshot.* The My Income, My Expenses, Previous Year Income Comparison, and Previous Year Expense Comparison graphs appear.

To view the fiscal year for your company:

1. On the title bar, click the Gear icon and then click *Account and Settings* in the *Your Company* column. The Account and Settings window appears.

2. At the Account and Settings window, click the Advanced tab on the left. The beginning of the company's fiscal year appears in the *Accounting* section of the Advanced tab. If the fiscal year for the company begins in January, this means that the fiscal year is January 1 through December 31.

3. Close the Account and Settings window by clicking the X or by clicking the Done button.

To set the closing date:

1. On the title bar, click the Gear icon and then click *Account and Settings* in the *Your Company* column.

2. At the Account and Settings window, click the Advanced tab on the left.

3. Click the *Accounting* section to expand it for editing.

4. Click the check box to the left of *Close the books* to insert a check mark. A blank field appears to enter the closing date.

5. In the *Closing date* field, key the closing date.

6. In the field under the *Closing date* field, click the drop-down arrow and click *Allow changes after viewing a warning and entering a password.*

7. In the *Password* and *Confirm Password* fields, key a password of your choosing.

8. Click the Save button.

9. Close the Account and Settings window by clicking the X or by clicking the Done button.

Key Concepts

Select the letter of the item that best matches each definition.

a. Export icon
b. fiscal year
c. Header/Footer section
d. recurring transactions
e. Retained Earnings
f. Rows/Columns section
g. Save customization button
h. debits and credits
i. Customize - New style
j. closing date

_____ 1. The 12-month financial reporting year of a company.

_____ 2. Not a default in QuickBooks Online but can be set up in the General Ledger Report using the *Rows/Columns* section of the Customize report window.

_____ 3. Button used to save the changes made to the settings in a report.

_____ 4. Used to customize a preestablished invoice in QuickBooks Online.

_____ 5. A setting that can be activated to protect the data for a fiscal year by restricting access to the records so no changes can be made after fiscal year end.

_____ 6. QuickBooks Online allows you to set up repetitive transactions referred to as this.

_____ 7. Section in the Customize report window used to add or delete the fields of information displayed in each column in a report.

_____ 8. Account created and used by QuickBooks Online at the start of the new fiscal year to automatically transfer the net income of the previous year into it.

_____ 9. Icon to export a report into a worksheet.

_____ 10. Section in the Customize report window used to disable the display of the date prepared or time prepared in a report.

Procedure Check

Write a response for each of the following prompts.

1. You are going to have a student assist you in entering some bills and invoices in QuickBooks Online, but you don't want the student to see your profit and loss, income, and expenses. What can you do in QuickBooks Online so the student will not see that information?

2. You notice that the Chart of Accounts List has an Accounting Expense account and an Accounting Company Expense account. Both these accounts are used to pay the monthly fee to your CPA. What can you do in QuickBooks Online to combine these two accounts into the Accounting Expense account?

3. Before sending the monthly invoices to your customers, you would like to prepare the invoice in a style you consider more attractive. List the steps you would take to customize an invoice in QuickBooks Online.

4. On the first of each month, you write a check for $100 for the liability insurance premium. How can you use QuickBooks Online to simplify this monthly process?

5. You are an accountant assistant working with a client whose Profit and Loss Report has net income in excess of a million dollars. You think displaying income and expenses on the Profit and Loss Statement to two decimal places for the cents is unnecessary and looks cumbersome on the financial statement. What can you do in QuickBooks Online to eliminate the cents to make the Profit and Loss Report more attractive? What can you do in QuickBooks Online so that you do not have to repeat this task every month?

6. Your manager, who has an accounting background, is new to QuickBooks Online and is reviewing the General Ledger Report. In her prior experience, there were always debit, credit, and balance columns on the General Ledger. She never saw a General Ledger Report that displays only amounts and balances, and many of the amounts and balances are preceded with a minus sign. Explain to the manager the default QuickBooks Online presentation for the General Ledger Report and what can be done to prepare the report in a format more commonly used by accountants.

 ## Case Problem

Demonstrate your knowledge of the QuickBooks Online features discussed in this chapter by completing the following case problem.

On September 30, 2019, Olivia Chen is reviewing her Olivia's Web Solutions company file account with QuickBooks Online and has decided to customize some procedures and documents.

1. Sign in to QuickBooks Online.
2. Change the company name to **OWS8 [*Your Name*] Olivia's Web Solutions**.
3. Prepare a customized document invoice.
   a. Open Invoice no. 1008 for Artie's Auto Repair.
   b. Create a new invoice style called *Friendly Company Invoice.*
   c. Use the Friendly template.
   d. Select the teal color.
   e. Save the template, apply the new style, and print the invoice.
4. Set up a recurring transaction for paying rent.
   a. The Transaction Type is *Check.*
   b The template name is Rent, and the payee is *ARC Management.*
   c. Schedule for the first day of the month beginning October 1, 2019.
   d. Charge to 6400 Rent Expense.
   e. The amount is $800.
5. Prepare a customized Account List Report.
   a. Remove the *DESCRIPTION* column.
   b. Widen the columns so the entire account names are displayed.
   c. Include the date prepared in the footer, but not the time prepared.
   d. Save the customization as *Account List - Custom.*
   e. Print the Account List - Custom Report.

6. Prepare a customized General Ledger Report (June 1, 2019 - September 30, 2019).
   a. Remove the *AMOUNT* column.
   b. Add a *DEBIT* column and a *CREDIT* column.
   c. Move the *BALANCE* column after the *CREDIT* column.
   d. Save the customized settings as *General Ledger - Debits - Credits.*
   e. Print the custom General Ledger Report.

CHAPTER 9

Payroll Setup

Activating the Payroll Feature and Customizing Payroll Settings

Objectives

- Review payroll terminology
- Activate the payroll feature
- Update the Chart of Accounts List for payroll
- Customize the Payroll Settings
- Transfer funds to the Checking - Payroll account

QuickBooks Online allows you to process payroll and track payroll information for your company's employees. The company that hires the workers is called the **employer**. The person hired by a company who will receive salary or wages on a regular basis is called the **employee**. Processing **payroll** involves computing each employee's gross earnings, determining each employee's **withholdings** and **deductions**, and calculating each employee's net pay. It also involves preparing employee paychecks or setting up direct deposit, properly recording payroll-related transactions (journal entries), submitting payroll withholdings and deductions to the appropriate tax agency or other entity, and preparing payroll compliance reports.

To process payroll in QuickBooks Online, the payroll must first be set up. Payroll setup involves enabling the payroll feature, customizing and adding payroll accounts to the Chart of Accounts List, choosing a QuickBooks Online payroll service, and customizing pre-established payroll items.

In this chapter, we will use the Test Drive sample company file to review the procedures for setting up payroll. After the payroll setup is complete, the payroll transactions for Craig's Design and Landscaping Services will then be illustrated in Chapter 10.

QuickBooks Online versus Manual Accounting: Payroll

In a manual accounting system, the process of preparing payroll is laborious and time-consuming. For each employee, the company has to tally the hours worked in a pay period, compute the gross pay for the pay period, and then determine all the withholdings and deductions from that employee's pay. After completing these computations, the company has to prepare paychecks, along with pay stubs showing all the earnings, withholdings, and deductions for the pay period, as well as all the year-to-date earnings, withholdings, and deductions. Without the use of computers, payroll withholdings are calculated manually using preprinted withholding tables. The gross pay, withholdings, and deductions for all employees then have to be totaled to record the payroll in a payroll journal, which subsequently is posted to the general ledger accounts. In addition, year-to-date earnings and withholdings need to be totaled for use in preparing government-required quarterly and year-end reports. In dealing with such a quantity and variety of computations, it is easy to make a mistake.

Payroll was one of the first accounting tasks to be performed digitally. Payroll preparation firms were formed for this sole purpose. A company simply prepares a list containing each employee's name and the hours that person worked during a pay period. This information is submitted to the payroll processing firm and the payroll is prepared; the company receives its properly completed paychecks and a summary report, usually by the next morning. The paychecks are distributed to the employees, and the summary report is used to record the appropriate journal entries for the payroll. Payroll processing firms also accumulate the necessary information for preparing government compliance reports. As personal computers and accounting software packages became available, companies were able to process their payroll in-house as part of their routine accounting tasks, rather than using an outside payroll preparation firm.

employer A company that hires workers.

employee A person hired by a company who will receive salary or wages on a regular basis.

payroll The computing of employees' gross earnings, withholdings and deductions, and net pay; preparation of paychecks or setting up direct deposit; proper recording of payroll-related transactions; submission of payroll withholdings to the appropriate agencies; and preparation of payroll compliance reports.

withholdings Generally refers to the payroll taxes the employer is required to take out of the employee's paycheck and submit to the appropriate government agency.

deductions Generally refers to amounts taken out of the employee's paycheck for various fringe benefits such as insurance, pension, and so on.

QuickBooks Online offers a subscription payroll service that allows for processing payroll with employees' gross earnings, withholdings, deductions, and net pay quickly and easily. The payroll transactions are recorded simultaneously in the journal. In addition, the paychecks can be immediately printed when the printer is set up to do so, or direct deposits can be set up and then immediately processed. QuickBooks Online also simultaneously prepares reports that summarize all quarterly and annual information needed for required filings and for required payments of employee withholdings to the appropriate agencies.

Part of what makes payroll processing in QuickBooks Online easier than in a manual system is the use of lists, which function as a database. Typical gross earnings, withholdings, and deductions are detailed in the Payroll Settings and the Employee List (discussed in Chapter 10). In addition, exact payroll taxes are maintained within the payroll feature of QuickBooks Online. When employees are to be paid, QuickBooks Online calls upon the information in the payroll service, the Payroll Settings, and the Employee List and quickly does all computations and prepares all related reports. Because QuickBooks Online computes the employee's pay by accessing information from the Payroll Settings and Employee List, it is important that all information be accurate and complete. Any errors in the Payroll Settings or Employee List will result in inaccurate computations in the payroll and the subsequent recording of incorrect entries in the journal.

Payroll Definitions and Terms

Whether payroll is processed manually or with a software package, the laws, procedures, filing requirements, definitions, and terminology remain the same. The following is a brief review of the more common payroll definitions.

Employee Payroll Information

To properly determine an employee's gross pay, tax withholdings, deductions, and net pay, and to meet federal and state record-keeping requirements, the employer needs specific information about the employee. This information includes but is not limited to the following:

- Name
- Address
- Social Security number
- Marital status
- Gross pay amount or hourly rate
- Tax withholding allowances
- Voluntary deductions (pensions, 401(k), insurance, and so on)

The employer uses this information along with the applicable tax rates to compute the employee's paycheck and track the employee's pay information.

Gross Pay

gross pay Total earnings for an employee for a specific pay period before withholdings and deductions.

Gross pay, also known as *gross earnings*, is the total earnings for the employee for a specific pay period before any withholdings and deductions. Compensation can be in the form of a salary, hourly wages, tips, commissions, bonus, and overtime earned during a pay period. If the employee is paid based on an annual salary, the annual amount is divided over the number of pay periods in the year. Gross pay for hourly workers is determined based on the number of hours worked during the pay period multiplied by the employee's hourly pay rate. The gross pay is subject to payroll taxes, for both the employer and employee.

FICA Tax (Social Security) and Medicare Tax

The Federal Insurance Contribution Act (FICA) tax, also known as Social Security, is a tax imposed on both the employer and employee at a rate of 6.2% of the first $128,400 (year 2018) of wages for each employee. Medicare tax is also imposed on both the employer and the employee at a rate of 1.45% for each—there is no wage maximum for the Medicare tax. Beginning in 2013, there is an Additional Medicare Tax of 0.9% (0.009) with different thresholds for different taxpayers ($250,000/$200,000). This additional tax is on employees only. The employer periodically remits both the employer and employee portion of the tax to the federal government.

Federal Income Tax (FIT)

Employers are required to withhold from each employee's pay the appropriate amount of federal income tax (FIT). The Internal Revenue Service (IRS) publishes tables and instructions to assist employers in determining the proper withholding amount for each employee. The withholding amount is determined based on the employee's gross pay, marital status, and exemption allowances claimed. The employer periodically forwards the tax withheld to the federal government along with the Social Security and Medicare taxes.

State Income Tax (SIT)

Many states impose an income tax and require employers to withhold the tax from the employees' pay, in a manner similar to that used for FIT. The employer will remit the state income tax periodically to the appropriate state taxing authority. Some local governments (city, county) may also impose income taxes. Rules for withholding local taxes for local governments are similar to those used by federal and state governments.

Federal Unemployment Tax Act (FUTA)

The Federal Unemployment Tax Act (FUTA) imposes a tax on the employer only. The tax is used to fund unemployment insurance programs administered by the federal government. The effective rate of the tax is 0.6% of the first $7,000 of each employee's wages.

State Unemployment Insurance (SUI)

In addition to paying the FUTA tax, employers are required by all states to contribute to a state unemployment insurance (SUI) fund. Rates and regulations vary from state to state. However, most states impose the tax only on the employer. The rates can vary from 1% to 11% based on the employer's location and unemployment experience, and the taxable amount varies from state to state.

State Disability Insurance (SDI)

Most states require employers to purchase an insurance policy, sometimes called *state disability insurance (SDI)*, that compensates employees if they are unable to work for an extended period due to illness or injury. Some states allow employers to withhold a small amount from each employee's pay to defray the employer's insurance premium cost.

Company Deductions

Many employers sponsor various fringe benefit programs and deduct amounts from an employee's pay to fund or offset the costs of the benefits. Programs such as 401(k) plans, medical and dental insurance, pension and profit-sharing plans, long-term disability, life insurance, and so on may be partially funded by these company deductions made by the company from an employee's paycheck.

Net Pay

net pay Total gross earnings for an employee minus all employee withholdings and deductions.

Net pay is the amount of the employee's gross pay less all employee withholdings and deductions. As anyone who has worked knows, net pay is only a fraction of the gross pay earned.

United States Treasury

The United States Treasury is the tax-collecting agency of the federal government. The United States Treasury is responsible for collecting the FICA tax, Medicare tax, FIT, and the FUTA tax. Most states have a similar department for collecting SIT, SUI, and SDI.

Chapter Problem

In this chapter, Craig's Design and Landscaping Services will set up the payroll in anticipation of hiring employees.

To begin, open the Test Drive sample company file for Craig's Design and Landscaping Services. Change the company name in the file to **EX9 [*Your Name*] Craig's Design and Landscaping Services** and key 12-3456788 in the *EIN* field. You may also want to extend the time-out period to three hours.

New Company Setup

QuickBooks Payroll Services

QuickBooks Online offers two different payroll services: QuickBooks Enhanced Payroll and QuickBooks Full Service Payroll. A company would choose the service that best fits its needs. For both services, QuickBooks Online computes the gross pay, all appropriate withholdings and deductions, and the net pay. QuickBooks Online uses the information in the Payroll Settings and Employee List to determine the computations. The journal entry for the payroll is automatically recorded in the Journal Entry window. If an employee has been set up for direct deposit, the direct deposit is made and is reflected in the journal entry. If the employee is issued a paper check, a check number is assigned and the payment by check is reflected in the journal entry. In addition to processing the payroll, QuickBooks Online also prepares the federal and state tax reporting information.

There are two primary differences between the two QuickBooks Online payroll services. The first difference is payroll setup. With Enhanced Payroll, the company sets up the payroll. With Full Service Payroll, you have the option to have QuickBooks Online set up the payroll for you.

The second difference is with the payment of the payroll taxes. With the Enhanced Payroll service, QuickBooks Online provides the federal and state tax reporting information, but it is the responsibility of the company to prepare the appropriate tax forms and remit the tax payments to the appropriate government agencies. With Full Service Payroll, QuickBooks Online files and remits the taxes on behalf of the company.

For both payroll services, a company subscribes to the payroll service and pays a monthly fee in addition to the subscription fee for QuickBooks Online. To use the payroll feature in QuickBooks Online, you first activate the payroll feature, and then you select the QuickBooks Online Subscription for payroll.

Activating the Payroll Feature in the Test Drive

When you activate payroll in the Test Drive sample company file for Craig's Design and Landscaping Services, payroll has already been set up. The Employee window appears with names already listed in the Employee List. In all other subscription accounts, including your student trial account, the Employee List would not yet have employee names. In addition, when you set up payroll for the first time, after you click the Turn on Payroll button, you will not be returned to the Employee List, but rather you will be asked to select one of the QuickBooks Online payroll services.

To activate the QuickBooks Online payroll feature in the Test Drive sample company file:

1. On the Navigation bar, click Workers. The Employees window appears. See Figure 9–A.

FIGURE 9–A Employees Window

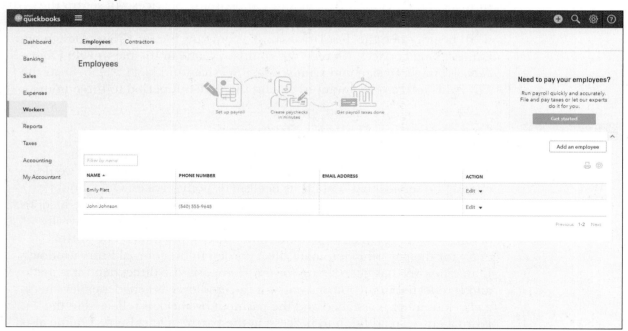

2. Click the Get started button. An updated Employee List appears. The Test Drive Employee List is prepopulated with sample employees. The Get started button switches to a Run payroll button. You will use this button in Chapter 10 when you learn how to process payroll. See Figure 9–B.

FIGURE 9-B Updated Employees Window

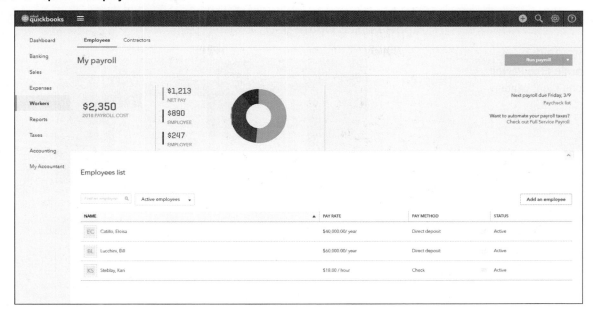

3. Return to the Dashboard.

Activating the Payroll Feature in a QuickBooks Online Subscription Account

To set up payroll in QuickBooks Online, you must first activate the payroll feature. Activating the payroll feature in a QuickBooks Online subscription account involves a few additional steps that you do not have to do in the Test Drive sample company file.

Note: The steps listed below will not appear in the Test Drive sample company file. You will need these steps to complete the Case Problem at the end of the chapter.

To activate the QuickBooks Online payroll feature and select a QuickBooks Online payroll service:

1. On the Navigation bar, click Workers. The Let's pay employees and get payroll taxes done window appears. See Figure 9–C.

FIGURE 9-C

Let's Pay Employees and Get Payroll Taxes Done Window

2. At the Let's pay employees and get payroll taxes done window, click the Get started button. The Hassle-free payroll, done right window appears. See Figure 9–D.

FIGURE 9–D

Hassle-Free Payroll,
Done Right Window

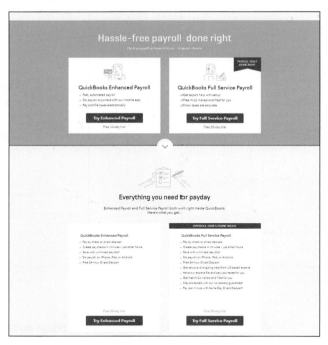

As noted earlier, QuickBooks Online offers two payroll services: QuickBooks Enhanced Payroll and QuickBooks Full Service Payroll. Scroll down the window and notice the comparison of the features available in the different payroll services plans.

3. Scroll to the top of the window, if necessary, and click the Try Enhanced Payroll button. The payroll feature is activated and you return to the Let's set you up to pay employees window.

4. If you click the Get set up button, the Get Ready for Payroll window appears. See Figure 9–E.

FIGURE 9–E

Get Ready for Payroll
Window

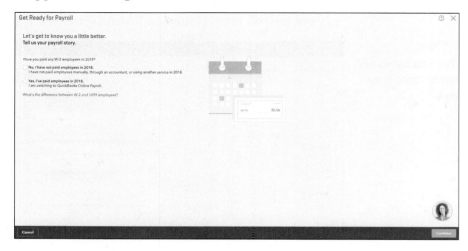

5. You will not use the Get Ready for Payroll window in this chapter. Click Cancel to exit out of the window.

6. Return to the Dashboard.

When the payroll feature is activated and payroll is processed, QuickBooks Online establishes one default general ledger liability posting account called Payroll Payable and one default general ledger expense account called Payroll Expenses. In addition, it creates subaccounts to these default accounts. If you were to process payroll, you would see these accounts on the Chart of Accounts List. If you have not yet processed payroll, the accounts are not displayed in the Chart of Accounts List.

Most companies usually create separate payroll liability accounts for FIT, SIT, Social Security, Medicare, and so on. Similarly, most companies usually create separate payroll expense accounts for Social Security, Medicare, FUTA, SUI, and so on. While QuickBooks Online does create some subaccounts, they may not be the specific subaccounts that a company would choose to create.

Since the accounts have not yet been created in QuickBooks Online, the next step will be to customize the Chart of Accounts List with the payroll accounts and subaccounts.

Craig's Design and Landscaping Services needs to add new accounts and subaccounts to process payroll. The company needs a separate checking account for payroll, the default payroll account Payroll Tax Payable with payroll liability subaccounts, and the default payroll account Payroll Expenses with payroll expenses subaccounts.

To add new payroll accounts:
1. On the Navigation bar, click Accounting and then click the See your Chart of Accounts button if it appears.
2. At the Chart of Accounts window, in the upper right corner, click the New button. The Account window appears.
3. At the Account window, in the *Account Type* field, click the drop-down arrow and then click *Bank*.
4. In the *Detail Type* drop-down list, click *Checking*.
5. In the *Name* field, key Checking - Payroll.
6. Click the Save and Close button. The Chart of Accounts List displays with the new account.
7. Return to the Dashboard.

Practice Exercise   9–1

Add the following accounts to the Chart of Accounts List:

Account Type:	Other Current Liabilities
Detail Type:	Payroll Tax Payable
Name:	Payroll Tax Payable
Account Type:	Expenses
Detail Type:	Payroll Expenses
Name:	Payroll Expenses

To add new payroll subaccounts:
1. On the Navigation bar, click Accounting.
2. Click the New button.

3. At the Account window, in the *Account Type* field, click the drop-down arrow and then click *Other Current Liabilities*.
4. In the *Detail Type* drop-down list, click *Payroll Tax Payable*.
5. In the *Name* field, key FIT and Social Sec/Medicare Payable.
6. Click the check box to the left of *Is sub-account* to insert a check mark.
7. At the subaccount drop-down list, click *Payroll Tax Payable*. See Figure 9–F.

FIGURE 9–F
Account Window—
Payroll Subaccount

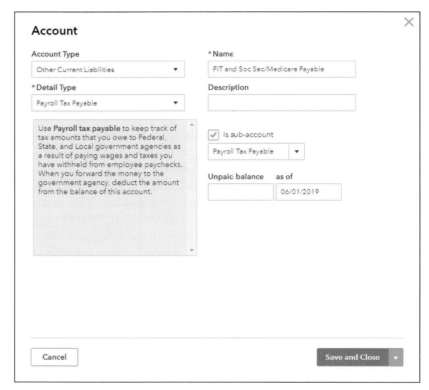

8. Confirm the information is correct and click the Save and New button.
9. Key in the accounts using the information in Table 9–1.

TABLE 9–1 Chart of Accounts List—New Payroll Subaccounts

Account Type	Detail Type	Account Name	Subaccount of
Other Current Liabilities	State/Local Income Tax Payable	SIT Payable	Payroll Tax Payable
Other Current Liabilities	Payroll Tax Payable	FUTA Payable	Payroll Tax Payable
Other Current Liabilities	Payroll Tax Payable	SUI Payable	Payroll Tax Payable
Expenses	Payroll Expenses	Salaries and Wages Expense	Payroll Expenses
Expenses	Payroll Expenses	Social Sec/Medicare Tax Expense	Payroll Expenses
Expenses	Payroll Expenses	FUTA Expense	Payroll Expenses
Expenses	Payroll Expenses	SUI Expense	Payroll Expenses

The partial updated Chart of Accounts List appears in Figure 9–G.

FIGURE 9–G
Updated Chart of
Accounts List—Partial

Checking - Payroll	Bank	Checking	0.00	View register ▼

Payroll Tax Payable	Other Current Liabilities	Payroll Tax Payable	0.00	View register ▼
FIT and Social Sec/Medicare Payable	Other Current Liabilities	Payroll Tax Payable	0.00	View register ▼
FUTA Payable	Other Current Liabilities	Payroll Tax Payable	0.00	View register ▼
SIT Payable	Other Current Liabilities	State/Local Income Tax Payable	0.00	View register ▼
SUI Payable	Other Current Liabilities	Payroll Tax Payable	0.00	View register ▼

Payroll Expenses	Expenses	Payroll Expenses		Run report ▼
FUTA Expense	Expenses	Payroll Expenses		Run report ▼
Salaries and Wages Expense	Expenses	Payroll Expenses		Run report ▼
Social Sec/Medicare Tax Expense	Expenses	Payroll Expenses		Run report ▼
SUI Expense	Expenses	Payroll Expenses		Run report ▼

10. Return to the Dashboard

Customizing the Payroll Settings

Each QuickBooks Online payroll service includes information to process payroll. It includes items such as Social Security (FICA tax) for both the company and the employee, Medicare (Medicare tax) for both the company and the employee, federal withholding, federal unemployment, and so on. It also includes information such as state and local taxes for the state in which the company operates.

When you activate the payroll feature, you can then access the Payroll Settings. As you know, the second level of operation in QuickBooks Online is to maintain background information using Lists. In earlier chapters, you added, deleted, and edited vendor, customer, accounts, and inventory item files to keep each List current for your company. While the Payroll Settings is not a List, it functions in a similar manner. You can customize and update the Payroll Settings to match the payroll information unique to your company. Then when payroll is processed, QuickBooks Online will call on your customized information to process and record payroll according to your preferences.

Payroll Settings is used to set up a broad range of activities related to payroll, including but not limited to identifying general ledger accounts to be used in the payroll journal entry, recording state tax rates, identifying special deductions such as pension and insurance plans, and setting up the electronic payment of taxes. We will use the Payroll Settings Preferences window to customize the Accounting preferences and Taxes preferences.

Accounting Preferences

The Accounting preferences in Payroll Settings are used to identify the general ledger accounts to be used in the payroll journal entry. QuickBooks Online automatically creates general ledger accounts, but a company can create its own accounts and set up the payroll so its custom accounts will be used. We will use the accounts just created in the Chart of Accounts List.

HINT

You can access the Payroll Settings only after payroll has been turned on.

FIGURE 9–H

Preferences Window

To customize the Accounting preferences in Payroll Settings:

1. On the title bar, click the Gear icon and then click *Payroll Settings* in the *Your Company* column. The Preferences main window appears. See Figure 9–H.

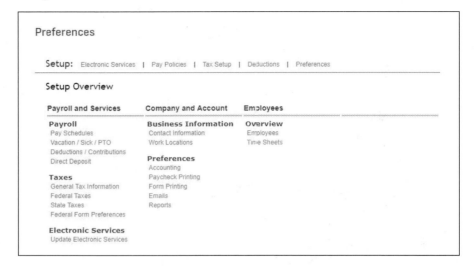

2. In the *Company and Account* column, under *Preferences*, click *Accounting*. The Accounting Preferences window appears.
3. Read the information in the Accounting Preferences window and then click the Next button. This displays Accounting Preferences fields that you can customize.
4. In the *Bank Account* section, click the drop-down arrow. An Account List box appears with the bank accounts from the Chart of Accounts List.
5. In the Account List box, click *Checking - Payroll - Checking*. See Figure 9–I.

FIGURE 9–I

Preferences Window—Accounting Preferences—Bank Account Completed

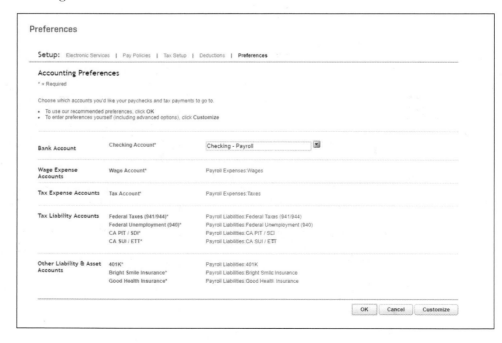

6. Click the Customize button. The sections in the Accounting Preferences window expand to allow for all accounting fields of information to be edited. See Figure 9–J.

FIGURE 9–J
Preferences
Window—Accounting
Preferences—Expanded

The bank account can be changed here also. Look at the account names in all the other fields. These are the account names QuickBooks Online would use when payroll is processed. If you processed payroll, these account names would appear in the Chart of Accounts List and in the payroll journal entries. You can update this window to include the account names just created in the Chart of Accounts List.

7. In the *Wage Expense Accounts* section, click the drop-down arrow to the right of the text box that displays *Payroll Expenses:Wages*. The Account List box appears with the Expenses accounts from the Chart of Accounts List.

8. In the Account List box, click *Payroll Expenses:Salaries and Wages Expense - PayrollExpenses.*

Only one expense account was set up for the Salaries and Wages Expense. Notice in the Tax Expense accounts there is only one text box, but a choice can be made to choose several expense accounts. See Figure 9–K.

Preferences

Setup: Electronic Services | Pay Policies | Tax Setup | Deductions | **Preferences**

Accounting Preferences
* = Required

Bank Account   Checking Account*   Checking - Payroll ▾

Wage Expense Accounts   How do you categorize wage expenses?*
○ All employees' wages go in the same accounts

Wage Account*   Expenses:Salaries and Wages Expense ▾

○ I use different accounts for different groups of employees
○ I use different accounts for different wages

9. In the *Tax Expense Accounts* section, click the radio button to the left of *I use different accounts for different groups of taxes.* The section expands with three text boxes. QuickBooks Online creates three expense accounts, but you can replace them with the subaccounts created in the Chart of Accounts List.

10. Click the drop-down arrow to the right of the text box for the *Federal Taxes (941/944)* field. The Account List box appears with the Expenses accounts from the Chart of Accounts List.

11. In the Account List box, click *Payroll Expenses:Social Sec/Medicare Tax Expense - PayrollExpenses.*

12. In a similar manner, in the *Federal Unemployment (940)* field, select the *Payroll Expenses:FUTA Expense - PayrollExpenses* account.

13. In the *CA SUI/ETT* field, select the *Payroll Expenses:SUI Expense - PayrollExpenses* account. See Figure 9–L.

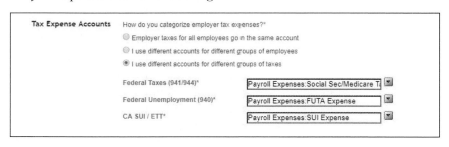

Tax Expense Accounts   How do you categorize employer tax expenses?*
○ Employer taxes for all employees go in the same account
○ I use different accounts for different groups of employees
● I use different accounts for different groups of taxes

Federal Taxes (941/944)*   Payroll Expenses:Social Sec/Medicare T ▾
Federal Unemployment (940)*   Payroll Expenses:FUTA Expense ▾
CA SUI / ETT*   Payroll Expenses:SUI Expense ▾

14. Edit the following Tax Liability accounts. See Figure 9–M.
Federal Taxes (941/944):   FIT and Social Sec/Medicare Payable
Federal Unemployment (940):   FUTA Payable
CA SUI/ETT: SUI Payable

Tax Liability Accounts   Federal Taxes (941/944)*   Payroll Tax Payable:FIT and Social Sec/M ▾
Federal Unemployment (940)*   Payroll Tax Payable:FUTA Payable ▾
CA PIT / SDI*   Payroll Liabilities:CA PIT / SDI ▾
CA SUI / ETT*   Payroll Tax Payable:SUI Payable ▾

15. Confirm the information is correct and then click the OK button. The sections of the Accounting Preferences Summary window collapse with all information updated. You may need to scroll to the top of the window. See Figure 9–N.

FIGURE 9–N
Accounting Preferences Summary Window

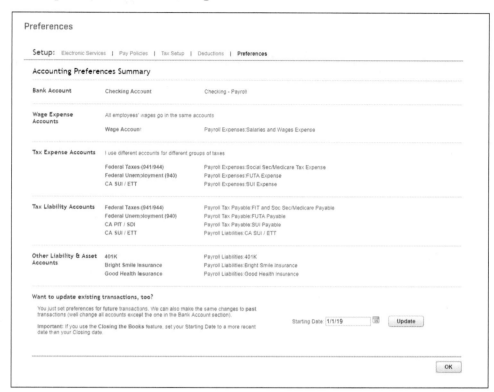

16. Click OK. You return to the Preferences main window.
17. Return to the Dashboard.

Taxes Preferences

The Taxes preferences in Payroll Settings are used to identify information that will be used when paying the payroll-related taxes. Similar to what was seen in the Accounting preferences, QuickBooks Online automatically sets up some of the taxes information, but a company can customize the settings to its own preferences.

To customize the Taxes preferences in Payroll Settings:
1. On the title bar, click the Gear icon and then click *Payroll Settings* in the *Your Company* column. The Preferences main window appears.
2. In the *Payroll and Services* column, under *Taxes*, click *General Tax Information*. The Company General Tax Information window displays.
3. In the *Company Type* section, at the *Are you a Sole Proprietor, 501c3, or Other?* field, click *Sole Proprietor* at the drop-down list.
4. In the *Filing Name* section, in the *Owner Name* field, key your first and last names. See Figure 9–O.

FIGURE 9–O
Company General Tax
Information Window

5. Confirm the information is correct and then click the OK button. You return to the Preferences main window.

6. In the *Payroll and Services* column, under *Taxes*, click *Federal Taxes*. The Company Federal Tax Information window displays. The tax ID as recorded in the Company Account and Settings is carried over to this field. If necessary, key the company tax ID 12-3456788.

7. In the *Filing Requirement & Deposit Schedule* field, click *Change or add new schedule*. A drop-down list appears.

8. Click the drop-down arrow. A list appears containing the different tax return numbers and the frequency with which the company—called the *depositor*—would pay the payroll taxes. See Figure 9–P.

FIGURE 9–P
Company Federal Tax
Information Window

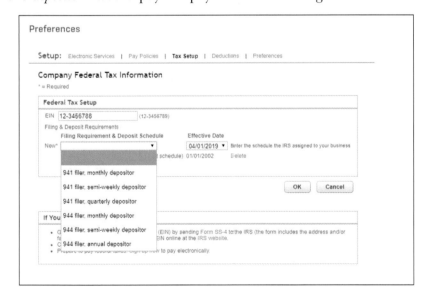

9. At the drop-down list, click *941 filer, monthly depositor*, and then click the OK button. At the warning message, click the OK button. You return to the Preferences main window.

10. In the *Payroll and Services* column, under *Taxes*, click *State Taxes*. The Company State Tax Information window appears.

11. In the *CA SUI* section, under 3.40%(current rate), click *Change or add new rate*. The section expands, allowing you to enter a different rate. See Figure 9–Q.

12. Click the Cancel button. You return to the Payroll Settings Preferences window.
13. Return to the Dashboard.

Preparing for Payroll Processing

After the payroll setup and customization is completed, funds will need to be transferred from the Checking account to the Checking - Payroll account before the payroll is processed.

To transfer funds:
1. On the title bar, click the Create icon and then click *Transfer* in the *Other* column.
2. At the *Transfer Funds From* drop-down list, click *Checking*. The balance in the account displays.
3. At the *Transfer Funds To* drop-down list, click *Checking - Payroll*.
4. In the *Transfer Amount* field, key 1000.
5. In the *Date* field, choose *06/01/2019* or the current year.
6. In the *Memo* field, key Funds Transfer. See Figure 9–R.

7. Confirm the information is correct and then click *Save and close* from the Save and new button list.

Reports

Payroll Reports

Reports, the fourth level of operation in QuickBooks Online, allows you to display and print a number of payroll reports, both for internal payroll management and for government and payroll tax compliance. You will create each of the reports relating to processing payroll in Chapter 10.

Exiting QuickBooks Online

HINT

Any work you do in the Test Drive sample company file is not saved when you exit out of the company file.

At the end of each session, you should exit QuickBooks Online and close the browser.

To exit QuickBooks Online and close the browser:
1. On the title bar, click the Gear icon.
2. At the Company window, click *Sign Out* in the *Profile* column. This closes the company file and exits QuickBooks Online.
3. Close your browser.

Chapter Review and Assessment

 Study Tools include a presentation and a glossary. Use these resources, available from the links menu in the student ebook, to further develop and review skills learned in this chapter.

Procedure Review

To activate the QuickBooks Online payroll feature in the Test Drive sample company file:
1. On the Navigation bar, click Workers. The Employees window appears.
2. Click the Get started button. An updated Employee List appears. The Get started button switches to the Run payroll button.

To activate the QuickBooks Online payroll feature and select a QuickBooks Online payroll service:
1. On the Navigation bar, click Workers. The Let's pay employees and get payroll taxes done window appears.
2. A the Let's pay employees and get payroll taxes done window, click the Get started button. The Hassle-free payroll, done right window appears.
3. Choose the payroll service that's right for you.

To add new payroll parent accounts:
1. On the Navigation bar, click Accounting and then click the See your Chart of Accounts button if it appears.
2. In the Chart of Accounts List in the upper right corner, click the New button. The Account window appears.
3. At the Account window, in the *Account Type* field, click the drop-down arrow and then click *Other Current Liabilities* or *Other Current Expenses.*
4. In the *Detail Type* drop-down list, click *Payroll Tax Payable, State/Local Income Tax Payable,* or *Payroll Expenses.*
5. In the *Name* field, key the payroll account name.
6. Click the Save and Close button.

To add new payroll subaccounts:
1. On the Navigation bar, click Accounting and then click the Chart of Accounts link, if necessary.
2. Click the New button.
3. At the Account window, in the *Account Type* field, click the drop-down arrow and then click *Other Current Liabilities or Other Current Expenses.*
4. In the *Detail Type* drop-down list, click *Payroll Tax Payable, State/Local Income Tax Payable,* or *State/Local Income Tax Payable,* or *Payroll Expenses.*
5. In the *Name* field, key the payroll subaccount name.
6. Click the check box to the left of *Is sub-account* to insert a check mark.
7. In the subaccount drop-down list, click *Payroll Tax Payable* or *Payroll Expenses.*
8. Click the Save and Close button.

To customize the Accounting preferences in Payroll Settings:

1. On the title bar, click the Gear icon and then click *Payroll Settings* in the *Your Company* column.
2. In the *Company and Account* column, under *Preferences*, click *Accounting*.
3. Click the Next button.
4. At the *Bank Account* section, click the text box drop-down arrow. An Account List box appears with the bank accounts from the Chart of Accounts List.
5. In the Account List box, click *Checking - Payroll - Checking*.
6. Click the Customize button to expand the remaining sections in the Accounting Preferences window for editing.
7. Use the radio buttons and drop-down arrows to customize the Wage Expense, Tax Expense, Tax Liability, and Other Liability and Asset accounts.
8. Click the OK button.

To customize the Taxes preferences in Payroll Settings:

1. On the title bar, click the Gear icon and then click *Payroll Settings* in the *Your Company* column.
2. In the *Payroll and Services* column, under *Taxes*, click *General Tax Information*.
3. In the *Company Type* section, at the *Are you a Sole Proprietor, 501c3, or Other?* field, click *Sole Proprietor* in the drop-down list.
4. In the *Filing Name* section, in the *Owner Name* field, key your first and last names. Click the OK button.
5. In the *Payroll and Services* column, under *Taxes*, click *Federal Taxes*.
6. In the *Filing Requirement and Deposit Schedule* field, click *Change or add new schedule*.
7. At the drop-down list, select the filing requirement and deposit schedule and then click the OK button. At the warning message, click the OK button.
8. In the *Payroll and Services* column, under *Taxes*, click *State Taxes*. The Company State Tax Information window appears.
9. In the *CA SUI* section, under 3.40% (current rate), click *Change or add new rate*.
10. Key in a rate and click the OK button.

To transfer funds:

1. On the title bar, click the Create icon and then click *Transfer* in the *Other* column.
2. At the *Transfer Funds From* drop-down list, select an account. The balance in the account is displayed.
3. At the *Transfer Funds To* drop-down list, select an account.
4. In the *Transfer Amount* field, key the amount.
5. In the *Date* field, choose the date.
6. In the *Memo* field, key Funds Transfer.
7. Click the Save and close button.

Key Concepts

Select the letter of the item that best matches each definition.

a. payroll
b. Payroll Settings - Preferences window
c. Social Security tax, Medicare tax, FUTA, and SUI
d. Tax Expense Accounts section
e. Social Security tax, Medicare tax, federal withholding, and state withholding

f. Taxes preferences
g. Payroll Tax Payable and Payroll Expenses
h. Accounting preferences
i. Transfer window
j. QuickBooks Payroll Services

_____ 1. Works like a List and is used to set up a broad range of activities related to payroll.

_____ 2. Offered by QuickBooks Online; it includes automatic processing of payroll and requires a monthly service fee.

_____ 3. Two general ledger parent accounts used in QuickBooks Online when the payroll feature is activated.

_____ 4. Payroll taxes imposed on the employee and collected by the employer.

_____ 5. When you select *I use different accounts for different groups of taxes*, the section expands to list separate payroll expense subaccounts.

_____ 6. Accessed in the Preferences window and used to identify the general ledger accounts to be used in the payroll journal entry.

_____ 7. Payroll taxes imposed on the employer.

_____ 8. Window used to transfer funds from the Checking account to the Checking - Payroll account before the payroll is processed.

_____ 9. Accessed from the Preferences window and used to identify information that will be used when paying the payroll-related taxes.

_____ 10. Involves computing each employee's gross earnings, withholdings and deductions, and net pay; preparing paychecks or direct deposit; recording payroll journal entries; and submitting payroll withholdings to the appropriate agency.

Procedure Check

Write a response for each of the following prompts.

1. You have decided to use the payroll feature of QuickBooks Online. How do you activate the payroll feature in an online subscription account?

2. After activating the payroll feature, which accounts would you create in the Chart of Accounts List?

3. Which Accounting preferences would you customize in the Payroll Settings Preferences window?

4. Which Taxes preferences would you customize in the Payroll Settings Preferences window?

5. What transaction would you record in preparation of payroll processing?

6. Your company has been using the services of an outside payroll processing firm. You, as a junior accountant, know that QuickBooks Online has a payroll feature; you wish to recommend to your manager that your company process payroll within the company. Prepare a summary of the steps involved in setting up payroll in QuickBooks Online.

Case Problem

Demonstrate your knowledge of the QuickBooks features discussed in this chapter by completing the following case problem.

In August, the third month of business for Olivia's Web Solutions, Olivia Chen has decided to hire two employees. To prepare for this, Olivia wishes to activate the payroll feature.

1. Sign in to QuickBooks Online.
2. Change the company name to **OWS9 [*Your Name*] Olivia's Web Solutions**.
3. Activate the payroll feature for Olivia's Web Solutions following the steps on pages 265–266.
4. Use Table 9–2 to add the following accounts to the Chart of Accounts List.

TABLE 9–2 Chart of Accounts List—New Payroll Accounts and Subaccounts

Account Type	Detail Type	Account Name	Number	Subaccount of
Bank	Checking	Cash - Payroll	1020	
Other Current Liabilities	Payroll Tax Payable	Payroll Tax Payable	2100	
Other Current Liabilities	Payroll Tax Payable	FIT and Social Sec/Medicare Payable	2110	2100 Payroll Tax Payable
Other Current Liabilities	State/Local Income Tax Payable	SIT Payable	2120	2100 Payroll Tax Payable
Other Current Liabilities	Payroll Tax Payable	FUTA Payable	2125	2100 Payroll Tax Payable
Other Current Liabilities	Payroll Tax Payable	SUI Payable	2130	2100 Payroll Tax Payable
Expenses	Payroll Expenses	Payroll Expenses	6560	
Expenses	Payroll Expenses	Salaries and Wages Expense	6565	6560 Payroll Expenses
Expenses	Payroll Expenses	Social Sec/Medicare Tax Expense	6610	6560 Payroll Expenses
Expenses	Payroll Expenses	FUTA Expense	6625	6560 Payroll Expenses
Expenses	Payroll Expenses	SUI Expense	6630	6560 Payroll Expenses

5. Customize the Accounting preferences in Payroll Settings:

    Bank Account: Checking - Payroll
    Wage Expense Accounts: Salaries and Wages Expense

Tax Expense Accounts:

    Federal Taxes (941/944):   Social Sec/Medicare Tax Expense
    Federal Unemployment (940):   FUTA Expense
    NYS Employment Taxes: SUI Expense

Tax Liability Accounts:

    Federal Taxes (941/944):   FIT and Social Sec/Medicare
                                    Payable
    Federal Unemployment (940):   FUTA Payable
    NYS Income Tax: SIT Payable
    NYS Employment Taxes: SUI Payable

6. Customize the Taxes preferences in Payroll Settings:

Company General Tax Information:

    Company Type: Sole Proprietor
    Filing Name: Olivia Chen

Company Federal Tax Information:

    EIN: 56-5656566
    Filing and Deposit
    Requirements: 941 filer, monthly depositor

Company State Tax Information:

    NY Withholding Number: 565656566
    NY Metropolitan Commuter
    Transportation Mobility
    Tax Rates: 0.11%
    Deposit Schedule: 3 Days After Payroll
    NY UI Number: 56565656
    NY SUI Rate::   4.025%

7. Transfer $6,500 from the Cash - Checking account to the Cash - Payroll account using today's date.

8. Display and print the following reports:

    a. Account List Report. Use the Account List - Custom Report from Chapter 8. Click the company name and change *OWS8* to *OWS9*. Save the customization as Account List - Custom - Chapter 9.

    b. Journal Report for today's date.

CHAPTER 10

Payroll Processing

Adding Employees and Processing Payroll

Objectives

- Review accounting for payroll transactions
- Update the Employees List
- Record payroll in the Run Payroll windows
- Record payment of payroll taxes in the Payroll Tax Center
- Display and print payroll-related and accounting reports

In Chapter 9, you learned how to activate the payroll feature, customize and update the Chart of Accounts List to include the appropriate payroll accounts required for payroll processing, set up the payroll, and customize payroll tax settings. Once payroll is activated and set up, QuickBooks Online allows you to process payroll and track payroll information for your company's employees. You can establish a file for each employee and then process payroll transactions. These employee files comprise the Employees List.

Once you have established an employee file, you can enter transactions for payroll in the Run Payroll window and the Payroll Tax Center. Every time your company processes payroll for employees in the activities windows, QuickBooks Online simultaneously updates the information in the Employees List. In addition, QuickBooks Online changes balance sheet and income statement accounts based on payroll transactions entered in the payroll activities windows

In this chapter, our sample company, Craig's Design and Landscaping Services, will hire new employees and pay all employees beginning with the first two pay periods after you access the Test Drive. Craig's Design will have to establish an employee file for each new employee in the Employees List.

QuickBooks Online versus Manual Accounting: Payroll Transactions

In a manual accounting system, employee pay transactions are usually recorded in a **payroll journal** or register. The employee's gross pay, tax withholding, and other payroll deductions are calculated in the journal using the employee's background information (pay rate, marital status, state of residency, and so on) along with the applicable tax schedules. Payroll checks and tax remittance checks are usually recorded in a cash payments journal.

payroll journal A journal used to calculate payroll and record payroll entries for each employee; also called a *register*.

In QuickBooks Online, the Employees List contains background information for each employee, such as name, address, Social Security number, pay rate, and applicable tax deductions. When the company processes payroll, the transactions are recorded in the Run Payroll window. QuickBooks Online uses the information entered in the Employees List to determine gross pay, payroll deductions, and net pay in the Pay Employees windows.

When payroll tax liabilities are paid, the Payroll Tax Center is used to record the transaction. These activities also simultaneously update the Chart of Accounts List (general ledger) and the employee's file.

In both manual and computerized systems, payroll reports are generated and forwarded periodically to the appropriate federal and state tax authorities. If you subscribe to one of QuickBooks Online's payroll services, these payroll forms are prepared using the Process Payroll Forms window.

Accounting for Payroll Transactions

When a company generates a paycheck, the transaction affects a number of expense and liability accounts. The employee's gross pay is an expense the company records at the payroll date. Additional expenses for the company include the various taxes imposed on the employer, including, but not limited to, Social Security tax (FICA), Medicare tax, Federal Unemployment Tax Act (FUTA) tax, and state unemployment insurance (SUI), recorded in the appropriate expense accounts at the payroll date.

The employee, at a minimum, will have amounts for FICA, Medicare, federal income tax, and state income tax (if applicable) deducted from his or her paycheck by the employer. These withheld taxes, along with the taxes imposed on the employer, are recorded as liabilities on the company books because the company is responsible for remitting these taxes to the appropriate governmental tax-collecting agency at a later date.

The gross pay less the employee deductions results in a net payroll check to the employee. The following example illustrates the effect one paycheck has on the general ledger:

> Company A has one employee who earns an annual salary of $48,000 per year. The company pays its employees semimonthly, on the 15th and last day of the month. Therefore, there are 24 pay periods in the year. Consequently, that employee will earn $2,000 of salary income for each pay period. The employee is subject to FICA (6.2% of $2,000 = $124), Medicare tax (1.45% of $2,000 = $29), FIT ($300), and SIT ($100)—with a resulting net pay of $1,447. The employer is also subject to the matching FICA tax and Medicare tax along with FUTA (0.6% of $2,000 = $12) and SUI (3% of $2,000 = $60).

The journal entry to record the employee's earnings, deductions, and net pay is as follows:

Salaries Expense	2000		
Social Sec/Medicare Tax Payable			153
($124 + $29)			
FIT Payable			300
SIT Payable			100
Cash – Payroll			1447

Many companies use a separate checking account for payroll transactions. Periodically, funds are transferred into this account from the operating account. Having a separate checking account helps track payroll transactions.

In addition, the journal entry of the employer's payroll tax expenses is recorded on the paycheck date as follows:

Social Sec/Medicare Tax Expense	153		
FUTA Expense (0.006 × $2,000)	12		
SUI Expense (0.03 × $2,000)	60		
Social Sec/Medicare Tax Payable			153
FUTA Payable			12
SUI Payable			60

When the company remits the employer and employee taxes to the federal and local governments, it records several journal entries. Payment for the employer and employee Social Security tax and Medicare tax, the employee federal withholding, and the FUTA tax will be forwarded to the federal government. The journal entry is as follows:

	Social Sec/Medicare Tax Payable	3 0 6			
	($153 + $153)				
	FIT Payable	3 0 0			
	FUTA Payable	1 2			
	Cash – Payroll			6 1 8	

Payment for the state withholding tax and the SUI is usually made with one check payable to the state taxing authority responsible for these taxes. In some states, two checks have to be sent because two different tax agencies are responsible. The journal entry is as follows:

	SIT Payable	1 0 0			
	SUI Payable	6 0			
	Cash – Payroll			1 6 0	

As you can see, the journal entries for the foregoing transactions can be complex, as several general ledger accounts are affected. In addition, federal and state payroll and compliance laws are detailed and burdensome, with costly penalties for noncompliance. As a result, payroll accounting is a time-consuming process that can result in costly errors and omissions.

Before the availability of low-cost, off-the-shelf accounting software, most small companies either processed payroll manually or used outside computerized payroll services that charged per check. With QuickBooks Online and other general ledger software packages, small companies can now process payroll; determine gross pay, tax expenses, and tax liabilities; and prepare employee paychecks and payroll data in compliance with federal and state payroll regulations.

 Chapter Problem

In this chapter, Craig's Design and Landscaping Services will hire additional employees and process payroll. You will enter information for the new employees in the Employees List. This information, along with the existing balances, is contained in the QuickBooks Online Test Drive sample company file.

To begin, open the Test Drive sample company file for Craig's Design and Landscaping Services. Change the company name to **EX10 [*Your Name*] Craig's Design and Landscaping Services** and key 12-3456788 in the *EIN* field. You may also want to extend the time-out period to three hours. In this chapter, you will use the current year to date transactions. You will process payroll for the first pay period due that appears when you access the Test Drive sample company file. Pay periods are weekly. The sample company will assign the pay period dates and year depending on the date you access the file.

Activating the Payroll Feature in Test Drive

As you did in Chapter 9, to process payroll for the Test Drive sample company, it will be necessary to customize the file in the following manner.

To prepare the Test Drive for payroll:
1. Update the Chart of Accounts List by adding a Checking - Payroll bank account.
2. Transfer $1,000 from the Checking account to the Checking - Payroll bank account using the current date.
3. Turn on the Payroll feature.

Lists ●——— ## The Employees List

The Employees List contains a file for each employee of the company. Information such as name, address, Social Security number, hire date, pay rate, and applicable payroll taxes are indicated for each employee. QuickBooks Online uses the information contained in each employee's file to calculate the employee's gross pay, deductions, and net paycheck.

Like all other Lists in QuickBooks Online, the Employees List needs to be updated as new employees are hired, employees leave the company, or applicable information about an employee changes.

To view the Employees List:
1. On the Navigation bar, click Workers and then click the Employees link, if necessary. The Employees List appears. See Figure 10–A.

FIGURE 10–A Employees List Window

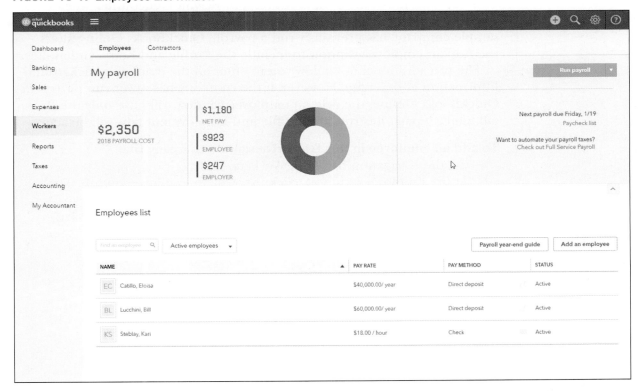

Make note of the following columns and features:

NAME column	This column lists the names of employees. You can display active employees, all employees, and/or inactive employees.
PAY RATE column	This column lists the employee's pay rate, which can be either annual or hourly.
PAY METHOD column	This column lists the methods of payment; the options are *check* or *direct deposit*.
STATUS column	This column displays each employee's current status, such as active, terminated, on leave, etc.
Run payroll button	Use this button to process the current payroll.
Add an employee button	Use this button to add new employees.

2. Close the Employees List by clicking Dashboard on the Navigation bar.

Craig's Design currently has three employees, whose background data has been entered in the Test Drive sample company file. The company will hire two new employees, Richard Henderson and Harry Renee, and terminate an employee, Bill Lucchini.

Adding an Employee in the Test Drive Sample Company File

When you add an employee in the Test Drive sample company file, the steps and windows will be different than those you'll encounter when using a QuickBooks Online subscription account. Since the Test Drive sample company has previously run a payroll, QuickBooks Online alters the Add an employee window to include the Profile and Employment tabs.

The two additional tabs allow you to enter all the employee background information at one time. However, if the company has never run payroll in QuickBooks Online, the Add an employee window will have only the Pay tab. Once a payroll is run, the Profile and Employment tabs will be active.

To add an employee in the Test Drive sample company file:
1. On the Navigation bar, click Workers.
2. At the Employees window, click the Add an employee button. The Add an employee window appears. See Figure 10–B.

   The Add an employee window has three information tabs: Pay, Profile, and Employment. The Pay tab is active.

FIGURE 10–B Add an Employee Window

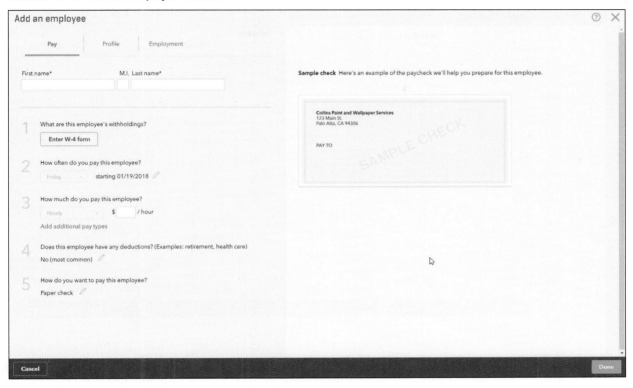

3. Enter the information listed below on the Pay tab:
    First name: Richard
    Last name: Henderson

    At the first question listed under the employee's name, click the
    Enter W-4 form button. A facsimile of the W-4 tax form appears.
    Enter the information below. See Figure 10–C.
    Home address: 551 Front Boulevard
                                      Menlo Park, CA 94025
    Social Security number: 112-55-9999
    Filing status: Married
    Number of allowances: 2
    California state taxes section
    Filing status: Married (one income)
    Allowances: 2

FIGURE 10–C W-4 Form—Completed

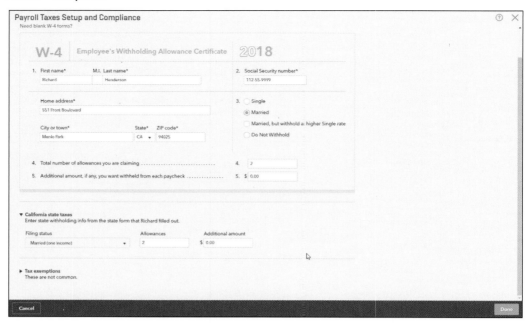

4. Confirm the information is correct and then click the Done button. You return to the Pay tab on the Add an employee window.

5. On the Pay tab, under the employee's name, answer questions 2–5 as follows:

    2: Accept *Friday* and the default starting date. Notice the payroll start date to the right. The start date is determined by the date you access the program.

    3: Accept *Hourly* and key 16 in the */hour* field.

    4: Accept *No.*

    5: Accept *Paper check.* See Figure 10–D.

FIGURE 10–D Add an Employee Window— Pay Tab—Complete

HINT

Notice the sample check to the right. You can compare this to the actual payroll when it is processed.

6. Confirm the information is correct and then click the Profile tab. The Profile tab displays. Close the Pay Stubs question window by clicking the X.

7. Enter the information below on the Profile tab. See Figure 10–E.

Home Phone:	650-555-3311
Mobile Phone:	650-555-0001
Gender:	Male
Birth date:	02/01/1990

FIGURE 10–E Add an Employee Window— Profile Tab—Completed

8. Confirm the information is correct and then click the Done button. The Employees List window displays. See Figure 10–F.

FIGURE 10–F Employees List Window

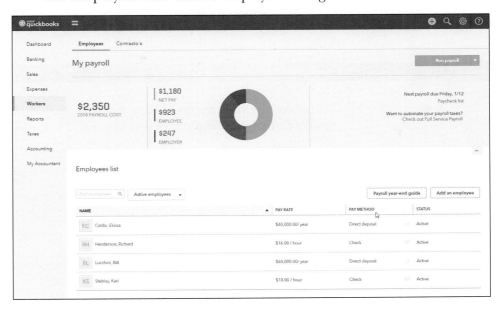

9. Confirm the information is correct and then return to the Dashboard.

Making An Employee Inactive

Employee Bill Lucchini has left the company, and Craig's Design must change his employment status to discontinue paying him.

To make an employee inactive:

1. On the Navigation bar, click Workers.
2. At the Employees window, click anywhere on the row for Bill Lucchini. This opens the Employee details window, displaying the employee file.
3. Click the Edit employee button and then click the Employment tab.
4. At the *Status* drop-down list, click *Terminated*.
5. In the *Termination date* field, key the current date. See Figure 10–G.

FIGURE 10–G Employment Tab

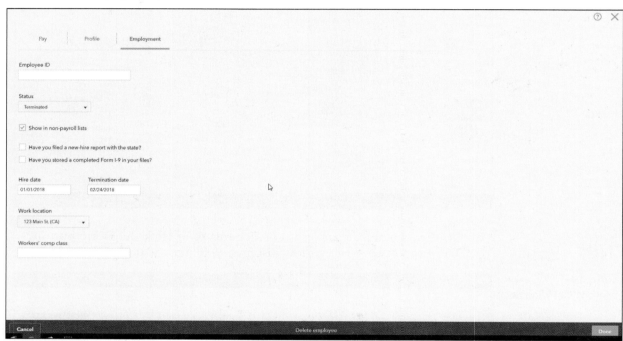

6. Confirm the information is correct and then click the Done button to return to the Employees window. Bill Lucchini's name should no longer appear.

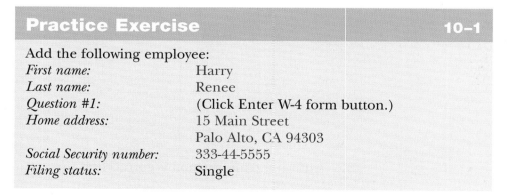

Practice Exercise	**10–1**

Add the following employee:

First name:	Harry
Last name:	Renee
Question #1:	(Click Enter W-4 form button.)
Home address:	15 Main Street
	Palo Alto, CA 94303
Social Security number:	333-44-5555
Filing status:	Single

Number of allowances:	1
California state tax section	
Filing status:	(Accept default.)
Question #2:	(Accept default.)
Question #3	
Pay type:	Salary
Rate:	40,000/year
Question #4:	(Accept default.)
Question #5:	(Accept default.)
Home phone:	650-555-6868
Mobile phone:	650-555-2541
Gender:	Male
Birth date:	08/01/1975

Remove Eloisa Catillo from the payroll.

QuickCheck: The updated Employees List appears in Figure 10–H.

FIGURE 10–H Updated Employees List Window

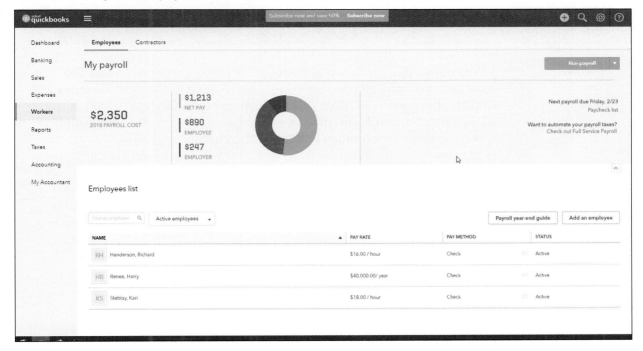

Adding an Employee in a QuickBooks Online Subscription Account

As previously discussed, since the Case Problem is processing payroll in QuickBooks Online for the first time, the procedure to add an employee will differ from the steps in the Test Drive. If the company is running payroll on QuickBooks Online for the first time, the Let's add one of your employees window will display. See Figure 10–I.

FIGURE 10–1 Let's Add One of Your Employees Window

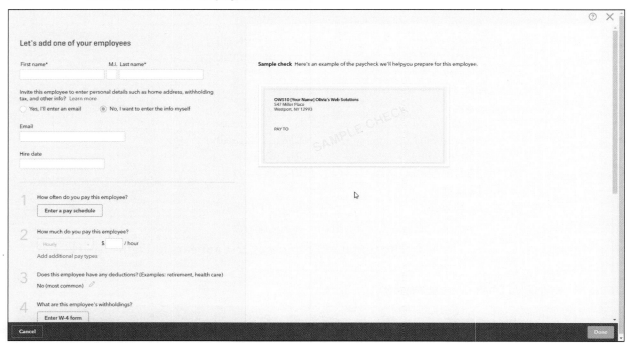

Notice that this window is similar to the Pay tab you saw in the Test Drive Add an employee window. However, unlike in the Add an employee window, there are no Profile or Employment tabs. Once a payroll is run, the Profile and Employment tabs will display and allow for data input.

For the Case Problem at the end of the chapter, since you will be processing payroll for the first time, you will enter background information in two steps. The information for the Pay tab will be entered prior to the first payroll run, while the information for the Profile and Employments tabs will be entered after the first payroll. Once you run the first payroll, you can return to the Employees List window to add the information required on the Profile and Employment tabs for each employee.

To add an employee in a QuickBooks Online subscription account:

1. On the Navigation bar, click Workers.
2. Click the Get set up button. The Get Ready for Payroll window appears.
3. Click the *No, I have not paid employees in 2018* (or the current year) option and then click the Continue button.
4. At the Get Ready for Payroll window, click the Add an employee link. The Let's add one of your employees window appears. This window is the first of several where you will enter employee information.
5. Enter the employee's name and then click the *No, I want to enter the info myself* option.
6. Enter the hire date (use the first day of the current month).
7. At Question #1, *How often do you pay this employee?*, click the Enter a pay schedule button. The What's the employee pay schedule? window appears.

8. At the *How often do you pay the employee?* drop-down list, choose *Twice a Month*.

9. In the *When's the next payday?* field, select the 15th of the current month if you access the program in the first half of a month. If you access the program in the last half of the month, choose the 15th of the next month.

10. In the *When's the last day of work (pay period) for the payday?* field, select the same date as the previous field.

11. In the *What do you want to name this pay schedule?* field, accept the default. See Figure 10–J.

FIGURE 10–J What's the Employee's Pay Schedule? Window—Completed

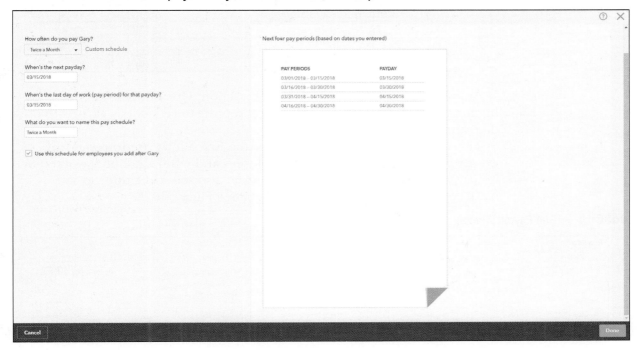

12. Confirm the information is correct and then click the Done button. You return to the Let's add one of your employees window.

13. At Question #4, *What are this employee's witholdings?*, click the Enter W-4 form button and enter the W-4 information using the information in Step 3 on page 289. Complete Question #5 using information in Step 5 on page 290.

14. Confirm the information is correct and then click the Done button.

15. Click the Add an employee link to continue to add employees as needed.

Activities — **The Run Payroll Windows**

The Run Payroll windows are used when calculating gross pay, taxes, and net payroll for employees, a daily business activity that is part of the third order of operations in QuickBooks Online. As in a manual accounting system, when you process payroll through the Run Payroll windows, a number of general ledger accounts are affected by the transaction.

As illustrated earlier in the chapter, it is common in a manual accounting system to record payroll using two journal entries. One journal entry records the salaries/wages expense, the employees' withholdings as liabilities, and the net pay. The second journal entry usually records the employer's related tax expense and liabilities.

In QuickBooks Online, the transaction is recorded as one compound journal entry instead of two separate journal entries. The transaction is recorded as follows:

Wages Expense (Gross pay)		XXX			
Payroll Tax Expense		XXX			
Federal Tax Payable					XXX
State Tax Payable					XXX
FUTA Payable					XXX
SUI Payable					XXX
Checking – Payroll					XXX

At the same time you record the transaction, QuickBooks Online updates the Employees List and payroll reports to reflect pay earned to date and taxes withheld.

There are two Run Payroll windows: the first allows you to review the weekly gross pay for the salaried employees and enter the hours worked by hourly workers for the pay period. You will also select the appropriate bank account, pay period, and pay date. See Figure 10–K.

FIGURE 10–K Run Payroll Window

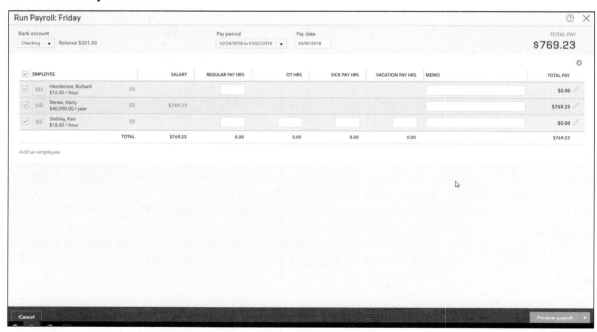

Once the pay information is confirmed, you will move to the Review and Submit window. Here you will review the gross pay, deductions, and net pay computations. See Figure 10–L. If the company has subscribed to a QuickBooks Online payroll service, tax figures and deductions are calculated and display automatically in the *EMPLOYEE TAXES AND DEDUCTIONS* column.

FIGURE 10–L Review and Submit Window

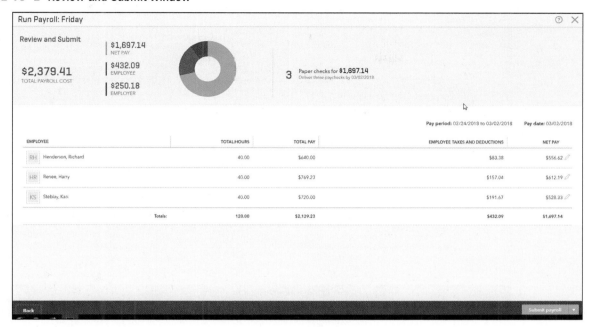

Paying an Employee

HINT

The Test Drive sample company has run a payroll for the week before you accessed the file. That data has been entered.

As discussed previously, you will use the default pay period and payroll date due for the Test Drive sample company, which will vary based on when you access the Test Drive. At the time this text was written, the Test Drive was accessed on February 24, 2018; therefore, the next pay period for the chapter problem is February 24, 2018, to March 2, 2018. The payroll date is March 2, 2018. Once the Test Drive is opened, the payroll functions will use your access date to set the pay dates.

On March 2, 2018, Craig's Design will pay the company's three employees for one week of pay. The salaried employee, Harry Renee, who has an annual salary of $40,000, will receive 1/52 of his annual salary ($769.23). Since Richard Henderson and Kari Steblay are hourly employees, the Run Payroll window will compute their pay based upon the rates contained in their employee files multiplied by the number of hours worked that week.

To pay all employees:
1. On the Navigation bar, click Workers, if necessary.
2. Click the Run payroll button. The Run Payroll window appears.
3. At the *Bank account* drop-down list, click *Checking - Payroll*. Note that the balance is only $1,000. Craig's Design will need to add funds prior to the payroll date.
4. In the *Pay period* field, accept the default period.
5. In the *Pay date* field, accept the default date.
6. In the row for Richard Henderson, key 40 in the *REGULAR PAY HRS* column. When you move to the next field or column, the *TOTAL PAY* column will fill automatically.
7. Key 40 in the *REGULAR PAY HRS* column for Kari Steblay. See Figure 10–M.

   Note that the *SALARY* column for Harry Renee was automatically filled based upon the salary entered in the Employees List.

HINT

Unlike in prior chapters, you will use the default pay period dates for the sample company, not the dates described above.

FIGURE 10–M Run Payroll Window—Completed

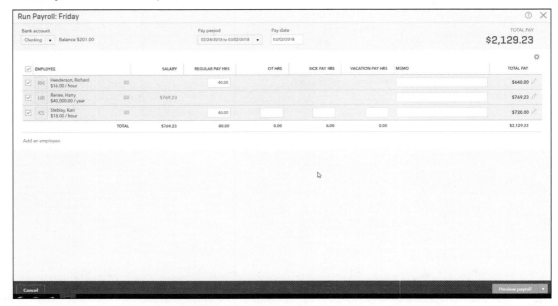

8. Confirm the information is correct and then click the Preview payroll button. The Review and Submit window appears.

9. Make sure the figures in the *TOTAL PAY* column are correct. The figures in the *EMPLOYEE TAXES AND DEDUCTIONS* column are calculated based on information contained in each employee's file in the Employees List. See Figure 10–N.

FIGURE 10–N Review and Submit Window

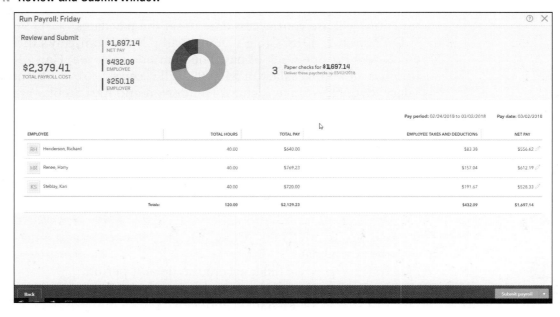

10. Confirm the information is correct and then click the Submit payroll button. The Got it! Your payroll is all set window appears.

11. In the *CHECK NUMBER* column for Richard Henderson, key 100 and then click the Auto-fill link to automatically assign numbers to the remaining checks. See Figure 10–C.

FIGURE 10–O Got It! Your Payroll Is All Set Window

12. Confirm the information is correct and then click the Finish payroll button. At the Tax payments due reminder window, insert a check mark in the *Don't show this reminder again* check box and then click the I'll do it later button. You return to the Employees window. Notice that in the upper right corner, the *Next payroll due* date is now one week later.

Accounting Concept

For the processing of a paycheck, the general ledger posting is as follows (the taxes payable accounts consist of both the employee and employer taxes; *er* represents the employer's share, and *ee* represents the employee's share):

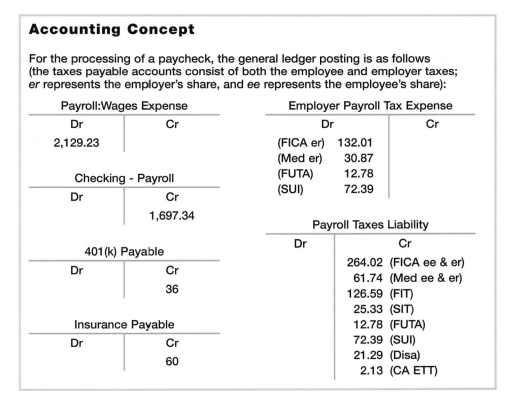

Payroll:Wages Expense	
Dr	Cr
2,129.23	

Checking - Payroll	
Dr	Cr
	1,697.34

401(k) Payable	
Dr	Cr
	36

Insurance Payable	
Dr	Cr
	60

Employer Payroll Tax Expense	
Dr	Cr
(FICA er) 132.01	
(Med er) 30.87	
(FUTA) 12.78	
(SUI) 72.39	

Payroll Taxes Liability	
Dr	Cr
	264.02 (FICA ee & er)
	61.74 (Med ee & er)
	126.59 (FIT)
	25.33 (SIT)
	12.78 (FUTA)
	72.39 (SUI)
	21.29 (Disa)
	2.13 (CA ETT)

Process payroll for the next pay period:

Harry Renee:	Regular Salary
Richard Henderson:	36 hours
Kari Steblay:	40 hours
Checks:	103–105

QuickCheck: Net pay $1,646.47

Activities

The Payroll Tax Center

Activities identified as paying employees were recorded in the Run Payroll windows. Subsequently, Activities identified as paying payroll liabilities are then recorded in the Payroll Tax Center window. As you process paychecks in the Run Payroll windows, QuickBooks Online tracks all payroll liabilities as they accumulate from each paycheck The Payroll Tax Center window then displays all payroll liabilities existing at a specified date and allows you to pay each to its appropriate tax-collecting agency.

The Payroll Tax Center window shown in Figure 10–P is designed for paying federal and local payroll tax liabilities. The default accounts are the various payroll tax liability accounts that have been credited during payroll processing in the Run Payroll windows. Once a liability is selected for payment, the transaction is recorded as follows:

	Payroll Liabilities		XXX	
	Cash – Payroll			XXX

FIGURE 10–P Payroll Tax Center Window

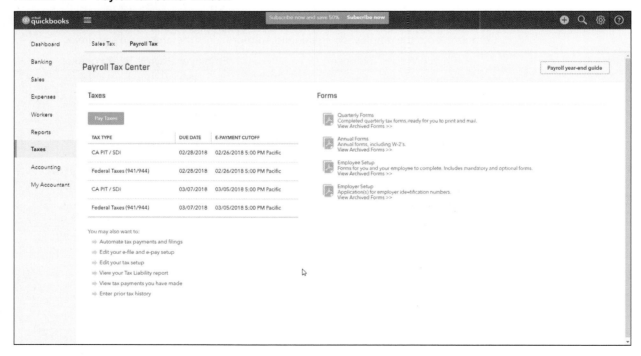

HINT

The first payroll for our chapter problem was for March 31, 2018. So the liabilities are due to be paid April 1.

Once you click the Pay Taxes button, QuickBooks Online displays all payroll tax liabilities accrued during that period, listed by due date.

Craig's Design wishes to remit the federal employer and employee payroll taxes owed to the United States Treasury for the pre-existing payroll processed for the period prior to your first payroll. The company and employee FICA, the company and employee Medicare tax, the employee's FIT, and the employer's FUTA tax are to be remitted to the federal government.

To pay federal payroll tax liabilities:

1. On the Navigation bar, click Taxes and then click the Payroll Tax link. The Payroll Tax Center window appears.
2. Click the Pay Taxes button. The Pay Taxes window appears, displaying the tax liabilities generated by the two payrolls. See Figure 10–Q.

FIGURE 10–Q Pay Taxes Window

TAX TYPE	DUE DATE	E-PAYMENT CUTOFF	AMOUNT	
Tax Payments Due (You need to take action on these tax payments soon.)				▶
CA PIT / SDI	04/18/2018	04/16/2018 5:00 PM Pacific	$71.92	Create payment
Federal Taxes (941/944)	04/18/2018	04/16/2018 5:00 PM Pacific	$464.10	Create payment
CA PIT / SDI	04/25/2018	04/23/2018 5:00 PM Pacific	$46.62	Create payment
Federal Taxes (941/944)	04/25/2018	04/23/2018 5:00 PM Pacific	$452.35	Create payment
CA PIT / SDI	05/02/2018	04/30/2018 5:00 PM Pacific	$44.58	Create payment
Federal Taxes (941/944)	05/02/2018	04/30/2018 5:00 PM Pacific	$436.17	Create payment
Upcoming Tax Payments (You don't need to pay these yet. We'll remind you when they are due.)				▶

Note: Some of these tax amounts are estimates based on accrual to date. You'll see the actual amount when you click Create Payment.

Automate tax payments and filings

HINT

Note the due date for the payment is 02/28/2018.

3. In the Federal Taxes (941/944) row for the first payroll, click *Create payment*. This is a federal payroll tax liability for a payroll processed for the first pay period. The Approve Payment window appears.
4. Click the radio button next to *Make Payment Myself*.
5. Accept the default dates in the *Liability Period* and *Due Date* fields.
6. At the *Bank Account* drop-down list, click *Checking - Payroll*, if necessary.
7. In the *Payment Date* field, accept the default date. The *AMOUNT* column should total $436.56. See Figure 10–R.

FIGURE 10–R Approve Payment Window—Completed

8. Confirm all information is correct and then click the Record payment button. The Payment Confirmation window appears, providing instructions on how to make the payment.
9. Confirm the information on the check is correct and then click the Skip for Now button.
10. Return to the Dashboard.

Accounting Concept

For a payment of payroll liability, the general ledger posting is as follows:

Payroll Liabilities: Federal Taxes		Checking - Payroll	
Dr	Cr	Dr	Cr
Pmt 436.56	436.56		436.56
	Bal 0		

Reports

Payroll Reports and Accounting Reports

Reports, the fourth level of operation in QuickBooks Online, allow you to display and print a number of payroll reports for internal payroll management as well as for government and payroll tax compliance.

The payroll management reports provide the company with valuable information concerning payroll costs—such as gross pay, payroll liabilities and withholding, and employer payroll taxes.

The government compliance reports (forms 941, W-2, and 940) are replications of the federal form 941, which is filed quarterly, and the federal forms W-2 and 940, which are filed annually. These reports are available only when you subscribe to a QuickBooks payroll service, but payroll management reports can provide information needed to complete state and local compliance reports that the company may be required to submit.

Payroll Management Reports

The following reports are available in QuickBooks Online to assist the company in managing and tracking the payroll process. These reports are accessed from the *Payroll* section of the Reports window. They are not required by law and therefore are not forwarded to a government agency. However, information contained in these reports is sometimes used to complete government-mandated payroll reports, especially at the state or local level.

Payroll Summary Report

The Payroll Summary Report lists the earnings, deductions, and employer payroll taxes for each employee for a specified period of time.

To view and print the Payroll Summary Report:
1. On the Navigation bar, click Reports.
2. In the *Payroll* section, click *Payroll Summary*.
3. At the *Date Range* drop-down list, click *This year* and then click the Run Report button. The report displays for the period.
4. To print the report, click *Printer Friendly* from the drop-down list in the top right corner and then click Print at the top of the report.
5. At the Print window, select the correct destination and then click the Print button. Your report should look like Figure 10–S.

FIGURE 10–S
Payroll Summary Report

6. Close the Print, email, or save as PDF window and then return to the Dashboard.

Payroll Tax Liability Report

The Payroll Tax Liability Report lists all payroll liabilities owed and unpaid for a specified period of time. If liabilities have been accrued and paid, a zero will appear in the *TAX OWED* column.

To view the Payroll Tax Liability Report:
1. On the Navigation bar, click Reports.
2. In the *Payroll* section, click *Payroll Tax Liability*.
3. At the *Date Range* drop-down list, click *This year* and then click the Run Report button. See Figure 10–T.

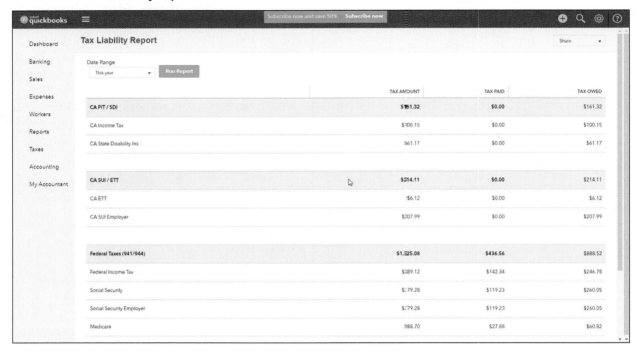

4. Return to the Dashboard.

Payroll Details Report

The Payroll Details Report provides detailed information for each payroll transaction (paychecks and payroll liability payments) recorded during the period. Information such as employee salary per paycheck, tax withholding, net pay, employer-paid taxes, and taxes remitted are presented in this report.

To view and print the Payroll Details Report:
1. On the Navigation bar, click Reports.
2. In the *Payroll* section, click *Payroll Details*.
3. At the *Date Range* drop-down list, click *This year* and then click the Run Report button.
4. To print the report, click *Printer Friendly* from the drop-down list in the top right corner and then click Print at the top of the report.
5. At the Print window, select the correct destination and then click the Print button. Your report should look like Figure 10–U.

FIGURE 10–U
Payroll Details Report

2/24/2018					Payroll Details Report					
Payroll Details Report				Print					**Collins Paint and Wallpaper Services**	
Jan 01 - Dec 31, 2018										
	PAY	HRS	AMT	DEDUCTIONS	AMT	EMPLOYEE-PAID TAXES	AMT	COMPANY-PAID TAXES	AMT	
	Regular	36.00	$576.00			FIT	$19.43	FUTA	$3.46	
Henderson, Richard						SS	$35.71	SS	$35.71	
Net $505.96 03/09/2018						Med	$8.35	Med	$8.35	
03/03/18 - 03/09/18						CA PIT	$0.79	CA ETT	$0.58	
						CA SDI	$5.76	CA SUI	$19.58	
	Sal	40.00	$769.23			FIT	$70.53	FUTA	$4.62	
Renee, Harry						SS	$47.69	SS	$47.69	
Net $612.19 03/09/2018						Med	$11.15	Med	$11.15	
03/03/18 - 03/09/18						CA PIT	$19.98	CA ETT	$0.77	
						CA SDI	$7.69	CA SUI	$26.15	
	Regular	40.00	$720.00	401K	$36.00	FIT	$30.23	FUTA	$4.32	
Steblay, Kari				Bright Smile Insurance	$10.00	SS	$44.64	SS	$44.64	
Net $528.33 03/09/2018				Good Health Insurance	$50.00	Med	$10.44	Med	$10.44	
03/03/18 - 03/09/18						CA PIT	$3.16	CA ETT	$0.72	
						CA SDI	$7.20	CA SUI	$24.48	
	Regular	40.00	$640.00			FIT	$25.83	FUTA	$3.84	
Henderson, Richard						SS	$39.68	SS	$39.68	
Net $556.62 03/02/2018						Med	$9.28	Med	$9.28	
02/24/18 - 03/02/18						CA PIT	$2.19	CA ETT	$0.64	
						CA SDI	$6.40	CA SUI	$21.76	
Renee, Harry	Sal	40.00	$769.23			FIT	$70.53	FUTA	$4.61	
Net $612.18 03/02/2018						SS	$47.69	SS	$47.69	
02/24/18 - 03/02/18						Med	$11.16	Med	$11.16	

6. Close the Print, email, or save as PDF window and then return to the Dashboard.

Payroll Government Compliance Reports

The Payroll Tax Center contains the basic government compliance reports all companies with payroll are required to file with the federal government (Internal Revenue Service).

To display and print government payroll compliance reports, you need to subscribe to a QuickBooks payroll service.

The Test Drive sample company provides copies of each form.

To view the forms:

1. On the Navigation bar, click Taxes and then click the Payroll Tax link, if necessary.
2. On the right side of the Payroll Tax Center window are the various government compliance forms, organized under *Quarterly Forms* and *Annual Forms*. See Figure 10–V.

FIGURE 10–V
Payroll Tax Center
Window

Form 941

Form 941—Employer's Quarterly Federal Tax Return is forwarded to the Internal Revenue Service quarterly. This report summarizes the total wages paid to all employees for the quarter, along with the federal tax withheld and employer's and employees' Social Security and Medicare tax liabilities.

Form 940

Form 940—Employer's Annual Federal Unemployment (FUTA) Tax Return is filed annually with the Internal Revenue Service. This form computes the FUTA tax liability for the company for the year and reconciles the amount to the tax payments made by the company during the year.

Form W-2

Form W-2—Wage and Tax Statement is prepared annually and furnished to each employee. This report totals the employee's earnings and tax withholding for the year. The employee uses this form to complete his or her personal income tax return. A copy of this form is also forwarded to the federal government to be reconciled with the quarterly Form 941 filings and the employee's tax return.

Accounting Reports

At the end of the month, the Journal Report should be displayed and printed. Print the Journal Report for the period of time covering the two payrolls you processed. See Figure 10–W.

FIGURE 10–W Journal Report

EX10 [Your Name] Craig's Design and Landscaping Services

JOURNAL

March 2018

DATE	TRANSACTION TYPE	NUM	NAME	MEMO/DESCRIPTION	ACCOUNT	DEBIT	CREDIT
03/02/2018	Payroll Check	101	Harry Renee	Pay Period: 02/24/2018-03/02/2018	Checking - Payroll		$612.18
				Gross Pay - This is not a legal pay stub	Payroll Expenses:Wages	$769.23	
				Employer Taxes	Payroll Expenses:Taxes	$90.39	
				CA SUI / ETT	Payroll Liabilities:CA SUI / ETT		$26.93
				CA PIT / SDI	Payroll Liabilities:CA PIT / SDI		$27.67
				Federal Unemployment (940)	Payroll Liabilities:Federal Unemployment (940)		$4.61
				Federal Taxes (941/944)	Payroll Liabilities:Federal Taxes (941/944)		$188.23
						$859.62	**$859.62**
03/02/2018	Payroll Check	102	Kari Steblay	Pay Period: 02/24/2018-03/02/2018	Checking - Payroll		$528.33
				Gross Pay - This is not a legal pay stub	Payroll Expenses:Wages	$720.00	
				Employer Taxes	Payroll Expenses:Taxes	$84.60	
				401K	Payroll Liabilities:401K		$36.00
				Bright Smile Insurance	Payroll Liabilities:Bright Smile Insurance		$10.00
				Good Health Insurance	Payroll Liabilities:Good Health Insurance		$50.00
				CA SUI / ETT	Payroll Liabilities:CA SUI / ETT		$25.20
				CA PIT / SDI	Payroll Liabilities:CA PIT / SDI		$10.36
				Federal Unemployment (940)	Payroll Liabilities:Federal Unemployment (940)		$4.32
				Federal Taxes (941/944)	Payroll Liabilities:Federal Taxes (941/944)		$140.39
						$804.60	**$804.60**
03/02/2018	Payroll Check	100	Richard Henderson	Pay Period: 02/24/2018-03/02/2018	Checking - Payroll		$556.62
				Gross Pay - This is not a legal pay	Payroll Expenses:Wages	$640.00	

continues...

FIGURE 10–W Journal Report...*continued*

DATE	TRANSACTION TYPE	NUM	NAME	MEMO/DESCRIPTION	ACCOUNT	DEBIT	CREDIT
				stub			
				Employer Taxes	Payroll Expenses:Taxes	$75.20	
				CA SUI / ETT	Payroll Liabilities:CA SUI / ETT		$22.40
				CA PIT / SDI	Payroll Liabilities:CA PIT / SDI		$8.59
				Federal Unemployment (940)	Payroll Liabilities:Federal Unemployment (940)		$3.84
				Federal Taxes (941/944)	Payroll Liabilities:Federal Taxes (941/944)		$123.75
						$715.20	$715.20
03/09/2018	Payroll Check	103	Richard Henderson	Pay Period: 03/03/2018-03/09/2018	Checking		$505.96
				Gross Pay - This is not a legal pay stub	Payroll Expenses:Wages	$576.00	
				Employer Taxes	Payroll Expenses:Taxes	$67.68	
				CA SUI / ETT	Payroll Liabilities:CA SUI / ETT		$20.16
				CA PIT / SDI	Payroll Liabilities:CA PIT / SDI		$6.55
				Federal Unemployment (940)	Payroll Liabilities:Federal Unemployment (940)		$3.46
				Federal Taxes (941/944)	Payroll Liabilities:Federal Taxes (941/944)		$107.55
						$643.68	$643.68
03/09/2018	Payroll Check	104	Harry Renee	Pay Period: 03/03/2018-03/09/2018	Checking		$612.19
				Gross Pay - This is not a legal pay stub	Payroll Expenses:Wages	$769.23	
				Employer Taxes	Payroll Expenses:Taxes	$90.38	
				CA SUI / ETT	Payroll Liabilities:CA SUI / ETT		$26.92
				CA PIT / SDI	Payroll Liabilities:CA PIT / SDI		$27.67
				Federal Unemployment (940)	Payroll Liabilities:Federal Unemployment (940)		$4.62
				Federal Taxes (941/944)	Payroll Liabilities:Federal Taxes (941/944)		$188.21
						$859.61	$859.61
03/09/2018	Payroll Check	105	Kari Steblay	Pay Period: 03/03/2018-03/09/2018	Checking		$528.33
				Gross Pay - This is not a legal pay stub	Payroll Expenses:Wages	$720.00	
				Employer Taxes	Payroll Expenses:Taxes	$84.60	
				401K	Payroll Liabilities:401K		$36.00
				Bright Smile Insurance	Payroll Liabilities:Bright Smile Insurance		$10.00
				Good Health Insurance	Payroll Liabilities:Good Health Insurance		$50.00
				CA SUI / ETT	Payroll Liabilities:CA SUI / ETT		$25.20
				CA PIT / SDI	Payroll Liabilities:CA PIT / SDI		$10.36
				Federal Unemployment (940)	Payroll Liabilities:Federal Unemployment (940)		$4.32
				Federal Taxes (941/944)	Payroll Liabilities:Federal Taxes (941/944)		$140.39
						$804.60	$804.60
TOTAL						**$4,687.31**	**$4,687.31**

Exiting QuickBooks Online

HINT

Any work you do in the Test Drive sample company file is not saved when you exit out of the company file.

At the end of each session, you should exit QuickBooks Online and close the browser.

To exit QuickBooks Online and close the browser:
1. On the title bar, click the Gear icon.
2. At the Company window, click *Sign Out* in the *Profile* column. This closes the company file and exits QuickBooks Online.
3. Close your browser.

Chapter Review and Assessment

 Study Tools include a presentation and a glossary. Use these resources, available from the links menu in the student ebook, to further develop and review skills learned in this chapter.

Procedure Review

To add an employee in a QuickBooks Online subscription account:
1. On the Navigation bar, click Employees.
2. Click the Get started with payroll button.
3. Click the *No, I have not paid employees ...* option and then click the Continue button.
4. At the Get Ready for Payroll window, click the Add an employee link.
5. Complete the fields with the appropriate information.
6. Click the Done button.
7. Continue to add employees, as needed. Once you run the first payroll, you can return to the Employees List window to add the information required at the Profile and Employment tabs for each employee.

To add an employee in the Test Drive sample company file:
1. On the Navigation bar, click Employees.
2. At the Employees List window, click the Add an employee button.
3. On the Pay tab, complete the information and then click the Profile tab.
4. Complete the information on the Profile tab.
5. Click the Done button.

To make an employee inactive:
1. On the Navigation bar, click Employees.
2. At the Employees window, click the appropriate employee.
3. Click the Edit employee button.
4. Click the Employment tab.
5. At the *Status* drop-down list, click *Terminated*.
6. Click the Done button.

To pay an employee:
1. On the Navigation bar, click Employees.
2. Click the Run payroll button.
3. Select the correct dates in the *Pay period* and *Pay date* fields.
4. In the *Bank account* field, click *Checking - Payroll*.
5. Key the hours worked in the *REGULAR PAY HRS* column for the hourly employees.
6. Click the Preview payroll button.
7. Click the Submit payroll button. The Got it! Your payroll is all set window appears.
8. Key the check numbers and click the Finish payroll button.
9. At the Tax payment due reminder window, insert a check mark in the *Don't show this reminder again* check box and then click the I'll do it later button.

To pay federal payroll tax liabilities:
1. On the Navigation bar, click Taxes and then click *Payroll Tax.*
2. At the Payroll Tax Center window, click the Pay Taxes button. The Pay Taxes window displays the tax liabilities generated by the payroll.
3. At the Pay Taxes window, on the line of the tax you wish to pay, click *Create Payment.* The Approve Payment window appears.
4. Click the radio button next to *Make Payment Myself* and accept the dates in the *Liability Period* and *Due date* fields.
5. At the *Bank Account* drop-down list, click *Checking - Payroll.*
6. Select the payment date.
7. Click the Record Payment button

To view and print reports from the Reports menu:
1. On the Navigation bar, click Reports.
2. In the *Payroll* section, click the desired report.
3. At the *Date Range* drop-down list, select the appropriate time period and then click the Run Report button.
4. To print the report, click *Printer Friendly* at the drop-down list in the top right corner, click Print at the top of the report, and then click *Print again.*
5. At the Print Reports dialog box, review the settings and then click the Print button.

Key Concepts

Select the letter of the item that best matches each definition.

a. Run Payroll windows	f. Payroll Summary Report
b. Pay tab	g. Form 941
c. Employees List	h. Payroll Details Report
d. Review and Submit window	i. Payroll Tax Liability Report
e. Add an employee button	j. Payroll Tax Center window

_____ 1. Tab in the Add an employee window where personal information such as name, address, etc., is entered.

_____ 2. Quarterly payroll report forwarded to the Internal Revenue Service.

_____ 3. Series of windows used to calculate gross pay, taxes, and net pay for an employee.

_____ 4. Appears at the Employees window and is used to set up employees for payroll processing.

_____ 5. Window used to review pay and tax information to calculate net pay.

_____ 6. Report that lists all payroll liabilities paid and unpaid as of a specified date.

_____ 7. Contains a file with each employee's payroll background information.

_____ 8. Report that displays information concerning details for selected paychecks, including gross pay, deductions, and taxes.

_____ 9. Window used to pay payroll liabilities accumulated when pay is processed.

_____ 10. Report that displays the earnings, deductions, and employer payroll taxes for each employee.

Procedure Check

Write a response for each of the following prompts.

1. Your company plans to convert from a manual payroll process to a computerized payroll processing system. What information must be assembled before you can process the first payroll?

2. Your company has hired a new employee. Describe the steps to add this employee to the Employees List.

3. After setting up a new employee in the Employees List, you want to prepare a paycheck for the employee. Describe the steps to pay an employee.

4. Your company's management wishes to have a report of the amount of each local payroll tax to which the company is subject. How would you use QuickBooks Online to gather this information?

5. Your company wishes to have a report that displays the details of the earnings, deductions, and employer payroll taxes paid for each employee for a specific period of time. Describe how you would use QuickBooks Online to obtain this information.

6. Your company's newly hired college intern has just received her first paycheck. She is disappointed that her net check is only a fraction of what she thought she was earning. Prepare a brief memo describing the taxes that must be withheld from her check.

 ## Case Problem

Demonstrate your knowledge of the QuickBooks Online features discussed in this chapter by completing the following case problem.

In the third month of business for Olivia's Web Solutions, Olivia Chen has decided to hire two employees. One employee will be a web page designer, who will be paid hourly. The other employee, an administrative assistant, will be paid a salary. Your company file should include the information for Olivia's Web Solutions you've added through Chapter 9.

As discussed in Chapter 9, QuickBooks Online's payroll year will be based on the date you access the QuickBooks Online program. For this case, the first payroll, labeled as payroll #1, will cover the period of time from the 1st day to the 15th day of the month and year you access the program. Payroll #2 will be the 16th day to month end. Since this text was written in the first quarter of 2018, you will see transaction dates during that period.

1. Sign in to QuickBooks Online.

2. Change the company name to **OWS10 [*Your Name*] Olivia's Web Solutions**.

3. Add the following employees:

First name:	Fiona
Last name:	Ferguson
Question #1:	Twice a Month (Start with the 15th of the month.)
Question #2	
Pay type:	Salary

Rate:	36,000/year
Question #3	No
Question #4:	(Click Enter W-4 form button.)
Question #5:	Paper check
Home address:	22 Sullivan Street
	Jericho, NY 11753
Social Security number:	449-99-3333
Filing status:	Single
Number of allowances:	1
New York state taxes section	
Filing status:	(Accept default.)
Local Tax:	(Accept default.)
First name:	Gary
Last name:	Glenn
Question #1:	Twice a Month
	(Start with the 15th of the month.)
Question #2	
Pay type:	Hourly
Rate:	25/hour
Question #3	No
Question #4:	(Click Enter W-4 form button.)
Question #5:	Paper check
Home address:	1050 York Avenue
	Woodmere, NY 11598
Social Security number:	101-55-3333
Filing status:	Married
Number of allowances:	2
New York state taxes section	
Filing status:	(Accept default.)
Local Tax:	(Accept default.)

4. Process pay for payroll #1 using the following information:

Check No.:	1
Check Date:	15th of month and year of access
Pay Period Ends:	15th of month and year of access
Employee:	Fiona Ferguson
Type of pay:	Salary
Check No:	2
Check Date:	15th of month and year of access
Pay Period Ends:	15th of month and year of access
Employee:	Gary Glenn
Type of pay:	Hourly
Hours:	80

5. Add the following information to the Profile tab for each employee:

Fiona Ferguson

Home phone:	631-555-1020
Mobile phone:	631-555-3814
Gender:	Female
Birth date:	08/08/1981

Gary Glenn

Home phone:	516-555-5447
Mobile phone:	516-555-7111
Gender:	Male
Birth date:	12/23/1975

6. Process pay for payroll #2 using the following information:

Check No.:	3
Check Date:	Last day of the month
Pay Period Ends:	Last day of the month
Employee:	Fiona Ferguson
Type of pay:	Salary

Check No:	4
Check Date:	Last day of the month
Pay Period Ends:	Last day of the month
Employee:	Gary Glenn
Type of pay:	Hourly
Hours:	88

7. Display and print the following reports for this year:
   a. Payroll Summary
   b. Payroll Details
   c. Payroll Tax Liability
   d. Journal

CHAPTER 11

Time Tracking

Tracking Time for Employees and Creating Customer Statements

Objectives

- Track employees' time using the Weekly Timesheet window
- Create invoices using time-tracking data
- Create customer statements
- Display and print time-tracking reports and accounting reports

Most service businesses track employee hours as part of the invoicing process. Customers are billed, usually at an hourly rate, for services provided by various company personnel. This is called *billable time* or *billable hours*. Time-tracking mechanisms can vary from a simple manual system that uses handwritten timesheets to stand-alone time-and-billing software. When activated, QuickBooks Online's time-tracking feature allows you to record time spent by company personnel by entering data in the Weekly Timesheet window. This data is then used to bill customers for work completed.

QuickBooks Online versus Manual Accounting: Time Tracking

QuickBooks Online has a time-tracking feature integrated into the existing accounting software. Time tracking is used to track employee time, which then determines the billable time allocated to customers. Billable time is recorded in the Weekly Timesheet window for each employee. This information is then carried to the Run Payroll window when payroll is processed. The payroll information can then be sent to the Invoice or Sales Receipts windows to bill customers based on the billable time and the rate for the service, which has been previously established in the Products and Services List.

 Chapter Problem

In this chapter, our sample company, Craig's Design and Landscaping Services, will use the time-tracking feature to allocate employee billable time to customers. The information will be entered in the Weekly Timesheet window.

To begin, open the Test Drive sample company file for Craig's Design and Landscaping Services. Change the company name in the file to **EX11 [*Your Name*] Craig's Design and Landscaping Services** and key 12-3456788 in the *EIN* field. You may also want to extend the time-out period to three hours.

Beginning this month, Craig's Design will use the time-tracking feature to account for time spent by the company's employees for various services provided by the company. Craig's Design will use the information entered in the Weekly Timesheet window to create invoices for customers for services provided and the billing rates contained in the Products and Services List. Use the procedures you learned in Chapter 6 to view the Products and Services List. See Figure 11–A.

Note that Custom Design is billed at a rate of $75, which is $75 per hour of employee time spent on that task for a customer. Landscape Installation is billed at $50 per hour; Tree and Shrub Trimming and Pest Control are billed at $35 per hour. The service provided and the number of employee hours are both entered in the Weekly Timesheet window. That information will be stored until the company prepares an invoice for the customer. The hours spent will then be multiplied by the billing rate to calculate the total amount to be billed.

FIGURE 11–A Products and Services List

The Weekly Timesheet Window

In QuickBooks Online, you can use the Weekly Timesheet window to enter the daily work activity of employees on a weekly basis. Each employee's timesheet is broken down first by customer and then by type of service and hours per day. This information does not in itself generate a transaction or journal entry. Instead, when you wish to invoice a customer or prepare the payroll, QuickBooks Online uses the information in the Weekly Timesheet to automatically complete fields in the Invoice, Sales Receipts, and Run Payroll windows. The QuickBooks Online Weekly Timesheet window appears in Figure 11–B.

FIGURE 11–B Weekly Timesheet Window

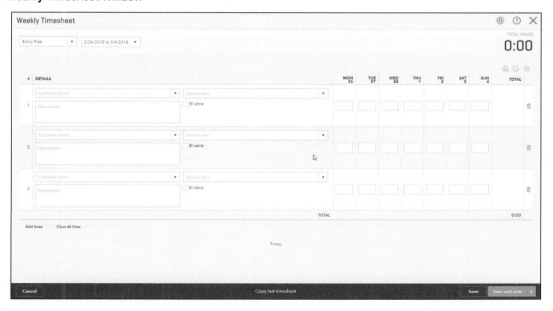

The Weekly Timesheet window allows you to select the name of the employee doing the work, the type of service to be invoiced, and the daily hours spent for each customer. Ideally, this information is entered daily by the employee. However, in this chapter, you will enter the data for an entire pay period at one time. Insert a check mark in the *Billable* check box, which appears under the *Service item* drop-down list, if the hours are billable to a customer. Note that the start of the pay period week is a Monday.

In order for the Weekly Timesheet window to display the service to be billed, the service setting must be turned on to allow that field to be added to the window. This will allow the Weekly Timesheet window to use the rate contained in the Products and Services List to bill the customer.

To activate the time-tracking feature:
1. On the title bar, click the Gear icon and then click *Account and Settings* in the *Your Company* column.
2. At the Account and Settings window, click the Advanced tab.
3. Click the Edit icon in the *Time tracking* section or click anywhere in the section. The *Add Service field to timesheets* option should indicate *On*. If it is not turned on, insert a check mark to the left of the text.
4. Confirm that the *First day of work week* drop-down list says *Monday*.
5. Click the Save button and then click the Done button to return to the Dashboard.

Craig's Design has been tracking time manually. Beginning now, the company wants to use the time-tracking feature and the Weekly Timesheet window.

As was the case in Chapter 10, the dates displayed will depend on when you access the Test Drive. In this chapter, Craig's Design will track the time of two employees, Emily Platt and John Johnson, to accurately invoice customers. Again, your first pay period dates will be determined by the date you access the Test Drive sample company.

During this week of work, the employees mentioned above performed Design and Landscaping services for three customers:

Bill's Windsurf Shop
Dylan Sollfrank
Jeff's Jalopies

Emily Platt provided Custom Design services, while John Johnson provided Landscape Installation services. You do not need to turn on the payroll feature or run payroll to use the Weekly Timesheet window to accumulate the billable time and create an invoice. Also, you can enter billable time spent for non-employees, such as the company owner or vendors who provide billable services to customers using the Weekly Timesheet window.

Tables 11–1 and 11–2 contain the work schedules completed by each employee during the first week:

TABLE 11–1 Emily Platt, Design Services

Customer Name	Hours per Customer by Day				
	Monday	Tuesday	Wednesday	Thursday	Friday
Bill's Windsurf Shop	8	4	4	0	0
Dylan Sollfrank	0	2	2	6	4
Jeff's Jalopies	0	2	2	2	4

TABLE 11–2 John Johnson, Landscaping Installation

	Hours per Customer by Day				
Customer Name	**Monday**	**Tuesday**	**Wednesday**	**Thursday**	**Friday**
Bill's Windsurf Shop	8	4	1	0	0
Dylan Sollfrank	0	0	0	4	4
Jeff's Jalopies	0	4	7	4	4

To enter time-tracking data in the Weekly Timesheet window:

1. On the title bar, click the Create icon and then click *Weekly Timesheet* in the *Employees* column.
2. Click *Emily Platt*, if necessary, at the *Select a Name* drop-down list.
3. Accept the pay period indicated.
4. In line 1 under the *DETAILS* column, click *Bill's Windsurf Shop* at the *Customer name* drop-down list.
5. Click *Custom Design* at the *Service item* drop-down list.
6. Insert a check mark in the *Billable* check box. Note that the $75 per hour rate fills automatically. Leave the *Taxable* check box unchecked, as services are not taxable.
7. In the *MON* column, key 8.
8. In the *TUE* column, key 4.
9. In the *WED* column, key 4.
10. Move to line 2 under the *DETAILS* column and click *Dylan Sollfrank* at the *Customer name* drop-down list.
11. At the *Service item* drop-down list, click *Custom Design*.
12. Insert a check mark in the *Billable* check box.
13. Key the hours for the appropriate dates as indicated in Table 11–1.
14. Move to line 3, and at the *Customer name* drop-down list, click *Jeff's Jalopies*.
15. At the *Service item* drop-down list, click *Custom Design*.
16. Insert a check mark in the *Billable* check box.
17. Key the hours for the appropriate dates as indicated in Table 11–1. See Figure 11–C. Note that the total hours for the week is *40*.

HINT

It is not necessary to enter a zero where no work is indicated for a customer on a specific date.

FIGURE 11–C Weekly Timesheet Window—Completed

18. Confirm the information is correct and then click the Save and new button. If the *Time activity saved!* message appears, click the Not Now button to close it.

19. At the *Select a Name* drop-down list at the top of the window, click *John Johnson*.

20. Confirm that the pay period dates are the same as your previous entry in Step 3.

21. In line 1 of the *DETAILS* column, click *Bill's Windsurf Shop* at the *Customer name* drop-down list.

22. At the *Service item* drop-down list, click *Installation of landscape design*.

23. Insert a check mark in the *Billable* check box. Note the rate is $50.

24. Complete the Weekly Timesheet for John Johnson using the information in Table 11–2. See Figure 11–D. Again, the total work hours should be *40*.

FIGURE 11–D Weekly Timesheet Window—Completed

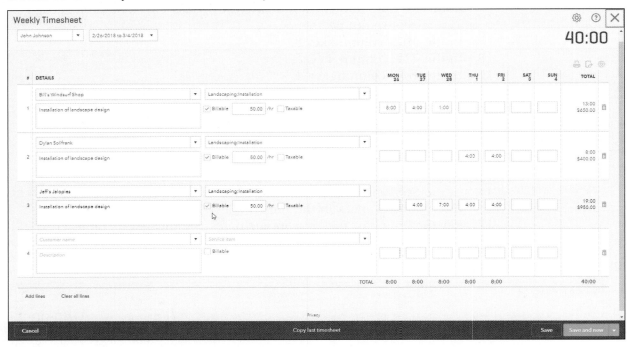

<table>
<tr><td colspan="2">HINT</td></tr>
<tr><td colspan="2">If the next timesheet for that employee is similar to the previous one entered, you can click Copy last timesheet at the bottom of the window.</td></tr>
</table>

25. Confirm the information is correct and then click *Save and close* from the Save and new button list. The time records for Emily Platt and John Johnson are now stored in the system for later use. When you bill the customers for the work done, QuickBooks Online will retrieve this information to assist in calculating billable time as part of creating an invoice for the work. In addition, this information will be part of the payroll processing.

HINT

Remember to change the pay period to the next week.

26. Use Tables 11–3 and 11–4 to complete the Weekly Timesheet windows for each employee during the second week of payroll.

TABLE 11–3
Emily Platt, Design
Services

	Hours per Customer by Day				
Customer Name	Monday	Tuesday	Wednesday	Thursday	Friday
Bill's Windsurf Shop	2	6	4	4	0
Dylan Sollfrank	6	0	0	4	6
Jeff's Jalopies	0	2	4	0	2

TABLE 11–4
John Johnson,
Landscaping Installation

	Hours per Customer by Day				
Customer Name	Monday	Tuesday	Wednesday	Thursday	Friday
Bill's Windsurf Shop	2	6	6	2	4
Dylan Sollfrank	4	2	0	4	0
Jeff's Jalopies	2	0	2	2	4

To print and review the data entered in a Weekly Timesheet:

1. On the title bar, click the Create icon and then click *Weekly Timesheet* in the *Employees* column.
2. Select *Emily Platt*, if necessary, from the *Select a Name* drop-down list.
3. Select the dates for the first pay period you processed.
4. Click the Print icon in the top right corner of the timesheet. QuickBooks Online opens a new browser tab.
5. Print the Weekly Timesheet. See Figure 11–E.

FIGURE 11–E
Timesheet

#	Details	Mon	Tue	Wed	Thu	Fri	Sat	Sun	Total
1	Name: Bill's Windsurf Shop Service: Design:Design Description: Custom Design Bill at $75.00/hr	8:00	4:00	4:00					16:00 $1,200.00
2	Name: Dylan Sollfrank Service: Design:Design Description: Custom Design Bill at $75.00/hr		2:00	2:00	6:00	4:00			14:00 $1,050.00
3	Name: Jeff's Jalopies Service: Design:Design Description: Custom Design Bill at $75.00/hr		2:00	2:00	2:00	4:00			10:00 $750.00
	TOTAL	**8:00**	**8:00**	**8:00**	**8:00**	**8:00**			**40:00**

2/27/2018   Print

6. Close the *Print* browser tab and return to the Weekly Timesheet window.
7. Close the Weekly Timesheet window to return to the Dashboard.

Review the timesheets to make sure the hours are correct and the correct service item is listed. The data on these timesheets will flow through to the Invoice window.

Activities

Creating an Invoice with Time-Tracking Data

You have entered the daily work information for Emily Platt and John Johnson in the Weekly Timesheet window. QuickBooks Online uses the information from the Weekly Timesheet window to total the hours spent for each customer. QuickBooks Online then allows you to generate invoices to bill the customers for services rendered. You do not have to process the payroll before you generate a customer invoice.

Craig's Design and Landscaping Services will create invoices for the three customers for work done by company personnel during the two payroll periods at the rates established in the Products and Services List.

To create an invoice using time-tracking data:

1. On the Navigation bar, click Sales and then click the Customers link, if necessary. The Customers window displays.
2. Click the UNBILLED ACTIVITY filter. The list of customers who have unbilled service time displays. Included in the list are the three customers for whom billable time was previously entered. See Figure 11–F.

FIGURE 11–F Customers Window—Filtered by Unbilled Activity

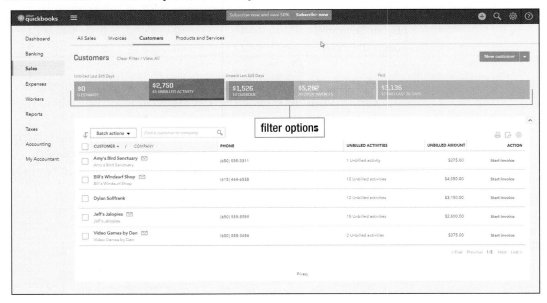

3. In the *ACTION* column for Bill's Windsurf Shop, click *Start invoice*. The Invoice window displays with all billable hours entered at the appropriate rate and time. See Figure 11–G.

FIGURE 11–G Invoice Window

4. Confirm the information is correct and then click *Save and close* from the Save and send button list.

As a result of this transaction, $4,050 of Custom Design and Landscaping Services revenue will be included in revenue for the period.

Practice Exercise	11-1

Invoice Dylan Sollfrank for all work done by the two employees for the hours entered for the two pay periods.

QuickCheck: $3,150

Invoice Jeff's Jalopies for all work done by the two employees for the hours entered for the two pay periods.

QuickCheck: $2,800

Activities

Creating a Customer Statement

As part of the management of accounts receivable, it is often advisable to forward a statement of activity to a customer. The statement lists all activity on that customer's account, such as sales on account or sales for cash, collections of receivables, and open balances, if any. The statement acts as a reminder to the customer if there is a balance due, especially if the balance is more than 30 days old. Often, the presentation of a statement will result in the payment of open invoices.

In QuickBooks Online, customer statements are prepared using the Create Statements window accessed either through the Customers window or from the Create icon. Use the Customers window to create a statement for a specific period for a specific customer. Alternatively, use the Create icon to create statements for all customers at one time, whether or not they have an open balance, or to individually select customers to receive a statement.

Craig's Design wishes to forward a statement to Amy's Bird Sanctuary, due to an overdue invoice.

HINT

An alternate method to generate a statement is to click the Create icon and then click *Statement* in the *Other* column to open the Create Statements window. Click to expand the *Recipients List* section and choose the customers to receive a statement.

To create a customer statement:
1. On the Navigation bar, click Sales and then click the Customers link.
2. In the *ACTION* column drop-down list for Amy's Bird Sanctuary, click *Create statement*. The Create Statements window appears.
3. At the *Statement Type* drop-down list, click *Balance Forward*, if necessary.
4. In the *Start Date* field, choose a date at least five months prior to the current date.
5. In the *End Date* field, accept the current date.
6. Click the Apply button. See Figure 11–H.

FIGURE 11–H Create Statements Window—Completed

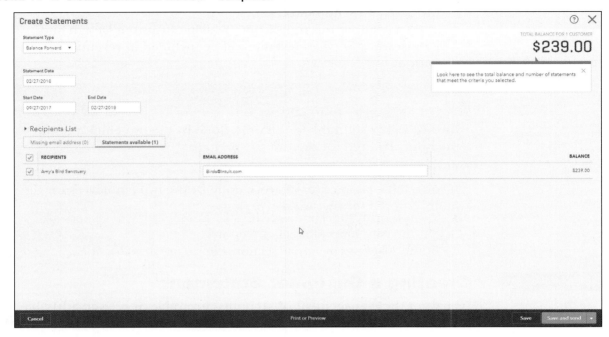

7. Click the Print or Preview button at the bottom of the screen.
8. Print the report. See Figure 11–I.

FIGURE 11–I

Customer Statement—Amy's Bird Sanctuary

EX11 [Your Name] Craig's Design and Landscaping
Services
123 Sierra Way
San Pablo, CA 87999
noreply@quickbooks.com

Statement

TO
Amy Lauterbach
Amy's Bird Sanctuary
4581 Finch St.
Bayshore, CA 94326

STATEMENT NO. 1025
DATE 01/19/2017
TOTAL DUE $239.00
ENCLOSED

DATE	ACTIVITY	AMOUNT	BALANCE
07/31/2016	Balance Forward		0.00
11/06/2016	Invoice #1025	205.00	205.00
12/01/2016	Payment: Amy claims the pest control did not occur	-105.00	100.00
12/02/2016	Invoice #1021	459.00	559.00
12/07/2016	Credit Memo #1026	-100.00	459.00
12/21/2016	Invoice #1001: Front yard, hedges, and sidewalks	108.00	567.00
12/22/2016	Payment #6552	-108.00	459.00
12/23/2016	Payment	-220.00	239.00

Current Due	1-30 Days Past Due	31-60 Days Past Due	61-90 Days Past Due	90+ Days Past Due	Amount Due
0.00	239.00	0.00	0.00	0.00	**$239.00**

9. Close the windows.
10. Return to the Dashboard.

Time-Tracking Reports and Accounting Reports

The time-tracking feature produces reports that companies find helpful in managing employee time and customer invoicing.

Time-Tracking Reports

Use the main time-tracking reports to organize information by employee, customer, or services most recently recorded. The payroll feature does not need to be active to access time-tracking reports.

Time Activities by Employee Detail Report

The Time Activities by Employee Detail Report lists the services and time provided by each employee, including hourly rate and duration.

To view and print the Time Activities by Employee Detail Report:
1. On the Navigation bar, click Reports.
2. In the *Employees* or *Payroll* section, click *Time Activities by Employee Detail.*
3. In the date fields, choose a period that includes your two pay periods and then click the Run report button. The report displays for the period. See Figure 11–J.

FIGURE 11–J Time Activities by Employee Detail Report

4. Print the report.
5. Return to the Dashboard.

Recent/Edited Time Activities Report

The Recent/Edited Time Activities Report lists the 25 products/services most recently entered to view services most recently provided by each employee, including hourly rate and duration.

To view and print the Recent/Edited Time Activities Report:
1. On the Navigation bar, click Reports.
2. In the *Employees* or *Payroll* section, click *Recent/Edited Time Activities.*
3. At the *Time Activity Date* drop-down list, select *All Dates*, if necessary. The report displays. See Figure 11–K.

FIGURE 11-K Recent/Edited Time Activities Report

4. Print the report.
5. Return to the Dashboard.

Time Activities by Customer Detail Report

The Time Activities by Customer Detail Report lists the services provided to each customer, including employees who provided the service, hourly rate, and duration.

To view and print the Time Activities by Customer Detail Report:
1. On the Navigation bar, click Reports.
2. In the *Sales and Customers* section, click *Time Activities by Customer Detail.*
3. In the date fields, choose the five-month period preceding the current date and then click the Run report button. The report displays. See Figure 11–L.

FIGURE 11-L Time Activities by Customer Detail Report

4. Print the report.
5. Close the report.

Accounting Reports

At the end of the month, the Journal Report should be displayed and printed. See Figure 11–M.

FIGURE 11–M
Journal Report

EX11 [Your Name] Craig's Design and Landscaping Services
JOURNAL
March 2018

DATE	TRANSACTION TYPE	NUM	NAME	MEMO/DESCRIPTION	ACCOUNT	DEBIT	CREDIT
03/09/2018	Invoice	1038	Bill's Windsurf Shop		Accounts Receivable (A/R)	$4,050.00	
				Installation of landscape design	Landscaping Services:Labor:Installation		$200.00
				Custom Design	Design income		$300.00
				Installation of landscape design	Landscaping Services:Labor:Installation		$100.00
				Custom Design	Design income		$300.00
				Installation of landscape design	Landscaping Services:Labor:Installation		$300.00
				Custom Design	Design income		$450.00
				Installation of landscape design	Landscaping Services:Labor:Installation		$300.00
				Custom Design	Design income		$150.00
				Installation of landscape design	Landscaping Services:Labor:Installation		$100.00
				Custom Design	Design income		$300.00
				Installation of landscape design	Landscaping Services:Labor:Installation		$50.00
				Custom Design	Design income		$300.00
				Installation of landscape design	Landscaping Services:Labor:Installation		$200.00
				Custom Design	Design income		$600.00
				Installation of landscape design	Landscaping Services:Labor:Installation		$400.00
						$4,050.00	$4,050.00
03/09/2018	Invoice	1039	Dylan Sollfrank		Accounts Receivable (A/R)	$3,150.00	
				Custom Design	Design income		$450.00
				Custom Design	Design income		$300.00
				Installation of landscape design	Landscaping Services:Labor:Installation		$200.00
				Installation of landscape design	Landscaping Services:Labor:Installation		$100.00
				Custom Design	Design income		$450.00
				Installation of landscape design	Landscaping Services:Labor:Installation		$200.00
				Custom Design	Design income		$300.00
				Installation of landscape design	Landscaping Services:Labor:Installation		$200.00
				Custom Design	Design income		$450.00
				Installation of landscape design	Landscaping Services:Labor:Installation		$200.00
				Custom Design	Design income		$150.00
				Custom Design	Design income		$150.00
						$3,150.00	$3,150.00
03/09/2018	Invoice	1040	Jeff's Jalopies		Accounts Receivable (A/R)	$2,800.00	
				Custom Design	Design income		$150.00
				Installation of landscape design	Landscaping Services:Labor:Installation		$200.00
				Installation of landscape design	Landscaping Services:Labor:Installation		$100.00
				Custom Design	Design income		$300.00
				Installation of landscape design	Landscaping Services:Labor:Installation		$100.00
				Custom Design	Design income		$150.00
				Installation of landscape design	Landscaping Services:Labor:Installation		$100.00
				Custom Design	Design income		$300.00
				Installation of landscape design	Landscaping Services:Labor:Installation		$200.00
				Custom Design	Design income		$150.00
				Installation of landscape design	Landscaping Services:Labor:Installation		$200.00
				Custom Design	Design income		$150.00
				Installation of landscape design	Landscaping Services:Labor:Installation		$350.00
				Custom Design	Design income		$150.00
				Installation of landscape design	Landscaping Services:Labor:Installation		$200.00
						$2,800.00	$2,800.00
TOTAL						$10,000.00	$10,000.00

Exiting QuickBooks Online

HINT

Any work you do in the Test Drive sample company file is not saved when you exit out of the company file.

At the end of each session, you should exit QuickBooks Online and close the browser.

To exit QuickBooks Online and close the browser:

1. On the title bar, click the Gear icon.
2. At the Company window, click *Sign Out* in the *Profile* column. This closes the company file and exits QuickBooks Online.
3. Close your browser.

Chapter Review and Assessment

 Study Tools include a presentation and a glossary. Use these resources, available from the links menu in the student ebook, to further develop and review skills learned in this chapter.

Procedure Review

To enter time-tracking data:
1. Click the Create icon and then click *Weekly Timesheets* in the *Employees* column.
2. From the *Select a name* drop-down list, click the appropriate employee.
3. Indicate the appropriate pay period.
4. In the first line of the *DETAILS* column, click the appropriate customer from the *Customer name* drop-down list.
5. At the *Service item* drop-down list, click the service item.
6. If the time is billable, insert a check mark in the *Billable* check box.
7. Key the hours in the appropriate columns for each date.
8. Move to the second line of the *DETAILS* column and click the second customer at the *Customer name* drop-down list.
9. Repeat the process for all successive customers and services for this time period.
10. Click the Save and close button.

To create an invoice with time-tracking data:
1. On the Navigation bar, click Sales and then click the Customers link.
2. Click the UNBILLED ACTIVITY filter.
3. On the line for the customer you wish to invoice, click *Start invoice* in the *ACTION* column. The invoice appears, and the billable hours will fill automatically.
4. Click the Save and close button.

To create and print a customer statement:
1. On the Navigation bar, click Sales and then click the Customers link.
2. On the line for the appropriate customer, click *Create statement* at the *ACTION* column drop-down list.
3. At the *Statement Type* drop-down list, click *Balance Forward*.
4. Indicate the dates covered by the statement in the *Start Date* and *End Date* fields.
5. Click the Apply button.
6. Click the Print or Preview button at the bottom of the screen and then click the Print button.

To view and print the Time Activities by Employees Detail Report:
1. On the Navigation bar, click Reports.
2. In the *Employees* or *Payroll* section, click *Time Activities by Employee Detail*.
3. Enter the appropriate dates in the date fields.
4. Print the report.
5. Close the report.

Key Concepts

Select the letter of the item that best matches each definition.

a. Unbilled Activity List
b. Time Tracking
c. Customers window
d. customer statement
e. *DETAILS* column
f. Weekly Timesheet window
g. Recent/Edited Time Activities
h. Time Activities by Customer Detail
i. Time Activities by Employees Detail
j. billable time

_____ 1. Section of the Weekly Timesheet window where the customer and service item provided are identified.

_____ 2. Window where UNBILLED ACTIVITIES filter is found.

_____ 3. Report that displays the services provided and time spent by employees for each customer.

_____ 4. Time worked by company personnel that can be billed to customers.

_____ 5. Process by which a company maintains records of time worked by employees for various customers.

_____ 6. Report that displays recent activities performed by employees, including time spent and services provided.

_____ 7. Report that displays employee time spent and services provided.

_____ 8. Contains a list of customers who have not yet been invoiced for work done by company personnel.

_____ 9. Window where time worked by company personnel is entered.

_____ 10. Report sent to a customer listing recent activities for that account.

Procedure Check

Write a response for each of the following prompts.

1. Your company wishes to keep a record of the time worked by company personnel to bill customers for services provided. How would you use QuickBooks Online to track time information?

2. Your company's new accounts receivable clerk wants to know how to inform customers of their account activity. How would you use QuickBooks Online to gather and share this information?

3. Explain why it is so important for a service business to keep accurate records of the time employees and others are spending for each customer.

Case Problem

Demonstrate your knowledge of the QuickBooks Online features discussed in this chapter by completing the following case problem.

In the fourth month of business for Olivia's Web Solutions, Olivia Chen has decided to use the time-tracking feature of QuickBooks Online so that the time spent by herself and one of her employees, Gary Glenn, can be tracked and allocated and billed to customers. As was the case in Chapter 10, the QuickBooks payroll year will be based on the date you access the program. Since this text was written in 2018, all transaction dates are recorded in that year.

HINT

Based on the way QuickBooks Online calculates payroll, you will need to use the current calendar year for dates in the Case Problem.

1. Sign in to QuickBooks Online.
2. Change the company name to **OWS11 [*Your Name*] Olivia's Web Solutions**.
3. Follow the procedures presented in Chapter 2 to update the Products and Services List.
   a. Add the following services (all non-taxable):

Name:	Web Page Design Services - Assistant
Sales information:	(Insert a check mark, if necessary.)
Description:	Web Page Design Services - Assistant
Sales price/rate:	50
Income account:	4010 Web Page Design Fees

Name:	Internet Consulting Services - Assistant
Sales information:	(Insert a check mark, if necessary.)
Description:	Internet Consulting Services - Assistant
Sales price/rate:	50
Income account:	4020 Internet Consulting Fees

   b. Change the Internet Consulting Services service name to *Internet Consulting Services - Owner.*
   c. Change the Web Page Design Services service name to *Web Page Design Services - Owner.*

> **HINT**
>
> Remember to click the Save and new button after entering time for each week.

4. Turn on the *Add Service field to timesheets* feature on the Advanced tab at the Account and Settings window and confirm *Monday* displays in the *First day of work week* drop-down list.
5. Enter the billable hours worked for two weeks in the Weekly Timesheet windows using Tables 11–5 and 11–6.

TABLE 11–5 Gary Glenn, Web Page Design Services—Assistant

Hours per Customer by Date										
Customer Name	9/3	9/4	9/5	9/6	9/7	9/10	9/11	9/12	9/13	9/14	Total
Breathe Easy	4	3	1	0	5	2	4	0	1	2	22
Sehorn & Smith	0	1	4	4	3	2	1	6	4	6	31
Thrifty Stores	4	4	3	4	0	4	3	2	3	0	27

TABLE 11–6 Olivia Chen, Web Page Design Services—Owner

Hours per Customer by Date										
Customer Name	9/3	9/4	9/5	9/6	9/7	9/10	9/11	9/12	9/13	9/14	Total
Breathe Easy	0	2	0	2	2	2	1	4	2	0	15
Sehorn & Smith	0	1	2	0	3	0	1	2	2	4	15
Thrifty Stores	2	1	1	2	0	1	2	2	3	0	14

6. Create the following invoices:

   Sep. 15 Create an invoice for Web Page Design Services for Breathe Easy A/C Contractors for services provided by Olivia Chen and Gary Glenn for the period September 1, 2018, to September 15, 2018 (your year may differ). Invoice no. 1017; $2,975. Terms Net 30 Days.

Sep. 15   Create an invoice for Web Page Design Services for Sehorn & Smith for services provided by Olivia Chen and Gary Glenn for the period September 1, 2018, to September 15, 2018. Invoice no. 1018; $3,425. Terms Net 30 Days.

Sep. 15   Create an invoice for Web Page Design Services for Thrifty Stores for services provided by Olivia Chen and Gary Glenn for the period September 1, 2018, to September 15, 2018. Invoice no. 1019; $3,100. Terms Net 30 Days.

7. Enter the billable hours worked for two weeks in the Weekly Timesheet window using Tables 11–7 and 11–8.

TABLE 11–7 Gary Glenn, Web Page Design Services—Assistant

Customer Name	Hours per Customer by Date										
	9/17	9/18	9/19	9/20	9/21	9/24	9/25	9/26	9/27	9/28	Total
Breathe Easy	4	3	6	4	2	0	1	2	3	0	25
Sehorn & Smith	2	3	1	2	4	6	5	5	4	1	33
Thrifty Stores	2	2	1	2	2	2	2	1	1	7	22

TABLE 11–8 Olivia Chen, Web Page Design Services—Owner

Customer Name	Hours per Customer by Date										
	9/17	9/18	9/19	9/20	9/21	9/24	9/25	9/26	9/27	9/28	Total
Breathe Easy	1	2	5	2	3	4	0	2	2	0	21
Sehorn & Smith	2	2	2	2	2	0	4	0	2	0	16
Thrifty Stores	4	3	0	3	1	4	2	1	1	0	19

8. Create the following invoices:

Sep. 30   Create an invoice for Web Page Design Services for Breathe Easy A/C Contractors for services provided by Olivia Chen and Gary Glenn for the period September 16, 2018, to September 30, 2018. Invoice no. 1020; $3,875. Terms Net 30 Days.

Sep. 30   Create an invoice for Web Page Design Services for Sehorn & Smith for services provided by Olivia Chen and Gary Glenn for the period September 16, 2018, to September 30, 2018. Invoice no. 1021; $3,650. Terms Net 30 Days.

Sep. 30   Create an invoice for Web Page Design Services for Thrifty Stores for services provided by Olivia Chen and Gary Glenn for the period September 16, 2018, to September 30, 2018. Invoice no. 1022; $3,475. Terms Net 30 Days.

Sep. 30   Display and print a customer statement for Thrifty Stores for September 1, 2018, to September 30, 2018.

9. Display and print the following reports for September 1, 2018, to September 30, 2018:
   a. Time Activities by Employee Detail
   b. Recent/Edited Time Activities (All Dates)
   c. Time Activities by Customer Detail
   d. Journal

Index

J

Journal. *See also* General journal; Special journals
    entering opening balances, 42–44
Journal entry. *See also* Adjusting journal entries
    entering opening balances, 42–44
Journal Entry window
    bank charges, 204, 206
    correcting adjusting journal entries in, 144–145
    elements of, 43
    entering opening balances, 42–44
    interest earned, 204, 205
    non-sufficient funds (NSF) check, 202, 209
    recent transaction window to view prior journal
        entry, 141
    recording adjusting journal entry, 140–141
    warning message for entry not in balance, 141
Journal Report
    correcting adjusting journal entries in, 143–145
    as period-end accounting report, 143–145
    printing, 47
    viewing, 47–48, 82–83, 117–119

L

Legal name field, 21
Liabilities category type, 27
Lists
    customizing, 228–229
    level of operation described, 3–4
Lists window, 34

M

Manual accounting systems
    compared to QuickBooks Online
        banking transactions, 198–200
        bank reconciliation, 199
        credit card charges, 199–200
        customer transactions, 92
        fiscal year closing, 247–249
        funds transfer, 199
        general journal entries, 128
        inventory transactions, 162
        journals and recording transactions overview,
            2–3
        New Company Setup, 20
        payroll, 260–261
        payroll transactions, 284
        time tracking, 314
        vendor transactions, 56
    General Ledger in, 26
Master Administrator, PRIVACY option, 228
Medicare tax
    accounting for payroll transactions, 285–286
    defined, 262

    payroll settings and, 272
Merging, two accounts, 228–229
Multi-user software, 14

N

Navigation bar, 8, 226
    accessing Chart of Accounts List under
        Transactions, 133–134
    hide and display, 227
Net pay, 263
New Company Setup
    Address, 22
    beginning balances, entering, 42–44
    company file, creating new, 7–10
    company legal name, 21
    company name, changing, 12–14, 21–22
    Company type, 22
    Contact info, 22
    Employer ID (EIN) field, 21
    extend time-out period, 24–26
    inventory preferences, enabling, 23–24
    level of operation described, 3–4
    QuickBooks Online compared to manual
        accounting, 20
New Vendor window, 68
Non-sufficient funds (NSF) checks, 199, 202, 209

O

Omission, bank reconciliation and, 199
Opening
    QuickBooks Online, 10
    saved customized report, 240–241
    Test Drive sample company, 11
Opening Balance Equity account, 32
Opening balances
    entering in Journal Entry window, 42–44
    New Company Setup, 42–44
Open Invoices Report, 115
Operating account, 198
Operations, levels of, 3–4
Outstanding check, 199

P

Parent: Subaccount
    flowing into financial statements, 152
    viewing, 131–133
Partial payment, making, 74–75
Pay Bills window
    automatic adjustment to
        Accounts Payable account, 57, 71, 73
        Cash/Credit Card account, 71, 73
    elements of, 72
    making partial payment of bill, 74–75

NOTES

NOTES